THE EUROPEAN COURT OF JUSTICE AND EXTERNAL RELATIONS LAW

This edited collection appraises the role, self-perception, reasoning and impact of the European Court of Justice on the development of European Union (EU) external relations law. Against the background of the recent recasting of the EU Treaties by the Treaty of Lisbon and at a time when questions arise over the character of the Court's judicial reasoning and the effect of international legal obligations in its case law, it discusses the contribution of the Court to the formation of the EU as an international actor and the development of EU external relations law, and the constitutional challenges the Court faces in this context. To what extent does the position of the Court contribute to a specific conception of the EU? How does the EU's constitutional order, as interpreted by the Court, shape its external relations? The Court still has only limited jurisdiction over the EU's Common Foreign and Security Policy: why has this decision been taken, and what are its implications? And what is the Court's own view of the relationship between court(s) and foreign policy, and of its own relationship with other international courts? The contributions to this volume show that the Court's influence over EU external relations derives first from its ability to shape and define the external competence of the EU and resulting constraints on the Member States, and second from its insistence on the autonomy of the EU legal order and its role as 'gatekeeper' to the entry and effect of international law into the EU system. It has not—in the external domain—overtly exerted influence through shaping substantive policy, as it has, for example, in relation to the internal market. Nevertheless the rather 'legalised' nature of EU external relations and the significance of the EU's international legal commitments mean that the role of the Court of Justice is more central than that of a national court with respect to the foreign policy of a nation state. And of course its decisions can nonetheless be highly political.

Volume 49 in the series Modern Studies in European Law

Modern Studies in European Law
Recent titles in this series:

Empowerment and Disempowerment of the European Citizen
Edited by Michael Dougan, Niamh Nic Shuibhne and Eleanor Spaventa

Legal Reasoning and the European Court of Justice
Gunnar Beck

Lawyering Europe: European Law as a Transnational Social Field
Edited by Antoine Vauchez and Bruno de Witte

Services and the EU Citizen
Edited by Frank S Benyon

The Accession of the European Union to the European Convention on Human Rights
Paul Gragl

Normative Patterns and Legal Developments in the Social Dimension of the EU
Edited by Ann Numhauser-Henning and Mia Rönnmar

The European Neighbourhood Policy and the Democratic Values
of the EU: A Legal Analysis
Nariné Ghazaryan

EU Security and Justice Law: After Lisbon and Stockholm
Edited by Diego Acosta Arcarazo and Cian C Murphy

EU Environmental Law, Governance and Decision-Making
Maria Lee

Shaping the Single European Market in the Field of Foreign Direct Investment
Philip Strik

Nationalism and Private Law in Europe
Guido Comparato

EU Asylum Procedures and the Right to an Effective Remedy
Marcelle Reneman

The EU Accession to the ECHR
Edited by Vasiliki Kosta, Nikos Skoutaris and Vassilis P Tzevelekos

**For the complete list of titles in this series, see
'Modern Studies in European Law' link at
www.hartpub.co.uk/books/series.asp**

The European Court of Justice and External Relations Law

Constitutional Challenges

Edited by

Marise Cremona
and
Anne Thies

·HART·
PUBLISHING

OXFORD AND PORTLAND, OREGON
2016

Published in the United Kingdom by Hart Publishing Ltd
16C Worcester Place, Oxford, OX1 2JW
Telephone: +44 (0)1865 517530
Fax: +44 (0)1865 510710
E-mail: mail@hartpub.co.uk
Website: http://www.hartpub.co.uk

Published in North America (US and Canada) by
Hart Publishing
c/o International Specialized Book Services
920 NE 58th Avenue, Suite 300
Portland, OR 97213-3786
USA
Tel: +1 503 287 3093 or toll-free: (1) 800 944 6190
Fax: +1 503 280 8832
E-mail: orders@isbs.com
Website: http://www.isbs.com

First published in hardback 2014
Paperback edition, 2016

Hart Publishing is an imprint of Bloomsbury Publishing plc.

British Library Cataloguing in Publication Data
Data Available

ISBN: HB: 978-1-84946-504-5
PB: 978-1-50990-990-2

Typeset by Compuscript Ltd, Shannon
Printed and bound in Great Britain by
Lightning Source UK Ltd

Table of Contents

List of Contributors

Loïc Azoulai, Professor of European law at the European University Institute, Florence.

Marise Cremona, Professor of European law at the European University Institute, Florence.

Bruno de Witte, Professor of European law at the University of Maastricht and the European University Institute, Florence.

Christina Eckes, Associate Professor of EU law at the University of Amsterdam and Senior Researcher at the Amsterdam Centre for European Law and Governance (ACELG).

Peter Van Elsuwege, Professor of European Union law at Ghent University.

Joni Heliskoski, Director of EU Litigation at the Finnish Ministry of Foreign Affairs, Finland, Helsinki.

Christophe Hillion, Professor of European law at the University of Leiden and Senior Researcher in EU law at the Swedish Institute for European Policy Studies (SIEPS), Stockholm.

Juliane Kokott, Advocate General at the Court of Justice of the European Union, Luxembourg.

Pieter Jan Kuijper, Professor of the Law of International Organisations at the University of Amsterdam.

Eleftheria Neframi, Professor of European law at the University of Luxembourg.

Jed Odermatt, PhD candidate at the University of Leuven.

Thomas Ramopoulos, PhD candidate at the University of Leuven.

Christoph Sobotta, Legal Secretary in the Chambers of AG Kokott, Court of Justice of the European Union, Luxembourg.

Anne Thies, Associate Professor of European and international law at the University of Reading.

Jan Wouters, Professor of International Law and the Law of International Organizations at the University of Leuven.

1

Introduction

MARISE CREMONA AND ANNE THIES

THIS BOOK DISCUSSES the contribution of the Court of Justice of the European Union (hereafter referred to as 'the CJEU' or 'the Court') to the formation of the European Union (hereafter referred to as 'the EU' or 'the Union') as an international actor, its approach to and responsibility for the development of EU external relations law, and the constitutional challenges the Court faces in this context. It seemed to us, as originators of the project of which this book is the result, to be an opportune moment to focus on the Court as a specific actor in the EU system of external relations. The Lisbon Treaty has been in force for five years and it is possible to reflect on the ways in which the allocation and categorisation of competence under the Lisbon Treaty affects the approach of the Court towards its own role as well as its interaction with other international courts and Member State courts.[1] The ever-increasing cross-policy nature of much EU external action (with its emphasis on policy coherence) is giving rise to both vertical and horizontal competence disputes and to questions over the relationship and boundaries between different policy areas. The engagement of the EU in international governance gives rise to practical questions over the implications of international legal obligations in the jurisprudence of the Court and its impact on the role of the EU as an international actor. These discussions are taking place against a background of debate over the character of judicial reasoning and law-making by the Court of Justice and invite us to consider whether there is, or should be, a specific framework for the development of 'external relations law'.

To what extent does the position of the Court contribute to a specific conception of the EU? Is it the Court's own activism or the need to fill normative gaps in the EU Treaties that have driven its contributions to the constitutional framework governing the external action of the EU and its Member States? The Court still has

---

[1] Throughout this book references to the Treaties as amended by the Treaty of Lisbon will be to the Treaty on European Union (TEU) and the Treaty on the Functioning of the European Union (TFEU); references to the Treaties prior to the Treaty of Lisbon will be to the Treaty on European Union (EU) and the EC Treaty (EC).

only limited jurisdiction over the EU's common foreign and security policy: why has this decision been taken, and what are its implications? What are the exceptions and how might they be used by the CJEU in the future? How does the EU's constitutional order, as interpreted by the Court, shape its external relations? And what is the Court's own view of the relationship between court(s) and foreign policy? The book aims, while taking a longer-term perspective, to present a series of reflections on these questions by a variety of legal scholars, offering an assessment of the way the Court is playing its role in the post-Lisbon constitutional environment.

The book will in particular explore two dimensions of the CJEU's role in the development of external relations law and related constitutional challenges. On the one hand, the collection demonstrates that the 'legalised' nature of EU external relations and the significance of the EU's external legal commitments mean that the role of the Court of Justice is more central than that played by a national court in the foreign policy of a nation state. To take one example: the Court's approach to the international legal system, international treaties and other international courts (the focus of Part IV but a recurrent theme in many other chapters) is regarded not simply as a technical matter but as of fundamental significance for the EU's self-image and international identity. And of course its decisions can be highly political. On the other hand, the contributions show that the main instruments of the Court's influence over EU external relations have been first its ability to shape and define the external competence of EU and the obligations and constraints on Member States' powers; and second its insistence on the autonomy of the EU legal order and its role as 'gatekeeper' to the entry and effect of international law into the EU legal order. It has not—in the external domain—overtly exerted influence through shaping substantive policy (as it has, for example in relation to the internal market).

The three chapters in Part I of the book introduce themes that are picked up in later chapters: Cremona discusses the 'internal' constitutional landscape within which the Court operates and which it shapes (objectives of external action, competences and inter-institutional relations). De Witte discusses the Court's response to 'external' challenges offered by other international dispute settlement mechanisms and its conception of the autonomy of the Union legal order. Hillion discusses the remaining constitutional limits placed on the Court's jurisdiction in relation to foreign policy and the impact of the new constitutional framework introduced by the Lisbon Treaty, including the reach of the general principles foundational to the EU legal order.

In contrast to the internal market, the EU has no external teleology; the treaties have not given the Union an external policy end-goal towards which to aim. Policy objectives certainly exist, both general and policy-specific, but these are orientations intended to guide action rather than end-goals and consist of broad objectives covering a range of issues applicable to all external action. In this context the Court of Justice has developed an approach which defers to the external policy choices made by the Commission, Council and Parliament, while at the same time ensuring that those institutions exercise their powers within the limits and according to the procedures established in the treaties. It is protective of the Union's autonomous international capacity, the decision-making space occupied by the institutions, and the balance between the institutions; and this extends to the protection of its own role as the exclusive forum in which disputes which impinge on the Union's legal order should be determined. According to de Witte, the Court's diffidence towards other international courts is reflected in the way in which the Court 'has reacted to initiatives taken by the EU's political institutions or by Member State governments to engage with new or existing international dispute settlement mechanisms'. As he points out, the Treaty itself establishes a potential tension between the jurisdiction given to the Court of Justice as the ultimate authority to interpret and determine the validity of Union law (including the provisions of international agreements binding the EU, which under the *Haegeman* doctrine become part of Union law[2]), and the explicit task of the Union to promote the development of international law—and thus to promote effective compliance and dispute settlement mechanisms. The Court's desire to protect its own jurisdiction and the autonomy of the Union legal order has, in several of the cases examined here, resulted in the separation rather than the engagement of the Union in international dispute settlement. In the most recent example of this diffidence—if not selfishness—the Court includes (in terms which emphasise its own authority) the national courts within this protected jurisdictional space.[3] The contrast with the Court of Justice's traditional exclusion from an important dimension of the EU's external action, the Common Foreign and Security Policy (CFSP), appears striking. However Hillion argues that the different role of the Court in relation to the CFSP may not be as entrenched as we have been used to assume. The exclusive jurisdiction of the Court of Justice founded inter alia upon Article 344 TFEU now applies equally to the CFSP; insofar as the Court is excluded from adjudicating on CFSP matters, the way is *not* opened to alternative forms of international dispute settlement. In fact, though, Hillion draws attention to the ways in which the Lisbon Treaty has enhanced the role of the Court of Justice in relation to the CFSP: (i) in allowing judicial review of the legality of certain types of CFSP act (which may be less restrictive than at first appears), and compatibility-review of treaties with a CFSP dimension; (ii) in recalibrating the Court's role in policing the boundary between the CFSP and other policy fields, thereby giving the Court a role in protecting the integrity (also) of the CFSP with its specific decision-making procedures and distinct institutional balance; and (iii) in generalising the application of the general principles (such as the principle of sincere cooperation) protected by the Court.

In these first chapters, then, a number of themes are introduced which are developed in subsequent chapters: the approach of the Court towards the Union's

---

[2] Case 181/73 *Haegeman v Belgian State* [1974] ECR 449.
[3] Opinion 1/09 on the draft agreement on the European and Community Patents Court [2011] ECR I-01137.

external objectives; the application of general principles to external action of the institutions and Member States; the institutional balance specific to external action and the ways in which this is preserved by the Court; the relationship between the Court, with its exclusive jurisdiction over the validity and interpretation of Union law, and other international courts and forms of international dispute settlement.

The second Part of this book approaches the fundamental issue of external competence from the perspective of the principle of conferral and the vertical division of powers between Union and Member States (Neframi), the role of the executive and the preservation of institutional balance in the negotiation, conclusion and implementation of treaties and determining the legal effect of treaties in the EU legal order (Kuijper), and inter-institutional conflicts (Van Elsuwege). It is clear from all three contributions that the issue of choice of legal basis is central to any discussion of delimitation of competence and one issue where the Court's influence can be clearly identified.

Neframi argues that the vertical division of competence, which is based on the principle of conferred powers, is linked to effectiveness and external objectives, and ultimately to the principle of unity of external action. She postulates, based on Articles 3(5) and 21 TEU, the existence of what might be called a general and ultimate objective: effective international action in the interest of the Union. Despite the codification of types of competence by the Lisbon Treaty, the Court still has an important role to play in defining competence with a view to furthering this objective, for example in determining when exclusivity arises. External competence is still 'fragmented'—there is no 'global' external competence of the EU and in addition to the express competences found in the Treaty, many external competences are still based on internal legal bases with internal objectives. What then is the relationship between external action objectives and external action based on internal competences and how does it impact the ultimate objective of enabling the EU to act effectively on the global stage? Neframi argues that the Court enforces the principle of conferral, with its resulting emphasis on internal objectives and fragmentation of competence, at the expense of the ultimate objective of effective external action. The Lisbon Treaty reform, while appearing to establish a more integrated and coherent system of external action with distinctive external objectives, has retained the underlying fragmented competence structures dependent on internal powers. However, in addition to delimiting the scope of Union powers and applying the principle of conferral, the Court is concerned with the *exercise* of competence by both the Union and Member States. In fact it is in cases where the issue is not the existence of competence but rather the question of when and how external competence is to be exercised, especially in the context of mixed agreements, that the Court has interpreted and enforced the duty of cooperation so as to further the effectiveness of the Union as an international actor.

In the following chapter Kuijper turns to another aspect of this question: the Court's role in maintaining what has been called institutional balance;

the reflection in the constitutional structures of the Union of the principle of separation of powers. Recalling the traditional importance of the executive and the relatively limited role for the legislature and the courts in the conduct of foreign policy by States—linked to the need to maintain a unitary position and to avoid internal divisions—he asks to what extent this also applies to the EU. Certainly, as Hillion points out in chapter 4, the Lisbon Treaty was concerned to preserve the specific procedures and institutional powers applicable to the CFSP, including a more limited role for the European Parliament.[4] Does the traditional preference for the executive power in foreign relations apply to EU external action as a whole, and to what extent is this reflected in the Court's case law? Two groups of cases help to answer this question: those connected with the status and effect of international law in the EU legal system, and those connected with ultra vires and legal basis disputes. The case law on the direct effect of treaties and customary international law, Kuijper argues, is evidence of the Court's respect for institutional balance. So too is the importance attached by the Court to the Treaty-based procedures for the negotiation and conclusion of treaties in Article 218 TFEU, so as to maintain the balance between the Council and the Commission. Inter-institutional conflicts have certainly been a feature of external relations case law and show no signs of diminishing as a result of the Treaty of Lisbon—on the contrary—and this theme is continued in chapter 7 by Peter Van Elsuwege, who agrees with Neframi that the Lisbon Treaty has by no means resolved all questions of competence.

Van Elsuwege points to several factors which are likely to lead to problems of competence delimitation: the typology of competence developed in the treaties is not best designed for external action and changes to the institutional balance brought about by the Lisbon Treaty will also need to be worked through. Debates over the role of the European Parliament in the procedure for the negotiation of treaties under Article 218 TFEU and disagreements over the inter-institutional agreement between the Commission and Parliament have already surfaced and may lead to litigation. Since the method developed by the Court for determining legal basis (which the Court is clear should be based not simply on political choice but on objective factors subject to judicial review) attaches importance to a measure's aims, the establishment of a single set of objectives governing all external action may create difficulty. However, Van Elsuwege rightly points out that most external policy fields also have specific objectives and since the ordinary legislative procedure has been generalised, removing one of the motivations for a legal basis challenge, the problem is not as great as might appear, although some tricky questions have arisen concerning comitology procedures. The exception

---

[4] *Cf* the Court's position in Case C-130/10 *European Parliament v Council*, not yet reported, judgment of 19 July 2012, at para 82: 'the difference between Art 75 TFEU and Art 215 TFEU, so far as the Parliament's involvement is concerned, is the result of the choice made by the framers of the Treaty of Lisbon conferring a more limited role on the Parliament with regard to the Union's action under the CFSP'.

is the divide between CFSP and non-CFSP actions and the revised relationship between the CFSP and other external policies established by Articles 24 and 40 TEU will need to be worked out: the CFSP no longer has policy-specific Treaty-based objectives and there are major decision-making differences, especially with respect to the role of the European Parliament. Article 40 TEU, with its reference to the 'application of the procedures and the extent of the powers of the institutions' is an expression of institutional balance and implicit in the judgment in Case C-130/10—albeit with no reference to Article 40—is a recognition of the Member States' decision to maintain specific CFSP decision-making procedures.[5]

Part III, in the chapters by Thies, Azoulai and Eckes, focuses on the ways in which the Court has built the constitutional framework for EU external action, its methodological approaches, reasoning techniques and its use of general principles. The concept of effectiveness and the unity of the EU in its external representation, expressed through the principle of loyal cooperation, have proved to be important instruments in this process.

In chapter 8 Thies examines the part played by general principles in the development of EU external relations law by the Court of Justice. General principles have proved to be an important tool in dealing with the impact and hierarchy of EU law norms (interpretative principles), the exercise of competence by the EU and its Member States (organisational principles), and as a foundation for the protection of fundamental rights in the EU legal order (benchmark principles). These functions and categories of general principles as well as the principles discussed here by Thies—the principle of direct effect, fundamental rights, and the principles of effectiveness and sincere cooperation—can be identified also within the case law on EU external relations. As Thies shows, the specificity of external relations—including external objectives, the impact of international legal obligations and the interests of third States—has influenced the function of general principles in this context. Thus, for example, the proportionality of restrictions on the right to property in the case law on restrictive measures is judged in the light of objectives 'fundamental for the international community'[6] including the fight against 'threats to international peace and security posed by acts of terrorism', established by the UN Security Council.[7] The principle of effectiveness, finding expression in the requirement of unity in international representation, imposes significant loyalty obligations on Member States in external fora. The discipline of external unity not

---

[5] See also the Opinion of Advocate General Bot of 30 January 2014 in Case C-658/11 *European Parliament v Council* [2012] OJ C58/2, at paras 4–5: 'It is nevertheless essential to define the respective boundaries of the Union's policies because of the specific nature of the CFSP compared with the Union's other policies. That specific nature is characterised, in particular, by the limited role played by the European Parliament in the CFSP. From this point of view, setting clear criteria to define the scope of that policy in relation to the other fields of the Union's external action represents a certain constitutional challenge'.

[6] Case C-84/95 *Bosphorus v Ministry of Transport, Energy and Communications* [1996] ECR I-3953, para 26.

[7] Joined Cases C-402/05 P and C-415/05 P *Yassin Abdullah Kadi and Al Barakaat International Foundation v Council and Commission* [2008] ECR I-6351, para 363.

only underpins the autonomy of the EU as an international actor; it also protects the space for internal policy-making and the internal legislative process.[8] Azoulai, in chapter 9, takes as his starting point the importance of effectiveness in the reasoning of the Court of Justice as a justification for asserting the Union's external competence and constraining the Member States' external action; a conception of effectiveness, as he points out, linked to achieving the (internal) objectives of EU law: 'the rationale of effectiveness is used to draw a link between internal objectives and external powers'.[9] He suggests, however, that although undoubtedly present in the Court's case law since AETR[10] this rationale is weakly justified; a stronger justification could be based upon the need (also recognised in AETR) to represent common interests internationally. Thus the basis for the EU's external power, as developed by the Court, is founded upon the Union's capacity and its autonomy: its personality and independence of action, implying the ability to act internationally independently of its Member States, to enter into contractual relations and incur obligations. There is a strong institutional dimension to the Union's capacity and autonomy—the existence of common institutions which may represent the Union's common interests—and the Court sees itself as the guarantor of the balance between the institutions and the Member States and the institutional balance which is at the heart of the EU. Azoulai rightly suggests that the challenge facing the Court—and the Union—is to find a paradigm which reflects the unity of international representation of the Union *and* its Member States,[11] reflecting both their independence and their inter-dependence.

The chapter by Eckes gives us another perspective on the reasoning of the Court of Justice, providing a bridge to Part IV, where the focus is on the Court within the international legal system. The starting point is again the connection between internal and external, as 'policy-making is increasingly externalised' and an increasing number of players claim the authority to govern a particular situation.[12] Multiple sites of authority require courts to assess the internal effects of external norms and the existence of multiple jurisdictions gives rise to judicial dialogue, or—as Eckes prefers—judicial discourse. Eckes questions whether lessons may be drawn from the practice of the Court of Justice in its internal discourse (with the Courts of the Member States) that may be applied in its external discourse with international judicial bodies such as the European Court of Human Rights, the European Free Trade Association (EFTA) Court and the World Trade Organization (WTO) Appellate Body. As she recognises, the Court of Justice's claim in its internal discourse to ultimate authority as regards EU law,

---

[8] R Post, 'Constructing the European Polity: *ERTA* and the *Open Skies* Judgments' in M Poiares Maduro and L Azoulai (eds), *The Past and Future of EU Law* (Oxford and Portland, Hart Publishing, 2010).

[9] L Azoulai, ch 9 of this volume.

[10] The European Agreement Concerning the Work of Crews of Vehicles Engaged in International Road Transport (AETR). See Case 22/70 *Commission v Council (AETR/ERTA)* [1971] ECR 263.

[11] C-246/07 *Commission v Sweden* [2010] ECR I-3317, para 104.

[12] C Eckes, ch 10 of this volume.

the interlocking relationship between national and EU law and the existence of a common integrative purpose represent important differences. Nonetheless some parallels may be drawn: in the ways in which courts may influence and exert pressure on political power; in the practice of 'conceptual borrowing'; and even—possibly—in placing the individual as a central point of reference.

As Eckes comments, 'examples are increasing in which external claims of authority affect individuals',[13] and in the following chapter Kokott and Sobotta explore one of the most well-known of such examples, an example which also exemplifies the interplay between courts (and specifically the European Court of Justice) and political power: the *Kadi* case.[14] The *Kadi* case has been the most controversial example of judicial reasoning by the Court of Justice in recent years. The authors of this chapter argue that the 'somewhat dualist' reasoning developed in *Kadi* arose not out of a generalised conceptual—and strictly dualist—approach to the relationship between international law and EU law, but was rather the result of the relative level of protection of fundamental rights in the specific context, leaving open the possibility of a 'Solange'-type solution in the future. They draw attention to the need for the Court to take account of the 'internal discourse' with national constitutional courts (to use Eckes' term) as well as its 'external discourse' vis à vis the UN Security Council, arguing that this balance is essential not only to 'integration through law' within the EU but also to maintaining the position of the EU towards international law—a position which, as we have seen, requires autonomy as well as capacity. In other words, the Union's competence to implement Security Council resolutions (also confirmed in the *Kadi* judgment) entails the duty to ensure that such implementation is compatible with the fundamental rights that have constitutional status for both the Union and its Member States. By the time of the second *Kadi* judgment,[15] important changes had been made to the delisting procedure at the UN level, including the appointment of an independent Ombudsperson. Kokott and Sobotta suggest that these developments might enable the emergence of another type of Solange-relationship, based on a requirement that action before the EU courts should be preceded by an (unsuccessful) application for delisting to the Office of the Ombudsperson. The Court could, it is suggested, borrow from its approach to Member States' national courts in cases involving autonomous sanctions, an approach based on the principle of loyal cooperation.[16] The principle of loyal cooperation, which applies to national and EU courts without compromising their autonomy,[17] could thus develop an external dimension.[18] This possibility illustrates the contribution

---

[13] C Eckes, ch 10 of this volume.

[14] Joined Cases C-402/05 P and C-415/05 P *Kadi* (n 7).

[15] Case C-584/10P *Commission v Kadi*, judgment of 18 July 2013, nyr.

[16] T-348/07 *Al-Aqsa v Council* [2010] ECR II-4575, para 163.

[17] *Cf* Opinion 1/09 (n 3), paras 84–85.

[18] *Cf* the argument of the Court in *Kadi* to the effect that although not legally bound by the UN Security Council resolution, the EU should observe undertakings given in the context of the UN: Joined Cases C-402/05 P and C-415/05 P *Kadi* (n 7), paras 292–94.

the CJEU could make to the international rule of law as (partially) represented by the UN and the system established by the European Convention and Court of Human Rights.

The European Court of Human Rights (ECtHR) is of course a close neighbour of the European Court of Justice and might perhaps appear as a competitor, provoking a 'selfish' response of the type identified by de Witte in chapter 3. In chapter 12, Heliskoski discusses the relationship between the Court of Justice and the ECtHR in the light of the projected accession of the Union to the Convention, and in particular Article 3(6) of the draft Accession Agreement.[19] According to this, in proceedings to which the EU is co-respondent, and where the CJEU has not yet assessed the compatibility of the relevant EU law with the Convention, 'sufficient time shall be afforded for the Court of Justice of the European Union to make such an assessment'. This procedure (the so-called 'prior involvement' mechanism) could be said to facilitate the type of local self-healing referred to by Kokott and Sobotta, although it can also be characterised as a concession to the Court's insistence on its exclusive jurisdiction as far as EU law is concerned, and as a form of EU exceptionalism or preferential treatment. Heliskoski's analysis of the rationale for the procedure leans towards the latter view. He shows that, on the one hand, it is not extraordinary for the EU to submit itself to external adjudication via an international agreement,[20] and, on the other hand, that in a number of Member States at least the possibility exists for the ECtHR to be required to rule on the compatibility of domestic law with the Convention without the constitutional court having first had the opportunity to do so.[21] The specificities of the relationship between the national courts, the CJEU and the ECtHR may provide some justification for this special procedure; certainly the drafting history of the Accession Agreement demonstrates the part played by the CJEU in developing the idea of such a provision. Heliskoski's conclusion is that this concern may evidence recognition by the CJEU that in the case of EU accession to the European Convention on Human Rights (ECHR) it would simply be impossible not to accept, in a subsequent case, a ruling by the ECtHR finding a violation of the Convention by the EU.

If so, this would stand in contrast to the approach of the CJEU to WTO dispute settlement mechanisms. Kuijper, in chapter 6, presents the Court's case law on the effect of international agreements in the EU legal order as a manifestation of its concern with the institutional balance of power and especially the power of the EU's legislative institutions, in particular the Council and the European

---

[19] A request has been made by the Commission under Art 218(11) TFEU for an opinion of the Court of Justice as to the compatibility of the Accession Agreement with the EU Treaties: Opinion 2/13, pending.

[20] See also the examples cited by de Witte in ch 3 of this volume. As Heliskoski points out, the ECtHR will not be adjudicating on the validity of EU law, but rather on possible breaches of Convention rights.

[21] See also de Witte, ch 3 in this volume, pointing out that this is a privilege not offered to national constitutional courts and citing both favourable and unfavourable commentary.

Parliament. In our final chapter, we return to this theme: the relationship between the Court and the legislature in their approach to international law. Wouters, Odermatt and Ramopoulos seek to contrast the approach of the Court to that of the legislature, which they argue is 'more open and receptive'. Whether one sees the CJEU's approach to international law as being a matter of loyalty or fidelity or one of openness and friendliness, or even unfriendliness, it is for the Court itself, as an expression of the autonomy of the EU legal order, to determine that relationship in accordance with Treaty provisions such as Article 3(5) and 21(1) TEU. Arguing that respect for international law should be included among the Union's fundamental constitutional principles the authors of this chapter contend that the Court should adopt a less reticent role than the one described by Cremona in chapter 2. This might, they suggest, take the form of a more flexible interpretation of the doctrine of 'functional succession', whereby in fields where there has been a complete transfer of competence, the EU may be found to have succeeded to the international obligations of the Member States. The doctrine has in practice been very rarely applied, and Wouters, Odermatt and Ramopoulos here suggest that the Court could adopt, in a wider range of cases where the EU exercises competence, a kind of voluntary self-binding to international obligations binding all the Member States. For the Court to take on this role would undoubtedly go beyond the principle of consistent interpretation—derived from the principle of sincere cooperation—and would have implications for legislative/judicial balance within the EU. At present such self-binding may be achieved via legislative reference.[22] The Court certainly seems to regard such policy choices as a matter for the legislature, and as this chapter demonstrates, the legislature has developed a practice in some fields of incorporating international standards although they are non-legally binding in character or are not directly binding on the EU.

We have here, then, a variety of different perspectives on the role of the Court of Justice in the development of EU external relations law. Naturally they do not all adopt the same conclusions but together they help to build up a complex picture with some identifiable features. The Court's reasoning (and its conception of the Union's external actorness) is based on its idea of the Union's legal capacity and the autonomy of its system of external legal relations. This capacity is exercised through an institutional framework and the Court sees itself as having a central position in that structure, maintaining the relative powers of the different actors—Member States as well as institutions—so as to ensure the effective exercise of the EU's powers. A number of core principles—such as effectiveness and the principle of sincere cooperation—operate on the articulation of these structures and have the potential to be further developed, for example, in the context of the CFSP, and in the Court's relations with other sources of international obligation, including courts. The autonomy of the Union's legal order is

---

[22] See, for example, the reference to the AETR in Regulation 561/2006/EC [2006] OJ L102/1.

an essential dimension of the Union's ability to be an independent actor within the international legal system: the Court asserts its exclusive jurisdiction over Union law and therefore its right to define the relationship between Union law and international law. But strikingly, in doing so the Court has emphasised both the importance of the choices made by the Union's political and legislative institutions and the constitutional structures within which those choices are made.

Part I

The CJEU's Role in the Development
of External Relations Law

2

A Reticent Court? Policy Objectives and the Court of Justice

MARISE CREMONA

I. INTRODUCTION

I T IS ALMOST a truism to refer to the Court of Justice (hereafter also referred to as 'the Court') as the motor of integration within the European Union legal order. In particular, the Court has played a crucial, even determinative role in the creation of the complex multi-layered form of governance that is now so characteristic of the European Union (hereafter referred to as 'the EU' or 'the Union'). In the external policy field, the Court has played an important role in defining the scope and nature of Community competence, and the legal effect of international obligations. It has not, however, been a driving force behind a policy agenda in the same way that the creation of the single market has influenced its approach to substantive treaty provisions on discrimination, competition policy or free movement. In the context of EU external action, the nature of the Treaty provisions, with a weaker set of policy objectives and fewer substantive legal obligations on the Member States, has left much to the agenda-setting of the political institutions.

This chapter examines the role that the Court of Justice has assumed—as evidenced by the approach taken in its case law—in relation to the Union's external policy objectives. The starting point is an observation: the Court appears to be reticent (non-interventionist) if not deferential as regards the policy choices of the political institutions in external relations. It tends to take those choices at face value (basing itself on statements in legal instruments and policy documents); it does not question them, nor seek to define or shape them. More than this, it emphasises the need for the political institutions to retain their policy discretion, their room for manoeuvre. This is in contrast to its interventionist—if not activist—stance in relation to the definition of the scope of EU external competence and its implications for Member States, and its 'gatekeeper'—if not defensive—role in relation to the status of international law within in the EU legal system (roles which are explored in other contributions).

The chapter seeks to establish a workable framework to understand this approach of the Court to EU external policy objectives by identifying some of the characteristics of those external objectives (see section II), and then placing the case law in the context of the Court's approach to EU internal policy objectives (see section III(A)) and to institutional and competence-related issues in external relations (see section III(B)). Its conclusion is that the Court, in the field of external relations, does not itself define the Union's objectives, nor derive them from the Treaty. It accepts them as defined by the political institutions and then uses the jurisdiction it exercises over the respective competences and obligations of the institutions and the Member States to enforce them.

II. THE NATURE AND FUNCTION OF FOREIGN POLICY OBJECTIVES

Although, as Larik has demonstrated,[1] the EU is by no means unique in enshrining foreign policy objectives in its constitution, these objectives play a distinctive role in the context of the EU, which remains an organisation of conferred powers. Union objectives authorise action and delimit powers; they provide the basis for the conferral of external powers in Article 216(1) TFEU, and thereby also define the limits of such powers.[2] Further, the EU institutions are required to specify the reasons on which a legal act is based (Article 296 TFEU), and the identification of objectives will help to determine the correct legal basis of EU instruments.[3] Union objectives are also the basis of the duty of sincere cooperation: the Member States are required by Article 4(3) TEU to 'facilitate the achievement of the Union's tasks and refrain from any measure which could jeopardise the attainment of the Union's objectives'. This has enabled the Court to impose an obligation on Member States not to depart from an agreed common negotiating strategy even where not laid down in a legally binding decision of the Council.[4]

The Court will refer to the objectives of international instruments in interpreting EU law and will interpret international instruments in the light of EU objectives. In the *Bosphorus* case the Court interpreted the scope of a sanctions Regulation in the light of the objectives of a UN Security Council Resolution.[5] In *Kadi* the Court affirmed that the EU, in drawing up measures implementing a Security Council resolution, was under a duty to take due account of the terms

---

[1] J Larik, 'Shaping The International Order as a Union Objective and the Dynamic Internationalisation of Constitutional Law', CLEER Working Paper 2011/5; J Larik, 'Worldly Ambitions: Foreign Policy Objectives in European Constitutional Law', PhD thesis defended at the European University Institute (EUI), June 2013.

[2] See, for example, Opinion 1/94 on the competence of the Community to conclude international agreements concerning services and the protection of intellectual property [1994] ECR I-5267, paras 81–86.

[3] Case C-370/07 *Commission v Council* [2009] ECR I-08917. Choice of legal basis must be based on objective factors amenable to judicial review and these include the aim and content of the measure.

[4] Case C-246/07 *Commission v Sweden* [2010] ECR I-03317; see further below.

[5] Case C-84/95 *Bosphorus v Ministry of Transport, Energy and Communications* [1996] ECR I-3953.

and objectives of the resolution.[6] The case law on the duty of conforming interpretation is based on the need to reconcile where possible the objectives of EU and international instruments: indeed, one of the EU's general external objectives is precisely to contribute to 'the strict observance and the development of international law, including respect for the principles of the United Nations Charter'.[7] As both *Bosphorus* and *Kadi* demonstrate, this applies even where the EU is not itself bound by the international instrument, if it is binding on the Member States. Thus in *Intertanko*, the Court held that 'the provisions of secondary law which fall within the field of application of Marpol' should be interpreted 'taking account' of Marpol.[8] However, this principle may work both ways: in *Lesoochranárske zoskupenie VLK* the Court said 'if the effective protection of EU environmental law is not to be undermined, it is inconceivable that Article 9(3) of the Aarhus Convention be interpreted in such a way as to make it in practice impossible or excessively difficult to exercise rights conferred by EU law'.[9]

What then is the nature of the Union's external objectives and where are they found? Prior to the Lisbon Treaty, although the EU was mandated to 'assert its identity on the international scene', there was no single set of objectives for the Union's external policy to help define what that identity might be. The Union had a number of external policies each with its own objectives, but there was no overall policy framework and consistency was left to the vigilance of the policy-makers; the objectives of the Community's implied external powers were inevitably defined in terms of internal policy objectives.[10] The Lisbon Treaty sought to move beyond this fragmented approach towards a more systematic account of overall external policy objectives. It did this by creating a set of general provisions governing the Union's external action, including a list of common objectives, and requiring that both specifically defined external policies such as the common foreign and security policy, the common commercial policy and development policy, and the external dimensions of other policies, pursue these objectives.[11] On the basis of these Treaty-based objectives, the European Council is to define the 'strategic interests and objectives' of the Union, and the Council and Commission assisted by the High Representative are to ensure consistency.[12] Within this overall framework we may identify four types of objective:

(i)   Objectives common to all Union action, external as well as internal. These include the promotion of equality between men and women (Article 8

---

[6] Joined Cases C-402/05 P and C-415/05 P *Yassin Abdullah Kadi and Al Barakaat International Foundation v Council and Commission* [2008] ECR I-06351, para 296; see also Joined Cases C-584/10 P, C-593/10 P and C-595/10 P *European Commission, United Kingdom and Council v Yassin Abdullah Kadi*, judgment of 18 July 2013, para 106.

[7] Art 3(5) TEU, *cf* also Art 21(2)(b) TEU; see below nn 13 and 15.

[8] Case C-308/06 *Intertanko* [2008] ECR I-4057, para 52.

[9] Case C-240/09 *Lesoochranárske zoskupenie VLK v Ministerstvo životného prostredia Slovenskej republiky*, 8 March 2011, para 49.

[10] See Opinion 1/94 (n 2).

[11] Art 21(3) TEU.

[12] Arts 21(3) and 22(1) TEU.

TFEU), the protection of human health (Article 9 TFEU), combating discrimination based on sex, racial or ethnic origin, religion or belief, disability, age or sexual orientation (Article 10 TFEU), the protection of the environment (Article 11 TFEU), and animal welfare (Article 13 TFEU).

(ii) Objectives general to all Union external action. These include the general statement of aims in Article 3(5) TEU[13] and the objectives listed in Article 21 TEU. Article 21 first of all sets out the principles (later in the same paragraph referred to as 'these values') which have 'inspired its own creation, development and enlargement'. Not only are these principles to guide EU external action; that action is to be designed to promote them 'in the wider world'. They include 'democracy, the rule of law, the universality and indivisibility of human rights and fundamental freedoms, respect for human dignity, equality and solidarity, and for international law'.[14] Article 21 in a second paragraph then sets out a series of more specific objectives for all Union external action.[15] The list incorporates objectives taken from specific policy areas in the pre-Lisbon treaties such as the Common Foreign and Security Policy (CFSP), development cooperation policy, common commercial policy and environment policy as well as some new references to stronger multilateral cooperation and good global governance.

(iii) Objectives that are mentioned in the context of specific external policies, including in particular 'the progressive abolition of restrictions on international trade and on foreign direct investment' (Article 206 TFEU, applying to the common commercial policy) and the eradication of poverty as the 'primary objective' of the Union's development cooperation policy (Article 208 TFEU). However, it is made clear that these specific policy objectives are to operate in the context of the general external objectives. Thus, although the

---

[13] Art 3(5) TEU: 'In its relations with the wider world, the Union shall uphold and promote its values and interests and contribute to the protection of its citizens. It shall contribute to peace, security, the sustainable development of the Earth, solidarity and mutual respect among peoples, free and fair trade, eradication of poverty and the protection of human rights, in particular the rights of the child, as well as to the strict observance and the development of international law, including respect for the principles of the United Nations Charter'.

[14] This statement in Art 21(1) in fact reflects Arts 2 and 3 TEU, which set out these principles—or values—as underpinning all Union activity (including external action).

[15] Art 21(2) TFEU: 'The Union shall define and pursue common policies and actions, and shall work for a high degree of cooperation in all fields of international relations, in order to: (a) safeguard its values, fundamental interests, security, independence and integrity; (b) consolidate and support democracy, the rule of law, human rights and the principles of international law; (c) preserve peace, prevent conflicts and strengthen international security, in accordance with the purposes and principles of the United Nations Charter, with the principles of the Helsinki Final Act and with the aims of the Charter of Paris, including those relating to external borders; (d) foster the sustainable economic, social and environmental development of developing countries, with the primary aim of eradicating poverty; (e) encourage the integration of all countries into the world economy, including through the progressive abolition of restrictions on international trade; (f) help develop international measures to preserve and improve the quality of the environment and the sustainable management of global natural resources, in order to ensure sustainable development; (g) assist populations, countries and regions confronting natural or man-made disasters; and (h) promote an international system based on stronger multilateral cooperation and good global governance'.

existing common commercial policy objective of the progressive abolition of restrictions on international trade is still there, the common commercial policy now also has an explicit sustainable development and human rights mandate derived from Article 21 TEU. The relationship between specific and general objectives is well expressed by the Court in the *Small Arms* case, while acknowledging that development cooperation policy will legitimately encompass the promotion of democracy and respect for human rights:

> While the objectives of current Community development cooperation policy should therefore not be limited to measures directly related to the campaign against poverty, it is none the less necessary, if a measure is to fall within that policy, that it contributes to the pursuit of that policy's economic and social development objectives ...'.[16]

(iv)   To these we may add a fourth type of objective: specific legislative objectives as expressed in legal acts, normally in the Preamble. As already mentioned, a legal act must include a statement of the reasons on which it is based and this will provide an indication of the legislature's objectives.[17] These legislative objectives are in fact engaged by the Court more readily than Treaty-derived objectives and are used to help determine competence and legal basis.[18] In this category we may also include objectives as expressed in non-legally binding Acts, such as strategy documents and Council Conclusions, which may also be referred to in the Preambles of legal Acts and which have also been used by the Court.[19]

Treaty-based objectives are open-ended, plural and (with the possible exception of Article 208 TFEU), unprioritised. Goals are acknowledged not to depend solely on the EU (the EU is to 'contribute' to peace, security, sustainable development and trade liberalisation). More important, although they reflect a perception that an enlarged Union with increasingly diversified fields of activity needs to be more explicit as to the overall direction of its policies, they are progressive objectives which help to define a policy direction or strategy, rather than end-goals. There is no external 'telos' or end purpose to which external policy is leading. In this it differs from the Union's internal policy objectives where specific goals are identified, especially in the context of the establishment of the internal market (freedom of movement, abolition of internal frontiers, common policies on agriculture, transport and competition, economic and monetary union), but is perhaps more like the foreign policy of a state, which has no defined end point although it may have directional or aspirational objectives.

---

[16] Case C-91/05 *Commission v Council* [2008] ECR I-3651, para 67.

[17] Art 296 TFEU.

[18] For an example, see Case C-411/06 *Commission v European Parliament & Council* [2009] ECR I-07585.

[19] See, for example, the use by the Court of the EU strategy on small arms and light weapons adopted by the European Council in December 2005 (Council doc. 5319/06 PESC 31 of 13 January 2006) in Case C-91/05 *Commission v Council* (n 16), to help determine the appropriate legal basis for a Council decision.

III. A RETICENT COURT

The characteristics of EU external objectives just outlined raise a number of questions: do they constrain the legislature/executive and empower the Court? Or do they—since they are so undefined—empower the legislature? Put differently, do these objectives help to sustain the principle of conferred powers, or do they undermine that principle by providing the basis for an almost unlimited external competence? Do they help to define a distinctive global role and international identity for the EU? Or do they simply exacerbate the capability—expectations gap[20] and invite accusations that the EU is cynically dressing up its interests in high-sounding but essentially meaningless words? The way in which the Court handles external policy objectives in its case law may help us to answer these questions.

A. Facilitating Union Objectives through a Flexible Use of Instruments

The Court has been willing to accept the use of European Community (now EU) instruments for purposes incidental to the policies in which they find their legal basis. This has been particularly striking with respect to trade measures, which have used to support development objectives;[21] for environmental and public health purposes;[22] and—in the case of economic sanctions adopted prior to the Maastricht Treaty—to further political and foreign policy objectives.[23] In *Werner*, which concerned the export of dual-use goods, the Court said that 'a measure ... whose effect is to prevent or restrict the export of certain products, cannot be treated as falling outside the scope of the common commercial policy on the ground that it has foreign policy and security objectives'.[24]

Nonetheless, there are limits: the Court in *Kadi* baulked at the idea that trade competence might be used as a legal basis for individual sanctions, on the ground that a measure falls within the common commercial policy 'only if it relates specifically to international trade in that it is essentially intended to promote, facilitate or govern trade and has direct and immediate effects on trade in the products

---

[20] C Hill, 'The Capability-Expectations Gap, or Conceptualizing Europe's International Role' (1993) 31 *Journal of Common Market Studies* 305.

[21] For example, the generalised system of preferences: Case 45/86 *Commission v Council* [1987] ECR 1493. See also Opinion 1/78/EEC on the International Agreement on Natural Rubber [1979] ECR 2871.

[22] Case C-62/88 *Greece v Council* [1990] ECR I-01527.

[23] See, for example, Council Regulation (EEC) 990/93 of 26 April 1993 concerning trade between the EEC and the Federal Republic of Yugoslavia (Serbia and Montenegro) [1993] OJ L102/14, interpreted without any allusion to competence or legal basis in Case C-84/95 *Bosphorus* (n 5). See also Case C-124/95 *R v HM Treasury and Bank of England ex p Centro-Com* [1997] ECR I-81.

[24] Case C-70/94 *Fritz Werner Industrie-Ausrustungen GmbH v Germany* [1995] ECR I-3189, para 10.

concerned'.[25] In this case, the Regulation's 'essential purpose and object' was combating international terrorism through freezing of the economic resources of individuals and entities, and although trade effects might be the result, '[h]aving regard to that purpose and object, it cannot be considered that the regulation relates specifically to international trade in that it is essentially intended to promote, facilitate or govern trade'.[26] And in the same case, although the Court accepted that Article 301 EC (now Article 215 TFEU) could be used as the basis for financial sanctions against individuals connected to a government, it held that that Article alone was an insufficient basis for sanctions against individuals and groups with no connection to the government of a third country. It nevertheless managed to find a means to accommodate the Union's desire to use a Union instrument to implement the UN sanctions by approving the combined use of Articles 60, 301 and 308 EC:

> Inasmuch as they provide for Community powers to impose restrictive measures of an economic nature in order to implement actions decided on under the CFSP, Articles 60 EC and 301 EC are the expression of an implicit underlying objective, namely, that of making it possible to adopt such measures through the efficient use of a Community instrument. That objective may be regarded as constituting an objective of the Community for the purpose of Article 308 EC.[27]

The Court here approves, through the use of Article 308 EC (now Article 352 TFEU), the use of powers granted for one purpose (restrictive measures against third countries) in order to achieve an extended objective which is non-explicit in the Treaty but which is derived from legislative choice: the Community objective is defined as 'implementing restrictive measures of an economic nature through the use of a Community instrument'.[28]

B. Identifying Legislative Objectives

The match between instruments and policy objectives also underlies the legal basis cases. Here too, although the Court insists on the need for objective criteria ('the choice of the legal basis for a measure, including one adopted in order to

---

[25] Joined Cases C-402/05P and C-415/05P *Yassin Abdullah Kadi and Al Barakaat International Foundation v Council and Commission* (n 6), para 183. For a recent reaffirmation of this definition of the scope of CCP powers in the context of Art 207 TFEU, while taking a sufficiently broad view of the 'specific relation' to trade so as to encompass the whole of the TRIPS agreement, see Case C-414/11 *Daiichi Sankyo Co Ltd v DEMO*, judgment 18 July 2013, paras 51–53.

[26] Joined Cases C-402/05P and C-415/05P *Yassin Abdullah Kadi and Al Barakaat International Foundation v Council and Commission* (n 6), paras 184–86. *Cf* the Court's ruling in its *Tobacco Advertising* judgment on the use of former Art 100a EC: 'a measure adopted on the basis of Article 100a of the Treaty must genuinely have as its object the improvement of the conditions for the establishment and functioning of the internal market': Case C-376/98 *Germany v European Parliament and Council* [2000] ECR I-08419, para 84.

[27] ibid, paras 226–27.

[28] ibid, para 229.

conclude an international agreement, does not follow from its author's conviction alone, but must rest on objective factors which are amenable to judicial review'[29]), in practice it tends to follow the legislature's choice. The objective factors it relies on include the aim and content of a measure. When ascertaining a measure's aim, the Court in practice accepts without question the legislature's own assertions. The author's conviction alone may not be enough, but when the author expresses that conviction in a Preambular statement—especially one that adopts the Court's own phraseology—that will be accepted. For example, in a case where it was accepted that a Regulation had an environmental purpose, the question being whether it also had a commercial policy purpose that was strong enough to require a joint legal basis, the Court said:

> In those circumstances, it is necessary to examine whether the objective and components of the contested regulation relating to the protection of the environment must be regarded as being the main or predominant objective and component. That is indeed the case. First, as regards the objective of the contested regulation, recital 1 in the preamble thereto states that '[t]he main and predominant objective and component of this Regulation is the protection of the environment'.[30]

In the *Small Arms* case, the Court also used the Preamble to the decision at issue in order to determine that the decision was designed to further both CFSP and development cooperation objectives 'without one of those objectives being incidental to the other'.[31] The same is true of the Court's analysis of the decision at issue in the *PNR* case.[32] In a more recent case on the correct legal basis for Regulation 1286/2009, which amended Regulation 881/2002 imposing restrictive measures against the Al-Qaida network, Advocate General Bot argued that the Regulation is not concerned with combatting terrorism *tout court*, but that its 'ultimate aim'—taken from the Preamble—'is to prevent terrorist crimes, including terrorist financing, in order to maintain international peace and security'. Since he then argued that the maintenance of international peace and security, although presented in the Treaty as a general objective of EU external action, is 'among those traditionally assigned to' the CFSP, he was able to conclude that Article 215 TFEU, because of its explicit link to the CFSP, is the correct legal basis.[33]

---

[29] Opinion 2/2000 on the conclusion of the Cartagena Protocol [2001] ECR I-9713, para 22.

[30] Case C-411/06 *Commission v European Parliament & Council* (n 18), paras 49–51. Indeed recital 1 even adds, 'its effects on international trade being only incidental'.

[31] Case C-91/05 *Commission v Council* (n 16), para 99.

[32] Joined Cases C-317/04 and C-318/04 *European Parliament v Council* [2006] ECR I-4721, para 55.

[33] Case C-130/10 *European Parliament v Council*, Opinion of AG Bot, 31 January 2012, paras 63–64. While the Court did not wholly follow this reasoning, it did take the view that the evidence of external objectives (*in casu*, combating international terrorism in order to preserve international peace and security) of an anti-terrorism measure supported the use of an external policy legal basis, in this case Art 215 TFEU as opposed to the Area of Freedom, Security and Justice legal basis Art 75 TFEU: judgment of 19 July 2012, para 61.

The above comments are not intended as a criticism of this reliance on Preambular statements of purpose. Once it has been decided that the aim of a measure is one of the key criteria for its legal basis, then it is reasonable to look to the Preamble to discover that aim. But clearly the move from 'author's conviction' to 'objective criterion' is rather easily satisfied once the author has learned to frame the Preamble in terms which reflect the Court's legal basis case law.[34] There is no sign in the Court's case law of a tendency to look behind these statements or to adopt 'substance over form' reasoning.

C. Prioritising Objectives

The Court has not sought to establish priorities among the external objectives expressed in the treaties—for example, by identifying certain ones as 'fundamental'—and has accepted the legislature's assessment of relative policy priorities. Thus, although the Treaty has from the start included among the objectives of trade policy the reductions of barriers to international trade, the legislature may decide how to balance this objective with the 'Union interest'. In *UK v Council*,[35] the Court held significantly that the objective of trade liberalisation was not a 'rule of law' binding the legislature and that therefore it could be departed from as a matter of policy discretion even in the case of a trade regulation whose primary objective was indeed liberalisation. We are used to the Court accepting a broad executive discretion and a corresponding reduction in its scope for judicial review in 'complex economic situations', including trade policy.[36] The point here is that the Court interprets the Treaty objective of liberalisation so as to leave room for that discretion; it 'cannot compel the institutions to liberalise imports from non-member countries where to do so would be contrary to the interests of the Community'.[37] And, crucially, the Court is willing to leave the assessment of the Community interest to the legislature. In *Bosphorus*, too, in the context of economic sanctions, the Court accepted the legislator's judgment in balancing

---

[34] Thus the framing of the Preamble can be critical if there is a potential legal basis dispute. See, for example, the original version of recital 1 to what became Regulation 1013/2006, proposed in COM (2003) 379 by the Commission: 'The primary objective of the Regulation is protection of the environment and the legal basis is therefore Article 175(1) of the EC Treaty. However, since the provisions of Titles IV, V and VI on exports out of, imports into and transit through the Community to and from third countries, are also rules on international trade, the legal basis as regards these specific provisions is Article 133 of the EC Treaty'. This was replaced in the final Regulation: 'The main and predominant objective and component of this Regulation is the protection of the environment, its effects on international trade being only incidental'. As we saw, this formulation was regarded as highly persuasive by the Court: see n 30 above.

[35] Case C-150/94 *United Kingdom v Council* [1998] ECR I-07235.

[36] See, for example, Case C-351/04 *Ikea Wholesale* [2007] ECR I-7723, para 40, 'in the sphere of the common commercial policy and, most particularly, in the realm of measures to protect trade, the Community institutions enjoy a broad discretion by reason of the complexity of the economic, political and legal situations which they have to examine ...'.

[37] ibid, para 67.

interests: 'the importance of the aims pursued by the regulation at issue is such as to justify negative consequences, even of a substantial nature, for some operators'.[38] Article 206 TFEU, which replaces Article 131 EC, adopts a more imperative language: the Union *shall* contribute to the progressive abolition of restrictions on trade; but the words used ('contribute', 'harmonious', 'progressive') still leave scope for legislative balancing of interests and it does not seem likely that the Court will take this as a mandate to prioritise liberalisation above all other Union interests or substantially fetter legislative discretion.

Just as the Court has not prioritised objectives, neither has it looked for opportunities to establish fundamental principles to guide external action akin to the principle of non-discrimination in the internal context. In the case of *Faust*, for example, the Court held that a Council Regulation granted the Commission a wide measure of discretion to adopt protective measures against imports and 'expressly permitted a selective application in favour or to the detriment of certain non-member countries'.[39] The Court argued that there is no general principle of non-discrimination with respect to non-Member States:

> Although Taiwan certainly appears to have been treated by the Commission less favourably than certain non-member countries, it should be remembered that there exists in the Treaty no general principle obliging the Community, in its external relations, to accord to non-member countries equal treatment in all respects.[40]

As these examples show, there is certainly no assumption that objectives and principles deemed fundamental at the 'internal' level, such as free movement and non-discrimination, are equally fundamental in external policy. But neither has the Court developed an alternative set of fundamental objectives and principles applicable to external policy. Instead it leaves room to the policy-makers. Could it be argued that the treaties themselves, after the Lisbon Treaty reform, now offer an opportunity for the Court to develop fundamental or overriding objectives? There is no sign that the Court will read the treaties in this way. In *Kadi II*, for example, the Court readily refers to the Article 21 TEU objectives, especially that of preserving peace and strengthening international security.[41] Despite having characterised the protection of fundamental rights as one of 'the principles that form part of the very foundations of the Community legal order',[42] and reaffirming the importance of judicial review in the context of anti-terrorism sanctions, it accepts the need to strike 'a fair balance between the maintenance of international peace and security and the protection of the fundamental rights and freedoms of

---

[38] Case C-84/95 *Bosphorus* (n 5), para 23.
[39] Case 52/81 *Offene Handelsgesellschaft in Firma Werner Faust v Commission* [1982] ECR 3745, para 9.
[40] ibid, at para 25.
[41] Joined Cases C-584/10 P, C-593/10 P and C-595/10 P *European Commission, United Kingdom and Council v Yassin Abdullah Kadi* (n 6), para 103, referring to Art 3(1) and (5) TEU and Art 21(1) and (2)(a) and (c) TEU.
[42] ibid (n 6), para 304.

the person concerned'.[43] The expressly-formulated objectives in Articles 3(5) and 21 TEU allow the Court to frame the issue in terms of Treaty-based principles but the Court does not use them to alter its previous approach or to derive a normative hierarchy.

D. Room for Manoeuvre and Negotiating Discretion

We thus find in the Court's judgments an emphasis on the need to preserve room for the exercise of political discretion and the policy choices of the legislature and the EU's negotiators. A clear example is the Court's case law on the World Trade Organization (WTO):

> To accept that the role of ensuring that those rules [ie WTO rules] comply with Community law devolves directly on the Community judicature would deprive the legislative or executive organs of the Community of the scope for manoeuvre enjoyed by their counterparts in the Community's trading partners.[44]

Agreements to resolve disputes within the framework of the WTO are the outcome of political negotiation; they are not 'designed to ensure the implementation in the Community legal order of a particular obligation assumed in the context of the WTO' and are thus not within the *Fediol* exception;[45] and even where *Fediol* does apply, the Court may conclude that the WTO only requires a negotiated solution without imposing any constraints on its outcome.[46]

In *Commission v Sweden* (PFOS), the key to Sweden's default, according to the Court, was that it had acted in a way that was 'likely to compromise the principle of unity in the international representation of the Union and its Member States and weaken their negotiating power with regard to the other parties to the Convention concerned'.[47] The Court emphasised the way in which Sweden's action, as it claimed, had effectively pre-empted the choice between exercising a collective Union vote and voting as individual Member States.

In the *ATAA* case Advocate General Kokott emphasises the need to allow policy-makers to determine how to fulfil the EU's international treaty obligations. She argues that although Article 2(2) of the Kyoto Protocol gives expression to the Contracting Parties' preference for a multilateral solution to the reduction of greenhouse gases from aviation, which should not be disregarded by the legislature, the attempt to achieve this multilateral outcome must be weighed against

---

[43] ibid (n 6), para 131.

[44] Case C-149/96 *Portugal v Council* [1999] ECR I-8395, para 46.

[45] ibid, para 51, referring to Case 70/87 *Fediol* v *Commission* [1989] ECR 1781.

[46] Case C-352/96 *Italy v Council* [1998] ECR I-06937, para 22, interpreting Article XXIV(6) GATT: 'the parties are required to achieve "mutually satisfactory compensatory adjustment". The concept of "mutually satisfactory compensatory adjustment" does not in itself constitute an objective criterion and the requirement to achieve a mutually satisfactory agreement must be regarded as fulfilled when an agreement embodying a solution is concluded by the parties concerned'.

[47] Case C-246/07 *Commission v Sweden* [2010] ECR I-03317, para 104.

meeting the objectives of the Kyoto regime, if necessary by adopting national or regional measures:

> Whether and when the European Union, working outside the framework of the ICAO [International Civil Aviation Organisation], should unilaterally take measures to limit or reduce greenhouse gases from aviation is ultimately a question of expediency, which it is for the European Union's political authorities to determine. Whilst this does not mean that the relevant EU institutions could in that respect act free from judicial scrutiny, it should nevertheless be noted that they have a wide discretion in decisions requiring assessment of complex economic and social matters, as well as in decisions on external action. It is precisely in the weighing up of the advantages and disadvantages of acting alone at a regional level to limit or reduce greenhouse gases from aviation and in choosing the timing of such action that the competent EU institutions must be given a discretion.[48]

In the paradigmatic *AETR* case, achieving the international negotiating objective is regarded by the Court as even more important than maintaining the principle of exclusive competence:

> The negotiations on the AETR are thus characterized by the fact that their origin and a considerable part of the work carried out ... took place before powers were conferred on the Community as a result of Regulation no 543/69. ... At that stage of the negotiations, to have suggested to the third countries concerned that there was now a new distribution of powers within the Community might well have jeopardized the successful outcome of the negotiations.[49]

The right solution was therefore for the Commission and Council to 'reach agreement ... on the appropriate methods of cooperation with a view to ensuring most effectively the defence of the interests of the Community'.[50]

It is noticeable that in each of these examples the Court shows itself aware of the political realities of international negotiation. It also entrusts the determination, as well as the defence, of the Community interest, to the political institutions.

IV. CREATING AND PRESERVING AN INSTITUTIONAL POLICY SPACE

In order to bring out more clearly this reticence of the Court in the face of external objectives we may contrast it with the approach of the Court to (A) 'internal' objectives; and (B) institutional and competence-related issues, including the 'protection' of the EU legal space. These contrasts will then help us to understand better the role of the Court in relation to external policy objectives.

---

[48] Case C-366/10 *The Air Transport Association of America and Others*, judgment of 21 December 2011, paras 184–85 (footnotes omitted).
[49] Case 22/70 *Commission v Council* [1971] ECR 263, paras 84–86.
[50] ibid, para 87.

A. Internal Objectives

Let us take just one example of the Court's handling of internal legislative objectives. The *TNT* case[51] concerned the interpretation of Regulation 44/2001 on jurisdiction, recognition and enforcement of judgments in civil and commercial matters, and in particular its Article 71(1):

> This Regulation shall not affect any conventions to which the Member States are parties and which in relation to particular matters, govern jurisdiction or the recognition or enforcement of judgments.[52]

In this particular case, the international convention to which the Member States are parties (but not the EU) was the Convention on the Contract for the International Carriage of Goods by Road (CMR) and the case concerned the application of the *lis pendens* rule in that Convention. According to recital 25, Article 71 is founded upon respect for international commitments entered into by the Member States, although as the Court pointed out,[53] the provision is not only concerned with the Member States' commitments vis-à-vis non-Member States, but also ensures the application of specialised conventions within the EU itself—and indeed the *TNT* case concerned intra-EU carriage of goods. Put very briefly for present purposes, the Court subordinated Article 71(1) to what it saw as the fundamental objectives of the Regulation linked to the creation of an Area of Freedom, Security and Justice. The non-affect clause—and therefore the CMR—could apply only conditionally, insofar as its application did not adversely affect those objectives:

> While ... Article 71 of Regulation No 44/2001 provides, in relation to matters governed by specialised conventions, for the application of those conventions, the fact remains that their application cannot compromise the principles which underlie judicial cooperation in civil and commercial matters in the European Union ... Observance of each of those principles is necessary for the sound operation of the internal market, which, as is apparent from recital 1 in the preamble, constitutes the raison d'être of Regulation No 44/2001.[54]

Thus, the Court holds, jurisdictional rules such as *lis pendens* contained in specialised conventions 'can be applied in the European Union only to the extent that ... they are highly predictable, facilitate the sound administration of justice and enable the risk of concurrent proceedings to be minimised'.[55] What appeared to be a clear derogation inserted into the Regulation by the legislature has been qualified by the Court in the name of the Regulation's objectives. The Court prioritises

---

[51] Case C-533/08 *TNT Express Nederland BV v AXA Versicherung AG* [2010] ECR I-04107.
[52] Council Regulation (EC) No 44/2001 of 22 December 2000 on jurisdiction and the recognition and enforcement of judgments in civil and commercial matters [2001] OJ L12/1.
[53] Case C-533/08 *TNT Express Nederland BV v AXA Versicherung AG* (n 51), para 42.
[54] ibid (n 51), paras 49–50.
[55] ibid (n 51), para 53.

those objectives which are linked to the establishment of the internal market (deeper integration), as opposed to the objective, likewise found in the Preamble, of preserving the application of sectoral rules which although they may be less integrationist, apply to a larger number of countries, including third countries. When what is at stake, as the Court sees it, is internal market integration (free movement of judgments in the EU) the Court does not hesitate to prioritise this objective over an international regime, although insofar as the derogation is explicit ('this Regulation shall not affect') it suggests a reverse preference by the legislature.

> Article 71 of Regulation No 44/2001 cannot have a purport that conflicts with the principles underlying the legislation of which it is part. Accordingly, that article cannot be interpreted as meaning that, in a field covered by the regulation, such as the carriage of goods by road, a specialised convention, such as the CMR, may lead to results which are less favourable for achieving sound operation of the internal market than the results to which the regulation's provisions lead.[56]

What is striking here is the Court's willingness to identify an objective—the internal market—which underlies the immediate objective of the Regulation—free movement of judgments, and then to derive from that the necessary conditions for achieving that objective (mutual trust, legal certainty, minimising risk of concurrent proceedings etc), elevating these to non-derogable principles. Where the EU legislature sought to preserve an international sectoral regime, the Court insists on the need to protect the unity of the Union's internal legal space.

B. Determining the Scope and Effects of Union Competence

In contrast to the Court's reticence when it comes to assessing Union action in the light of its external policy objectives, it has had no hesitation in establishing principles and far-reaching rules governing the scope of Union competence, institutional questions concerning the exercise of that competence, and the obligations on the Member States, both of compliance and cooperation. As several other contributions demonstrate,[57] the Court confidently asserts the scope and nature of Union external competence, protects the institutional balance, and determines and enforces the Member States' obligations. For example: its insistence that legal basis is a matter of constitutional significance and subject to judicial control, inter alia since it determines the relative scope of Union and Member State powers;[58] its insistence on the importance of judicial review and the priority of EU primary law;[59] its development of the doctrines of exclusivity and pre-emption, thereby

---

[56] ibid (n 51), para 51.
[57] See, for example, the contributions by de Witte, Neframi and Van Elsuwege.
[58] Eg Opinion 2/2000 [2001] (n 29); Case C-91/05 *Commission v Council* (n 16).
[59] Eg the *Kadi I* and *Kadi II* cases (n 6).

curtailing the Member States' treaty-making powers;[60] its development of the duty of cooperation, now based on Article 4(3) TEU, requiring the Member States to exercise their own powers in ways which are compatible with EU law,[61] which do not hinder the exercise of its competence by the Union,[62] and which do not jeopardise the 'unity of international representation' of the Union.[63]

The Court also has no hesitation—and why should it?—in protecting what we might call its legal space. Here I have in mind its case law on international dispute settlement (explored here by Bruno de Witte);[64] on the interpretation of EU law, including EU agreements;[65] on the direct effect of international agreements;[66] and more generally on the effects of international law in the EU legal system.[67] The institutions, which as we have seen are allowed great latitude to determine and prioritise their external policy objectives, are subject to strict control when it comes to procedural requirements,[68] and defining the scope of EU law.[69]

C. Preserving a Policy Space

These seemingly contrasting positions of the Court (its willingness to identify and further internal Union objectives, and its confidence in defining the competences and duties of the institutions and the Member States) in fact provide a contextual explanation for the Court's reticence in relation to external policy objectives.

First, as we have seen, the EU's external objectives lack a 'telos'. There is no end point to which they seek to move the Union. Where the Treaty contains such a 'telos' (such as the internal market) the Court will promote and protect it. But in its external action the EU is given a task—to develop relations and

---

[60] Eg Case 22/70 *Commission v Council* (n 49); Case C-45/07 *Commission v Greece* [2009] I-00701; Opinion 1/03 on the competence of the Community to conclude the new Lugano Convention on jurisdiction and the recognition and enforcement of judgments in civil and commercial matters [2006] ECR I-1145.

[61] Case C-476/98 *Commission v Germany* [2002] ECR I-9855.

[62] Case C-266/03 *Commission v Luxembourg* [2005] ECR I-4805; Case C-433/03 *Commission v Germany* [2005] ECR I-6985; Case C-205/06 *Commission v Austria* [2009] ECR I-01301; Case C-249/06 *Commission v Sweden* [2009] ECR I-01335; Case C-118/07 *Commission v Finland* [2009] ECR I-10889.

[63] Case C-246/07 *Commission v Sweden* (n 4).

[64] Opinion 1/91 on the draft agreement between the Community, on the one hand, and the countries of the European Free Trade Association, on the other, relating to the creation of the European Economic Area [1991] ECR 6079; Opinion 1/2000 on the proposed agreement establishing a European Common Aviation Area [2002] ECR I-3493; Case C-459/03 Commission v Ireland [2006] ECR I-4635; Opinion 1/2009 on the draft agreement on the European and Community Patents Court [2011] ECR I-01137.

[65] Case 104/81 *Hauptzollampt Mainz v Kupferberg* [1982] ECR 3641.

[66] Case C-265/03 *Simutenkov* [2005] ECR I-2579.

[67] Case C-162/96 *Racke GmbH & Co v Hauptzollamt Mainz* [1998] ECR I-3655; Case C-239/03 *Commission v France* [2004] ECR I-9325; Case C-308/06 *Intertanko* (n 8).

[68] Case C-370/07 *Commission v Council* (n 3); Opinion 1/08 on the General Agreement on Trade in Services (GATS) [2009] ECR I-11129.

[69] Case C-240/09 *Lesoochranárske zoskupenie VLK* (n 9).

build partnerships with third countries and international, regional or global organisations,[70] it is given a number of policy fields in which to operate, a range of instruments, and a set of orienting, open-ended and non-prioritised objectives. Against this background the direction and goals of EU external policy must be set by the institutions themselves, and the Court is extremely rarely driven to find that the Union's powers have been misused.[71]

Instead, and this is the second point, it ensures that the institutions act within their powers, and that the Member States do not obstruct the formation and implementation of EU policy. It is in fact engaged in establishing and protecting an institutional space within which policy may be formed, in which the different actors understand and work within their respective roles.[72] Two recent well-known examples may illustrate this argument.

In the *PFOS* case[73] the Court found that Sweden, by taking unilateral action in the context of the Stockholm Convention, a mixed agreement, was in breach of the duty of cooperation established in what is now Article 4(3) TEU. Sweden, the Court said, had dissociated itself from a concerted common strategy within the Council. The Stockholm Convention is an international environmental agreement concluded by the Union on an environment legal basis, and Sweden argued that its action had not jeopardised the Union's environmental objectives. The Court, however, took account not only of the environmental objectives established in the treaties, but also of the objectives of the Council as defined in its 'common strategy'; these included 'economic factors' linked to listing under the Stockholm Convention and the decision to propose PFOS first for listing under a different international instrument, the Aarhus Protocol. These objectives were not even established in a formal legal act, but only in Council conclusions. Nevertheless they created an obligation of loyalty for the Member States. As has already been mentioned, the Court also drew attention to the effects of Sweden's action on the Union's position within the Convention's decision-making structures. The Court, then, was protecting the Council's policy-making process and the Union's room for manoeuvre under the Convention. It, unsurprisingly, did not try to evaluate the environmental risks and benefits of the Swedish action versus the Council's strategy.

In the Bilateral Investment Treaty cases,[74] the Court held that Sweden, Austria and Finland had failed to comply with their obligations under Article 307 EC (now

---

[70] Art 21(1) TEU.

[71] It is striking that one of the few cases in which the Court did find that the Community had acted outside its (external) powers (Joined Cases C-317/04 and C-318/04 *European Parliament v Council* [2006] ECR I-4721) concerned the use of an internal market legal basis for purposes that fell outside internal market objectives.

[72] *Cf* R Post, 'Constructing the European Polity: *ERTA* and the *Open Skies* Judgments' in L Azoulai and M Poiares Maduro (eds), *The Past and Future of EU Law* (Oxford, Hart Publishing, 2010).

[73] Case C-246/07 *Commission v Sweden* (n 4).

[74] Case C-205/06 *Commission v Austria* [2009] ECR I-01301; Case C-249/06 *Commission v Sweden* [2009] ECR I-01335; Case C-118/07 *Commission v Finland* [2009] ECR I-10889.

Article 351 TFEU) by not taking appropriate steps to eliminate incompatibilities between EU law and the provisions on transfer of capital contained in a number of their bilateral investment agreements or BITs. The incompatibility identified by the Court was based on the failure of the BITs to provide for restrictions on capital movements in case such a restriction might be required under EU law (for example, where legislative action is taken under Article 66 TFEU in case of serious difficulties in the management of the economic and monetary union, or under Article 215 TFEU in case of economic sanctions). No such restrictions were then envisaged, so the problem related to the possible future need to take immediate action: the effectiveness of such future action would require the measure to apply immediately. The Court here interprets the notion of incompatibility in such a way as to protect the ability of the Council to act swiftly should it deem this necessary, although such an act by the Council would itself derogate from a Treaty-based principle of freedom of capital movements. It is the freedom to take action in the future which is being protected.[75]

V. CONCLUSIONS

The EU's external policy objectives are non-teleological, non-prioritised, open-ended, and concerned more with policy orientation than goal-setting. They are defined at a number of levels (general Treaty objectives, general external objectives, sectoral objectives, and institutional or legislative objectives). The Court has tended to focus more on institutional/legislative objectives and uses them in the context of defining competences, distribution of powers, and obligations. In its focus on institutional objectives it has not sought to (re)define them or to impose overriding Treaty-based objectives or priorities; it has tended to accept at face value their objectives as expressed by the legislature or institutions, and has stressed the importance of political discretion. It has accepted the use of Treaty-based external instruments (such as trade instruments) for broader external policy objectives. It is perhaps less amenable to the use of internal (market) instruments to achieve external policy objectives.[76] In its case law on Union competence, institutional and Member State powers and obligations, the Court has asserted its jurisdiction not only over EU law per se, but also over the institutional space within which that law is made and policy objectives are set, and this includes establishing compliance and cooperation obligations designed to protect that space and resultant decisional outcomes.

Let us return to the questions posed earlier. Do the EU's external objectives constrain the legislature/executive and empower the Court? Or do they—since they are so undefined—empower the legislature? Do they help to sustain the

---

[75] *Cf* also Opinion 1/03/EC (n 60), para 126.
[76] See, for example: Joined Cases C-317/04 and C-318/04 *European Parliament v Council* (n 32); Case C-533/08 *TNT Express Nederland BV v AXA Versicherung AG* (n 51).

principle of conferred powers? Or do they undermine that principle by providing the basis for an almost unlimited implied competence? The answer here must be nuanced. On the one hand, the Court's approach does empower the legislature and political institutions (the *PFOS* and *Bilateral Investment Treaty* cases are examples of this). On the other hand, the Court itself is also empowered, in that it defines the institutional space and the framework of rules within which policy is made. The *Kadi* cases are a good example of both effects: that is to say, the Court manages to find a way to accommodate the legislature's desire to use Union powers to implement the UN Security Council Resolution despite the lack of a clear legal basis in the Treaty;[77] at the same time, the Court insists that the resultant legislation is subject to its own judicial control. And this approach of the Court does not in fact result in unlimited competence for the EU, for two reasons. First, part of the Court's role as institutional power-broker (for want of a better term) is to demonstrate the constitutional dimension of this function and it is quite willing to remind the institutions of the limits of conferred powers.[78] Second, the Court will defend internal objectives,[79] and will also take care that external competences implied from internal powers are used for the relevant Treaty-defined purposes.[80] So the more clearly-defined internal objectives impose some outer limits to external action.[81]

Do the Union's external objectives help to define a distinctive identity for the EU? Since the Court does not—at least so far—actively promote specific objectives, nor does it—at least so far—enforce Treaty objectives against policy judgments by the political institutions, we cannot argue that the Court itself promotes a distinctive external identity or agenda. But on the other hand, it leaves the other institutions free to use the Treaty-based objectives to do so, and it has been instrumental in shaping the structures within and through which the political institutions may define a strategy—how successfully they do so is another question.

[77] See text at n 27 above; for a critique of the legal basis reasoning in *Kadi I*, see M Cremona, 'EC Competence, "Smart Sanctions" and the Kadi Case' (2009) 28 *Yearbook of European Law* 559.

[78] Eg in Opinion 2/94 on the accession by the Community to the European Convention for the Protection of Human Rights and Fundamental Freedoms [1996] ECR I-1759; Joined Cases C-402/05 P and C-415/05 P *Yassin Abdullah Kadi and Al Barakaat International Foundation* (n 6); Case C-403/05 *European Parliament v Commission* [2007] ECR I-9045.

[79] *Cf* Case C-533/08 *TNT Express Nederland BV v AXA Versicherung AG* (n 51).

[80] Opinion 1/94 (n 2); Joined Cases C-317/04 and C-318/04 *European Parliament v Council* (n 32).

[81] See further M Cremona, 'EU External Relations: Unity and Conferral of Powers' in L Azoulai (ed), *The EU as a Federal Order of Competences?* (Oxford, Oxford University Press, 2014), 65.

3

A Selfish Court? The Court of Justice and the Design of International Dispute Settlement Beyond the European Union

BRUNO DE WITTE

I. INTRODUCTION

A MINOR BUT recurring theme in the external relations case law of the Court of Justice (hereafter also referred to as 'the Court' or 'the CJEU') is its diffidence towards other international courts and, more broadly, towards international dispute settlement mechanisms. The Court of Justice does not feel bound to follow closely the interpretations adopted by international courts or dispute settlement bodies, whether the World Trade Organization (WTO) Appellate Body or the European Free Trade Association (EFTA) Court or even (despite the apparent deference shown to it) the European Court of Human Rights.[1] I will not revisit that part of the Court's jurisprudence here. I will rather examine another facet of that same diffidence towards 'rival' dispute settlement mechanisms, namely *the way in which the Court of Justice has reacted to initiatives taken by the European Union's (hereafter referred to as 'the EU' or 'the Union') political institutions or by Member State governments to engage with new or existing international dispute settlement mechanisms.* On several occasions, the Court has sought to fend off the threat to the integrity of the EU legal order which those initiatives posed, as seen from its perspective. This diffident attitude raises the

---

[1] See generally M Bronckers, 'The Relationship of the EC Courts with Other International Tribunals: Non-Committal, Respectful or Submissive?' (2007) 44 *CML Rev* 601. On the Court's attitude towards WTO dispute settlement decisions, see A Thies, Case annotation in (2006) 43 *CML Rev* 1145, and A Tancredi, 'On the Absence of Direct Effect of the WTO Dispute Settlement Body's Decisions in the EU Legal Order' in E Cannizzaro, P Palchetti and R Wessel (eds), *International Law as Law of the European Union* (Leiden, Martinus Nijhoff, 2012) 249. For the argument that the ECJ makes a rather selective use of the case law of the ECtHR, see B de Witte, 'The Use of the ECHR and Convention Case Law by the European Court of Justice' in P Popelier, C Van de Heyning and P Van Nuffel (eds), *Human Rights Protection in the European Legal Order: The Interaction between the European and the National Courts* (Antwerp, Intersentia, 2011) 17.

question whether the Court might have been acting 'selfishly', i.e. acting to protect its own authority and prerogatives against rival international dispute settlement mechanisms. In this contribution, I will address that question by examining, one by one, the relevant Court rulings. Most of them are Opinions pursuant to what is now Article 218(11) TFEU, which allows the Court to decide on whether proposed EU external agreements are compatible with primary EU law.[2] Those compatibility assessments have repeatedly concerned, among other things, the possibility for the EU[3] to create a new international court together with other countries; or the possibility for the EU to accede to an existing international regime with a binding dispute settlement mechanism.

Those rulings generally address a tension between two sets of constitutional norms of EU law, both of which are clearly expressed in the text of the Treaties:[4]

> On the one hand, the principle emerging from various provisions in the Treaties that the ECJ has the ultimate authority on questions of interpretation and validity of EU law, coupled with the express rule (which is outside the TFEU chapter dealing with the Court) that 'Member states undertake not to submit a dispute concerning the interpretation or application of the Treaties to any method of settlement other than those provided for therein.' (Article 344 TFEU). The latter article can be considered, from an overall international perspective, as the 'archetypal exclusive jurisdiction clause'.[5]

> On the other hand, the constitutional value emerging from various provisions in the Treaties but now expressly laid down in Article 3 (5) TEU that the European Union shall contribute to international cooperation and to the development of international law. This duty logically implies that the EU should favour initiatives that strengthen the effectiveness of international treaties by means of adjudicatory or other compliance mechanisms, so as to help improving the current situation of 'uneven judicialisation'[6] of international law.

If one puts side by side these two sets of legal norms, they do not seem to conflict with each other. When looking at the same issues in national constitutional law, one would normally not consider that a constitutional provision encouraging openness to international cooperation could pose a threat to the authority of the supreme courts of the country. However, in EU law, the two constitutional norms have repeatedly interfered with each other. One structural factor contributing to

---

[2] For a thorough analysis of the law and practice of the Opinion procedure, see S Adam, *La procédure d'avis devant la Cour de justice de l'Union européenne* (Brussels, Bruylant, 2011).

[3] In this contribution, generic references to 'European Union' (EU) or 'EU law' should be understood as comprising also the European Community (EC) and EC law of pre-Lisbon times. The term 'European Community' (and related terms) will be used only when specific reference is made to legal facts that took place before the entry into force of the Lisbon Treaty.

[4] I use the term Treaties to indicate the TEU and TFEU taken together, in accordance with its usage in those Treaties themselves.

[5] Y Shany, *The Competing Jurisdictions of International Courts and Tribunals* (Oxford, Oxford University Press, 2003) at 180.

[6] B Kingsbury, 'International Courts: Uneven Judicialisation in Global Order' in J Crawford and M Koskenniemi (eds), *The Cambridge Companion to International Law* (Cambridge, Cambridge University Press, 2012) 203.

this interference is the monist doctrine[7] of the Court of Justice. Since its *Haegeman* judgment,[8] the Court has held that international agreements concluded by the EU form part of the EU legal order and fall within the Court's competence to interpret EU law which—according to Article 344 TFEU—is in principle exclusive. If those agreements provide for their own dispute settlement mechanisms, there will be a situation of competing jurisdiction between those mechanisms and the Court of Justice. Whereas international law has no clear conflict rules for cases of competing jurisdiction,[9] the Court of Justice has developed its own conflict rules in the course of time. As we shall see, it has not excluded the possibility of creating new dispute settlement mechanisms to ensure compliance with international agreements concluded by the EU, but it has carefully sought (whenever it had the occasion to do so) to avoid limitations being made to its own authority to interpret and enforce EU law. In order to achieve the latter objective, it has nipped in the bud a number of international tribunals.

II. OPINION 1/76: THE FUND TRIBUNAL

Although this Opinion is well known for the general statements made by the Court about EU external relations law,[10] the draft international agreement which it examined in this Opinion was very trivial: it aimed at creating a small international organisation between the European Economic Community (EEC), six of its Member States and Switzerland, to run a 'Laying up Fund' to compensate shippers using the Rhine basin who were prepared to withdraw their ships in times of overcapacity. The agreement also created a mini-court, the Fund Tribunal, to decide on the validity and interpretation of decisions of the Fund organs. Whereas the Court of Justice did not object to the creation of that Tribunal as such, it did object to the fact that six of its seven judges were to be members of the European Court of Justice (ECJ) itself. Instead of showing appreciation for the occasion thus offered to control and 'streamline' the activity of the Fund Tribunal, the ECJ held that this composition could create problems if the same legal question would arise first before the Fund Tribunal and later before the Court of Justice (or vice versa), as the 'double hatted' judges could then no longer act impartially.[11] So, despite the

---

[7] In a recent contribution, Cannizzaro proposes the term 'neo-monism', to emphasise the fact that the Court of Justice regulates, and limits, the impact of international law in the EU legal order despite the formal recognition that international treaties become part of the EU legal order upon their ratification: E Cannizzaro, 'The Neo-Monism of the European Legal Order' in *International Law as Law of the European Union* (n 1), 35.

[8] Case 181/73 *R & V Haegeman v Belgian State,* judgment of 30 April 1974.

[9] For an exhaustive discussion of this question, see Shany, *The Competing Jurisdictions of International Courts and Tribunals* (n 5).

[10] On which, see for example P Koutrakos, *EU International Relations Law* (Oxford, Hart Publishing, 2006) 92–96.

[11] ECJ, Opinion 1/76 *Draft Agreement establishing a European laying-up fund for inland waterway vessels* [1977] ECR 471. The part of the Opinion dealing with the Fund Tribunal is in paras 17–22.

fact that the Court rejected the way in which the Commission and the Member States had envisaged the creation of an international tribunal, this Opinion is not an example of 'selfishness' as defined above, but rather of perhaps exaggerated attention to detail.

III. OPINION 1/91: THE EEA COURT

This Opinion is known for its lofty constitutional language, which the Court used eventually to veto the creation of a new international court. The original version of the Agreement creating a European Economic Area (EEA) covering the EC and a number of EFTA states provided for the creation of a new court, the EEA Court (with a court of first instance added to it) which would be tasked with dispute settlement between the contracting parties, and with the enforcement of the EEA Agreement and its later implementing acts with regard to EFTA states. The Agreement did not take away any part of the existing jurisdiction of the ECJ. In Opinion 1/91, the Court of Justice held that the system of judicial supervision created by the Agreement was incompatible with the EEC Treaty.

In its relevant part, the Opinion started by making a generous statement which the Court has repeated in several later rulings:

> An international agreement providing for (…) a system of courts is in principle compatible with Community law. The Community's competence in the field of international relations and its capacity to conclude international agreements necessarily entails the power to submit to the decisions of a court which is created or designated by such an agreement as regards the interpretation and application of its provisions.[12]

Yet, even if the creation of an international court was not, by itself, considered impermissible, this particular court, the EEA Court, did not pass muster for a number of reasons.

The EEA Agreement did not regulate a specialised domain (as in Opinion 1/76) but took over a large amount of existing Community internal market rules 'which constitute, for the most part, fundamental provisions of the Community legal order'.[13] Although the EEA Court was not given jurisdiction to interpret EC law as such, the fact that it would interpret and apply identically-worded rules of EEA law (even if only with regard to cases stemming from the EFTA states) could lead to a 'contamination' of the EC legal order:

> in so far as it conditions the future interpretation of the Community rules on free movement and competition the machinery of courts provided for in the agreement conflicts with article 164 of the EEC Treaty and, more generally, with the very foundations of the Community.[14]

---

[12] Opinion 1/91Agreement on the European Economic Area [1991] ECR 6079, para 40.
[13] ibid, para 41.
[14] ibid, para 46.

The fact that the activity of an 'external' court would affect the interpretation of EU law can, by itself, not be enough to disqualify it; indeed, the Court admitted, in the passage quoted above, that an international agreement could establish a court that can give binding rulings on that agreement (which, in view of the *Haegeman* doctrine, are at the same time rulings about EU law). The decisive element, which damned the EEA Court, seems to have been that the role given to that external court affected the interpretation of *core* provisions of EC law: the Court of Justice wanted to retain full control in respect of that core.

The creation of the EEA Court was vetoed by the ECJ for another reason as well. By providing that the EEA Court would be competent to hear disputes 'between Contracting Parties', and given that both the EC and its Member States were among those contracting parties, the EEA Court would be led to rule on the respective competences of the EC and its Member States within the context of the EEA Agreement and would thus adversely affect the autonomy of the EC legal order and the exclusive jurisdiction of the ECJ.[15] The reasoning in this part of the Opinion seems rather far-fetched. It does not show much confidence in the capacity of an 'external' court to incidentally interpret EC law in the few disputes in which the question of division of competences would arise (whereas the ECJ itself very often interprets other international agreements when this appears useful for the application of EU law, and rightly so).

As a result of Opinion 1/91, the EEA Court disappeared from the legal scene. The original EEA Agreement was revised so as to create a split adjudication system, which was then approved by the Court in its subsequent Opinion 1/92. Under the revised agreement, an EFTA Court was created which was invited to follow as closely as possible the case law of the Court of Justice, and it has tried to do so ever since.[16] Its interpretations of internal market law may even, occasionally, influence the case law of the ECJ,[17] but at least the ECJ has no duty, under the Agreement, to consider the interpretations of its little sister, so that its ultimate authority is fully preserved. As a consequence of Opinion 1/91, the EEA Agreement also lacks an adjudication mechanism for disputes between the contracting parties, with the result that outside mechanisms can come into play. For example, Norway decided

---

[15] ibid, paras 14–15.

[16] There is an extensive literature exploring the way in which the EFTA Court has pursued this so-called homogeneity objective. See among others: C Baudenbacher, 'The EFTA Court: An Actor in the European Judicial Dialogue' (2004–05) 28 *Fordham International Law Journal* 353; C Timmermans, 'Creative Homogeneity' in M Johansson, M Wahl, U Bernitz (eds), *Liber Amicorum in Honour of Sven Norberg. A European for All Seasons* (Brussels, Bruylant, 2006) 471; H Haukeland Fredriksen, 'One Market, Two Courts: Legal Pluralism vs. Homogeneity in the European Economic Area' (2010) 79 *Nordic Journal of International Law* 481; S Magnússon, 'Judicial Homogeneity in the European Economic Area and the Authority of the EFTA Court' (2011) 80 *Nordic Journal of International Law* 507.

[17] See the analysis of EFTA Court influence on CJEU case law by C Baudenbacher, 'The EFTA Court, the ECJ, and the Latter's Advocates General—A Tale of Judicial Dialogue' in A Arnull, P Eeckhout and T Tridimas (eds), *Continuity and Change in EU Law—Essays in Honour of Sir Francis Jacobs* (Oxford, Oxford University Press, 2007) 90.

to challenge an EU regulation imposing a marketing ban on seal products before the WTO Dispute Settlement Body,[18] since the EEA Agreement—which is clearly relevant to the facts of the dispute—does not contain a binding dispute settlement mechanism. This example may show how the Court of Justice, by being unduly rigid towards the creation of quasi-EU jurisdictions, may paradoxically have favoured the use of dispute settlement mechanisms that are situated entirely outside the EU legal order.

IV. OPINION 2/94 (AND REFLECTION DOCUMENT OF 2010): THE EUROPEAN COURT OF HUMAN RIGHTS

In its famous Opinion 2/94, given in 1996, the ECJ denied to the Community the competence to accede to the European Court of Human Rights (ECtHR). It read in the text of the then Article 235 EC Treaty (the 'gap-filling clause', now Article 352 TFEU), which seemed like a possible legal basis for accession, an implied limit. Measures based on that Treaty article could not 'be used as a basis for the adoption of provisions whose effect would, in substance, be to amend the Treaty without following the procedure which it provides for that purpose'.[19] Accession to the European Convention on Human Rights (ECHR) would have such an effect and was thus not permissible on the basis of Article 235 (nor on any other legal basis).

It is obvious that the gap-filling competence of Article 235 could not be used to amend the Treaty, since amendment was subject to a separate procedure in the (then) next Article 236. But why would accession to the ECHR have meant a Treaty amendment 'in substance', if the existing text of the EC Treaty contained no wording prohibiting such accession? For the Court, accession would have entailed 'a substantial change in the present Community system for the protection of human rights in that it would entail the entry of the Community into a distinct international institutional system (...)', and this could only be done through a formal amendment of the EC Treaty. The 'distinct institutional system' to which the ECJ coyly referred was essentially the Convention's system of dispute settlement and adjudication, consisting at that time of a Commission and a Court. So, the substantial change—as identified by the ECJ—would consist in allowing outside adjudicatory bodies to examine possible human rights violations by the EC institutions. Although the ECJ did not refer explicitly to its own role in this

---

[18] Request for the Establishment of a panel by Norway, *European Communities—Measures Prohibiting the Importation and Marketing of Seal Products*, WT/DS401/5, 15 March 2011. A similar request was introduced by Canada. For discussion of the substantive issues raised by the dispute, see R Howse and J Langille, 'Permitting Pluralism: The *Seal Products* Dispute and Why the WTO Should Accept Trade Restrictions Justified by Noninstrumental Moral Values' (2012) 37 *Yale Journal of International Law* 367; T Perišin, 'Is the EU Seal Products Regulation a Sealed Deal? EU and WTO Challenges' (2013) 62 *ICLQ 373*.

[19] ECJ, Opinion 2/94 *Accession by the Community to the European Convention for Human Rights* [1996] ECR I-1759, para 30.

Opinion, it seems to have been worried mainly by the fact that it would have to relinquish, after accession, its own ultimate authority on questions of validity of EC law. Whereas the Opinion uses the language of constitutional integrity, there is a subtext of selfishness, which several commentators have noted.[20] The Court decided to (provisionally) close the door for accession to the ECHR, without stopping to consider the benefits of this accession for the protection of the rights of individual European citizens. The Court's preoccupation with its own role is even more striking when compared with what happened, in the same period, in the many countries of Central and Eastern Europe that acceded to the ECHR. In none of them was accession seen as requiring a constitutional amendment or as unduly affecting the authority of the domestic supreme courts.

A recent echo of the ECJ's concern for its own authority in the human rights field can be found in the Discussion Document of 5 May 2010 which the Court adopted in view of the upcoming negotiations of accession of the EU to the ECHR (now that the Treaty of Lisbon had made the pro-accession amendment which the Court had required in Opinion 2/94).[21] One may note that the Court very rarely adopts policy documents which are not strictly related to its own powers and procedures: this shows the importance which the Court attaches to the question of its future relations with the ECtHR. The discussion document asked the EU negotiators to provide for a 'privileged dialogue' route between the ECJ and the ECtHR, in the sense that the Strasbourg Court should not decide on applications directed against the EU without first allowing the ECJ to examine those cases in the light of the EU's own human rights standards. Later on, the President of the ECJ convinced the President of the Strasbourg Court to adopt a joint communication that reaffirmed the essence of the Discussion Document,[22] and the accession negotiation has, indeed, proceeded on this basis and has introduced a special interlocutory procedure allowing for a ECJ ruling on human rights compatibility of EU law whilst a case is pending in Strasbourg.[23] This is a truly privileged treatment

---

[20] See, for example, the case comment by G Gaja in (1996) 33 *CML Rev*, at 988: 'what is here at stake is the conservation by the Court of Justice of its present functions, although understandably the Court has not stressed this point in order not to emphasize its concern with its own prerogatives'. See also P Wachsmann, 'L'avis 2/94 de la Cour de Justice relatif à l'adhésion de la Communauté européenne à la Convention de sauvegarde des droits de l'homme et des libertés fondamentales' (1996) *Revue trimestrielle de droit européen* 467, at 484: 'une juridiction qui, jalouse de son pouvoir, adopte les réflexes mêmes qu'elle avait reproché aux juridictions nationales d'entretenir à son égard'.

[21] Discussion document of the Court of Justice of the European Union on certain aspects of the accession of the European Union to the European Convention for the Protection of Human Rights and Fundamental Freedoms, 5 May 2010, curia.europa.eu/jcms/jcms/P_64268/.

[22] Joint communication from the presidents of the European Court of Human Rights and the Court of Justice of the European Union, further to the meeting between the two courts in January 2011, 24 January 2011 (available on same webpage as in n 21).

[23] Art 3(6) of the draft accession Agreement, Council of Europe document 47+1(2013)008rev2 of 10 June 2013. The initiative of the ECJ, and the prior involvement of the ECJ in Convention cases which was provided, as a result, in the various drafts of the accession agreement, have been abundantly commented, with a good mix of favourable and unfavourable views. See, among others, T Lock, 'Walking on a Tightrope: The Draft ECHR Accession Agreement and the Autonomy of the EU Legal Order' (2011) 48 *CML Rev* 1025, 1045. See, further, the contribution by J Heliskoski to this volume.

since national constitutional courts do not have a similar guarantee for a 'first bite of the apple' when cases involving their state are pending in Strasbourg.[24] The Accession Agreement will also create a co-respondent mechanism between the EU and its Member States in cases brought against either of them before the ECtHR.[25] In this way, the Strasbourg Court will not have to rule on the respective competences of the Union and the Member States which was, precisely, one of the unacceptable elements in the first EEA Agreement which the ECJ had vetoed in its Opinion 1/91. In this manner, we could say that the old Opinion of 1991 still affects, in an important way, the regime of EU accession to the ECHR.[26]

V. CASE C-459/03 *COMMISSION V IRELAND (MOX PLANT)*[27]

In contrast with the previous rulings, this one did not originate from a request for an Opinion about a possible international agreement to be concluded by the Union. It arose, instead, from infringement proceedings brought by the Commission against a Member State for having submitted a dispute with another Member State to extra-EU dispute settlement mechanisms. The ECJ held in this case that Ireland had acted in breach of its EU law obligations by submitting a bilateral dispute with the United Kingdom about environmental pollution caused by a nuclear waste plant to the dispute settlement mechanism provided by the UN Convention on the Law of the Sea (UNCLOS). There was no doubt that the subject matter of the dispute was covered by UNCLOS and that the arbitral tribunal of UNCLOS could therefore adjudicate it. But the Commission argued, and the Court agreed, that by using the UNCLOS dispute settlement mechanism Ireland had breached the rule now laid down in Article 344 TFEU, according to which EU Member States may not submit disputes between themselves, relating to EU law, to outside dispute settlement mechanisms. Indeed, the facts of the dispute fell within the scope of UNCLOS but also, in part, within the scope of EU environmental law. The drafters of the original EEC Treaty provision, which is now Article 344 TFEU, had probably wanted to create a 'self-contained regime' whereby the judicial enforcement of EEC law would not be shared between the special court

---

[24] Indeed, although individual complaints are only admissible before the ECtHR after exhaustion of the available national judicial remedies, those remedies do not necessarily include a judgment by the country's constitutional court. This is particularly the cases for the numerous countries (including France and Italy) where there is no direct individual recourse to the Constitutional Court and where the Constitutional Court must be seized of a fundamental rights issue through a reference by one of the lower national courts—which does not always happen.

[25] Art 3 of the draft accession Agreement (n 23).

[26] See, for this point, C Eckes, 'The European Court of Justice and (Quasi-) Judicial Bodies of International Organisations' in RA Wessel and S Blockmans (eds), *Between Autonomy and Dependence—The EU Legal Order under the Influence of International Organisations* (Dordrecht, Springer, 2013) 85, at 97.

[27] Case C-459/03 *Commission v Ireland*, judgment of 30 May 2006. Among the many comments of the judgment, see N Lavranos, 'The Scope of the Exclusive Jurisdiction of the Court of Justice' (2007) 32 *EL Rev* 83.

created for the EEC and general judicial authorities such as the International Court of Justice (ICJ); but did they also seek to ensure that, if a future dispute would fall within the scope of two overlapping special legal regimes, the dispute settlement of the EEC would entirely pre-empt the use of the other dispute settlement regime? This was, anyway, the radical interpretation adopted by the ECJ in *Mox Plant*. It added that 'the institution and pursuit of proceedings before the arbitral tribunal (…) involve a manifest risk that the jurisdictional order laid down in the treaties, consequently, the autonomy of the Community legal system may be adversely affected'.[28] This is strong language! If two Member States occasionally bring a dispute before an international tribunal instead of bringing an infringement action under the TFEU, where the subject matter of the dispute is only partly within the scope of EU law, and where the international tribunal has specialist knowledge of the subject, does this really form a threat to the autonomy of the EU legal order? Surely, a decision adopted in such circumstances by the 'outside' adjudicator would not bind the EU and would not prevent the CJEU from adopting its own interpretation of the relevant rules of EU law in a later case? The Court was, in fact, criticised by some commentators of this judgment for adopting a hegemonic posture on the issue of regime overlap.[29]

VI. OPINION 1/09: THE EUROPEAN AND COMMUNITY PATENTS COURT

The most recent of the Court's diffident rulings in relation to international dispute settlement is also one of the most striking (and arguably most selfish) of them all. In Opinion 1/09, the Court held that the projected creation of a European and Community Patents Court, to adjudicate disputes arising under a set of Europe-wide patent rules, was unlawful for being incompatible with the integrity of the EU legal order.[30] Thereby, the Court prevented the creation of a useful and specialised international adjudication system in a domain in which

---

[28] Case C-459/03 *Commission v Ireland* (ibid) para 154.

[29] M Prost, *The Concept of Unity in Public International Law* (Oxford, Hart Publishing, 2012) at 42–43, who further argues that 'this decision artificially 'Communitarises' whole portions of the law of the sea and asserts, in absolute terms, the autonomy and superiority of the Community system over the universal regime of the UN'. See also S Adam, 'Het Europees Hof van Justitie en andere internationale rechtsprekende organen. Enkele opmerkingen naar aanleiding van het *Mox-fabriek arrest*' (2007) *Revue belge de droit international* 113, at 147.

[30] Opinion 1/09 of 8 March 2011, Agreement on a European and Community Patents Court, [2011] ECR I-1137. Among the comments on this Opinion (so far), see R Baratta, 'National Courts as "Guardians" and "Ordinary Courts" of EU Law: Opinion 1/09 of the ECJ' (2010) 38 *Legal Issues of Economic Integration* 297; S Adam, 'Le mécanisme prejudiciel, limite fonctionnelle à la compétence externe de l'Union—Note sur l'avis 1/09 de la Cour de justice' (2011) *Cahiers de Droit Européen* 277; J Alberti, 'Il parere della Corte di giustizia sul Tribunale dei brevetti europeo e comunitario' (2012) *Il Diritto dell'Unione Europea* 367; LN González Alonso, 'Fundamentalismo constitucional en Luxemburgo? El Tribunal de Justicia y los límites de la autonomía del sistema jurídico de la Unión Europea a la luz del Dictamen 1/09' (2012) *Revista Española de Derecho Europeo* 251; and also the Editorial, 'The Court of Justice as the Guardian of National Courts—or not?' (2011) 36 *EL Rev* 319.

forum shopping between national courts has had a detrimental impact on the international protection of intellectual property rights.

The remote origins of this Opinion are situated in the 1970s. In 1973, a number of European countries, including the EC Member States of that time, signed the European Patent Convention (EPC), which provides for a unitary procedure for the granting of patents by a European Patent Office (EPO) based in Munich. The EPC has now 38 contracting parties.[31] The patents granted by the EPO have a Europe-wide validity, but the actual rights of the patent holder remain defined by the domestic law of the contracting states, and must be enforced through their domestic courts. The EPC did not then, and does not today, provide for a system of international litigation.

The EC, and later the EU, have attempted for many years to go further than this, and to establish a truly harmonised and uniformly applicable patent system, similar to the EU trademark system.[32] The absence of such a system has repeatedly been described, in Commission documents and in the scholarly literature, as an important missing element in the regulation of the internal market. The Council finally reached political agreement on such a unitary EU patent in 2010, but, due to the opposition of Italy and Spain to the restricted language regime that was chosen, this EU Patent Regulation was eventually adopted by means of the enhanced cooperation mechanism.[33]

Since all EU states are also parties to the EPC, the Commission and Council sought to build on that existing and well-tested regime: EU patents would be granted by the EPO, and rules of the EPC would apply to those EU patents except where the EU regulation contains specific rules. In order to allow for the harmonious application and enforcement of this bifurcated European patent regime, the Council drafted an international agreement, to be concluded between the EU, its Member States and the third countries which are parties to the EPC, creating a *European and Community Patents Court* (ECPC) with exclusive jurisdiction to hear individual actions related to 'European' and 'Community' patents, in particular actions for infringement.[34] The ECPC would thus have served both the EU (with its Member States) and the other EPC countries that would decide to

---

[31] The original text of the EPC Convention, as well as its current revised version, can be found at www.epo.org/law-practice/legal-texts/epc.html.

[32] For discussions of the long and winding history of EU patent regulation initiatives, see, among many others: V Di Cataldo, 'From the European Patent to a Community Patent' (2002) 8 *Columbia Journal of European Law* 19; H Ullrich, 'Patent Protection in Europe: Integrating Europe into the Community or the Community into Europe?' (2002) 8 *European Law Journal* 433; H Ullrich, 'National, European and Community Patent Protection: Time for Reconsideration' *EUI Working Papers*, LAW 2006/41; T Jaeger, 'The EU Patent: *cui bono et quo vadit?*' (2010) 47 *CML Rev* 63.

[33] Regulation of the European Parliament and of the Council No 1257/2012 of 17 December 2012 implementing enhanced cooperation in the area of the creation of unitary patent protection OJ [2012] L361/1, and the accompanying Council Regulation No 1260/2012 of 17 December 2012 OJ [2012] L361/89, which deals with the translation arrangements.

[34] This draft agreement was prepared before the entry into force of the Treaty of Lisbon, hence the reference to the 'Community' instead of the 'Union' in the denomination of the court.

participate in its creation. It would be composed of a court of first instance (itself comprising a central division and local and regional divisions) and a Court of Appeal. Although negotiations on this agreement had not yet started, the scheme was submitted to the Court of Justice in order to seek its approval in principle. The Court, in its Opinion 1/09 of 8 March 2011, decided that the agreement was incompatible with the EU legal order.

It could have seemed that the EU institutions, when designing the agreement, had taken due account of the severe lessons imparted by the ECJ in its previous Opinions. In particular, and unlike the ill-fated EEA Court, the ECPC would not have jurisdiction for the settlement of disputes between the contracting states, but would only deal with cases brought by private parties. Also, the danger of the ECPC drifting away from the general case law of the ECJ was minimised by the fact that its court of first instance would have been *enabled* to request preliminary rulings from the Court of Justice on matters of EU law (including the interpretation of the new EU patent regulation), and its Court of Appeal would have been *obliged* to request such rulings. So, the ultimate authority of the ECJ to apply and interpret EU law could seem to have been guaranteed under the draft agreement. However, this time, the Court of Justice used an entirely new and surprising[35] 'fundamental objection': it held that, by vesting exclusive jurisdiction in the ECPC for a number of patent disputes, the agreement would have limited the normal role of national courts in applying EU law (namely, the future EU patent regulation) and would therefore also have limited their power and duty to ask preliminary rulings from the ECJ. By doing so, the agreement would have altered 'the essential character of the powers which the Treaties confer on the institutions of the EU and on the Member States and which are indispensable to the preservation of the very nature of European Union law'.[36]

One may wonder whether there really is such an essential difference between the 'normal' system in which the national courts are mandated to apply EU law and to ask preliminary questions from the ECJ, and the special mechanism proposed for patents in which a specialised international court would also (but not only) apply EU law and be required to ask preliminary questions from the ECJ in that context? The main difference, according to the Court of Justice, seems to be that the national courts of the Member States can be disciplined more effectively in performing that role by the threat of 'punishment' if they do not perform their duties, by means of 'Köbler' liability actions or by means of infringement actions by the Commission; whereas there is no such judicial sanction for 'disobedience' by an international court![37] The strange logic of that argument is that national courts can (only) be trusted to be faithful actors of the EU legal order because they must fear sanctions if they do not perform their duties. Does this logic reflect

---

[35] The surprising nature of the objection is shown by the fact that the Advocates General, in their submission to the Court, had not mentioned it at all.

[36] Opinion 1/09 (n 30), para 89.

[37] ibid (n 30), paras 86–88.

the spirit of judicial cooperation and dialogue that is supposed to underpin the preliminary reference mechanism?

Note that the choice made by the jurists of the Council, and of the Member States, to bypass the national court systems and to entrust the application of patent law to a new international court was not born out of a capricious desire to undermine the existing system of judicial enforcement of EU law. It sprang, instead, from the wish to preserve the integrity of the EPC and to integrate the non-EU parties to the EPC within a common system of patent adjudication.

As a result of this Opinion, the EU institutions and the Member States had to return to the drawing board. Their subsequent deliberations eventually led to the signature, on 19 February 2013, of an Agreement on a Unified Patent Court.[38] In this new version, the Union itself is no longer a party to the agreement. The non-EU state parties to the EPC are no longer welcome to participate in the activities of the new court, whose judgments will apply only within the territory of the EU (except Italy and Spain), and whose jurisdiction will no longer include the judicial review of EPO patent grant decisions. Still, in substance, the new court will continue to apply the EPC in addition to the new EU patent regulation. It will acquire exclusive jurisdiction—instead of the national courts—for the settlement of a number of disputes relating to the (old) European patents and the (new) 'European patents with unitary effects'. The link of the new court with the EU legal order is made stronger than in the earlier version. In fact, the new court is defined as 'a court common to the Contracting Member States and thus subject to the same obligations under Union law as any national court of the Contracting Member States'[39]—most importantly, the obligation to make preliminary references to the ECJ on matters of EU (patent) law. Its errors in the application of EU law are expressly declared to allow for liability actions and for infringement actions, both of which will be directed against the Member States, as the 'masters' of the Unified Patent Court.[40] By means of this acrobatic and entirely unprecedented construction, the Member States have sought to respond, in the narrowest possible way, to the objections made by the ECJ in Opinion 1/09, whilst keeping the new Patent Court 'safely' outside the *immediate* jurisdiction of the Court of Justice (in accordance, apparently, with the wishes of the patent law 'community').[41] One may conclude that a project that held the promise of improving the effective application of a well-established international agreement (the EPC) was sacrificed on

---

[38] The final text of the Agreement—after many earlier drafts had been debated and then modified within the Council, and after discussions with the European Parliament—was approved in December 2012. See the text of the Agreement in Council doc. 16351/12 of 11 January 2013.

[39] Agreement on a Unified Patent Court, Art 1(2).

[40] See ch IV (Arts 20–23) which is significantly entitled '*The Primacy of Union Law, Liability and Responsibility of the Contracting Member States*'.

[41] In the new 'package', substantive rules on patent infringements were excised from the text of the Patent Regulation (and therefore from EU law) and re-inscribed in the Agreement on the Unified Patent Court, so that they are no longer part of EU law, and are therefore not subject to the interpretation of the CJEU. This move was decided at the highest political level, see European Council Conclusions of 28/29 June 2012, point 3.

the altar of the ECJ's self-referential view of the autonomy of the EU legal order, although the final result is still the creation of a separate court, and with the ECJ being denied a major role in the new litigation system.[42] Since the new Agreement (unlike the previous version) is not one to be concluded by the EU, the Court of Justice cannot exercise its usual legal control power by means of an Opinion based on Article 218 (11) TFEU. It would seem that the Member State governments, by concocting their almost surrealist design for the Unified Patent Court, have sought to retaliate against the Court of Justice for its veto against the creation of the ECPC.

VII. A CONCLUDING ASSESSMENT

From the analysis of the Court rulings above, three main legal rules emerge. Firstly, the ECJ has repeatedly held that it is acceptable for the EU and its Member States to conclude international agreements providing for compulsory dispute settlement, including the creation of new international courts whose decisions will bind the EU; indeed, from the perspective of strengthening the international rule of law (which is an objective supported by Article 3(5) EU Treaty), the fact that some international treaties are equipped with a mechanism of compulsory adjudication is to be applauded. Secondly, the ECJ has also consistently held, since the *Haegeman* judgment, that international agreements concluded by the EU institutions form an integral part of the EU legal order. Thirdly, the ECJ has also taken very seriously the Treaty provision that vests in it an exclusive jurisdiction for disputes between Member States; it has added to this, in Opinion 1/09, an exclusive jurisdiction for the Member State courts to hear disputes between individuals on matters of EU law.

These three legal propositions cannot easily be combined, though. If EU agreements form part of EU law, and if the ECJ and Member State courts, taken together, have a complete and exclusive jurisdiction to interpret and apply EU law, how much room is there then for the participation by the EU in international dispute mechanisms set up by treaties concluded by the EU or to which the EU wishes to accede? In practice, though, there is still room for such forms of international adjudication, either because some agreements slipped through the net (most remarkably the WTO Agreements, whose dispute settlement mechanism was not scrutinised by the ECJ in Opinion 1/94); or because the EU institutions and the third states try to accommodate the wishes of the ECJ as best they can (as is happening with accession to the ECHR); or, more simply, because the EU or its Member States become engaged in an international dispute settlement

---

[42] In the words of one observer, the new regime is 'designed as an international law exclave from the Union's legal order, within which, however, it is supposed to operate and to produce its effects' and it 'only adds to the byzantine complexity of the overall system' (H Ullrich, 'Select from within the System: The European Patent with Unitary Effect', *Max Planck Institute for Intellectual Property and Competition Law Research paper* No 12-11, at 45).

mechanism without anybody bothering to ask the ECJ's permission. Indeed, the Court of Justice can only pronounce itself if seized in accordance with one of the procedures provided by the European Treaties. If a 'rival' international dispute settlement exists, without its existence being submitted to the Court's scrutiny, the potential incompatibility can remain in existence for a long time. An example of this is provided by the bilateral investment treaties (BITs) concluded between countries that are now Member States of the EU; these are mostly agreements concluded during the 1990s between 'old' EU Member States and future EU Member States from Central and Eastern Europe. Those 'intra-EU BITs' typically provide for the possibility of investors to bring claims for violation of the BIT to an independent arbitration tribunal. In so far as, after accession of the host state to the EU, the subject matter of the BIT overlaps with norms of EU law, one could consider that an arbitration tribunal would breach the jurisdictional monopoly of the Court of Justice, following the *Mox Plant* doctrine. This point was argued, for example, in the submission by Slovakia in the *Eureko* case, but the investment tribunal that heard the case confirmed its own jurisdiction, and the German *Oberlandesgericht Frankfurt,* in front of which the arbitration award was challenged by Slovakia, upheld the decision of the investment tribunal without feeling the need to refer this question to the Court of Justice for a preliminary ruling.[43] In this way, the Court of Justice was not (yet) put in a position to decide the question of whether, or to what extent, bilateral investment dispute resolution is still permissible under an investment treaty concluded between two EU Member States.

Nevertheless, the jurisprudence of the Court of Justice on the permissibility of creating new international courts certainly casts a shadow on the international initiatives of the EU and of its Member States. Nobody can criticise the Court of Justice for wanting to preserve the unique nature of the adjudication system established by the European Treaties, and fine-tuned by the Court itself in the course of time. But we would nevertheless conclude by arguing that the Court, in preserving the autonomy of the EU legal order in the face of rival international adjudication systems, has occasionally been a little selfish, showing more concern for its own role than for the advancement of the broader agenda of promoting the international rule of law.

[43] *Eureko BV v The Slovak Republic,* Award on jurisdiction, arbitrability and suspension, PCA Case No. 2008-13, of 26 October 2010; Oberlandesgericht Frankfurt-am-Main, Decision of 10 May 2012. For discussion of this issue, and of the *Eureko* case in particular, see K von Papp, 'Clash of "Autonomous Legal Orders": Can EU Member State Courts Bridge the jurisdictional Divide between Investment Tribunals and the ECJ? A Plea for Direct Referral from Investment Tribunals to the ECJ' (2013) 50 *CML Rev* 1039; and see also S Hindelang, 'Circumventing Primacy of EU Law and the CJEU's Judicial Monopoly by Resorting to Dispute Resolution Mechanisms Provided for in Inter-se Treaties? The Case of Intra-EU Investment Arbitration' (2012) 39 *Legal Issues of Economic Integration* 179.

4

A Powerless Court?
The European Court of Justice and
the Common Foreign and Security Policy

CHRISTOPHE HILLION[1]

I. INTRODUCTION

W HILE DECONSTRUCTING THE old pillar architecture of the
European Union (hereafter referred to as 'the EU' or 'the Union'),
the Treaty of Lisbon maintained the traditional dichotomy between
the Union's Common Foreign and Security Policy (CFSP) (including the
Common Security and Defence Policy), and its other external competences,
encompassing the previous European Community (EC) 'external relations'
and the external facet of the Police and Judicial Cooperation in Criminal
Matters (PJCCM) (ie former Title VI TEU).[2] Not only did the authors of the
Treaty entrench the procedural specificity of the CFSP, they also attempted
to circumscribe its effects, notably on Member States' foreign policies.[3] And
yet, this is a policy that is arguably more incorporated than ever within the
EU constitutional order, as its definition and implementation are increasingly

---

[1] I have greatly benefited from the insightful discussions held at the Florence conference where the
chapter was presented as a paper, and more particularly from the comments made by Irene Blazquez,
to whom I am especially grateful. All mistakes are mine.
[2] Further on this dichotomy, see eg: G De Baere, *Constitutional Principles of EU External Relations*
(Oxford, Oxford University Press, 2008), especially ch 6; P Van Elsuwege, 'EU External Action after the
Collapse of the Pillar Structure: In Search of a New Balance Between Delimitation and Consistency'
(2010) 47 *CML Rev* 987; D Thym, 'The Intergovernmental Constitution of the EU's Foreign, Security
& Defence Executive' (2011) 7 *European Constitutional Law Review* 453; A Dashwood, 'Article 47
TEU and the Relationship between First and Second Pillar Competence' and M Cremona, 'Defining
Competence in EU External Relations' in A Dashwood and M Maresceau (eds), *Law and Practice of
EU External Relations—Salient Features of a Changing Landscape* (Cambridge, Cambridge University
Press, 2008) 34 and 70, respectively; J-C Piris, *The Lisbon Treaty—A Legal and Political Analysis*
(Cambridge, Cambridge University Press, 2010).
[3] See Art 24 TEU, Art 40(2) TEU, and Declarations 13 and 14 attached to the Final Act of the
Intergovernmental Conference which adopted the Treaty of Lisbon, OJ [2010] C83/335.

determined by the Union's structures.[4] A useful barometer to gauge the degree of such incorporation is the role that has been assigned to the EU judicature with respect to that policy.

In at least three different ways, the Treaty of Lisbon has reformulated the Court of Justice's (hereafter also referred to as 'the Court') jurisdiction in relation to the CFSP.[5] First, it has made it possible for the Court, albeit within limits, to *exercise judicial control* with regard to certain CFSP acts, thus abolishing the policy's traditional immunity from judicial supervision. Second, it has recalibrated the Court's role in *patrolling the borders* between EU (external) competences based on the TFEU and the CFSP, turning it into the guarantor of the latter's integrity. Third, the Treaty has generalised the Court's capacity to *enforce the principles underpinning the Union's legal order*. The chapter will examine these three levels of jurisdiction in turn and argue that while constitutional restrictions remain as regards judicial intervention in the CFSP area,[6] the Court of Justice is nevertheless *not* as powerless as one might posit on a cursory look at the TEU and TFEU.

[4] See eg: A von Bogdandy and M Nettesheim, 'Ex Pluribus Unum: Fusion of the European Communities into the European Union' (1996) 2 *ELJ* 267; Editorial comments, 'The CFSP under the Constitutional Treaty? Issues of Depillarization' (2005) 42 *CML Rev* 325; D Curtin and I Dekker, 'The European Union from Maastricht to Lisbon: Institutional and Legal Unity Out of the Shadows' in P Craig and G de Búrca (eds), *The Evolution of EU Law* (Oxford, Oxford University Press, 2011) 155; C Hermann, 'Much Ado about Pluto? The "Unity of the European Legal Order" revisited' in M Cremona and B de Witte (eds), *EU Foreign Relations Law—Constitutional Fundamentals*, Essays in European Law (Oxford, Hart Publishing, 2008) 20; P Eeckhout, 'The EU's Common Foreign and Security Policy after Lisbon: From Pillar Talk to Constitutionalism' in A Biondi, P Eeckout and S Ripley (eds), *EU Law after Lisbon* (Oxford, Oxford University Press, 2012) 265; E Cannizzaro, 'Unity and Pluralism in the EU's Foreign Relations Power' in C Barnard (ed), *The Fundamentals of EU Law Revisited—Assessing the Impact of the Constitutional Debate* (Oxford, Oxford University Press, 2005) 193; C Hillion, 'Cohérence et action extérieure de l'Union' in E Neframi (ed), *Objectifs et compétences de l'Union européenne* (Bruxelles, Bruylant, 2012) 229.

[5] On the background, see eg: L Saltinyté, 'Jurisdiction of the European Court of Justice over Issues Relations to the Common Foreign and Security Policy under the Lisbon Treaty' (2010) 119 *Jurisprudence* 261; M Brkan, 'The Role of the European Court of Justice in the field of Common Foreign and Security Policy after the Treaty of Lisbon: New Challenges for the Future' in PJ Cardwell (ed), *EU External Relations Law and Policy in the post-Lisbon Era* (The Hague, TMC Asser Press, 2012) 97; A Hinarejos, *Judicial Control in the European Union—Reforming Jurisdiction in the Intergovernmental Pillars* (Oxford, Oxford University Press, 2009); T Tridimas, 'The European Court of Justice and the Draft Constitution: A Supreme Court for the Union?' in T Tridimas and P Nebbia (eds), *European Union Law for the Twenty-First Century: Rethinking the New Legal Order. Vol 1: Constitutional and Public Law. External Relations* (Oxford, Hart Publishing, 2004) 128.

[6] On the rationale behind the restricted jurisdiction of the Court of Justice in relation to the CFSP, see eg: E Denza, *The Intergovernmental Pillars of the European Union* (Oxford, Oxford University Press, 2002) especially ch 9; M-G Garbagnati Ketvel, 'The Jurisdiction of the European Court of Justice in respect of the Common Foreign and Security Policy' (2006) 55 *ICLQ* 77; De Baere, *Constitutional Principles* (n 2), especially ch 5; Van Elsuwege, 'EU External Action' (n 2). For a general critique of the abdicationist position of courts as regards foreign policy, see T Franck, *Political Questions/Judicial Answers. Does the Rule of Law Apply to Foreign Affairs?* (Princeton, Princeton University Press, 1992), and on the EU context, see P Eeckhout, *Does Europe's Constitution Stop at the Water's Edge?* (2005) Walter van Gerven Lectures (5).

Indeed, it has been noted that the Lisbon Treaty introduced a shift of perspective in the Court's role within the EU legal order.[7] Under the previous dispensation, the judicature only had jurisdiction where it was explicitly provided (ex-Article 46 TEU). The post-Lisbon rule is the reverse: the Court has jurisdiction except where the latter is explicitly excluded. Hence, any lack of jurisdiction is now framed as an exception to that rule[8] which, like any exception in EU law, is arguably to be interpreted restrictively. Another connected evolution is the generalisation of the Court's exclusive jurisdiction as regards EU law. The rule enshrined in Article 344 TFEU, whereby 'Member States undertake not to submit a dispute concerning the interpretation or application of the Treaties to any method of settlement other than those provided for therein', is applicable to the whole of the EU legal order, thereby barring the previously available legal option for Member States to solve any dispute regarding the CFSP through, for example, the International Court of Justice.[9]

More generally, the Lisbon Treaty has modified the legal landscape in which the Union is to develop its CFSP, but also within which the Court is to exercise its judicial powers. Constitutional norms (democracy, the rule of law, and respect for fundamental rights), and organising principles have been emboldened by EU primary law (eg principles of sincere cooperation, consistency),[10] with plausible effects on the Courts' jurisprudence, notably as regards the Union's external policy.[11]

II. THE COURT'S CONTROL OVER CFSP ACTS

Since the entry into force of the Treaty of Lisbon, the Court of Justice has had jurisdiction to control the legality of 'restrictive measures' adopted in the context of the CFSP (A). Also, it appears that the Court may have a say on EU international agreements having a CFSP dimension (B).

A. Restrictive Measures

Article 24(1) TEU stipulates that the European Court of Justice has jurisdiction 'to review the legality of certain decisions as provided for by the second paragraph of Article 275 of the Treaty on the Functioning of the European Union'. The

---

[7] A Rosas and L Armati, *EU Constitutional Law—An Introduction* (Oxford, Hart Publishing, 2012) 264, Tridimas, 'The European Court of Justice and the Draft Constitution' (n 5), Hinarejos, *Judicial Control in the European Union* (n 5), especially ch 3.

[8] Hinarejos, *Judicial Control in the European Union* (n 5) at 150. This has recently been confirmed by the ECJ in Case C-658/11 *European Parliament v Council*, judgment of 24 June 2014, at paras 70–73.

[9] See eg Denza, *The Intergovernmental Pillars of the European Union* (n 6).

[10] On the significance of EU principles on the Court's exercise of its jurisdiction, see eg T Horsley, 'Reflections on the Role of the Court of Justice as the Motor of European Integration: Legal Limits to Judicial Lawmaking' (2013) 50 *CML Rev* 931–64.

[11] Something the Court has acknowledged, eg in its judgment in Case C-414/11 *Daiichi Sankyo Co Ltd*, judgment of 18 July 2013, nyr.

latter Article foresees more specifically that the Court is 'to rule on proceedings, brought in accordance with the conditions laid down in the fourth paragraph of Article 263 of this Treaty, reviewing the legality of decisions providing for restrictive measures against natural or legal persons adopted by the Council on the basis of Chapter 2 of Title V of the Treaty on European Union'.

This empowerment comes in addition to the jurisdiction that the Court already had over EC acts *implementing* CFSP measures, including those targeting individuals[12] (now based on Article 215(2) TFEU).[13] Henceforth, natural or legal persons are entitled to contest the legality of *any* EU restrictive measures adopted in the context of the CFSP,[14] such as restrictions on entry or transit. In acknowledging the right to challenge the CFSP decision itself, the Treaty has made it possible to remedy the possible 'public opprobrium and suspicion of [the] person [concerned] which those measures provoke'.[15]

It is the first time that the EU judicature is enabled, outside inter-pillar disputes in the context of former Article 47 TEU,[16] to control the legality of certain CFSP acts against EU law in general, including the constitutionalised EU Charter of

---

[12] See eg Joined Cases C-402/05P and C-415/05P *Kadi and Al Barakaat Foundation v Council and Commission* [2008] ECR I-6351 (hereinafter, the '*Kadi I*' judgment).

[13] Case 130/10 *European Parliament v Council*, judgment of 19 July 2012, nyr.

[14] See eg: Cases T-86/11 *Bamba v Council*, judgment of 8 June 2011, nyr, C-417/11 *Bamba*, judgment of 15 November 2012, nyr; T-348/11 *Gbagbo v Council* [2011] ECR II-227, C-478/11 P to C-482/11 P *Gbagbo and Others*, judgment of 24 April 2013, nyr; T-316/11 *Mathieu Kadio Morokro v Council* [2011] ECR II-00293; T-218/11 *Dagher v Council*, judgment of 17 February 2012, nyr; T-439/10 and T-440/10, *Fulmen and Mahmoudian v Council*, judgment of 21 March 2012, nyr, under appeal—Case C-280/12P; T-509/10 *Manufacturing Support & Procurement Kala Naft Co*, judgment of 25 April 2012, nyr, under appeal—Case C-348/12 P; T-63/12 *Oil Turbo Compressor Co (Private Joint Stock) v Council*, judgment of 26 October 2012, nyr; T-421/11 *Qualitest FZE v Council*, judgment of 5 December 2012, nyr; T-15/11 *Sina Bank v Council*, judgment of 1 December 2012, nyr; T-496/10 *Bank Mellat v Council*, judgment of 29 January 2013, nyr, under appeal—C-176/13P; T-494/10 *Bank Saderat Iran v Council*, judgment of 5 February 2013, nyr, under appeal—C-200/13P; T-495/10 *Bank Saderat plc v Council v Council*, judgment of 20 March 2013, nyr; T-392/11 *Iran Transfo v Council*, judgment of 16 May 2013, nyr; T-200/11 *Fahed Mohamed Sakher Al Matri v Council*, judgment of 28 May 2013, nyr; T-187/11 *Trabelsi and Others*, judgment of 28 May 2013, nyr; T-188/11 *Mohamed Slim Ben Mohamed Hassen Ben Salah Chiboub v Council*, judgment of 28 May 2013, nyr; T-128/12 and T-182/12 *HTTS Hanseatic Trade Trust & Shipping GmbH v Council*, judgment of 12 June 2013, nyr; T-493/10 *Persia International Bank plc v Council*, judgment of 6 September 2013, nyr; T-4/11 and 5/11 *Export Development Bank of Iran v Council*, judgment of 6 September 2013, nyr; T-12/11 *Iran Insurance Company v Council*, judgment of 6 September 2013, nyr; T-13/11 *Post Bank Iran v Council*, judgment of 6 September 2013, nyr; T-24/11 *Bank Refah Kargaran v Council*, judgment of 6 September 2013, nyr; T-434/11 *Europäisch-Iranische Handelsbank AG v Council*, judgment of 6 September 2013, nyr; T-42/12 and T-181/12 *Naser Bateni v Council*, judgment of 6 September 2013, nyr; Case T-57/12 *Good Luck Shipping LLC v Council*, judgment of 6 September 2013, nyr, T-110/12 *Iranian Offshore Engineering & Construction Co v Council*, judgment of 6 September 2013, nyr; Case T-489/10 *Islamic Republic of Iran Shipping Lines*, judgment of 16 September 2013.

[15] See Cases C-584/10 P, C-593/10 P and C-595/10 P *European Commission and Others v Yassin Abdullah Kadi* ('*Kadi II*'), judgment of 18 July 2013, nyr, para 132; Case C-239/12P *Abdulbasit Abdulrahim*, judgment of 28 May 2013, nyr, paras 70ff. Further, on such damage, see C Eckes, 'EU Counter-Terrorist Sanctions against Individuals: Problems and Perils' (2012) 17 *European Foreign Affairs Review* 113.

[16] See section III, below.

Fundamental Rights. Such a development suggests that, to some extent at least, the rule of law, proclaimed as one of the Union's founding 'values' (Article 2 TEU), applies throughout the EU legal order including the CFSP.[17]

The envisioned judicial control is nevertheless circumscribed in various ways. Firstly, EU primary law limits the *type* of CFSP acts that can be challenged. According to Article 275 TFEU, the Court of Justice may review the legality of CFSP 'decisions providing for restrictive measures against natural or legal persons'. While the notion of restrictive measures against individuals could be interpreted broadly, if only to include CFSP sanctions against *states*,[18] other (non-restrictive) CFSP measures cannot, in principle, be challenged before the Court.[19] If judicial control is an essential element of the rule of law principle,[20] the latter's application remains therefore limited when it comes to the CFSP terrain.[21]

Secondly, in referring to the provisions of Article 263 (4) TFEU, Article 275(2) TFEU seemingly restricts the *proceedings* available to bring those specified CFSP acts before the Court. This has been understood as allowing only 'proceedings brought by private parties *under* Article 263(4) TFEU' (emphasis added).[22] As a result, other courses of action, such as disputing the validity of CFSP restrictive measures through the preliminary ruling procedure, the plea of illegality, let alone claims for damages, would not be accessible.[23]

The view that action should *not* be limited to annulment proceedings has nevertheless been defended.[24] And indeed, various elements could support a more open reading of Article 275(2) TFEU. To begin with, neither Article 24(1) TEU nor Article 275(2) TFEU explicitly limits the proceedings to 'direct actions'. Instead, the Court is empowered 'to rule on proceedings *brought in accordance with the conditions laid down* in the fourth paragraph of Article 263'.[25] Arguably, Article 275(2) TFEU does not seem to restrict the Court's intervention only to the

---

[17] P Eeckhout, *EU External Relations Law* (Oxford, Oxford University Press, 2011) 498). It has been suggested that it was already the case since the Treaty of Amsterdam, see R Gosalbo Bono, 'Some Reflections on the CFSP Legal Order' (2006) 43 *CML Rev* 337 at 347.

[18] See eg: Case T-57/12 *Good Luck Shipping LLC v Council* (n 15); Case T-489/10 *Islamic Republic of Iran Shipping Lines* (n 14); Case T-383/11 *Eyad Makhlouf v Council* (13 September 2013).

[19] But see further below, section II(B).

[20] De Baere, *Constitutional Principles* (n 2) at 176.

[21] Eeckhout, *EU External Relations Law* (n 17) at 499.

[22] Rosas and Armati, *EU Constitutional Law* (n 7) at 264.

[23] The General Court does not appear to reject such claim in principle; though in practice it might seldom be successful, see eg: Cases T-187/11 *Trabelsi and Others*, judgment of 28 May 2013, nyr and T-218/11 *Dagher v Council*, judgment of 17 February 2012, nyr. On the difficulty to obtain damages in relation to EC restrictive measures, see eg Case T-341/07 *Sison* [2011] ECR II-7915.

[24] See eg: Tridimas, 'The European Court of Justice and the Draft Constitution' (n 5) at 128; De Baere, *Constitutional Principles* (n 2) at 190.

[25] According to this paragraph: 'any natural or legal person may, under the conditions laid down in the first and second paragraphs, institute proceedings against an act addressed to that person or which is of direct and individual concern to them, and against a regulatory act which is of direct concern to them and does not entail implementing measures'. The conditions of the first and second paragraphs relate to the jurisdiction of the court, and the grounds on which the application for annulment can be made.

proceedings of Article 263(4) TFEU, but rather establishes the 'conditions' under which its control is to be exercised, namely the *locus standi* requirements, and the grounds of review. Moreover, both Article 275(2) TFEU and Article 24(1) TEU entrust the Court with the power of 'reviewing the legality' of CFSP sanctions. The case law indicates that such a review of legality is not limited to annulment proceedings. Instead, 'requests for preliminary rulings which seek to ascertain the validity of a measure constitute, like actions for annulment, *means for reviewing the legality of European Union acts*'.[26]

In challenging the application by a Member State's authorities of a CFSP restrictive measure, the applicant could thus invoke the latter's invalidity, in which case the national judge concerned would turn to the Court of Justice, particularly since national courts do not have the power to invalidate EU rules.[27] Similarly, in contesting the legality of restrictive measures based on Article 215 TFEU before the Court of Justice, an applicant ought to be able to plea the illegality of the preliminary CFSP decision upon which it has been adopted. It is indeed noticeable that, in making a cross reference only to the conditions of paragraph 4 of Article 263 TFEU, which themselves refer to the first and second paragraphs thereof, but not to the condition of paragraph 6, Article 275(2) appears not to subject all legality control of CFSP restrictive measures to the two-month time limit enshrined in Article 263(6) TFEU. While action for annulment of the restrictive measures remain subject to the said time limit specific to that procedure, Article 275(2) TFEU does not as such preclude a review of the legality of CFSP restrictive measures in the contexts of a preliminary ruling procedure, and/or a plea of illegality,[28] at least for those that are not explicitly mentioned in, but are nevertheless affected by the restrictive measure.[29]

That judicial control of CFSP restrictive measures should not be limited to direct actions under Article 264(3) TFEU would indeed be consistent with the notion

---

[26] See: Case C-583/11 P *Inuit Tapiriit Kanatami and Others*, judgment of 3 October 2013, nyr, para 95; Joined Cases C-143/88 and C-92/89 *Zuckerfabrik Süderdithmarschen and Zuckerfabrik Soest* [1991] ECR I-415, para 18; and Joined Cases C-453/03, C-11/04, C-12/04 and C-194/04 *ABNA and Others* [2005] ECR I-10423, para 103.

[27] Case 314/85 *Foto-Frost v Hauptzollamt Lübeck-Ost* [1987] ECR 04199.

[28] Indeed, in contrast to the provisions of Art 275 TFEU, the Council's notice to addressees of restrictive measures would typically mention the possibility for the persons and entities concerned of challenging its decision 'before the General Court of the European Union, in accordance with the conditions laid down in Article 275 [TFEU], second paragraph, and Article 263 [TFEU], fourth and sixth paragraphs', see eg Case C-417/11P *Nadiany Bamba*, judgment of 15 November 2012, nyr, para 80.

[29] The plea of illegality based on Article 277 TFEU does not seem to be excluded, as a matter of principle, by the General Court: Case T-70/12 *Ali Divandari v Council*, judgment of 17 June 2013, nyr except when coming from the addressee(s) of the impugned act, based on the *TWD* jurisprudence (Case C-188/92 *Textilwerke Deggendorf GmbH (TWD) v Bundesrepublik Deutschland* [1994] ECR I-833), see: Case T-15/11 *Sina Bank v Council*, judgment of 11 December 2012, nyr, para 43; Case T-120/12 *Shahid Beheshti University v Council*, judgment of 20 November 2012, nyr, para 24. Based on the same *TWD* approach, it is unlikely that the Court would not admit indirect applications involving addressees of the measures whose legality is questioned particularly in view of its strict reading of the two-months' time limit related to direct applications for annulment: Cases T-348/11 *Gbagbo v Council* [2011] ECR II-227, C-478/11 P to C-482/11 P *Gbagbo and Others*, judgment of 24 April 2013, nyr.

that the treaties establish a 'complete system of judicial remedies', a notion coined by the Court of Justice to compensate for its strict reading of the admissibility conditions of Article 263(4) TFEU.[30] If the other avenues of the 'complete system' were foreclosed, the very notion of *completeness* to which the Court has recurrently referred in the post-Lisbon EU context,[31] would then become relative. Indeed, the compatibility of the CFSP related judicial review with the requirement of effective judicial remedies of Article 47 of the Charter of Fundamental Rights would be debatable, in view of the connection the Court usually establishes between the availability of alternative remedies and the fulfilment of that requirement. As would its consistency with the constitutional requirement of Article 19(1) TEU according to which 'Member States shall provide remedies sufficient to ensure effective legal protection *in the fields covered by Union law*' (emphasis added). As the Court recalled, 'the national courts and tribunals, in collaboration with the Court of Justice, fulfil a duty entrusted to them both of ensuring that in the interpretation and application of the Treaties the law is observed',[32] so that 'it is ... for the Member States to establish a system of legal remedies and procedures which ensure respect for the fundamental right to effective judicial protection'.[33]

Excluding other remedies would moreover introduce a rather arbitrary distinction in terms of judicial protection between those individuals that are subject to restrictive measures of economic and/or financial nature, who would be able to challenge the implementing measures based on Article 215 TFEU using all available remedies, and those who would be the target of other types of restrictive measures (eg visa restrictions) founded (and possibly implemented) under the CFSP chapter, whose remedies would be limited to the more restricted annulment procedure. More generally, it would be paradoxical that such proceedings be excluded in relation to EU measures that arguably are amongst the most corrosive on individual freedoms. Precluding the availability of other judicial remedies in relation to CFSP restrictions would further tone down the already limited

---

[30] See eg Case C-50/00 P *Unión de Pequeños Agricultores v Council* [2002] ECR I-6677.

[31] In Case C-533/10 *Compagnie internationale pour la vente à distance (CIVAD) SA*, judgment of 14 June 2012, nyr, para 32: 'those [TEU and FEU] *treaties* have established a complete system of legal remedies and procedures designed to confer on the Court of Justice jurisdiction to review the legality of acts of the institutions, bodies, offices and agencies of the European Union'. In Case C-59/11 *Association Kokopelli*, judgment of 12 July 2012, nyr, the Court emphasised: 'the complete system of legal remedies and procedures *established by the TFEU Treaty* with a view to ensuring judicial review of the legality of acts of the institutions, where natural or legal persons cannot, by reason of the conditions for admissibility laid down in the fourth paragraph of Article 263 TFEU, directly challenge acts of the European Union of general application, they are able, depending on the case, either indirectly to plead the invalidity of such acts before the EU judicature under Article 277 TFEU or to do so before the national courts and ask them, since they have no jurisdiction themselves to declare those measures invalid, to make a reference to the Court of Justice for a preliminary ruling on validity'. See also, Case C-583/11 P *Inuit Tapiriit Kanatami and Others* (n 26).

[32] Opinion 1/09 *Unified Patent Litigation System* [2011] ECR I-1137, para 69, Case C-583/11 P *Inuit Tapiriit Kanatami and Others* (n 26), para 99.

[33] Case C-50/00 P *Unión de Pequeños Agricultores v Council* [2002] ECR I-6677, para 41, and Case C-263/02 *Commission v Jégo-Quéré* [2004] ECR I-3425, para 31, Case C-583/11 P *Inuit Tapiriit Kanatami* and Others (n 26), para 99.

significance of the Article 275(2) TFEU in rule of law terms, which was evoked earlier, it would make the provisions of Article 2 TEU sound rather hollow in the context of the CFSP.

In sum, literal, systemic and principled arguments point towards a judicial control under Article 275(2) TFEU that should not be limited to the annulment proceedings under Article 263(4) TFEU. If, however, the reading of Article 275(2) TFEU suggested above was incorrect, thus allowing a structural differentiation between CFSP measures and other EU acts in the Court's legality control,[34] it could be expected that the exercise of this specific CFSP control be adjusted so as to meet the requirements of Article 47 of the Charter.[35] In particular, the *locus standi* conditions of Article 263(4) TFEU applied to the context of proceedings against CFSP acts would have to be adjusted so as to comply with the imperative of effective judicial remedies. Such a differentiation would be consistent with the distinct legality review envisaged by Article 275(2) TFEU, and would compensate, as it were, for the lack of compensation for the strictness of the Court's reading of the *locus standi* requirements of Article 263(4) TFEU, which the 'complete system of judicial remedies' incarnates. This would be particularly important for applicants who are not addressees of a restrictive measure but who could, like family members, be significantly affected by it, and who as such would be subject to the standing requirements of the second or third limbs of Article 263(4) TFEU.

In this respect, since CFSP acts cannot be of a legislative nature,[36] could it be suggested that they are by definition conceived as 'regulatory' for the purpose of Article 263(4) TFEU?[37] If so, the applicant, who would not be the addressee of the measure, would only have to demonstrate 'direct concern' for his/her application to be admissible, the other condition, namely individual concern, being then of

---

[34] Even if the above reading of Art 275(2) TFEU was accepted, a degree of differentiation between CFSP acts and other EU acts would exist too, in terms of legality review. For the conditions of Art 263(4) TFEU, including standing requirements, would remain applicable even in the context of other remedies, as required by Art 275(2) TFEU. To be sure, admissibility requirements are not foreign to the preliminary ruling procedure, but in this particular case, they would be more stringent, which suggests that, in any event, though to a lesser degree, the EU 'complete system of judicial remedies' does not operate the same way in relation to challengeable CFSP measures.

[35] In line with the principle reiterated by the Court that 'the conditions of admissibility laid down in the fourth paragraph of Article 263 TFEU must be interpreted in the light of the fundamental right to effective judicial protection, *but such an interpretation cannot have the effect of setting aside the conditions expressly laid down in that Treaty*' (emphasis added), see Case C-583/11 P *Inuit Tapiriit Kanatami and Others* (n 26), para 98.

[36] Art 24(1) TEU.

[37] The Court has characterised the restrictive measures as: measures 'which at the same time resemble both measures of general application in that they impose on a category of addressees determined in a general and abstract manner a prohibition on, inter alia, making available funds and economic resources to persons and entities named in the lists contained in their annexes and also a bundle of individual decisions affecting those persons and entities', adding that 'as regards measures adopted on the basis of provisions relating to the Common Foreign and Security Policy, such as the contested measures, it is the individual nature of those measures which, in accordance with the second paragraph of Article 275 TFEU and the fourth paragraph of Article 263 TFEU, permits access to the Courts of the European Union'; see Joined Cases C-478/11 P to C-482/11 P *Gbagbo and Others*, judgment of 24 April 2013, nyr.

no relevance.[38] If that were the case, the *locus standi* requirements would amount to a lower admissibility threshold in relation to CFSP restrictive measures, which could mitigate the effects of the absence of alternative remedies.[39] Admittedly, some CFSP restrictive measures have to be implemented by decisions adopted on the basis of Article 215 TFEU, or indeed through so-called 'implementing CFSP decisions'.[40] The condition of the third limb of Article 263(4) TFEU would thus be fulfilled only if the impugned CFSP restrictive measure 'affect[s] directly the legal situation of the applicant and leaves no discretion to its addressees, who are entrusted with the task of implementing it, such implementation being purely automatic and resulting from European Union rules without the application of other intermediate rules'.[41]

B. EU International Agreements

While EU primary law explicitly entrusts the Court to control the legality of CFSP restrictive measures against natural and legal persons, the question has been raised as to whether it might also be in the position to inspect EU external agreements covering CFSP matters. Like judicial control in relation to CFSP restrictive measures, this is an issue that was considered in the *Discussion Circle on the European Court of Justice* set up in the context of the Convention on the Future of Europe.[42]

Article 218 TFEU establishes the procedure for the EU to conclude external agreements, irrespective of whether they concern the CFSP or other areas of EU competence. Thus, EU agreements in the area of CFSP are also acts adopted, at least in part, on the basis of the TFEU,[43] even if their substantive legal basis would in principle be located in the CFSP chapter of the TEU (viz Article 37 TEU). As such, they can be subject to judicial control given that EU primary law does not otherwise limit the Court's jurisdiction with respect to the provisions of Article 218 TFEU.[44] In particular, the decision on the conclusion of an agreement including CFSP elements, which would have been adopted in violation of the procedural requirements established in Article 218 TFEU, could be challenged before the Court.

---

[38] Cp Brkan, 'The role of the European Court of Justice' (n 5) at 110.

[39] See Case C-340/08 *M and Others v HM's Treasury* [2010] ECR I-03913.

[40] For references, see cases mentioned above (n 14).

[41] Joined Cases T-454/10 and T-482/11 *Associazione Nazionale degli Industriali delle Conserve Alimentari Vegetali*, judgment of 30 May 2013, nyr, see also Case C-125/06 P *Commission v Infront WM* [2008] ECR I-1451.

[42] Supplementary report on the question of judicial control relating to the Common Foreign and Security Policy, CONV 689/1/03.

[43] Eeckhout, *EU External Relations Law* (n 17) at 498.

[44] De Baere, *Constitutional Principles* (n 2) at 190. See also Tridimas, 'The European Court of Justice and the Draft Constitution' (n 5).

Thus, the European Parliament has challenged an EU decision concluding an international agreement between the EU and Mauritius on the ground that the procedural requirement of Article 218(10) TFEU, which appears to apply to all EU agreements, has not been complied with in the negotiations and/or conclusion of the agreement. The Parliament also contested the Council's view that the agreement 'relates exclusively to the CFSP', and required that its consent be requested in accordance with Article 218(6) TFEU.[45] Admittedly, the latter situation relates to the question of delimitation between the CFSP and non-CFSP aspects of the agreement under Article 40 TEU, to which this discussion will return later.[46]

That the Court should have jurisdiction to control the legality of EU agreements in the area of CFSP has been further supported by reference to paragraph 11 of Article 218 TFEU.[47] The latter provision establishes an ex ante judicial control of compatibility with the founding treaties of 'envisaged' EU external agreements.[48] Phrased in general terms, paragraph 11 does not seem to exclude EU agreements that relate 'exclusively or principally' to the CFSP from the Court's scrutiny.[49] Indeed, while the procedural requirements for the negotiation and conclusion of EU agreements vary depending on the degree of their CFSP content, no such differentiation is envisaged in paragraph 11 as regards the judicial involvement. Could this then entail that the Court's control extends to examining the compatibility of the specific CFSP components of EU agreements with the treaties, including if the agreement 'relates exclusively' to the CFSP?

The provisions of Article 24(1) TEU could suggest otherwise, given that they appear to set out an exhaustive list of Court's powers in relation to the CFSP provisions. If Article 218(11) were to be read against this backdrop, and considering the rule of Article 40(2) TEU, only the non-CFSP provisions of an EU agreement could be examined in the light of the treaties (outside the CFSP), including agreements deemed to be 'predominantly' about the CFSP. For in view of the provisions of Article 40(1) TEU, such an agreement could not be subtracted altogether from the jurisdiction of the Court under paragraph 11 as regards its TFEU aspects. It would then be the task of the Court of Justice first to distinguish the CFSP and non-CFSP contents of the agreement, and then to limit its compatibility check to the latter. While this approach would respect scrupulously the constitutional limitations of the Court's jurisdiction with respect to the CFSP provisions, it would nonetheless require the Court, as it will be suggested later, first to look at *all* the

---

[45] Since these lines were written, the procedural argument based on Art 218(10) TFEU was upheld by the European Court of Justice in Case C-658/11 *European Parliament v Council*, judgment of 24 June 2014, see esp paras 69ff.

[46] See section III below.

[47] Eeckhout, *EU External Relations Law* (n 17) at 498.

[48] Further on this point, see S Adams, *La procédure d'avis devant la Court de Justice de l'Union européenne* (Bruxelles, Bruylant 2011) especially 462ff.

[49] As De Baere points out, Art 218 itself provides no derogation for the CFSP as regards the application of the ex ante control, while establishing derogations for the CFSP on other matters (see paras 3, 6 and 8 of Art 218); De Baere, *Constitutional Principles* (n 2) at 190.

provisions of the agreement in order to establish their possible CFSP nature. In other words, while the Court would not venture into a compatibility control of the CFSP provisions, it would nevertheless exercise an interpretative function over the whole agreement, so as to characterise its content, and in turn establish the scope of its control.[50] Here, the case law on the Court's jurisdiction in the context of mixed agreements springs to mind.

Yet, it may be wondered whether such a restricted reading of the Court's precautionary control would be satisfactory in view of the latter's rationale.[51] If a (wholly or partly) CFSP agreement were to be negotiated and concluded in violation of the treaties, the EU international commitment would arguably be vitiated, raising questions of a possible international responsibility of the Union as a whole and not only qua CFSP.[52] Another reading of Article 218(11) TFEU could thus be that it allows the judiciary to test the compatibility of the *whole* agreement, including its CFSP content, with the treaties. It is arguably the only way for the Court fully to exercise the unqualified mandate it is endowed with under this provision, and to ensure the latter's effectiveness.[53] Indeed, Article 107(2) of the rules of procedure of the Court of Justice stipulates that in its ex ante control, the Court may also examine 'whether the Union or any Union institution has the power to enter into that agreement'.[54] Hence, only a full compatibility check would permit the Court to establish, in particular in relation to hybrid agreements containing both CFSP and non-CFSP aspects, that while the EU acting through TFEU competences would not have the power to enter into that agreement, the EU qua CFSP could.

It may be recalled that the previous (ie pre-Lisbon) ex ante jurisdiction of the Court was not subject to the condition that the 'envisaged agreement' be a 'pure' Community agreement. Often the purpose of the requested opinion has been precisely to determine whether the agreement in question was to be concluded by the Community only.[55] That such agreements covered areas for which the Member States were competent did not prevent the Court from scrutinising the

---

[50] See section III, below.

[51] Opinion 1/75 *Local Cost Standards* [1975] ECR 1355 especially 1360 and 1361; Opinion 2/94 *European Convention on Human Rights* [1996] ECR I-1759, paras 3–6; Opinion 2/00 *Cartagena Protocol* [2001] ECR I-9713, para 6.

[52] Incidentally, as the EU budget covers the administrative costs of the CFSP, would the EU budget be used for covering any damages that the EU could have to pay for compensating other parties' possible losses?

[53] This option would indeed echo what the *Discussion Circle* envisaged in its final report. See: *Discussion Circle* (n 42). According to Tridimas, 'The European Court of Justice and the Draft Constitution' (n 5), that option had support within the *Circle*.

[54] Art 107(2) of the rules of procedure of the European Court of Justice foresees that: The Opinion may deal not only with the question whether the envisaged agreement is compatible with the provisions of the treaties but also with the question whether the Union or any Union institution has the power to enter into that agreement.

[55] See Opinion 1/75 *Local Cost Standard* [1975] ECR 1355, especially 1360; Opinion 1/78 *International Agreement on Natural Rubber* [1979] ECR 2871 para 30; Opinion 2/91 *Convention No 170 ILO on Safety in the Use of Chemicals at Work* [1993] ECR I-1079, para 3; and Opinion 1/94 *World Trade Organisation* [1994] ECR I- 5267; Opinion 2/00 *Cartagena Protocol* [2001] ECR I-9713, para 3.

whole agreement's compatibility with the EC Treaty, not least to establish the degree to which the Community had the competence to negotiate and conclude such an agreement. Based on this, and on the Court's jurisdiction over the rules of Article 40 TEU, it would seem that any EU agreement could be submitted to its a priori scrutiny. At the very least, the Court should be able to control the compatibility of the agreement with the distribution of competence foreseen in the treaties. It would be the only way a priori to guarantee compliance with the requirements of Article 40 TEU, which is the second task the Lisbon Treaty has conferred on the Court of Justice in relation to the CFSP.

III. THE COURT'S DEFENCE OF THE CFSP

According to Article 275(2) TFEU and Article 24(1) TEU, the Court also has jurisdiction to 'monitor compliance with the provisions of Article 40 TEU', according to which:

> The implementation of the common foreign and security policy shall not affect the application of the procedures and the extent of the powers of the institutions laid down by the Treaties for the exercise of the Union competences referred to in Articles 3 to 6 of the Treaty on the Functioning of the European Union.

> Similarly, the implementation of the policies listed in those Articles shall not affect the application of the procedures and the extent of the powers of the institutions laid down by the Treaties for the exercise of the Union competences under this Chapter.

These provisions contain a reformulated version of the pre-Lisbon non-contamination requirement of Article 47 TEU. In its applicable formulation, the rule is that EU competences based on the TFEU should be protected against the exercise of CFSP competence. They also introduce the reverse rule in paragraph (2), that CFSP competence should be protected against TFEU interference. As it has been suggested, 'the Court can [thus] be asked to review … whether an act adopted under the TFEU is in reality a CFSP act'.[56] The EU judicature is therefore not only the guardian of the integration acquis against CFSP intrusion, it also protects the CFSP integrity against possible (ab)use of TFEU competence and procedures,[57] for fulfilling the Union's objectives.

Like in the previous dispensation, it should be noted that the Court's 'border patrol' jurisdiction is not formally limited to a particular course of action. The case law relating to previous Article 47 TEU suggests that the Court of Justice could be asked to exercise that jurisdiction not only in the context of the annulment

---

[56] Eeckhout, *EU External Relations Law* (n 17) at 498.

[57] Further on this, see eg: Cremona, 'Defining Competence in EU External Relations' (n 2) at 45; also: Hinarejos, *Judicial Control in the European Union* (n 5); Dashwood, 'Article 47 TEU' (n 2), Elsuwege, 'EU External Action' (n 2); B Van Vooren, 'The Small Arms Judgment in an Age of Constitutional Turmoil' (2009) 14 *European Foreign Affairs Review* 231.

proceedings, but also through the plea of illegality.[58] On this basis, and in view of the case law mentioned earlier,[59] it may be assumed that the preliminary ruling procedure could equally be practiced for ascertaining compliance with Article 40 TEU.[60] This means that in case of doubts about the validity of an EU act on the ground that it may have been adopted in violation of Article 40 TEU, a national court would have to turn to the Court of Justice.[61] As suggested above, the Court could also control whether an envisaged EU agreement is compatible with the rules of Article 40 TEU.

That the Court should protect the integrity of the CFSP was arguably conceivable prior to the Treaty of Lisbon. The first ever 'inter-pillar' case under the Maastricht version of the TEU made it clear that the contested application of an 'intergovernmental' decision-making procedure (in casu a provision of Title VI TEU) would be upheld by the Court where the alleged Community competence to take the contested measure would be legally lacking.[62] Indeed, the Court annulled an EC Decision to conclude the EU's agreement on Passenger Names Records with the United States on the ground that the agreement fell outside the scope of Community competence, implicitly opening the way for the adoption of a new Decision on the basis of ex-Title VI TEU.[63] Given the precedence which the previous EU treaties granted to the 'Community method', the exercise of pre-Lisbon border control jurisdiction under Article 47 TEU consisted for the Court in establishing whether the Community had the competence for taking the measure under review, considering the latter's objective and content, and if so, to favour the exercise of such competence, even if the measure would equally fulfil an objective of the Union qua CFSP and/or PJCCM.[64] If, conversely, such scrutiny revealed that the EC did not have the relevant competence, then a course of action under Title V or VI would be, at least implicitly, made possible.[65] In other words, the integrity of the second and third pillars was ensured by default, viz by establishing first that the Community did not have the competence.[66]

As pointed out above, the post-Lisbon duty to protect the specific CFSP procedures and institutions' powers is formulated in similar terms as the duty to protect TFEU procedures and institutions' powers. Moreover, the legal nature of both clusters of competence is deemed to be equivalent, as a result of the principle enshrined in Article 1 TEU, that the TEU and the TFEU have the same

---

[58] See Case C-91/05 *Commission v Council (ECOWAS)* [2008] ECR I-3651.

[59] See eg Case C-583/11 P *Inuit Tapiriit Kanatami and Others* (n 26).

[60] Further: C Hillion and RA Wessel, 'Competence Distribution in EU External Relations After ECOWAS: Clarification or Continued Fuzziness?'(2009) 46 *CML Rev* 551.

[61] Case 314/85 *Foto-Frost v Hauptzollamt Lübeck-Ost* (n 27), Case C-344/04 *IATA and ELFAA* [2006] ECR I-403.

[62] See Case C-170/96 *Commission v Council (Airport Transit Visas)* [1998] ECR I-2763.

[63] Joined Cases C-317/04 and C-318/04 *European Parliament v Council* (PNR) [2006] ECR I-4721.

[64] Case C-91/05 *Commission v Council (ECOWAS)* (n 58).

[65] See also Case C-440/05 *Commission v Council (ship-source pollution)* [2007] ECR I-9097.

[66] Case C-170/96 *Commission v Council (Airport Transit Visas)* (n 62), para 17; cp Case C-91/05 *Commission v Council (ECOWAS)* (n 58).

legal value.[67] Thus in the context of Article 40 TEU, the EU judicature is asked to ascertain whether the implementation of the TFEU policies affects the application of the procedures and the extent of the powers of the institutions as set out in the CFSP chapter and if so to annul the impugned TFEU act. Arguably, this cannot be secured only by default, as previously. Faced with the contention that a TFEU measure ought to have been adopted as a CFSP act in line with the rule of Article 40(2) TEU, the Court's approach should go beyond the mere determination of whether the TFEU establishes the relevant competence, because that in itself would not ipso facto foreclose the use of the CFSP procedure and thus would not ensure compliance with Article 40(2) TEU.[68] Instead, the Court should actively examine whether a specific CFSP procedure exists for adopting the act in question, and if so determine whether such procedure ought to have been followed either in combination with,[69] or rather than the TFEU procedure altogether. Only thus would the Court be able to guarantee that the identified CFSP procedure, and the institutions powers it encapsulates, is not affected by the implementation of the TFEU. In monitoring compliance with the provisions of Article 40(2) TEU, the Court is therefore entrusted, albeit implicitly, with an interpretative function as regards CFSP provisions, a task it has seemingly begun to perform, as suggested further below.

One known difficulty in relation to the Court's jurisdiction under Article 40 TEU is the determination of the specific circumstances under which a CFSP procedure should be chosen over of a TFEU course of action, if and where the two are conceivable.[70] In particular, the judicial techniques practiced under pre-Lisbon Article 47 TEU, combining the 'centre of gravity' approach and the precedence of the EC competence, are no longer entirely pertinent. As recalled earlier, the two EU Treaties are legally equal, thereby precluding precedence being given a priori to the TFEU. And since all the objectives of the EU external action have been combined in Article 21(2) TEU, the identification of specific CFSP objectives for the purpose of establishing competence has become more complex.

Several approaches have been mooted to address such difficulty. For example, it has been contended that the CFSP, defined in Article 24(1) TEU as 'cover[ing] all areas of foreign policy and all questions relating to the Union's security' may be envisaged as *lex generalis*, while other external policies such as trade, development cooperation, humanitarian aid, set out in the TFEU, would amount to *lex*

---

[67] Eg Dashwood, 'Article 47 TEU' (n 2), Cremona, 'Defining Competence in EU External Relations' (n 2), Piris, *The Lisbon Treaty* (n 2).

[68] Case C-91/05 *Commission v Council (ECOWAS)* (n 58).

[69] Within the limits set out by the Court in Case C-130/10 *European Parliament v Council* (n 13); see further below.

[70] Editorial comments, 'Mind the Gap!' (2008) 45 *CML Rev* 317, Van Elsuwege, 'EU External Action' (n 2), Cremona, 'Defining Competence in EU External Relations' (n 2), Dashwood, 'Article 47 TEU' (n 2), Eeckhout, *EU External Relations Law* (n 17) at 180, van Vooren, 'The Small Arms Judgment' (n 57).

specialis.[71] The Treaties provide some support to this approach in that, unlike the CFSP, most external policies based on the TFEU include their own specific aims, trade and development cooperation being cases in point.[72] Only the Common Security and Defence Policy (CSDP), which is a sub-chapter of the CFSP, would appear to include its own purposes, particularly in Articles 42 and 43 TEU.[73] Disagreement over the choice between the CSDP or TFEU legal basis could thus be resolved on the basis of the traditional 'centre of gravity' approach.

The practical consequence of this is that TFEU-based external policies are more identifiable and thus exercisable than the CFSP, save in its CSDP dimension. Title V chapter 2 TEU (outside the CSDP) would thus be relied upon for the EU to act externally if and when other policy frameworks would prove to be inappropriate. Indeed, the ensuing residual character of the CFSP, squeezed as it is between the TFEU and the CSDP, could be even more pronounced. Not only because the objectives of TFEU policies are broadly formulated, thus paving the way for a potentially wide interpretation by the Court,[74] but also because all such policies have to be implemented while respecting the principles and pursuing the objectives set out in Article 21(2) TEU, which incorporated the previously distinct CFSP objectives of pre-Lisbon Article 11 TEU. Cross-references included in several TFEU provisions related to external policies specifically require that the latter be 'conducted within the framework of the principles and objectives of the Union's external action'.[75] All EU external policies, including the CFSP-CSDP, have thus become instrumental to achieving the general external objectives of the EU, whether they relate to the old CFSP goals or the previously scattered aims of EC external relations. Pushed further, this discussion raises the question of what

[71] See eg Cremona, 'Defining Competence in EU External Relations' (n 2); cp Dashwood, 'Article 47 TEU' (n 2). Monitoring compliance with Art 40 could also be performed in consideration of the *nature* of the act under review and of the specific powers of the institutions involved (Eeckhout, *EU External Relations Law* (n 17) at 183). As the Council and the European Council cannot adopt 'legislative acts' in the context of the CFSP, any such act can only be adopted by institutions operating under TFEU, provided of course it can be related, in terms of aim and content, to a EU competence under the TFEU. The Court's jurisdiction under Article 40 TEU could thus entail an assessment of CFSP acts with a view to determining whether they have such a 'legislative' nature (possibly in the light of the case law regarding the nature of reviewable acts under Art 263(4) TFEU, eg: Case C-583/11 P *Inuit Tapiriit Kanatami and Others* (n 26); see also Case C-77/11 *Council v Parliament*, judgment of 17 September 2013, nyr), and if so, to annulling them.

[72] Thus, Art 206 TFEU on the Common Commercial Policy foresees that '… the Union shall contribute, in the common interest, to the harmonious development of world trade, the progressive abolition of restrictions on international trade and on foreign direct investment, and the lowering of customs and other barriers', while Art 208(1) TFEU on Development Cooperation stipulates that 'Union development cooperation policy shall have as its primary objective the reduction and, in the long term, the eradication of poverty'. Further on this, see: Cremona, 'Defining Competence in EU External Relations' (n 2), Hillion, 'Cohérence et action extérieure de l'Union' (n 4).

[73] For a thorough analysis of the CSDP, see eg P Koutrakos, *EU Common Security and Defence Policy* (Oxford, Oxford University Press, 2013).

[74] In this sense, see the Court's interpretation of EU development objectives in Case C-377/12 *Commission v Council*, judgment of 11 June 2014, reiterating the broad pre-Lisbon reading provided in Case C-91/05 *Commission v Council (ECOWAS)* (n 58).

[75] On the significance of those objectives, see J Larik, 'Worldly Ambitions: Foreign Policy Objectives in European Constitutional Law' (PhD Thesis, EUI, Florence, 2013).

in the end remains of the CFSP in substantive terms; which in turn questions the actual significance of Article 40(2) TEU on the protection of the CFSP integrity that the Court of Justice is called upon to guarantee.

The pronouncement in Case C-130/10 *European Parliament v Council* of July 2012 gives some indication of the Court of Justice's approach to these questions.[76] In particular the judgment offers some glimpses of how the EU judicature may exercise the interpretative and protective functions that underpin its border patrolling jurisdiction. The Court found that Article 215 TFEU, which establishes the legal basis for EU restrictive measures based on preliminary CFSP decisions, was the appropriate foundation for adopting the amended text of the 'Regulation imposing certain specific restrictive measures directed against certain persons and entities associated with Usama bin Laden, the Al-Qaeda network and the Taliban'.[77] It thereby rejected the claim made by the European Parliament that the Regulation ought to have been adopted on the basis of Article 75 TFEU,[78] relating to the area of freedom, security and justice (AFSJ).

While admitting that 'the combating of terrorism and its financing may well be among the objectives of the area of freedom, security and justice, as they appear in Article 3(2) TEU', the Court of Justice opined that 'the objective of combating international terrorism and its financing in order to preserve international peace and security corresponds, nevertheless, to the objectives of the Treaty provisions on external action by the Union'.[79] Then, as 'terrorism constitutes a threat to peace and international security', it was held that 'the object of actions undertaken by the Union in the sphere of the CFSP, and the measures taken in order to give effect to that policy in the Union's external actions, in particular, restrictive measures for the purpose of Article 215(2) TFEU, can be to combat terrorism.'[80]

Remarkably, the Court referred explicitly to Article 43 TEU included in the CSDP chapter, and to its express allusion to the possible contribution of CSDP missions to combating terrorism to corroborate its findings. Reference was also made to the first subparagraph of Article 24(1) TEU according to which 'the Union's competence in matters of [the CFSP] shall cover all areas of foreign policy and all questions relating to the Union's security'. It is one instance, if not the first

---

[76] See Case C-130/10 *Parliament v Council* (n 13).

[77] Council Regulation (EU) No 1286/2009 of 22 December 2009 amending Regulation (EC) No 881/2002 imposing certain specific restrictive measures directed against certain persons and entities associated with Usama bin Laden, the Al-Qaeda network and the Taliban OJ [2010] L346/42.

[78] According to Art 75 TFEU: 'Where necessary to achieve the objectives set out in Article 67, as regards preventing and combating terrorism and related activities, the European Parliament and the Council, acting by means of regulations in accordance with the ordinary legislative procedure, shall define a framework for administrative measures with regard to capital movements and payments, such as the freezing of funds, financial assets or economic gains belonging to, or owned or held by, natural or legal persons, groups or non-State entities.

The Council, on a proposal from the Commission, shall adopt measures to implement the framework referred to in the first paragraph.

The acts referred to in this Article shall include necessary provisions on legal safeguards'.

[79] Para 61.

[80] Para 63.

time, that the all-encompassing character of the CFSP is evoked in the case law,[81] here to substantiate that a particular policy goal, namely counterterrorism, cannot be excluded from its ambit.

This, in turn, formally permits the EU to rely on Article 215 TFEU to adopt restrictive measures against terrorists/terrorist organisations, despite the provision's silence on the matter. Considering that Article 75 TFEU is '[i]ncorporated in Part Three of the FEU Treaty on Union policies and internal actions',[82] while Article 215 TFEU is included in the external action part of the Treaty,[83] and formally linked to the CFSP, the Court found that 'Article 215(2) TFEU constitutes the appropriate legal basis for measures ... directed to addressees implicated in acts of terrorism who, having regard to their activities globally and to the international dimension of the threat they pose, affect fundamentally the Union's external activity'. The EU judicature thereby sets out a significant CFSP dimension of the EU external fight against terrorism, while seemingly circumscribing the external dimension of the AFSJ,[84] and particularly its ability to underpin an implied external power.[85]

It is also noticeable that, in this case, the Court points out that adopting measures like the contested one only on the basis of Article 75 TFEU 'would render Article 215(2) TFEU largely redundant'.[86] It thereby safeguards the *raison d'être* of Article 215 TFEU, and by doing so indirectly preserves the integrity of the CFSP, at least in terms of its counterterrorism dimension. Had the Court decided otherwise, it would not only have emptied Article 215(2) TFEU of much of its relevance, it would also have considerably reduced the size of the CFSP in

---

[81] The Court thus appears to place considerable importance upon the separation now enshrined in the TFEU between internal policies and external action, for the purposes of determining the correct legal basis of an act. Consequently, faced with a conflict between a TFEU and CFSP legal basis, the possible inclusion of the TFEU competence in the Treaty section devoted to internal policies may have a bearing on the Court's analysis (See also, in this respect, the judgment of the Court of Justice in Case C-414/11 *Daiichi Sankyo Co Ltd* (n 11), para 50; and Advocate General Kokott's Opinion in Case C-137/12 *Commission v Council*, judgment of 27 June 2013, nyr.

[82] Para 54.

[83] Para 56.

[84] The Court first established that Art 215 TFEU replaces the combination of Arts 60, 301 and 308 EC that serves as legal basis for the pre-Lisbon regulation which the impugned act was deemed to replace, distinguishing it from the more restricted function of Article 75 TFEU: '54. (...) its context and tenor differ from those of Articles 60 EC and 301 EC. Article 75 TFEU does not, in fact, refer to the interruption or reduction, in part or completely, of economic relations with one or more third countries. Incorporated in Part Three of the TFEU Treaty on Union policies and internal actions, and more specifically in Title V thereof, entitled "Area of freedom, security and justice", that Article simply refers to the definition, for the purpose of preventing terrorism and related activities and combating the same, of a framework for administrative measures with regard to capital movements and payments, when this is necessary to achieve the objectives set out in Article 67 TFEU'. Further on the external dimension of the AFSJ, see eg: M Cremona, J Monar and S Poli (eds), *The External Dimension of the Area of Freedom, Security and Justice* (Brussels, Peter Lang-PIE, 2011); J Monar, 'The External Dimension of the EU's Area of Freedom, Security and Justice', SIEPS Report 2012: 1.

[85] Indeed, the Court fails to expound the purpose of Art 75 TFEU in the fight against terrorism.

[86] Para 84.

view of the quantitative and qualitative significance sanctions represent in CFSP activities.[87]

In sum, this judgment could be read as the nascent judicial safeguard of the CFSP integrity in line with the post-Lisbon arrangements. Although the Court of Justice does not mention Article 40 TEU,[88] in contrast to the Council and the Advocate General,[89] its interest in various CFSP provisions, displays how it may exercise the protective and implicit interpretative jurisdiction in relation to the CFSP, with which it is endowed under Article 40(2) TEU.[90]

In this respect, it should be observed that the EU judicature did not follow Advocate General Bot's suggestion that the external objectives of a CFSP nature contained in Article 21(2) TEU could be singled out based on their previous inclusion in Article 11 TEU pre-Lisbon,[91] eg Article 21(2)(c) on 'consolidat[ion] and support [for] democracy, the rule of law, human rights and the principles of international law'.[92] Instead, the Court underlined that Article 21(2)(c) forms 'part of Chapter 1 laying down general provisions on the Union's external action in Title V of the EU Treaty'.[93] It thereby confirmed that the preservation of peace, prevention of conflicts and strengthening international security does not relate exclusively to the CFSP province. Any other EU external initiative is equally determined by, and may thus contribute to fulfilling the objectives enounced in Article 21(2) TEU.[94]

Arguably, the Advocate General's suggestion to rely on the pre-Lisbon dispensation for establishing the CFSP nature of some of the external objectives contained in Article 21(2) TEU would water down, if not contravene the legal modifications introduced by the Treaty of Lisbon. In effect, this would restore the teleological dichotomy that the Treaty abolished through the introduction of a single set of external objectives enshrined in the '*General provisions* on the Union's external action' (emphasis added). Had these objectives been specifically CFSP, they would

---

[87] See Eckes, 'EU Counter-Terrorist Sanctions' (n 15).

[88] I Bosse-Platière, 'L'action extérieure de l'Union européenne - 3. La Cour confirme le rattachement de la lutte contre le terrorisme international et son financement à la PESC' (2013) 2 *Revue Trimestrielle de Droit Europeen* 118 at 120.

[89] Para 41 of the judgment as regards the Council's argument, and para 67 of Advocate General Bot's Opinion.

[90] It may be wondered whether para 77 of the judgment could be read as an indication that the legal basis of the Common Position, on which the contested measure is founded, could be altered should this common position be replaced. The Court held that: 'although, in connection with the second plea in law, the Parliament denies that Common Position 2002/402 can possibly amount to a decision under the CFSP for the purpose of Article 215(2) TFEU, it has not, however, called in question whether it was possible for that Common Position, having enabled adoption of Regulation No 881/2002 in accordance with Articles 60 EC and 301 EC, to be validly based on Title V of the EU Treaty, as it stood before the Treaty of Lisbon, that is to say, the title of that treaty concerning the CFSP'.

[91] See Opinion of Advocate General Bot in Case C-130/10 *Parliament v Council* (31 January 2012). See also Dashwood, 'Article 47 TEU' (n 2).

[92] Para 64, Opinion of Advocate General Bot in Case C-130/10 *Parliament v Council* (31 January 2012).

[93] Para 62.

[94] A point also made by Advocate General Bot at para 77 of his Opinion.

have logically found their home in the Chapter entitled '*Specific provisions* on the common foreign and security policy' (emphasis added), the way the particular aims of the CSDP are spelled out in Articles 42 and 43 TEU.

An additional illustration of the Court's engagement with the protection of the CFSP integrity is its deference to the constitutional choice of the Treaty authors that is embodied in the CFSP specific institutional arrangements. The European Parliament argued that Article 75 TFEU ought to have been chosen as the appropriate legal basis, in view of 'the general scheme and the spirit of the Treaties', and given that it better reflected 'the intention of the Member States' when drafting the Lisbon Treaty 'to enhance the democratic nature of the European Union'. Invoking the Court's decision in *Kadi I*, the Parliament claimed that in view of the nature of the regulation, and notably its impact on individuals, the legal basis of the contested Regulation ought to be Article 75 TFEU given that it enables the Parliament to take part in the decision-making process'.[95] But the Court rejected this line of argument, based notably on the intention of the authors of the Treaty regarding the institutional specificity of the CFSP, which it is entrusted to safeguard:

> Admittedly, participation by the Parliament in the legislative process is the reflection, at Union level, of the fundamental democratic principle that the people should participate in the exercise of power through the intermediary of a representative assembly ...

> Nevertheless, the difference between Article 75 TFEU and Article 215 TFEU, so far as the Parliament's involvement is concerned, *is the result of the choice made by the framers of the Treaty of Lisbon conferring a more limited role on the Parliament with regard to the Union's action under the CFSP* (emphasis added).[96]

In view of the above discussion, it appears that in safeguarding the integrity of the CFSP, the Court is also in a position to articulate the circumstances where its specific procedures are to be used. The difficulty in operating Article 40 TEU resulting from the reformulation of the relationship between the CFSP (TEU) and other EU competences (TFEU), and the reduced suitability of previous judicial tools, leaves the Court with a broad margin of manoeuvre, inasmuch as it has become the authoritative exegetist of CFSP treaty norms and procedures, and the guardian of their authenticity.[97] That the Treaty authors have entrusted the Court with this particular authority looks paradoxical in view of the aim of Article 40(2), namely to shield the CFSP from the integration spin. Rather, the resulting arrangement epitomises the notion that the CFSP is being further integrated with(in) the EU constitutional order, and that perhaps EU constitutionalism does not 'stop at the water's edge'.[98]

---

[95] Paras 28 and 33.

[96] See paras 81 and 82.

[97] The General Court has equally shown eagerness to make interpretative use of the CFSP provisions, and 'secondary' acts, see in particular Case T-395/11 *Elti doo v Delegation of the European Union to Montenegro*, order of 4 June 2012, nyr, paras 31ff.

[98] Eeckhout, *Does Europe's Constitution Stop at the Water's Edge?* (n 6).

IV. THE COURT'S SAFEGUARD OF EU CONSTITUTIONAL PRINCIPLES

The Treaty of Lisbon has not only opened the CFSP to the Court of Justice's jurisdiction, it has also modified the constitutional landscape within which the Court adjudicates[99]—notably by adding emphasis on, for example, democratic principles and respect for fundamental rights, the principle of sincere cooperation and the requirement of consistency. In this last section, the chapter discusses whether the Court's jurisdiction in relation to these *constitutional* principles[100] might have an impact on the exercise of CFSP competence, and on its normative effects.

The Court of Justice has already established that such principles apply to, and can be judicially enforced against EU institutions acting in the context of CFSP. Thus, it has been held that the principle of transparency/access to documents covers all Council documents, including when acting in the field of CFSP.[101] The horizontal application of other principles such as the protection of fundamental rights or the principle of cooperation also finds support in the case law.

As regards the former, suffice to recall that the Court held in its 2012 pronouncement in the case *European Parliament v Council* discussed above, that 'the duty to respect fundamental rights is imposed, in accordance with Article 51(1) of the Charter of Fundamental Rights of the European Union, on all the institutions and bodies of the Union',[102] thus emphasising the unqualified character of such a duty, at least as regards the institutions. Indeed, it held that the 'respect for fundamental rights equally bears on Union measures giving effect to resolutions of the Security Council',[103] making no difference whether such implementing measures are CFSP or TFEU-based. In principle therefore, the choice between a TFEU or CFSP course of action should have no bearing on the institutions' obligation to respect fundamental rights protected under EU law.[104] But the same holds true as regards Member States. Whether they apply CFSP or TFEU measures, they 'implement … Union law' for the purpose of Article 51(1) of the EU Charter, and as such they must comply with EU fundamental rights requirements.[105] That respect for fundamental rights is also required in the CFSP area is confirmed by the provisions of Article 275 TFEU. As discussed above, these provisions allow the Court to

---

[99] Further on this, see: M Dougan, 'The Treaty of Lisbon 2007: Winning Minds, Not Hearts' (2008) 45 *CML Rev* 617; JP Jacqué, 'Le traité de Lisbonne. Une vue cavalière' (2008) 3 *Revue Trimestrielle de Droit Europeen* 444; F Jacobs in Dashwood and Maresceau, *Law and Practice of EU External Relations* (n 2).

[100] Further on such principles, see A von Bogdandy, 'Constitutional Principles' in A von Bogdandy and J Bast (eds), *Principles of European Constitutional Law* (Oxford, Hart Publishing, 2006).

[101] See: Case T-14/98 *Hautala v Council* [1999] ECR II- 2489; Case C-353/99 P *Council v Hautala* [2001] ECR I-9565, although within limits, see: Case T-301/10 *In 't Veld v Commission* (19 March 2013); Case T-331/11 *Leonard Besselink* (12 September 2013). Further, see: De Baere, *Constitutional Principles* (n 2) at 181; Eeckhout, *EU External Relations Law* (n 17).

[102] Para 83.

[103] Para 84.

[104] The same cannot be said about democratic control, as confirmed by the Court's judgment in Case C-130/10 (n 13).

[105] See, in this regard, Case C-617/10 *Fransson*, judgment of 26 February 2013, nyr.

exercise judicial control over restrictive measures adopted in the context of CFSP, in line with the *Kadi I* jurisprudence, and thus to guarantee that fundamental rights are respected when adopting these measures.[106]

Moreover, as set out in Article 19(1) TEU, and as confirmed in the Court's Opinion 1/09,[107] the judicial system of the Union involves not only the Court of Justice, but also Member States' judiciaries, which are together 'the guardians of [the EU] legal order'. Thus 'in collaboration with the Court of Justice, [they] fulfil ... a duty entrusted to them both of ensuring that in the interpretation and application of the Treaties the law is observed'. As a result, Member States' courts can be expected to step in if and when the Court of Justice's jurisdiction is restricted or non-existent.[108] In particular, they are entrusted to ensure the application by national authorities of, for example, fundamental rights enshrined in the Charter, when acting in the context of the CFSP and as such 'implementing Union law'.[109] The Court of Justice could then be asked to intervene by way of a preliminary ruling procedure to help the Member State court apply the Charter or other EU principles relevant to the situation.[110]

The application of the principle of cooperation is equally transversal,[111] as confirmed by the Lisbon Treaty. Article 4(3), included in the Common Provisions of the TEU, makes clear that the rebranded 'principle of sincere cooperation' relates to all the objectives of the Union, and all the 'tasks which flow from the *treaties*' (emphasis added). The positive obligations of support and obligations to refrain from taking action that could jeopardise the fulfilment of EU tasks, which derive from Article 4(3) TEU, are therefore not limited in their application to non-CFSP objectives and tasks. Should it be considered that a Member State is failing to fulfil its duties under Article 4(3) TEU, because its failure to comply with a CFSP obligation are jeopardising the attainment of the Union's external action objectives, the question may be raised as to whether the enforcement mechanisms made available by primary law should be triggered. Here, the Commission would not be suing a state for failure to comply with the CFSP obligation as such, but because

---

[106] See, Joined Cases C-402/05 P and C-415/05 P *Kadi and Al Barakaat International Foundation v Council and Commission* (n 12), and judgment of 18 July 2013 in Cases C-584/10P, C-593/10 and C-595/10 P *Commission, Council, United Kingdom v Kadi ('Kadi II')*, as well as Advocate General Bot's Opinion, 19 March 2013, nyr.

[107] Opinion 1/09 (n 32).

[108] See Case C-50/00 P *Unión de Pequeños Agricultores v Council* (n 30), Case C-583/11 P *Inuit Tapiriit Kanatami and Others* (n 26).

[109] Further on the role of national courts in guaranteeing compliance with EU fundamental rights, see A von Bogdandy, M Kottmann, C Antpöhler, J Dickschen, S Hentrei and M Smrkolj, 'Reverse Solange—Protecting the Essence of Fundamental Rights against EU Member States' (2012) 49 *CML Rev* 489.

[110] EU accession to the European Convention on Human Rights (ECHR) would possibly add pressure to the involvement of the EU judiciary in relation to the CFSP, in view of the intention of the draft agreement to allow the Strasbourg Court to control the EU CFSP compliance with the ECHR.

[111] See Case C-105/03 *Pupino* [2005] ECR I-5285. Further, see eg, C Hillion and RA Wessel, 'Restraining External Competences of EU Member States under CFSP' in Cremona and de Witte, *EU Foreign Relations Law* (n 4) at 79.

of its violation of the principle of sincere cooperation which, in view of the recent case law, is able to generate obligations of itself, without necessary recourse to any other specific obligations in the Treaty.[112]

The principle of sincere cooperation equally binds EU institutions in accordance with Article 13(2) TEU, whereby they shall also 'practice mutual sincere cooperation'. In other words, institutions are too bound by obligations of conduct, akin to those applying to Member States, notably the duty to consult, inform, if not to refrain from acting if action may jeopardise the fulfilment of a Union objective.[113] As a result, EU institutions acting within the context of the CFSP are bound to cooperate with those acting in the framework of the TFEU, and vice versa.[114] Thus, it may be asked whether the Commission or Parliament could sue the Council or European Council on the ground that they fail to comply with the provisions of Article 13(2) TEU, by consistently omitting to transmit information related to the CFSP, or to consult, where the CFSP provisions so stipulate. Indeed, institutions operating in the context of the CFSP are subject to the obligation of consistency enshrined in Article 21(3) TEU, which imposes procedural obligations between the Council and the Commission, assisted by the High Representative, to strive to achieve synergies between the different areas of its external action and between these and its other policies.[115] Arguably, these two principles located outside the specific TEU chapter on CFSP, and particularly the procedural obligations derived therefrom are in principle enforceable before the Court of Justice, irrespective of the fact that EU institutions are operating within the CFSP context,[116] the way the principle of transparency has previously been enforced against the Council acting in the area of foreign policy.

The question could immediately be raised as to whether the transversal application and enforcement of principles underpinning the EU legal order would

---

[112] See, in this respect: Case C-266/03 *Commission v Luxembourg* [2005] ECR I-4805, para 60; Case C-433/03 *Commission v Germany* [2005] ECR I-6985, para 66; and Case C-246/07 *Commission v Sweden* [2010] ECR I-03317. Further: M Cremona, 'Case C-246/07, *Commission v Sweden* (PFOS), Judgment of the Court of Justice (Grand Chamber) of 20 April 2010' (2011) 48 *CML Rev* 1639; A Delgado Casteleiro and J Larik 'The Duty to Remain Silent: Limitless Loyalty in EU External Relations?' (2011) 36 *EL Rev* 522; M Cremona, 'Defending the Community Interest: the Duties of Cooperation and Compliance' in Cremona and de Witte, *EU Foreign Relations Law* (n 4) at 125; E Neframi, 'The Duty of Loyalty: Rethinking its Scope through its Application in the Field of EU External Relations' (2010) 47 *CML Rev* 323; C Hillion, 'Mixity and Coherence in EU External Relations: the Significance of the Duty of Cooperation' in C Hillion and P Koutrakos (eds), *Mixed Agreements Revisited—The Union and its Member States in the World* (Oxford, Hart Publishing, 2010); G De Baere, 'O, Where is Faith? O, Where is Loyalty? Some Thoughts? On the Duty of Loyal Co-operation and the Union's External Environmental Competences in the light of the PFOS Case' (2011) 36 *EL Rev* 405. Whether the Commission would be inclined to use this tool remains to be seen, in view of its stance on, eg Member States' compliance (or lack thereof) with the rule of law requirements.

[113] See in this regard, pending Case C-409/13 *Council of the European Union v European Commission*.

[114] Case C-77/11 *Council v Parliament* (n 71).

[115] Further, see eg Hillion, 'Cohérence et action extérieure de l'Union' (n 4) at 229.

[116] ibid (n 4); also in this sense, see the Court's findings in Case C-658/11 *European Parliament v Council* (24 June 2014) on the Parliament's right to be informed in relation to CFSP agreements, in order to 'exercise democratic scrutiny of the European Union's external action'.

be contrary to the rule set out in Article 24(1) TEU that the CFSP 'is subject to specific rules and procedures', and to the restriction it contains on the Court's jurisdiction.

A close reading of Article 24(1) TEU does not appear to restrict the general application of EU constitutional principles to the CFSP domain. Taken literally, the provision formulates the CFSP specificity only in terms of 'rules and procedures', not in terms of 'principles'. Arguably therefore, while the exercise of EU competence is subject to specific procedures and rules, it is not immune from the general application of EU organising principles. Indeed, as pointed out above, the Court of Justice has already emphasised the horizontal application of, for example, fundamental rights, whose respect it guarantees in relation notably to CFSP restrictive measures. In any event, restrictions to the Court's jurisdiction in relation to other CFSP acts have no bearing on the question of whether EU principles apply or not to the CFSP context. They merely indicate that the Court itself is not in a position to scrutinise general CFSP acts against EU constitutional principles.

Moreover, Article 40(2) TEU foresees that the implementation of the policies listed in Articles 3–6 TFEU, which enounce EU competences, cannot affect the application of CFSP procedures. As EU constitutional principles do not amount to EU policies or competence, the provisions of Article 40 TEU are of no relevance as regards the effects of, for example, Article 4(3) TEU, or fundamental rights in the context of CFSP. Therefore, the constitutional limitations to the Court's jurisdiction in CFSP (eg Article 275) do not entail restrictions to its jurisdiction as regards the application of other EU constitutional principles that could have effects on the CFSP. In the same vein, Declarations 13 and 14 on the CFSP, that are annexed to the Treaty of Lisbon, only concern the effect of 'the provisions in the Treaty on European Union covering the Common Foreign and Security Policy, including the creation of the office of High Representative of the Union for Foreign Affairs and Security Policy and the establishment of an External Action Service', and 'the provisions governing the Common Security and Defence Policy';[117] they have no bearing on the application of EU constitutional principles, and on the jurisdiction of the Court to enforce them.

V. CONCLUDING REMARKS

While CFSP competence and procedures remain distinct from mainstream EU arrangements, such distinctiveness should be nuanced. One of the hallmarks of this policy's specificity has been the restricted involvement of EU supranational institutions, and particularly of the European Court of Justice. The above discussion has hopefully demonstrated that although its jurisdiction is more restricted in the CFSP context than on the TFEU terrain, the Union's judiciary is certainly

---

[117] See Declaration 13 'concerning the common foreign and security policy', and Declaration 14 'concerning the common foreign and security policy' (n 3).

less powerless as regards the former than it used to be, and arguably less powerless than it might be surmised under the post-Lisbon dispensation.

Hence, in examining the provisions of Article 275 TFEU, several elements were spelled out which point towards a judicial control in relation to CFSP that is not as restricted as it may look. It was also argued that the Court's border patrolling function under Article 40 TEU could bolster its interpretative power in the relation to the CFSP. Indeed, it was suggested that in asking the Court to protect its specificity, the authors of the Treaty may paradoxically have eroded it, by entrenching the policy and its governance further in the EU constitutional order, characterised by the authority of a powerful judicature. Finally and more generally, the chapter contended that the evolution of EU constitutional law strengthens the overarching role of the Union's judiciary. In particular, it allows the Court of Justice to enforce EU constitutional principles across the whole legal order, without infringing the limitations of its jurisdiction in relation to the CFSP specifically.

The Court of Justice might be less of a Community creature than it used to be. It is the judicature for the whole of the EU, in charge of preserving the latter's *grands équilibres* as set out by the Treaty of Lisbon. As such, it has the constitutional task of ensuring the rule of law throughout the Union's legal order, in collaboration with the Member States' courts. Hence, the question might be less of whether it is desirable for the judiciary to control EU foreign policy measures, but how far it should exercise such a control in a Union deemed also to be founded on the value of democracy.

Part II

Jurisprudence and the Allocation
of External Competence

5

Vertical Division of Competences and the Objectives of the European Union's External Action

ELEFTHERIA NEFRAMI

I. INTRODUCTION

T HE TREATIES ENABLE the Court of Justice (hereafter also referred to as 'the Court') to exercise the constitutional function of patrolling the verti-cal division of competences between the European Union (EU) and the Member States and therefore to act as a guardian of the constitutional principle of conferral.[1] In the field of the EU's external action, the Court of Justice has to ensure respect of the principle of conferral while pursuing the objective of unity in the international area.

Unity in the international area is not an explicit objective but a condition to attain the objective of asserting the identity of the Union in the international scene[2] the objective of shouldering its responsibilities in the governance of glo-balisation according to the Laeken declaration. The Lisbon Treaty sets out the Union's external action objectives in Article 21 TEU. The list in paragraph (2) covers substantive and specific external action objectives ((a) to (g)) and an objec-tive which could be considered as general or ultimate (under (h)), to 'promote an international system based on stronger multilateral cooperation and good global governance'.

Whereas substantive specific objectives correspond to specific external action competences conferred to the Union in Part V of the Treaty on the Functioning of the European Union (TFEU), the objective to promote an international system based on stronger multilateral cooperation and good global governance is not linked to a specific competence of the Union. This objective is to be attained through the

---

[1] A Dashwood, 'The Limits of European Community Powers' (1996) 21 *EL Rev* 113; D Wyatt, 'Is the European Union an Organisation of Limited Powers?' in A Arnull, C Barnard, M Dougan, E Spaventa (eds), *A Constitutional Order of States?, Essays in EU Law in Honour of Alan Dashwood* (Oxford, Hart Publishing, 2011) 3.

[2] Former Art 2 TEU.

credibility and efficiency of the Union's external action, general horizontal objective which presuppose horizontal and vertical coherence in the exercise of external competences. Both horizontal coherence, in the sense of alignment of the exercise of competences to the Union's fundamental values and transversal objectives, and vertical coherence, in the sense of alignment of the Member States' external action to the objectives of the Union, meet the question of the vertical division of external competences between the Union and the Member States. Furthermore, the attainment of the external specific and ultimate objectives meet the question of vertical division of competences which are not linked to the objectives set out in Article 21(2) TEU. Indeed, according to Article 21(3) TEU, external action objectives are to be pursued also in the development of the external aspects of internal policies of the Union, where the competence of the Union is linked to internal objectives.

The link between the external action objectives and the vertical division of competences raises a number of questions. The starting point should be the definition of the principle of conferral under the Lisbon Treaty. Article 5(2) TEU reads:

> The Union shall act only within the limits of the competences conferred upon it by the Member States in the Treaties to attain the objectives set out therein.

It follows that when considering external action, the Union must give precedence to considerations of competence over considerations of effectiveness.[3] Therefore, the ultimate objective of promoting an international system based on stronger multilateral cooperation and good global governance is not capable of legitimating the Union's external action beyond the exercise of specific competences corresponding to specific, external or internal objectives.

Despite progress made in the definition and conferral of competences in the Treaty of Lisbon, the Court of Justice still has to face the constitutional challenge of allocating competences by establishing the extent of exclusivity and regulating their exercise according to the objectives set out in the treaties.[4] The Court of Justice deals with external competences in a fragmented way, in order to determine the level of exercise of competence in a specific area. The Court underlines its attachment to the principle of conferral, considering specific competences in relation to the corresponding objectives. In such a context, is it likely for the Court of Justice to adopt a global view of external action competence and objectives, beyond specific policy fields? Can we affirm such a global view in the framework of coexistence of the Union's competence alongside with the Member States' competence? Is such a global view linked to the ultimate objective, beyond the allocation of specific competences?

---

[3]   G De Baere, K Gutman, 'Federalism and International Relations in the European Union and the United States: A Comparative Outlook' in E Cloots, G De Baere, S Sottiaux (eds), *Federalism in the European Union* (Oxford, Hart Publishing, 2012) 139.

[4]   R Schütze, 'Dual Federalism Constitutionalised: The Emergence of Exclusive Competences in the EC Legal Order' (2007) 32 *EL Rev* 3; E Sharpston, G De Baere, 'The Court of Justice as a Constitutional Adjudicator' in A Arnull, C Barnard, M Dougan, E Spaventa (eds), *A Constitutional Order of States?, Essays in EU Law in Honour of Alan Dashwood* (Oxford, Hart Publishing, 2011) 123.

In order to rethink the role of the Court of Justice in the vertical allocation of competences with the perspective to attain external action objectives, the following should be taken into consideration.

The competences conferred upon the Union in order to attain external action objectives (external action competences) are not necessarily exclusive; the Court intervenes to clarify the extent of exclusivity. Moreover, external action objectives may be pursued through the exercise by the Union of competences linked to internal objectives (external aspect of internal competence). In such a case, the extent of exclusivity has also to be determined by the Court of Justice. In both cases (external competence and external aspects of internal competence) the Court of Justice is asked to determine the allocation of competences according to the principle of conferral; in both cases, the Court does not define the scope of the specific objectives, which is a political question, but considers the allocation of competences in relation to the objective clearly linked to the envisaged measure; in both cases the Court considers the specific objective pursued through the exercise of the competence in question.

In the case of shared competence, where the Union and Member States may act jointly, the Court of Justice has to determine the extent to which the Member States have the obligation to avoid jeopardising the external action objectives. Furthermore, in the case of interference of objectives, the Court of Justice has to appreciate the scope of the objectives in order to decide on the competence to be exercised. In both cases, the Court of Justice adopts a global approach to the objectives, either the specific objectives, or in relation to the ultimate external objective, to be a global and influential international actor.

It is proposed to review these issues through the case law on vertical allocation of competences. The Court of Justice defines the vertical allocation when a competence is clearly linked to an objective. In such a case the Court of Justice sets out the boundaries of the EU external action competences (section II) and develops the doctrine of exclusivity beyond external action policies (section III). However, the Court of Justice also has to deal with the vertical allocation of competences when the parallelism between competences and objectives has to be defined. In that case, a global approach to the objectives is necessary (section IV).

II. VERTICAL DIVISION OF EXTERNAL COMPETENCES PURSUING EXTERNAL ACTION OBJECTIVES

In external action policy fields, defined in Part V of the TFEU, the competence conferred to the Union is linked to the external action specific objectives. The Treaty allows the Union to exercise its external competence regardless of its nature. However, in the case of exclusive external competence of the Union, the Member States are retired from the international scene. The autonomous action of the Union is thus a function of the question of exclusivity.

The Court of Justice has been called to determine, before the entry into force of the Lisbon Treaty, the scope of the Treaty provisions conferring exclusive external competence to the Union, the former Community.

In the field of Common Commercial Policy (CCP), the Court of Justice has first affirmed the exclusive nature of the Community's competence. The Court held in Opinion 1/75[5] that the CCP was conceived in the context of the operation of the common market, for the defense of the common interests of the Community. This conception was considered incompatible with the Member States' action, which could endanger the internal market structure of the Community, and led to the exclusion of the exercise of concurrent powers by the Member States. The reasoning of the Court in order to establish exclusivity has been based on the consideration of an internal objective: the common interest that should be preserved according to the principle of loyalty. Exclusivity in the field of CCP has thus been established and has therefore been considered, regardless of its internal link. The Treaty of Lisbon confirms that the Union is exclusively competent with regard to external trade.[6] The exclusive external competence conferred by the Treaty is linked to external action objectives such as the contribution to the harmonious development of world trade and to the progressive abolition of restrictions on international trade.[7] The external action orientation of the new CCP is further confirmed by the statement, in the second sentence of Article 207(1) TFEU, that it will be conducted in the context of the principles and objectives of the Union's external action. Therefore the exclusivity of the competence conferred on the Union is derived from its link to an external action objective, and no longer needs to be considered with respect to internal objectives.

However, the Court of Justice has had to define the scope of the CCP, and as a consequence the scope of the exclusive competence of the Union. The extent of exclusivity determines the vertical allocation of competences. Before the entry into force of the Lisbon Treaty, the definition of the scope of the CCP was not necessarily guided by a consideration of external action objectives. In Opinion 1/94 on the World Trade Organization (WTO) agreement,[8] the Court ruled with respect to the General Agreement on Trade in Services (GATS) and the Agreement on Trade-Related Aspects on Intellectual Property Rights (TRIPs), that only some aspects of trade in services and trade-related intellectual property rights were covered by the CCP and, as a consequence, by exclusive Community competence. The non-exclusive nature of Community competence should not prevent the Community from exercising it, as the largest part of the WTO agreements were covered by the CCP, but the Community could not act alone on the basis of the former Article 113 EC.

---

[5] Opinion 1/75 *Draft Understanding on a Local Cost Standard drawn up under the auspices of the OECD* [1975] ECR 1355.

[6] Art 3(1)(e) TFEU.

[7] Art 206 TFEU.

[8] Opinion 1/94 *World Trade Organization (WTO) agreement* [1994] ECR I-5267.

As is well known, Opinion 1/94 was not eagerly received by scholars and led to the reform of the CCP.[9] It should be pointed out that the reasoning of the Court when determining the scope of the CCP was not externally oriented. Although the objective linked to the Community's competence is an external one, related to international trade, and although in Opinion 1/75 and in Opinion 1/78[10] the Court considered the scope of the CCP in relation to international trade and to the objective of the Community to be an influent international actor,[11] in Opinion 1/94 the Court did not take into consideration the international law conception of commercial policy. Instead of permitting the Community to act as a commercial power in the international scene, by accepting a wide reading of the objectives of the CCP, the Court showed its attachment to a strict respect for the principle of conferral. Opinion 1/94 is based on the functioning of the internal market and the objectives of internal policies, the scope of Community powers being defined according to the internal system of competences. Since services and intellectual property rights are internal policies, pursuing internal market objectives, the objectives of the GATS and the TRIPs could not be considered as externally oriented, to be pursued through the competence based on the former Article 113 EC. Consequently there is a parallelism between internal and external competence, as shared internal competence concerning services and incomplete harmonisation of intellectual property rights could not lead to exclusive external competence. In other words, GATS and TRIPs were not to be considered in relation to external trade objectives and the CCP competence, because services and intellectual property rights fall under internal competence and internal objectives. The Court of Justice adopted a subject-matter based approach, considering the objective of each provision and not of the GATS and the TRIPs as a whole. Opinion 1/94 shows a fragmented conception of external competence, regardless of the ultimate objective to be an international actor, and the vertical allocation of competences depended on the horizontal policy-based division of powers.

The Court of Justice was also required to interpret the reform by the Nice Treaty of the scope of the Community competence in this field.[12] Indeed, the Community has been entrusted with the competence to conclude agreements concerning trade in services and commercial aspects of intellectual property, although these fields were not included in the scope of Article 133(1) EC. Thus

---

[9] T Tridimas, P Eeckhout, 'The External Competence of the Community and the Case Law of the Court of Justice: Principle versus Pragmatism' (1994) *YEL* 143; P Pescatore, 'Opinion 1/94 on Conclusion of the WTO Agreement: Is There an Escape from a Programmed Disaster?' (1999) 36 *CMLRev* 387.

[10] Opinion 1/78 *International Agreement on Natural Rubber* [1979] ECR 2871.

[11] In Opinion 1/75 the Court held that the concept of commercial policy has the same content whether it is applied in the context of the international action of a state or to that of the Community.

[12] M Cremona, 'A Policy of Bits and Pieces? The Common Commercial Policy after Nice' (2002) *Cambridge Yearbook of European Legal Studies* 61; W Herrmann, 'Common Commercial Policy after Nice: Sisyphus Would Have Done a Better Job' (2002) 39 *CMLRev* 7; E Neframi, 'La politique commerciale commune selon le traité de Nice' (2001) *Cahiers de droit européen* 605.

the Nice Treaty enlarged the scope of the Community competence, but not the scope of the CCP. The Nice Treaty distinguished the external objectives pursued by the GATS and the TRIPs from the internal objectives pursued by competence in services and harmonisation of intellectual property rights. Article 133(5) EC conferred on the Community an express external competence pursuing an external action objective, to reinforce the role of the Community in the WTO, but this competence was not exclusive. At the same time, liberalisation of services and harmonisation of intellectual property protection were still considered to be linked to internal market objectives, giving rise to an implied external competence, the exclusivity of which being determined by the pre-emption doctrine.

However, the conferral of an express external competence allowed the Community to act regardless of the question of exclusivity. This is how Advocate General Kokott interpreted Article 133(5) EC in Case C-13/07 *Commission v Council*,[13] concerning the legal basis of the Union's decision on the approval of Vietnam's accession to the WTO:

> The new powers in respect of external trade conferred upon the Community by Article 133(5) EC are not parallel, but concurrent. A characteristic of *concurrent competence* (also referred to as *shared competence*) is that the Member States exercise their competence in so far as the Community has not exercised its competence. However, if the Community does exercise its competence, it acts *alone*, so far as that competence is sufficient.[14]

Although the Court of Justice did not take a position on this point, the case having been removed from the register, we should note that explicit external competence may be exercised by the Community alone, regardless of its exclusive nature, if it is associated to the external action objective. It follows that when external and internal objectives are dissociated the pre-emption doctrine is not required to authorise the exercise of the Community's external competence. However, the exercise by the Community of its external competence pursuing an external action objective affects the allocation of competences in the internal field, linked to internal market objectives.

The first and only ruling of the Court on the scope of the reform of the CCP by the Nice Treaty is the *GATS Schedules* Opinion.[15] The Court confirmed the non-exclusive nature of the Community competence in the field of services and pointed out that the former Article 133(6) EC conferred a shared competence in the fields of culture, education, social and human health services. However, in contrast to paragraph (5), paragraph (6) did not empower the Community to act alone, referring explicitly to the joint conclusion of the agreements. The Court interpreted this provision as the basis of a shared competence including instances

---

[13] Case C-13/07 *Commission v Council*, Opinion of AG Kokott 26 March 2009, case withdrawn.
[14] ibid, para 76.
[15] Opinion 1/08 *GATS Schedules* [2009] ECR I-11129. See M Cremona, 'Balancing Union and Member State Interests: Opinion 1/2008, Choice of Legal Base and the Common Commercial Policy under the Treaty of Lisbon' (2010) 35 *EL Rev* 678.

of horizontal agreements covering other fields of services, where the Community could exercise its competence alone. The Court adjudicated on the vertical division of competences regardless of the ultimate objective of being an influential actor in the international scene and remains attached to the principle of conferral in regard to the specific objectives. The Court recalled that the resolution of the issue of the allocation of competence could not be determined by problems which might possibly arise in the administration or the conclusion of agreements.[16] It follows that under the Nice Treaty an externally-oriented measure could be adopted either on the basis of internal competence as linked to an internal market objective, under the conditions of the pre-emption doctrine, or on the basis of external competence based on Article 133(5) EC if the measure was considered to serve an international trade objective.

The reform of the CCP by the Lisbon Treaty separates clearly the external and internal aspects of the Union's objectives in the field of services and intellectual property rights. The Lisbon Treaty extends the field of exclusivity, the CCP according to Article 207(1) TFEU covering agreements relating to trade in goods and services and the commercial aspects of intellectual property, as well as foreign direct investment.[17] In the field of trade in services and commercial aspects of intellectual property, exclusivity is therefore granted by the Treaty following an external action objective, that is to act in international trade relations, and not as a result of the necessity criterion stemming from the exercise of the competence in the internal field.

Consequently, an externally-oriented measure in the field of services or intellectual property rights now falls under the scope of the CCP and thus under the exclusive competence of the Union. It follows that measures in the field of trade in services and the commercial aspects of intellectual property, if linked to international trade, are considered to pursue an exclusively external objective. They cannot be considered as falling under the external aspect of the internal market competence, even if the adoption of these measures may lead to the harmonisation of internal provisions. If internal provisions may be harmonised through the exercise of the CCP competence, the same internal provisions no longer give rise to an external competence as the latter is linked to international trade. As the Court of Justice points out in the *Daiichi Sankyo* case, Article 207 TFEU, while

---

[16] Opinion 1/08 (ibid), para 127.

[17] M Bungenberg and C Herrmann, 'Common Commercial Policy after Lisbon' (2013) *European Yearbook of International Economic Law* Special issue; M Cremona, 'Defining Competences in EU External Relations: Lessons from the Treaty Reform Process' in A Dashwood, M Maresceau (eds), *Law and Practice of EU External Relations* (Cambridge, Cambridge University Press, 2008) 34; M Krajewski, 'The Reform of the Common Commercial Policy' in A Biondi, P Eeckhout, S Ripley (eds), *EU Law after Lisbon* (Oxford, Oxford University Press, 2012) 292; P-C Müller-Graff, 'The Common Commercial Policy Enhanced by the Reform Treaty of Lisbon?' in A Dashwood, M Maresceau (eds), *Law and Practice of EU External Relations* (Cambridge, Cambridge University Press, 2008) 188.

linked to the external action objective of trade with non-member countries, differs noticeably from the former Article 133 EC.[18]

The *Daiichi Sankyo* judgment underlines the link between international trade objectives and commercial aspects of intellectual property in the sense of Article 207 TFEU. The question raised was whether Article 27 of the TRIPs, a provision setting out the framework for patent protection, falls within the field of the CCP. The subject of patentability concerns international trade only indirectly, being covered by shared competence in the field of the internal market. According to Advocate General Cruz Villalón, Article 27 of the TRIPs should not be considered as falling under the CCP competence. However, the Court of Justice did not follow the Opinion of the Advocate General. The Court emphasises the international trade objective of the TRIPs, resulting from its specific place in the WTO system.[19] The question of patentability cannot be isolated from the external action objective of the agreement containing Article 27. Admitting the dissociation of Article 27 from the CCP could allow the use of an internal market based external competence, according to the conditions of exercise of implied competences, in order to conclude agreements related to patentability issues, despite their link to international trade. It follows from the *Daiichi Sankyo* judgment that the meaning of 'commercial aspects of intellectual property rights' is associated to the external action objective of the Union to be an international trade actor. While a CCP measure may lead to harmonisation of internal provisions, internal provisions can no longer be the legal basis of an international trade linked measure.

The same objective-oriented approach is followed by the Court of Justice in *Commission v Council*, a case concerning the legal basis of the Council decision concluding the European Convention on the legal protection of services based on, or consisting of, conditional access.[20] The Court insisted on the criterion of the specific link to international trade in order to determine the scope of Article 207 TFEU. Despite the existence of internal market provisions covering the same subject and thus liable to establish an implied external competence, the Court dissociated the internal market-oriented measures, aiming at improving the functioning of the internal market from those specifically linked to international trade. Considering that the principal objective of this Council of Europe Convention is to promote international trade in services, the Court annulled the decision based on Article 114 TFEU, considering that Article 207 TFEU should be the corresponding legal basis. As Advocate General Kokott pointed out,[21] a CCP measure may lead to harmonisation of national legislation. However, harmonisation of national legislation may no longer give rise to an external competence to pursue an international trade, external action objective, this objective being covered by the specific externally-oriented exclusive EU competence based on Article 207 TFEU.

---

[18] Case C-414/11 *Daiichi Sankyo Co Ltd and Sanofi-Aventis Deutschland GmbH v DEMO Anonymos Viomichaniki kai Emporiki Etairia Farmakon*, judgment of 18 July 2013, para 46.

[19] ibid, para 53.

[20] Case C-137/12 *Commission v Council*, judgment of 22 October 2013.

[21] Opinion of AG Kokott 27 June 2013, para 66.

In the field of foreign direct investment, the exclusive external competence conferred to the Union under Article 207 TFEU is also linked to an international trade objective.[22] As a consequence, internal provisions related to the freedom of capital movements are no longer the basis of the external Union competence. However, the external trade orientation means that Article 207 TFUE is limited to trade-related aspects of investments and does not address foreign investments in general, although the CCP competence covers investment protection provisions to the extent that harmonisation is not excluded.

It follows that the Union has the possibility to exercise its external competence in the field covered by the CCP, in order to attain an international trade objective, regardless of the exercise of the internal competence and the attainment of internal objectives. However according to Article 207(6) TFEU the international action of the Union should not affect the Member States' competence in the internal field: exclusivity in the field of CCP appears only in relation to an external action objective, provided that the Union is vested with the power to take measures internally in the same field.

The CCP is the only field of external action competence where the competence of the Union is expressly conferred as exclusive. In the field of development cooperation and humanitarian aid the Union has, as reflected in Article 4(4) TFEU, shared competence[23] that does not lead to pre-emption, and could thus be considered as parallel competence.[24]

With respect to development cooperation policy, it should be noted that the primary objective on the basis of the conferral of competence is the external action objective of reduction and eradication of poverty in developing countries. As the Court pointed out,[25] it is an objective that can be broadly interpreted and encroach other fields of competence. That is why this objective is mainly pursued through instruments such as association agreements, in the framework of which more than one Union and Member States' competences are exercised. In that sense, development cooperation can be considered as both a field of competence (namely in case of adoption of unilateral measures) and a framework for the global exercise of competences. The question is no longer the vertical but the horizontal allocation of competences.

Finally, the fields of economic, financial and technical cooperation with third countries, as well as neighbourhood policy, do not correspond to a substantive

---

[22] JA Bischoff, 'Just a Little *BIT* of Mixity? The EU's Role in the Field of International Investment Protection Law' (2011) 48 *CML Rev* 1534; A Dimopoulos, *EU Foreign Investment Law* (Oxford, Oxford University Press, 2011) 111. P Eeckhout, 'Exclusive External Competences: Constructing the EU as an International Actor' in *The Court of Justice and the Construction of Europe: Analyses and Perspective on Sixty Years of Case Law* (The Hague, Springer, 2013) 613.

[23] The Court has considered that development cooperation is a non-exclusive competence: Cases C-181/91 and C-248/91 *Parliament v Council* [1993] ECR I-3685.

[24] Opinion of AG Mengozzi in Case C-91/05 (n 25) and Opinion of AG Kokott in Case C-13/07 (n 13).

[25] Case C-268/94 *Portugal v Council* [1996] ECR I-6177; Case C-91/05 *Commission v Council* [2008] ECR I-3651.

objective giving rise to a specific competence. The pragmatic objective to create special relationships with third countries is to be pursued within the scope of other policies. In that sense there is no question of specific vertical allocation of competences, but rather of a global approach to specific competences, which however contributes to the ultimate external action objective of being a coherent international actor.

III. VERTICAL DIVISION OF EXTERNAL COMPETENCES PURSUING INTERNAL OBJECTIVES

The doctrine of implied external powers results from a constructive case law, developing the *ERTA* doctrine.[26] The Court of Justice established the existence of external Community competence in order to pursue internal objectives, despite the absence of express external competence.[27] In the *ERTA* judgment the Court linked the existence of external Community competence to its exclusive nature, establishing the doctrine of exclusivity according to the criterion of the effect on common rules.[28] According to this judgment, when common rules exist, the Community alone is capable of assuming and carrying out any contractual obligations arising out of international agreements with third countries and affecting the whole sphere of application of the Community legal system. Exclusivity results from Article 4(3) TEU (former Article 10 EC, former Article 5 EEC) reflecting the duty of loyalty or loyal cooperation to take all appropriate measures to ensure fulfillment of the obligations arising out of the treaties and to refrain from any measure which could jeopardise the attainment of the Union's objectives. As the internal competence has been exercised in enacting common rules, the duty of loyalty operates in the context of implementation of the common rules and the principle of effectiveness of EU law.

The objectives that are to be preserved or pursued through the duty of loyalty, leading to exclusivity, are, in the case of the *ERTA* doctrine, internal. The case law that followed the *ERTA* judgment completed the criterion of effect on common rules. In Opinion 2/91,[29] Opinion 1/94, the *Open Skies* cases[30] and Opinion 1/03,[31] the Court developed its reasoning on the ground that Member States may not enter into international obligations outside the framework of the Community

---

[26] Case 22/70 *Commission v Council* [1971] ECR 263.

[27] M Cremona, 'External Relations and External Competence of the European Union: The Emergence of an Integrated Policy' in P Craig and G de Búrca (eds), *The Evolution of EU Law* (Oxford, Oxford University Press, 2011) 217; P Eeckhout, *EU External Relations Law* (Oxford, Oxford University Press, 2011) 70.

[28] G De Baere, *Constitutional Principles of EU External Relations* (Oxford, Oxford University Press, 2008) 38; R Holdgaard, *External Relations Law of the European Community*, (The Netherlands, Kluwer Law International, 2007) 101.

[29] Opinion 2/91 *Convention no 170 of the International Labour Organization concerning safety in the use of chemicals at work* [1993] ECR I-1061.

[30] Cases C-467/98 [2002] ECR I-9519; C-468/98 [2002] ECR I-9575; C-469/98 [2002] ECR I-9627; C-471/98 [2002] ECR I-9681; C-472/98 [2002] ECR I-9741; C-475/98 [2002] ECR I-9797; C-476/98 [2002] ECR I-9855; C-523/04 [2007] ECR I- 3267.

[31] Opinion 1/03 *Competence of the Community to conclude the new Lugano Convention* [2006] ECR I-1145.

institutions if these obligations fall within the scope of the common rules, or within an area which is already largely covered by such rules, even if there is no contradiction between these commitments and the common rules.[32] The vertical allocation of competences and the establishment of exclusivity depend on whether international commitments are liable to affect common rules or alter their scope. In that sense, exclusive external competence of the Union results from the exercise of the internal competence, and exclusivity in the external field is liable to preserve and pursue internal objectives. The Treaty of Lisbon reflects this criterion in order to establish the exclusive external competence of the Union (Article 3(2) TFEU) and the possibility of the Union to conclude international agreements (Article 216(1) TFEU).

The interpretation of the *ERTA* effect relies on a case law that does not guarantee legal certainty and predictability. Consequently, the Court of Justice is still the final adjudicator. Indeed, in the *Open Skies* judgment the Court stated when it should be considered that international obligations fall within an area which is already largely covered by common rules,[33] but in Opinion 1/03 it pointed out that these instances were only examples, formulated in the light of the particular contexts with which the Court was concerned.[34] The Court considered that exclusivity according to the *ERTA* effect should be based not only on the scope of the common rules, but also on their nature and content. The Court added that it is also necessary to take into account not only the current state of Community law in the area in question but also its future development, insofar as that is foreseeable at the time of that analysis.[35] As a result the application of the criterion of effect on common rules is not easy and predictable, but depends on a circumspect approach. Nevertheless, the Court emphasised the importance of the principle of conferral and held that exclusive implied external competence must have its basis in conclusions drawn from a specific analysis of the relationship between the agreement envisaged and the Community law in force and from which it is clear that the conclusion of such an agreement is capable of affecting Community rules.[36]

---

[32] P Mengozzi, 'The EC External Competences: From the *ERTA* Case to the Opinion in the Lugano Convention' in M Poiares Maduro, L Azoulai (eds), *The Past and Future of EU Law* (Oxford, Hart Publishing, 2010) 213; B Van Vooren, 'The Principle of Pre-emption after Opinion 1/2003 and Coherence in the EU Readmission Policy' in M Cremona, J Monar, S Poli (eds), *The External Dimension of the European Union's Area of Freedom, Security and Justice* (Berlin, Peter Lang, 2011) 163.

[33] 'Whenever the Community has included in its internal legislative acts provisions relating to the treatment of nationals of non-member countries or expressly conferred on its institutions powers to negotiate with non-member countries, it acquires an exclusive external competence in the spheres covered by those acts. The same applies, even in the absence of any express provision authorising its institutions to negotiate with non-member countries, where the Community has achieved complete harmonisation in a given area, because the common rules thus adopted could be affected within the meaning of the *AETR* judgment if the Member States retained freedom to negotiate with non-member countries': Case C-467/98 *Commission v Denmark* [2002] ECR I-9519, paras 83, 84.

[34] Opinion 1/03 (n 31), para 121.

[35] ibid (n 31), para 126.

[36] ibid (n 31), para 124.

The same link between exclusive implied external competence and internal objectives results from another criterion of exclusivity, that of pragmatic necessity according to Opinion 1/76.[37] The Court held that the Community has exclusive competence to conclude an international agreement, even in the absence of Community provisions in the area concerned, where the conclusion of such an agreement is necessary in order to attain the objectives of the Treaty in that area, such objectives being incapable of being attained merely by introducing autonomous common rules. In that sense, internal and external aspects of the policy area can only be exercised effectively together. This criterion of pragmatic necessity leading to exclusivity has also been codified in the Lisbon Treaty.[38] Finally, the link between exclusive external competence and internal objectives is also obvious in the third case of exclusive implied external competence according to Article 3(2) TFEU, that of exclusivity arising out of internal legislative acts.

The fact that exclusive implied external competence of the Union derives from the consideration of its internal objectives shows that the general external action objective to promote international cooperation and to be a globally influential actor is not to be considered beyond the principle of conferral. This is also confirmed by the Court's interpretation of Article 352 TFEU. According to the case-law, this provision cannot in itself vest exclusive competence of the Union at international level in the name of a general external action objective, insofar as specific competence is conferred with a view to an internal objective.[39]

However, implied external competence of the Union exists beyond exclusivity. The Court removed all doubt in Opinion 1/03, making it clear that an implied competence may be either shared or exclusive, a question which is separate from its existence.[40] The mere existence of an external implied competence does not allow the Union to exercise this competence alone, insofar as exclusivity does not derive from internal objectives. Nevertheless, the implied external non-exclusive competence of the Union may be exercised jointly with Member States, by means of the conclusion of a mixed agreement. The Court of Justice, in the *Mox Plant–Sellafield* case,[41] distinguished between the scope of the Community competence and the scope of exclusivity and held that the Community had elected to

---

[37] Opinion 1/76 *Draft Agreement establishing a European laying-up fund for inland waterway vessels* [1977] ECR 741.

[38] According to Art 3(2) TFEU, the Union has exclusive competence to conclude an agreement when the conclusion of the agreement is necessary to enable the Union to exercise its internal competence.

[39] A Dashwood, 'Article 308 EC as the Outer Limit of Expressly Conferred Community Competence' in C Barnard and O Odudu (eds), *The Outer Limits of European Law* (Oxford, Hart Publishing, 2009) 35.

[40] Opinion 1/03 (n 31), paras 132–34.

[41] Case C-459/03 *Commission v Ireland* [2006] ECR I-4657. See E Neframi, 'La mixité éclairée dans l'arrêt *Commission contre Irlande* du 30 mai 2006 (affaire Mox): une double infraction, un triple apport' (2007) 3 *Revue du droit de l'Union européenne* 687; L S Rossi, 'De l'avis 1/03 à l'arrêt MOX: communautarisation des relations extérieures de la Communauté européenne en raison de la cohérence du système' in M Dony and L S Rossi, *Démocratie, cohérence et transparence: vers une constitutionnalisation de l'Union européenne* (Bruxelles, Editions de l'Université de Bruxelles, 2008), 155.

exercise its shared competence by becoming a party to a mixed agreement (UN Convention on the Law of the Sea (UNCLOS)).[42] In that way, the Community could be considered as having assumed international obligations beyond the field of its exclusive competence, and the mixed agreement could be considered in its entirety as a source of EU law.

The possibility of exercising implied external competence beyond exclusivity, jointly with the Member States, shows that the external aspect of an internal competence may also be linked to an external action objective. This external action objective would be the general one to act as an international actor, the specific objective corresponding to the competence exercised being internal. We could thus affirm that the external aspect of an internal competence exists even if the consideration of the internal objective does not lead to exclusivity. In this case, the external aspect of the internal competence may be considered as oriented to the ultimate external action objective.

The distinction between the existence and the exclusivity of the external competence of the EU and the possibility to exercise it beyond exclusivity but jointly with the Member States, concerns not only implied external competence, but also express external competence, when it is the external aspect of an internal one. In other words, express external competence is not necessarily linked to an external action policy. It may be conferred to the EU in order to attain an internal objective, as for instance in the case of readmission agreements. In such cases, the EU may exercise its external competence regardless of the question of exclusivity. According to Article 216(1) TFEU, the Union may conclude an international agreement where the Treaty so provides. However, whether the Union will act alone or jointly with its Member States depends on the conditions of exclusivity.[43]

The exercise of an express external competence, even where linked to an internal objective, is also to be considered in the light of the EU's ultimate external action objective to be an international actor. In the case of environmental policy, the objective is included in the list in Article 21 TEU.[44] However it is not dissociated from internal objectives as the conditions of exclusivity still depend on the exercise of the internal competence and environmental competence is not included in Part V of the TFEU together with the other external action policies.

---

[42] Advocate General Maduro held that the Community exercised both its exclusive and its non-exclusive external competence in the area of environmental protection when it acceded to UNCLOS (para 27 of the AG's Opinion) and that the conclusion of an international agreement can itself be a form of exercising a non-exclusive competence of the Community, independently of the previous adoption of Community internal legislation (para 33 of the AG's Opinion).

[43] As far as readmission agreements are concerned, it is considered that the EU can act alone according to the necessity criterion of Opinion 1/76. See Van Vooren, 'The Principle of Pre-emption after Opinion 1/2003' (n 32); S Peers, *EU Justice and Home Affairs Law* (Oxford, Oxford University Press, 2011) 586.

[44] According to Art 21(2)(f) TEU, the EU will help develop international measures to preserve and improve the quality of the environment and the sustainable management of global resources, in order to ensure sustainable development.

From the perspective of a specific competence, express external environmental competence seems to be the external aspect of the internal competence. In relation to external action objectives, the external aspect of the environmental competence seems to be sufficiently important to be explicitly codified. Furthermore, as the environmental objective is of a transversal nature, it is part of the ultimate external action objective to contribute to good global governance and it is to be taken into account in a global approach to objectives and competences.[45]

The distinction between the existence of an external competence of the Union, implied or express, linked to an internal objective, and exclusivity, may explain why the case law is codified in two different provisions in the Lisbon Treaty: Article 3 TFEU deals with exclusivity, while Article 216 TFEU deals with existence, which may authorise the exercise of the Union competence beyond exclusivity, jointly with the Member States. Where not exclusive, the exercise of the external competence of the Union is indeed independent on the internal objectives. While Article 3 TFEU provides that exclusive external competence is established in order to attain an internal objective, Article 216 TFEU provides that the Union may exercise its competence in order to achieve one of the objectives referred to in the treaties. Such an objective may be the ultimate external action objective, which may be pursued through the exercise of a non exclusive external competence of the Union.

The result is that in allocating external competences, the Court of Justice, attached to the principle of conferral, does not link external aspects of internal competences to specific external action objectives. However, the general external action objective seems to be subsidiary where the Union exercises an exclusive specific competence, and autonomous where the Union exercises an external non-exclusive competence. Besides, the distinction between exercise and exclusivity of an external competence may contribute to a coherent external dimension of both external and internal policies, which is also the basis of the search for unity in the regulation of the exercise of external competences.

IV. VERTICAL DIVISION OF EXTERNAL COMPETENCES AND THE QUESTION OF A GLOBAL APPROACH OF THE UNION'S OBJECTIVES AND COMPETENCES

Vertical allocation of external competences may stem from a context where the parallelism between competence and objective is not clear. In such a case, the Court of Justice appreciates the different specific objectives in question through a global approach and establishes the parallelism through the choice of the appropriate legal basis, which may determine at the same time the vertical allocation of external competences (A). Besides, the Court adopts a global approach to the

---

[45] See below, section IV.

Union's objectives when regulating the exercise of external competences already allocated. This approach may lead to the prevalence of the general external action objective and the global approach to competences (B).

A. External Competences and Specific Objectives

Case law on the appropriate legal basis is mainly linked to the horizontal division of competences. However, the constitutional significance of the choice of the legal basis which corresponds to the main objective pursued by the action in question is not limited to the question of institutional balance.[46] The choice of the appropriate legal basis determines the exclusivity of the competence of the Union and the possibility for the Union to conclude an international agreement alone or jointly with the Member States. At the same time, the choice of the appropriate legal basis is imposed by the principle of conferral. In other words, the principle of conferral has the significance, not only that the Union has the competence to conclude an international agreement, but also that the Union exercises the competence which corresponds to the main objective pursued by the agreement to be concluded.

The choice of the appropriate legal basis thus preserves both the vertical and the horizontal constitutional balance sought by the authors of the treaties.[47] With regard to the vertical division of competences, it is to be noticed that the Court of Justice is still guided by the strict implementation of the principle of conferral. The European judge is invited to consider the aim and the content of the measure envisaged in order to determine its objective in relation to other objectives assigned to the Union. For this purpose, a global approach to the Union's objectives is necessary, in order to define the main objective. However, overlapping objectives do not lead to overlapping competences. The Court of Justice considers the specific objectives, corresponding to specific competences, in order to choose the appropriate legal basis in accordance with the predominant objective.[48] Transversal objectives, such as the preservation of the environment, development cooperation policy, the consolidation of the rule of law and the protection of human rights, as well as the global objectives and the requirement of coherence, allow the Court to favour an instrumental approach.[49] Such an approach is based on the characteristics of the measure envisaged; it is a fragmented approach to the specific competences regardless of the overall objective of strengthening the Union's international action.

---

[46] P Koutrakos, 'Legal Basis and Delimitation of Competence in EU External Relations' in M Cremona and B de Witte (eds), *EU Foreign Relations Law—Constitutional Fundamentals* (Oxford, Hart Publishing, 2008) 177. See further PJ Kuijper in this volume.

[47] K Lenaerts, 'EU Federalism in 3-D' in E Cloots, G De Baere and S Sottiaux (eds), *Federalism in the European Union* (Oxford, Hart Publishing, 2012) 25.

[48] Holdgaard, *External Relations Law of the European Community* (n 28) 41.

[49] V Michel, 'Les objectifs à caractère transversal' in E Neframi (ed), *Objectifs et compétences dans l'Union européenne* (Brussels, Bruylant, 2012) 177.

For example, in Opinion 2/00,[50] the Court established that the main purpose of the Cartagena Protocol on Biosafety is environmental protection. While the Protocol aims to ensure the safe handling, transport and use of living modified organisms, and could thus be considered in relation to an international trade objective, the Court of Justice did not link this to the exercise of exclusive competence in the field of CCP. Elaborated in the framework of the Convention on Biological Diversity, the Cartagena Protocol was considered to be an instrument of environmental policy. Even though commercial measures may integrate non-commercial considerations, the Court insisted on an instrumental approach in order to determine the predominant objective and thus the appropriate legal basis for the Community's competence. Its consideration of the specific objectives, environmental or international trade objectives, led the Court to assert the exercise of a shared external competence through the conclusion of a mixed agreement, without taking into consideration the overall objective of strengthening the international role of the Community, which could have led the Court to advantage the commercial objective. The Court recalled that practical difficulties associated with the exercise of a shared external competence and the implementation of mixed agreements cannot be accepted as relevant when selecting the legal basis for a Community measure and cannot justify recourse to the CCP competence.[51]

Another example of the instrumental approach of the Court derives from the judgment on the legal basis of the *Energy Star agreement* case.[52] Pursuing simultaneously a commercial-policy objective and an environmental-protection objective, the agreement is considered as an instrument of CCP. The Court came to this conclusion regardless of the vertical division of competences and the strengthening of the international position of the Community through the exercise of the exclusive competence in the field of CCP.[53]

Moreover, in the *Rotterdam Convention* case on the prior informed consent procedure for certain hazardous chemicals and pesticides in international trade,[54] the Court of Justice established that the trade and environmental objectives of this Convention are indissociably linked and thus the Convention should be concluded on a dual legal basis. The Court emphasised the explicit link established by the Convention between trade and environment: although the main objec-

---

[50] Opinion 2/00 *on the legal basis of the proposal for a regulation of the European Parliament and of the Council amending Regulation (EC) No 562/2006 of the European Parliament and of the Council establishing a Community Code on the rules governing the movement of persons across borders (Schengen Borders Code) and the Convention implementing the Schengen Agreement* [2001] ECR I-9713.

[51] ibid, para 41.

[52] Case C-281/01 *Commission v Council* [2002] ECR I-12049.

[53] The Court considered the specific objectives and pointed out that the 'Energy Star labeling program is essentially intended to enable manufacturers to use, in accordance with a procedure for the mutual recognition of registrations, a common logo to identify for consumers certain products complying with a common set of energy-efficiency specifications which they intend to sell on the American and Community markets. An instrument having a direct impact on trade in office equipment is therefore involved' (para 40).

[54] Case C-94/03 *Commission v Council* [2006] ECR I-1.

tive is the protection of the environment, the control procedure applies only to certain hazardous chemicals and pesticides which are traded internationally and the implementation is governed by provisions which directly regulate trade in goods. The instrumental approach behind the recourse to the commercial policy legal basis does not prevail over the consideration of the specific environmental objective. Regardless of the effectiveness of the establishment of an exclusive external competence, the recourse to a dual legal basis leads to the conclusion of the Convention jointly by the Community and the Member States, as a mixed agreement. The Court pointed out that by basing the decision approving the Convention on a dual legal basis, 'the Community is also giving indications to the other parties to the Convention (...) with regard to the division of competences between the Community and its Member States'.[55]

The choice of the appropriate legal basis is not necessarily linked to the vertical division of external competences.[56] However, it follows from the foregoing that even where the vertical division of external competences is concerned, the choice is based on a consideration of the specific objectives of the instrument and not on the consideration of the global, ultimate objective of favouring the international action of the Union. Article 40 TEU also confirms the fragmented approach to competences through the consideration of specific objectives, excluding the inter-action of common foreign and security policy objectives with objectives linked to other policies.[57] Nevertheless, it could be argued that the objective-oriented approach in the case concerning the conclusion of the European Convention on the legal protection of services based on, or consisting of, conditional access[58] derives from a consideration of the ultimate external objective of efficient international action. The specific connection between the Convention's provisions and international trade in services prevailed over the internal market link deriving from the parallelism with the provisions of the harmonisation Directive. As a consequence, the Court decided that the appropriate legal basis for the conclusion of the Convention was Article 207 TFEU and not Article 114 TFEU.

The external objective oriented approach in Case C-137/12 *Commission v Council* can be explained by the need to clarify the scope of the reformed CCP through the emphasis on international trade-related matters. However, in *Portugal v Council*[59] the Court pointed out that the Cooperation Agreement

---

[55] ibid, para 55.

[56] For example, in Case C-155/07 *Parliament v Council* [2008] ECR I-8103, the Court admitted the dual legal basis of a measure pursuing objectives of both development cooperation and economic, financial and technical cooperation with third countries. In this case, only the horizontal constitutional balance was at stake.

[57] The reasoning of the Court in Case C-130/10 *Parliament v Council*, judgment of 19 July 2012, concerning the horizontal constitutional balance through the consideration of internal and international security objectives, confirms the fragmented approach of the competences regardless of the interest of the Union to be strengthened as an international actor through the exercise of its competence in the field of the common foreign and security policy.

[58] Case C-137/12 *Commission v Council* (n 20).

[59] Case C-268/94 *Portugal v Council* [1996] ECR I-6177.

between the European Community and India could be concluded by the Community on the basis of its competence in the field of the development cooperation policy, although the agreement contained conditionality clauses on respect for human rights and democratic principles. The Court interpreted broadly the development policy objective, in the sense of taking account of the objective of respect for human rights. Consequently, human rights clauses do not give rise to another field of competence requiring the participation of the Member States in the agreement (nor the need to use the flexibility clause). The question of respect for human rights and democratic principles is not a specific field of cooperation provided for in the agreement, but is covered by the development cooperation objective, allowing thus the Community to exercise a political and normative influence through the exercise of the development cooperation competence. Hence, such influence contributes to the attainment of the ultimate external action objective to be an influential and global international actor.

The global approach to external action objectives in Article 21 TEU and Article 205 TFEU, stemming from the Lisbon Treaty, implies that specific objectives can also be pursued incidentally through the exercise of an external competence corresponding to another main specific objective, external or internal.[60] Each specific external action objective can therefore be considered as transversal, the inclusion of which in the context of another objective/competence parallelism does not change the vertical allocation of powers. Thus, the inclusion of environmental or human rights clauses in trade agreements concluded by the Union does not affect the exclusive nature of the Union's competence. If not a normative actor in environmental or human rights policy, the Union can therefore be considered as a normative power when exercising its commercial policy competence. In that way, the Union's action pursues the general objective of promoting an international system based on stronger multilateral cooperation and good global governance.

B. Regulation of the Exercise of External Competences and the Ultimate External Action Objective

The attainment of external action objectives depends not only on the allocation of competences, but also on the regulation of the exercise of the external competences of the Union and the Member States, once the division of external competences is established. While allocation of external competence is modeled according to the principle of conferral, the Court of Justice plays the game of activism by regulating the exercise of the Union and Member States' external competences through

---

[60] See E Neframi, 'Le rapport entre objectifs et compétences: de la structuration et de l'identité de l'Union européenne' in E Neframi (ed), *Objectifs et compétences dans l'Union européenne* (Brussels, Bruylant, 2012) 5.

the principle of loyalty (Article 4(3) TEU). The constitutional function of the Court of Justice is thus reinforced.[61]

The scope of the duty of loyalty is extended through a constantly developing case law which constrains the Member States' external action.[62] The scope of EU law is understood beyond exclusivity, the Member States having the obligation, going from a best efforts obligation to an obligation of result, to facilitate the exercise of the Union competence and to ensure unity of external representation in case of mixity.

The duty to facilitate the exercise of the Union competence applies in the case of exclusive as well as in the case of shared competence.

When the Union has exclusive external competence which cannot be exercised, because of international law or political reasons, Member States have the obligation to act on behalf of the Union.[63] Such an obligation derives from the same aspect of the duty of loyalty that leads to exclusivity, to fulfil Treaty obligations and abstain from jeopardising the attainment of the Union objectives. In the *IMO* judgment the Court recalled that the fact that the Community is not a member of an international organisation does not prevent its external competence from being exercised, in particular through the Member States acting jointly in the Community interest.[64] In this case, the Commission brought an infringement procedure against Greece for having submitted a non-binding proposal for consideration to a committee of the International Maritime Organisation (IMO) regarding maritime safety, an issue falling within the Union's exclusive competence.[65] The Court found that Greece violated its duty to abstain from any individual action likely to affect the common rules. The EU's lack of membership of the IMO creates a situation where Member States may act in the international scene, but only as trustees of the Union's interest. In other words, the duty of loyalty requires that Member States' external action is oriented towards the attainment of the EU's objectives, both the specific objective pursued by the competence conferred in the field of action and the ultimate objective of an effective international action in the interest of the Union.

When the Union has shared competence, the duty to facilitate the exercise of this competence is linked to the aspect of the duty of loyalty to facilitate the

---

[61] L Azoulai, 'Le rôle constitutionnel de la Cour de justice des Communautés européennes tel qu'il se dégage de sa jurisprudence' (2008) 1 *RTDE* 39.

[62] M Cremona, 'Defending the Community Interest: the Duties of Cooperation and Compliance' in M Cremona and B de Witte (eds), *EU Foreign Relations Law—Constitutional Fundamentals* (Oxford, Hart Publishing, 2008) 125; E Neframi, 'The Duty of Loyalty: Rethinking its Scope through its Application in the Field of EU External Relations' (2010) 47 *CML Rev* 323.

[63] M Cremona, 'Member States Agreements as Union Law' in E Cannizzaro, P Palchetti and R Wessel (eds), *International Law as Law of the European Union* (Boston/Leiden, Martinus Nijhoff Publishers, 2011) 291.

[64] Case C-45/07 *Commission v Greece* [2009] ECR I-701, para 31.

[65] M Cremona, 'Extending the Reach of the *AETR* Principle: Comment on *Commission v Greece*' (2009) 34 *EL Rev* 754; E Neframi 'Renforcement des obligations des Etats membres dans le domaine des relations extérieures' (2009) 3 *Revue trimestrielle de droit européen* 601.

achievement of the Union's tasks and to abstain from jeopardising the attainment of its objectives. In the *Inland Waterways* judgments[66] the Court found that the exercise by the Member States of a retained external competence, without cooperating or consulting with the Commission, although negotiations at Community level had been initiated, constituted a failure to comply with the duty of cooperation. The Court recalled that this duty is of general application and does not depend either on whether the Community competence is exclusive or on any right of the Member States to enter into obligations towards non-member countries. Consequently, according to the Court, the adoption of a decision authorising the Commission to negotiate an agreement marks the start of a concerted Community action at international level and requires, if not a duty of abstention on the part of the Member States, at the very least a duty of close cooperation between the latter and the Community institutions in order to facilitate the achievement of the Community tasks and to ensure the coherence and consistency of the action and its international representation.[67]

If the Court established in the *Inland Waterways* cases a best endeavours obligation, Advocate General Maduro in the *PFOS* case[68] sees an obligation of result to refrain from action in the case of a concerted common strategy within the Council in a field of shared competence. *PFOS* concerned the making of a proposal for the nomination of the inclusion of a new substance within the structures of a mixed agreement, the Stockholm Convention on Persistent Organic Pollutants. The Advocate General took the view that Sweden's proposal risked undermining the Community decision-making process which had already been triggered.

In both cases, the duty of loyalty regulates the exercise of the Member States competence with a view to facilitate the exercise of Union competence, and the constraints on the Member States' action are related not only to the specific objective in the area concerned, but also to the ultimate external action objective. Indeed, by limiting the Member States' external action (whether they exercise the Union's or their own competence), the Court adopts a global approach to the external action of the Union and the Member States, which favours the conception of the Union as a global and credible external actor.

In the *PFOS* judgment, the Court of Justice clarified further the scope and the effects of the duty of loyalty. The Court did not simply consider that Sweden dissociated itself from a concerted common strategy within the Council and thus failed to facilitate the exercise of the Union's competence. It went further in

---

[66] Case C-266/03 *Commission v Luxembourg* [2005] ECR I-4805; Case C-433/03 *Commission v Germany* [2005] ECR I-6985. See Eeckhout, *EU External Relations Law* (n 27) 246.

[67] Case C-266/03 *Commission v Luxembourg* (ibid), paras 57–60; Case C-433/03 *Commission v Germany* (ibid), paras 63–66.

[68] Case C-246/07 *Commission v Sweden* [2010] ECR I-3317. See M Cremona (2011) 48 *CML Rev* 1639; G De Baere, 'O, Where is Faith? O, Where is Loyalty? Some Thoughts on the Duty of Loyal Co-operation and the Union's External Environmental Competence in the Light of the *PFOS* case' (2011) 36 *EL Rev*. 405; A Delgado Casteleiro, J Larik, 'The Duty to Remain Silent: Limitless Loyalty in EU External Relations?' (2011) 36 *EL Rev* 524.

finding that such a situation was likely to compromise the principle of unity in the international representation of the Union and its Member States and weaken their negotiating power with regard to other parties to the Convention.[69]

The unity of international representation in the case of mixity[70] is a requirement, qualified as a principle in the *PFOS* case, linked to the ultimate external action objective to be an influential international actor. In fact, credibility relies on unity, and based on the duty of loyalty, it implies the obligation of the Member States to refrain from individual action (or to cooperate with the institutions before individual action, as in the *Sellafield* case), beyond exclusivity and regardless of the area where the action is situated (external policy or an external aspect of internal policy). In the *PFOS* case, one could raise the question of whether the unilateral proposal of Sweden could affect the Community regulation in the field concerned.[71] In such a case, the duty to refrain from unilateral action would be linked to the internal policy objective and the *ERTA* effect. However, the Court insisted on the fact that once a mixed agreement has been concluded under shared competence, it is difficult to tolerate unilateral action by a Member State. Unilateral action constitutes a breach of the duty of cooperation, stemming from the duty of loyalty, not in the sense that unilateral action affects common rules and thus breaches the obligation to implement EU law, but in the sense that unilateral action jeopardises the attainment of the objectives of the Union, unity in the international scene being linked to the ultimate objective to be a credible and influential international actor through a strong negotiating position. Therefore, the duty of loyalty underscores the distinction between the scope of EU law and the scope of EU competences.[72] Member States have to refrain from unilateral action in order to preserve the attainment of a specific objective, pursued by the exercise of a specific competence, but also in order to preserve the ultimate external action objective, regardless of the exercise of a Union competence.

Furthermore, the ultimate external action objective may also explain the jurisprudence on the status and implementation of mixed agreements.[73] The vertical division of competences does not affect the interpretative jurisdiction of the Court with regard to a mixed agreement in its entirety. As the Court of Justice

---

[69] Case C-246/07 *Commission v Sweden* (ibid), para 102.

[70] C Hillion, 'Mixity and Coherence in EU External Relations: The Significance of the Duty of Cooperation' in C Hillion and P Koutrakos (eds), *Mixed Agreements Revisited—The EU and its Member States in the World* (Oxford, Hart Publishing, 2010), 87.

[71] Eeckhout, *EU External Relations Law* (n 27) 254.

[72] M Cremona, 'Defending the Community Interest: the Duties of Cooperation and Compliance' (n 62) 168.

[73] P Koutrakos, 'Interpretation of Mixed Agreements' in C Hillion and P Koutrakos (eds), *Mixed Agreements Revisited* (Oxford, Hart Publishing, 2010) 116; E Neframi, 'Mixed Agreements as a Source of EU Law' in E Cannizzaro, P Palchetti and R Wessel (eds), *International Law as Law of the European Union* (Boston/Leiden, Martinus Nijhoff Publishers, 2011) 325.

held in the *Dior*,[74] *Merck*[75] and *Lesooschranarske*[76] cases, mixed agreements are indeed considered as a source of EU law subject to a uniform application which contributes to the efficiency of its implementation and that of the external action of the Union.[77] Besides, the Court of Justice contributes to the unity of external representation by considering that the allocation of international responsibility in the context of mixed agreements is not tied to the vertical division of competences.[78] Finally, the Court remains exclusively competent to define the allocation of powers in the implementation of mixed agreements.[79]

Such a global approach to the Union and Member States' external competences and the regulation of their exercise through the duty of loyalty goes further than the specific allocation of competences through the principle of conferral. Judicial activism through Article 4(3) TEU may lead to a broader conception of external competences. External action competences and the external aspects of internal competences can be considered beyond specific policy objectives. We may consider the external competence of the Union and the Member States as a whole, linked to the ultimate external action objective. Such a competence is not to be exercised solely by the Union, the exercise of the Union's competence being dependent on the principle of conferral, but could be conceived as a collective exercise of external competences through cooperation under the auspices of the Court of Justice. In that sense, the Court can be considered as a constitutional adjudicator of competences[80] in the constitutionalisation process.

---

[74] Cases C-300 and 392/98 *Dior* [2000] ECR I-11307.

[75] Case C-431/05 *Merck* [2007] ECR I-7001.

[76] Case C-240/09 *Lesooschranarske Zoskupenie VLK* [2011] ECR I-1255.

[77] In the *Lesooschranarske* (The Slovak Brown Bear) (ibid) case, the Court of Justice considered that Art 9(3) of the Aarhus Convention on Access to Information, Public Participation in Decision Making and Access to Justice in Environmental Matters, fell under its interpretative jurisdiction, despite the fact that this provision had not been implemented by the EU as far as access to national judge is concerned, and fell, therefore, under the Member States' competence. The Court held that the dispute before the national courts fell within the scope of EU Law, following a reasoning based on the need to ensure effective implementation of the EU environmental law and the Aarhus Convention, being a mixed agreement. See M Klamert, 'Dark Matter: Competence, Jurisdiction and the area largely covered by EU Law—Comment on *Lesooschranarske*' (2012) 37 EL Rev 340.

[78] In the *Hermès* case (Case C-53/96 [1998] ECR I-3603) the Court pointed out that the WTO Agreement was concluded by the Community and ratified by its Member States without any allocation between them of their respective obligations towards the other contracting parties (para 24).

[79] In the *Merck* case (n 75) the Court established that the TRIPs Agreement having been concluded by the Community and its Member States by virtue of joint competence, the Court, hearing a case brought before it in accordance with the provisions of the EC Treaty has jurisdiction to define the obligations which the Community has thereby assumed and, for that purpose, to interpret the provisions of the TRIPs Agreement (para 33).

[80] Sharpston, De Baere, 'The Court of Justice as a Constitutional Adjudicator' (n 4).

6

The Case Law of the Court of Justice of the EU and the Allocation of External Relations Powers

Whither the Traditional Role of the Executive in EU Foreign Relations?

PIETER JAN KUIJPER[1]

I. INTRODUCTION

TRADITIONALLY THE GOVERNMENT has had a special role in the foreign relations of States. It was generally believed that the executive power and especially its Ministry of Foreign Affairs, disposed of an expertise that was not to be found in the other branches of government. Moreover, the general sentiment was that foreign policy required quick reactions, adaptability and fast mobilisation of many different resources of the State, including if necessary, the armed forces, in order to confront challenges from outside, which could arise almost instantaneously and might in some instances directly affect the economic or physical survival of the State. The executive power was believed to be uniquely suited to take on such challenges and should not be 'hindered' unduly in doing so. Moreover, ideally the State should act externally as a unitary actor without even the slightest hint of internal division. Hence: hands-off for the legislative power and the judiciary.[2]

This attitude found its expression in the relations between the legislative and the executive power of most States in that considerable restraint on foreign policy[3]

---

[1] Thanks are due to Marieke Vreeken and Emma Bree for research assistance.

[2] This attitude—which is prevalent, in varying intensity, in many democratic states that uphold the rule of law—is directly linked to the Westphalian State system and its governing rule of sovereign equality between States, where the foreign policy of States was originally the task of the sovereign King and nowadays of the government, ie primarily the executive.

[3] In this chapter terms such as 'foreign policy', 'foreign relations' and 'external relations' will be used interchangeably in a non-technical sense. In order to make distinctions in a non-technical manner we will use the well-used and well-understood terms of 'high politics' and 'low politics' in order to distinguish between purely political foreign policy and the more mercantile and soft power aspects

was considered necessary on the part of the legislature. Parliament should restrict itself to broad policy debates on foreign affairs; it should not use the budgetary power to interfere with the details of foreign affairs. Acts of Parliament on foreign affairs are few and far between. At best, parliamentary questions, both written and oral, could be resorted to in order to obtain clarification of details of foreign policy.[4] In respect of the approval of treaties, this restraint shows up in various ways in different constitutional systems. Sometimes a distinction is created between treaties that need the approval of Parliament and others that do not, such as the distinction between 'treaties' and 'executive agreements' in the US.[5] Or the distinction between treaties that need to be transformed into national law and international agreements that are not in need of such transformation and thus do not need to be submitted to Parliament, as in the different 'dualist' systems of Italy and Germany and formerly the UK.[6] In other constitutional systems, mechanisms have been introduced that avoid explicit prior approval by Parliament of *all* international agreements (Netherlands).[7] In nearly all States different parts of the executive power, such as ministries and quasi-independent administrations, regularly conclude international arrangements that are supposed to be non-binding (although in reality they may sometimes create legally binding obligations) and hence considered outside the remit of the legislative power.[8] In reaction to that, legislatures in some countries have established special notification procedures of

of foreign relations. If it is considered necessary, for legal reasons, terms such as 'external action' and Common Foreign and Security Policy (CFSP) will be used.

[4] Just to give a nationally inspired historical example: one of the greatest parliamentary scandals in the Netherlands occurred when protestant representatives managed in a late night session in 1925 to have the budget item for the delegation to the Holy See eliminated. This so-called 'Night of Kersten' is still cited as a negative example in present day texts on constitutional law. The number of Acts of Parliament that directly relate to foreign affairs in the Netherlands is presently five, of which three are largely used to implement UN and EU sanctions and EU rules on admission of aliens and asylum seekers.

[5] For a brief sketch of the development of so-called congressional executive agreements and sole executive agreements next to the constitutional category of treaties, see EA Purcell jr, 'Varieties and Complexities of Doctrinal Change' in DL Sloss et al (eds), *International Law in the US Supreme Court. Continuity and Change* (Cambridge, Cambridge University Press, 2011) 285–313, at 288.

[6] See P Kiiver and N Kornet, *Selected National, European and International Provisions from Public and Private law: The Maastricht Collection* 3rd edn (Groningen, Europa Law Publishing, 2013) Part I Constitutional law 1–90, at 31 (Germany) and 10 (France); LFM Besselink, 'Italiaanse Republiek' in LFM Besselink et al (eds), *Staatsrecht van landen van de Europese Unie* 8th edn (Deventer, Kluwer, 2012) 191–255 at 204 (Italy). In the UK the Constitutional Reform and Governance Act 2010 in section 20 introduced a system that closely resembles the Dutch system described in n 7 below.

[7] See Rijkswet goedkeuring en bekendmaking van verdragen (Act on the approval and proclamation of Treaties) of 1994, arts 2, 3 and 5, which introduced a system that provides for the laying before Parliament of all international agreements, which will be deemed to have been tacitly approved, if no action is taken by Parliament. If the government or one-fifth of Parliament so desire, there will be explicit approval before ratification, see http://wetten.overheid.nl/BWBR0006799/geldigheidsdatum_19-12-2013.

[8] On this practice, see A Aust, *Modern Treaty Law and Practice* 2nd edn (Cambridge, Cambridge University Press, 2011) ch 3.

all agreements 'concluded' by ministries and administrations or at least of those agreements that are supposed to have binding force.[9]

Where the relations between the judiciary and the executive in the field of foreign policy and international agreements are concerned, these are characterised by a great measure of caution on the part of the judiciary in most constitutional systems. Usually there is no formal exclusion of the courts from this terrain, as is presently the case for the 'high politics' area of the Common Foreign and Security Policy (CFSP) in the European Union (hereafter referred to as 'the EU' or 'the Union'),[10] but there is undeniably a strong voluntary restraint on the part of the judiciary. In some cases this goes as far as a self-imposed 'political question doctrine', as the judges feel that in the field of foreign policy choices 'judicially discoverable and manageable criteria' may be lacking.[11] These words were, of course, first used by the US Supreme Court in the famous case of *Baker v Carr*.[12] As has been pointed out in the literature, the political question doctrine as practiced by courts in the US, and possibly also elsewhere, is in most cases an extreme form of judicial deference to the executive based on the separation of powers.[13]

The first aim of this chapter is to find out to what extent a similar approach to foreign policy as an area from which the legislature and the judiciary should keep a respectful distance has existed and perhaps still exists in the EU. To this end it is important to give a brief sketch of the provisions of primary law that seem to confirm this tendency and of the evolution that primary law has gone through as a consequence of the major Treaty modifications.

The second objective is to fix the attention on the case law of the Court of Justice (hereafter referred to as 'the Court' or 'CJEU') in the domain of external relations and to analyse it in some depth with a view to coming to an assessment of the contribution of the Court's case law to the allocation of foreign relations powers between the major institutions, that is to say the Council of Ministers, the European Parliament and the Commission.[14] This will require a brief analysis

---

[9] In the US, for example, the Case Act, see Aust, *Modern Treaty Law and Practice* (ibid) 39–42.

[10] Art 275 TFEU.

[11] In reality courts from European countries have shied away from going so far, even in the highly politicised cruise missile debate of the late 1980s, see PJ Kuyper and KC Wellens, 'Deployment of Cruise Missiles in Europe: The Legal Battles in the Netherlands, the Federal Republic of Germany and Belgium' (1987) XVIII *Netherlands Yearbook of International Law* 145–228; LFM Besselink, 'Entrapped by the Maximum Standard: On Fundamental Rights, Pluralism and Subsidiarity in the European Union' (1998) 35 (3) *CML Rev* 629–680.

[12] *Baker v Carr* 369 US 186 (1962). This was not a foreign affairs case; it concerned an equal protection complaint on state redistricting of electoral districts, but was to have considerable influence in the foreign affairs domain. Nonetheless, the US Supreme Court in an earlier case concerning the Presidential requisitioning of the steel industry during the Korean war did not have recourse to the doctrine, *Youngstown Sheet & Tube Co v Sawyer* 343 US 579 (1952). See PB Stephan, 'Treaties in the Supreme Court 1946–2000' in Sloss et al (eds), *International Law in the US Supreme Court* (n 5) 317–352, at 331–335.

[13] CM Vazquez, '*Breard* and the Federal Power to Require Compliance with ICJ Orders of Provisional Measures' (1998) *American Journal of International Law* 92, 683.

[14] The position of the EU agencies and the extent to which they have foreign policy powers, especially with respect to the negotiation and conclusion of international agreements without supervision

of the separation of powers doctrine, or what the Court has called 'the balance between the institutions'.

II. SUMMARY OF THE DEVELOPMENT OF THE ALLOCATION OF POWERS IN THE CONSTITUTIONAL LAW OF FOREIGN RELATIONS

It is important to recall, even before beginning our summary, that there have been two lines of development that have influenced the place that foreign policy holds in the government of modern democracies since the Second World War. First, foreign policy has become so much more technical in many of its aspects and demands nowadays that it can be conducted only with the help of experts in economics, trade, finance, development, agriculture, science, culture etc.[15] At the same time there has been a process of democratisation of foreign policy. This implies that foreign policy in a broad sense has turned from the *chasse gardée* of a small number of civil servants and diplomats from the Ministry of Foreign Affairs into a much broader operation in which the Ministry of Foreign Affairs can only aspire to be the coordinator of a large operation in which many ministries of the government cooperate.[16] This also implies that a larger circle of people from industry, the banking sector, agriculture etc are directly affected by foreign policy, in short that the public at large shows a greater interest in the substance of foreign policy.[17] This in turn has led to a greater interest from national parliaments in foreign policy. It is safe to say that in all the countries of the EU, national parliaments are much more active and inquisitive about the conduct of foreign policy now than they were at the time of the beginning of the European Communities, which spells a certain tension with the 'classical' hands-off position of parliaments. It is only logical that this should have had an influence on the Member States' position in the constant succession of inter-governmental conferences amending the EC Treaties since the Single Act of 1986.

The Treaty of Rome of 1958 contained only a minimal external relations power that was restricted to the competence to conclude trade and association agreements and the capacity to maintain relations (of a technical nature) with other international organisations at Secretariat/Commission level.[18] The Court in principle had jurisdiction over the whole EEC Treaty and hence there was no constitutional restriction to its power in this field and it is general knowledge

by the major institutions will be left out of consideration. See for this problem: A Ott, 'EU Regulatory Agencies in EU External Relations: Trapped in a Legal Minefield between European and International Law' (2008) *European Foreign Affairs Review* 515–540.

[15] See JP Pancracio, *Droit et institutions diplomatiques* (Paris, Pedone, 2007) 157ff.

[16] *Cf* the coordinating role of the EU High Representative, Art 18(4) TEU.

[17] This is certainly also linked to the phenomenon of the increased technocratic character of foreign policy mentioned above.

[18] See Arts 113 (trade), 238 (Association agreements), 229–231 (relations with different international organisations) of the Treaty of Rome 1958.

that the Court has used this power to a very large extent from the moment of its *ERTA* judgment in 1970.[19] The European Parliament was handicapped by the fact that initially it had only an advisory power on all legislation and that insofar as it gained power (primarily in the budgetary field alone), this had very little influence on external relations, since the budget was a blunt instrument in this respect. In the field of commercial policy, the core business of EU foreign policy during the first 40 years of its existence, the treaties formally excluded any parliamentary power until the entry into force of the Lisbon Treaty.

It was only the combination of the development of the implied powers doctrine by the Court of Justice, which led to internal legal bases being used for the conclusion of many EU and mixed agreements,[20] and the co-legislative powers for the European Parliament, which increased step by step after the Maastricht Treaty, that permitted the EU to follow the trend of democratisation of foreign policy that took place in the Member States at the same time. The constitutional aspect of this democratisation of foreign policy was, for the moment, completed, but at the same time severely circumscribed, by the Treaty of Lisbon. It was completed by giving the European Parliament full co-legislative powers in the field of trade policy (which was, moreover, expanded to include direct foreign investment) and in basically all internal policy areas that matter to external relations under the TFEU. It was, however, strictly limited in the domain of the CFSP, where the European Parliament can rely only on its budgetary powers,[21] its powers of general political oversight and on parliamentary questions. At the same time the Court, too, was being excluded from the CFSP and Common Security and Defence Policy (CSDP) domains, except insofar as it remained in charge of patrolling the boundaries between the Union competences laid down in the TFEU and the competences inherent in CFSP and CSDP: a political question doctrine imposed by Treaty.[22]

The picture under the Lisbon Treaty is complicated by the new rules laid down for the configuration of the executive power in the field of foreign affairs. The new post of the High Representative (HR) of the Union for Foreign Affairs and Security Policy—assisted by a diplomatic service, the European External Action

---

[19] Case 22/70 *Commission* v *Council* (*ERTA*) [1970] ECR 263.

[20] This recourse to internal legal bases was also stimulated by the narrow interpretation that the Court gave in its Opinion 1/94 WTO Agreements [1994] ECR I-5267, to the notion of the common commercial policy. See PJ Kuijper, 'Fifty Years of EC/EU External Relations: Continuity and the Dialogue Between Judges and Member States as Constitutional Legislators' (2007–2008) 31 *Fordham International Law Journal* 1571.

[21] This follows by implication from Art 41 TEU, insofar as operational expenditure is not allocated to the Member States. The European Parliament actually used budgetary threats in the discussions with the Council and the Commission on the creation of the EEAS. See European Parliament, document reference 2009/2133(INI), para N, at http://www.europarl.europa.eu/sides/getDoc.do?pubRef=-//EP// NONSGML+REPORT+A7-2009-0041+0+DOC+PDF+V0//EN.

[22] See Art 40 TEU and Art 275 TFEU. On the possibilities that the Court may still have to exercise some control over the CFSP with the help of an extended interpretative power of Art 40 TEU and insisting more on the structural principles of the treaties, see Christophe Hillion, ch 4 of this volume.

Service (EEAS)—who sits astride the Commission and the Council, while also presiding the Foreign Affairs Council,[23] falls in part under the full democratic and judicial discipline of the TFEU, insofar as the HR and the EEAS act under that Treaty. Insofar, however, as CFSP and CSDP are concerned, the HR and the EEAS are outside judicial control and largely outside democratic control as well. The same applies to the tasks of the European Council[24] and of its President[25] in the field of foreign relations. There is no doubt, on the other hand, that insofar as external policy and representation of the EU in the field of the TFEU remain in the hands of the Commission, although subject to the overall coordinating power of the HR,[26] they are fully subject to the political control (and the approval of any international agreement) by the European Parliament and to the judicial control of the Court of Justice.

After this summary overview of the allocation of powers in the field of foreign relations according to the treaties, it is time to turn to the Court's role in it all. It is telling that it has already proved impossible even in this brief overview to leave the Court's case law entirely out of the narrative in order to arrive at a truthful picture of the situation. There is, however, one preliminary issue that must be dealt with first, namely the Court's position in respect of the issue of the 'separation of powers' or 'the balance between the Institutions'.

III. THE COURT AND THE SEPARATION OF POWERS IN THE EU

As has been pointed out abundantly in the literature, the Court has long had recourse to the principle of what it called the 'institutional balance' inside the Union.[27] It has always studiously avoided speaking of a separation of powers or hinting at such notions as the *trias politica* or anything else that could smack of constitutional concepts used within States.

A classical, or perhaps it is better to speak of a naive, approach to the separation of powers is to see it as a separation between the executive, legislative and judicial powers that can each be fully identified with one of the institutions of the State, respectively the government, the Houses or Chambers of Parliament and the courts. There are not even many modern States that correspond fully to this simplistic view of the separation of powers.[28] Governments, by proposing bills, participating in parliamentary discussions about them and by openly or often

---

[23] Art 18 TEU.

[24] Arts 15 and 22 TEU.

[25] Art 15(6) *in fine* TEU.

[26] See Art 18(4) TEU.

[27] JP Jacqué, 'The Principle of Institutional Balance' (2004) 41 *CML Rev* 383–391; J Monar, 'The European Union's Institutional Balance of Power after the Treaty of Lisbon', at http://www.fpn.co.me/fajlovi/fpn/attach_fajlovi/lat/studentske-informacije/obavjestenja/2013/12/pdf/Institutional_balance.pdf.

[28] For this point I am indebted to Robert Schütze, *European Constitutional Law* (Cambridge, Cambridge University Press, 2012) 82–85.

implicitly brandishing the question of confidence, have to a certain extent become co-legislators. Parliaments, by subjecting governments to onerous conditions when they implement laws and supervising these very tightly through parliamentary committee procedures, have been turned into a co-executive power.

The EU founding treaties go even further than the mere practices of modern government; they institutionalise both before and after the Treaty of Lisbon the granting of a mix of powers to the different institutions of the Union. Thus the Commission can be said to possess a mix of executive, legislative and even (quasi-) judicial powers. The Commission certainly has some implementing and executive powers, but, as the Treaty of Lisbon states more firmly than its predecessors, the Member States' authorities are the real implementers of EU law (Article 291 TFEU). However, in the field of external action of the Union the Commission, partly through the EEAS, partly on the basis of its right of external representation in the domain of the TFEU (Article 17(1) *in fine* TEU) has considerable executive power in TFEU-based external relations. The Commission with its guaranteed right of proposal (Article 17(2) TEU and Article 294(2) TFEU) and now that Lisbon regulates the exercise of delegated legislative powers more clearly in Article 290 TFEU, also shares in the legislative power. Moreover, in the infringement procedure, where its reasoned opinion (Article 258 TFEU) determines the scope of the alleged breach of the Treaty, which the Court will be asked to rule on, it has been also bestowed with a modicum of judicial powers.

Similarly the Council is co-legislator with the European Parliament (Article 294 TFEU), but within the TFEU it can reserve certain implementation powers to itself (Article 291(2) TFEU), while within the TEU it is, together with or through the EEAS, the exclusive executive power in the CFSP, and co-executive with the Commission of the EU's external action more generally. In the relationship with the Council, the European Parliament, since the introduction of direct elections in 1979, has served primarily as the Europe-level democratic legitimiser of the legislative power.

Within the EU's constitutional system, only the European Parliament as co-legislator (Article 294 TFEU) and the courts of the Union as judiciary (Article 19 TEU) are largely restricted to exercising only one power of government; the Court more so than the European Parliament.

In the light of this peculiar situation, the Court's tendency to avoid such terms as 'separation of powers' appears at least comprehensible.[29] The Treaty of Lisbon, with a full recognition of co-legislative powers to the European Parliament in a kind of bi-cameral system and with, at least in principle, greater clarity provided on the delegation of legislative power, seemed to have made the separation of powers between the institutions more stringent. Nevertheless nothing much has

---

[29] In the same sense, Schütze, *European Constitutional Law* (ibid) 85. Contra: G Conway, 'Recovering a Separation of Powers in the European Union' (2011) 3 *European Law Journal* 304–322. Conway has laid down his ideas more broadly in: Conway, *The Limits of Legal Reasoning and the European Court of Justice* (Cambridge, Cambridge University Press, 2012).

changed in the multi-power character of both the Commission and the Council. Hence it is certainly not wrong to continue to speak of the 'balance between the institutions'. Moreover, as a consequence of the 'multi-power character' of some institutions, litigation on so-called 'separation of powers issues' often takes the character of ultra vires claims in respect of the powers allocated to individual institutions and seems closer to questions of the constitutional attribution of precise powers to these institutions than to questions related to broad constitutional principles, such as the distribution and separation of powers among and between institutions. 'Wrong legal basis' claims often serve the same function in EU external relations law. And although the Court's Opinions on international agreements notionally serve to verify their compatibility with the founding treaties, this procedure in reality often serves to maintain the proper balance between the institutions.

In the following discussion, we will turn to the cases of the Court, which can be considered relevant to maintaining the balance between the institutions in the field of the external action of the Union. Part of the analysis of these cases will be devoted to the question whether the Court shows itself to be broadly a defender of the traditional view that gives a certain preference for the institutions endowed with executive power in external relations as being *the* preferred institution in this field. To this end the cases will be split into two major categories. The first category is that of cases broadly relating to the position and the rank order of international law (treaty law as well as general international law) in the law of the EU. The second group of cases falls into what we have called ultra vires and legal basis cases, ie cases where the Court is asked to rule on an alleged mistake in the allocation of powers by one of the institutions in the field of the external action of the Union.

IV. AN ANALYSIS OF THE CASE LAW OF THE COURT OF THE EU

A. Cases of a General Nature: The Relationship between International Law and EU Law

It is perhaps trite to say so, but *anything* the Court decides on the relation between international law and EU law has an influence on the relations between the institutions and the powers allocated to them. The relation between international law and EU law is defined by three questions:

(1)   Is international law—customary as well as treaty law—the law of the land, ie an integral part of EU law?
(2)   If so, what is the hierarchy between international law and secondary EU law? Is international law of a higher rank than the secondary law of the EU or of the same rank? In the latter hypothesis, will later EU law override earlier treaties of the EU?

(3)   If international law is of higher rank, will EU law be interpreted so as to be
in harmony with international law or will the Courts, if necessary, go so far
as to set aside EU law in favour of international law?

It is easy to see that even a positive answer by the courts to the first question,
could potentially have an explosive influence on the position of the legislator and
destabilise the separation of powers in its classical manifestation, since it could
easily lead to an acceptance by the courts into the Union legal system of international law rules that have never had to pass the scrutiny of part of the legislative
power, which was the case of the European Parliament during the period that it
had no or very little true legislative power, ie until the entry into force of the Treaty
of Maastricht. However, that was a general problem of secondary Community law
at the time, given that the system of the treaties limited this branch of the legislature to consultative power in all legislative spheres, except to a certain extent in
the budgetary field. The true legislator at the time was the Council, which also
approved treaties negotiated by the Commission on behalf of the Community.

Hence, it was natural for the Court to consider international agreements of
the Community at the time as comparable to Community regulations, namely as
directly applicable acts, as law of the land, without any transformative measure
being necessary at either the Community or the national level.[30] Similarly, it was
coherent with this view that certain provisions of European Community (EC)
international agreements, just as certain provisions of Community acts, could
be regarded as having direct effect, insofar as they satisfied specific conditions,
namely containing a clear and precise obligation and not requiring any subsequent measure.[31] In short the obligation is of such a nature that it can be applied
by a court.[32] In other words, the obligation is literally self-executing and further
legislative or executive action for its implementation is not necessary. Moreover,
later Community legislation could not override international agreements, just as
later national legislation could not override EU secondary legislation.

Such an approach by the CJEU fitted entirely with the scheme of the
Community treaties in force at the time. This approach to direct effect or the
self-executing-ness of provisions of international agreements concluded by the
EC is also clearly respectful of the balance between the institutions. In those times
that meant the balance between the Court itself, the Council as legislator that had
concluded the agreement and enacted the Community implementing legislation
or other legislation affected by the direct effect granted by the Court, and the
Commission as executive that had taken further implementing measures.

The situation has not changed fundamentally after the entry into force of the
Lisbon Treaty, except that the European Parliament has become a full-fledged
co-legislator with the Council both in the approval of international agreements

---

[30] See Art 288 TFEU. Case 181/73 *Haegemann v Commission* [1974] ECR 449, paras 3–6.
[31] Case 12/86 *Demirel v Stadt Schwäbisch Gmünd* [1987] ECR 3719, para 14.
[32] Case 104/81 *Hauptzollamt Mainz v Kupferberg* [1982] ECR 3641, para 26.

(including trade agreements) and in the enactment of implementing legislation or of other legislation set aside by the Court because of the direct effect of a treaty provision. Thus the correction, not to say condemnation, of the legislative power, which is inherent in the granting of such direct effect by the Court,[33] has become starker in the EU, now that the democratic legitimacy of the former has been reinforced. However, this is a situation that is encountered in many States having a monist approach to international law and is generally considered acceptable.

It is a situation that is also rendered acceptable to the legislative power (and to a lesser extent to the executive), as we saw above, by the Court carefully circumscribing the conditions under which direct effect may be granted to a treaty provision.[34] On that basis this strain of case law continues until the present day without much change.[35]

In addition, the Court has also developed conditions linked to the fundamental nature of a treaty, as in its case law originally limited to the General Agreement on Tariffs and Trade (GATT) and the World Trade Organization (WTO), but later extended to the UN Convention on the Law of the Sea (UNCLOS) and the Chicago Convention.[36] The middle case is the most straightforward: UNCLOS was considered to be a treaty creating rights and obligations only between States. Hence individuals were inherently incapable of invoking any of these rights and obligations.[37] The EU is not yet a party to the Chicago Convention on Civil Aviation and cannot be considered to have succeeded automatically to *all* the rights and duties of its Member States and thus none of the provisions can be granted direct effect in the Union.[38] As for the GATT and the WTO, it was in a large number of cases relating to these organisations that the Court developed an important argument against self-executing-ness that is directly linked to the balance between institutions. In particular in cases before it that were related to the so-called banana dispute that raged in the GATT and the WTO over almost two decades, the CJEU could observe very clearly that, even after the dispute had been

---

[33] Implicit in a declaration of direct effect of certain treaty provisions and the non-application of provisions of EU law flowing from it, is the condemnation of the legislature for after the approval an international agreement having left on the books or enacted certain provisions of Union law that are incompatible with this agreement.

[34] See above nn 32 and 33 and accompanying text.

[35] This is borne out of such cases as Case C-265/03 *Simutenkov v Ministerio de Educación y Cultura, Real Federación Española de Fútbol* [2005] ECR I-2579 and Case C-228/06 *Mehmet Soysal and Ibrahim Savatli v Bundesrepublik Deutschland* [2009] ECR I-1031.

[36] In light of the dilemma of democratic legitimacy mentioned above, it is useful to recall that the Chicago Convention and the WTO were never subjected to approval by the European Parliament. However, UNCLOS was approved in 1998 with the assent of the European Parliament. See Council Decision of 23 March 1998 concerning the conclusion by the European Community of the United Nations Convention of 10 December 1982 on the Law of the Sea and the Agreement of 28 July 1994 relating to the implementation of Part XI thereof (98/392/EC), para 3.

[37] Case C-308/06 *Intertanko and Others v Secretary of State for Transport* [2009] ECR I-4057, paras 55–65.

[38] Case C-366/10 *Air Transport Association of America and Others v Secretary of State for Energy and Climate Change*, judgment of 21 December 2011, nyr, paras 69–72.

'definitively' decided by panels and Appellate Body reports, negotiations between the EU, represented by the Commission, the US and three different groups of banana-producing countries continued, while there were also still discussions ongoing in the Council about the reform of the EU banana regime. This was an important reason for the Court not to grant direct effect to provisions such as Article XI of the GATT, as that would have implied depriving the Commission as negotiator and the Council as co-legislator of their possibility to negotiate a provisional agreement on compensation or of their margin of manoeuvre as enjoyed by their counterparts from other WTO members.[39]

It is important to note that the so-called 'harmonious or conforming interpretation technique' of national law in the light of international agreements is used by the Court also in cases where it denies direct effect to agreements for systemic reasons, as in the case of the WTO.[40] This technique tries to avoid conflict between national law and international law by interpreting the former in conformity or harmony with the latter. It is an approach that is often congenial to the Court, since it can thus manage to stay clearly within its normal remit of interpreting EU law, while avoiding international problems of non-compliance, which would land primarily on the co-legislators or the executive powers, ie the other three main institutions. Again, the balance between the institutions is thus safeguarded.

When courts are confronted by the question whether rules of general international law, in particular customary international law, are part of the law of the land and whether they may or may not be granted direct effect and set aside national law, the problem of democratic legitimacy, as mentioned earlier, is stronger than in the case of international agreements, since parliaments normally have had nothing to do with the gestation of these rules of international law. This is equally true for the European Parliament, especially after the treaties of Maastricht, Amsterdam and Lisbon have successively given it more legislative powers, also in the international domain. This democratic deficit of customary international law is all the more acute, as customary international law is nowadays often derived by international courts and tribunals from declarations, UN resolutions and multilateral conventions that are insufficiently ratified (also by the EU) to have entered into force.[41]

Hence it is not surprising that the Court of Justice's favourite approach to customary international law is one of conforming to interpretation, since this avoids

---

[39] Case C-377/02 *Léon Van Parys NV v BIRB* [2005] ECR I-01465 paras 42–54. The final solution of the banana dispute was negotiated between the EU, the US and banana producing countries and finally ratified by all concerned in late 2012: European Union and Brazil, Colombia, Costa Rica, Ecuador, Guatemala, Honduras, Mexico, Nicaragua, Panama and Venezuela—Notification of a Mutually Agreed Solution (8 November 2012), WT/DS364/3 G/L/822/Add.1.

[40] See Case C-53/96 *Hermès v FHT* [1998] ECR I-3603; Joined Cases C-300 and 392/98 *Parfums Christian Dior v Tuk Consultancy* [2000] ECR I-11307; Case C-89/99 *Schieving-Nijstad vof and Others v Robert Groeneveld* [2002] ECR I-5851, paras 55, 60–61, 69, 71.

[41] See Case C-286/90 *Anklagemyndigheden v Poulsen and Diva Navigation* [1992] ECR I-6019, in which the Court based itself on customary law of the sea derived from UNCLOS, which at that time had not yet been concluded by the EU.

the question of direct effect and thus the chance of having to set aside an EU legal rule because of a rule of international law that the EU legislator never even had the opportunity to see pass under its eyes. This is particularly true in cases concerning the limits customary international law sets to the exercise of legislative or executive jurisdiction of the Union. Thus, by resorting to conforming interpretation, the Court maintained the balance between itself and the legislative power in relation to Union legislation restraining salmon fishing in the North Atlantic.[42] Similarly, the Court avoided a clash with the Commission as enforcer of competition law by reinterpreting what seemed to be the application by the Commission of an effects doctrine to non-EU enterprises so that it was in conformity with the territorial principle of jurisdiction, which at least until the 1990s was less controversial as the basis for executive jurisdiction in this field in Europe.[43]

Even when the question of direct effect was posed directly and could not be avoided the Court created wiggle room for itself in its relations with the other institutions by positing that the level of precision of rules of customary international law is such that the other institutions, normally the Commission and the Council, had a right to greater discretion in their acts than normal.[44] This approach was recently confirmed in the case concerning the unilateral application of the system of EU carbon taxes on foreign aviation corporations with flights into and from the territory of the EU; this was again a legislative jurisdiction case.[45]

B. Specific Competence Cases: The EU Treaty Procedure and the Doctrine of 'Ultra Vires' and Legal Basis Cases

Ultra vires cases can tell us how strongly the Court defends the Treaty allocation of powers in the field of external relations, and whether in doing so, the Court showed any of the favouritism to the executive power (mostly the Commission, but in some instances the Council) that was inherent in the classical view of foreign relations prevailing for a long time in the Member States. In some instances 'legal basis' cases can give the same information. Here there has been, especially in the environmental field, a tendency in the Court's case law to give priority to the legal basis that guaranteed the best democratic legitimacy to the Community acts adopted, at least in cases involving the possibility of a double legal basis.[46]

---

[42] See Case C-286/90 *Anklagemyndigheden v Poulsen and Diva Navigation* (ibid).

[43] See for the last such case, Cases C-89,104,114,116,117,125–129/85 *Ahlstrom and Others v Commission* [1988] ECR 5193, paras 11–18.

[44] See Case C-162/96 *Racke v Hauptzollamt Mainz* [1998] ECR I-3655, paras 50–61. This case concerned the immediate suspension contrary to the rules of the treaty itself of the Cooperation Agreement—Yugoslavia at the moment of the outbreak of the Yugoslav civil war, which the Commission and the Council based on the so-called *clausula rebus sic stantibus*, which was asserted to be part of customary international law.

[45] Case C-366/10 *Air Transport Association of America and Others v Secretary of State for Energy and Climate Change* (n 38).

[46] Case C-300/89 *Commission v Council* (*Titanium dioxide*) [1991] ECR I-2867, paras 17–21.

Precisely in the external relations field this would be an interesting tendency in the light of the 'classical view' referred to above. Moreover, during the period up to the Treaty of Lisbon the legal basis of the EC trade policy was not democratically legitimised at all, whilst the legal basis for external environmental policy provided for the European Parliament-Council co-legislation (Article 175 TEC). Opinions, the special instrument of the Court in the field of external relations, may also from time to time indirectly say something about the balance between the institutions in that field,[47] in particular about the position of the Court itself.

After these introductory remarks, the analysis will concentrate on the different phases of the treaty-making procedure: (i) negotiation; (ii) conclusion; (iii) suspension; and (iv) termination. Next to that, in some instances autonomous action in the external relations field may be brought into the analysis.

(i) Negotiation

Leaving to one side the new complications introduced by the Lisbon Treaty with the notion of the 'negotiator' who can vary in composition in different situations, the negotiation phase of an agreement to be concluded by the Union (alone or together with its Member States), consisted of the recommendation from the Commission, the opening of and, if necessary, the guidelines for negotiations decided by the Council, and the ensuing negotiation by the Commission.

The balance inherent in this negotiation phase between the Commission and the Council has been safeguarded indirectly by the Court in the celebrated *ERTA* case.[48] That case is mostly considered as deciding a question of competence, but it is also about the role of the Commission and the Council in arriving at the point that the Commission could have started to participate in the ERTA negotiations in the name of the Community. Here the Court called on the principle of Community loyalty (now the duty of sincere cooperation), on the one hand, to excuse the Council from adopting the arrangement on the parallel action by the Member States in the ERTA negotiations, given that at the relatively late stage of the negotiations this was the only remaining approach open to it. On the other hand, this approach was all the more excusable in the light of the fact that the Commission had hesitated too long in advancing its recommendation for the opening of negotiations.[49] In this way, by berating the Commission for its lack of action in the face of the Treaty rules and supporting the Council in its improvisation, the Court stimulated that henceforth the allocation of powers in starting negotiations on behalf of the Union would be respected.

A recent occasion demonstrates that the old *ERTA* judgment is perhaps not capable of mitigating passions under the new Lisbon Treaty. During the transition

---

[47] In practice, Opinions have been used principally to receive an answer on the question of the division of powers in the external relations field between the EU and Member States.

[48] Case 22/70 *Commission v Council (ERTA)* (n 19).

[49] ibid (n 19), paras 87–91.

period from the Nice to the Lisbon Treaty, the Commission considered itself forced to withdraw a recommendation for an EU position on the negotiations on mercury in the framework of the UN Environment Programme (UNEP), when it judged that the Council had totally perverted its proposal by ignoring the predominance of the Union's competence on this subject, given the considerable EU legislation on mercury.[50] As a consequence the EU could not negotiate at all during the first stages of the negotiations. A year later, however, a new Commission recommendation was issued and the Council adopted directives for negotiations, according to which the Union was to be represented by the Commission in the negotiations.[51] It would seem likely that in the long run a new court case may be necessary to reinstall some discipline in the application of the provision of Article 218(3) under the Lisbon Treaty.

A comparable situation arises, when the Commission must initiate the procedure for the definition of the position of the Union to be taken in a treaty body or an organ of an international organisation, when that body or organ is about to lay down acts having legal effects.[52] This provision so far has had a checkered history, punctuated by conflicts between the Council and the Commission. Thus the provision has been advanced once by a Member State in a vain attempt to sideline the global directives for negotiations for the Doha Round trade negotiations in the WTO by arguing that the negotiations had reached a critical phase in which acts having legal effects would be taken and that thus a position of the Union within the meaning of this provision was necessary in order to be able to continue the negotiations.[53] This attempt failed, probably because it was made in the context of the WTO, where it is common currency that 'nothing is agreed until everything is agreed'. This made the argument that one phase of the negotiations was more critical than another inherently implausible. On the other hand, the Commission and the Council are not averse from using the procedure of Article 218(9) in the WTO, when there is really an act to be adopted by the General Council that will have legal effects, such as the accession of Russia and other countries.[54]

In the field of mixed competences the Council has displayed a tendency to react ambiguously to proposals from the Commission with a view to establishing the position of the Union in a treaty body. In the field of environmental policy, where many multilateral environmental agreements have treaty bodies with the power to take acts with legal effects, the Council often decides to leave the Commission proposal to one side and adopt a general declaration on how Member States and

---

[50] Compare the first Commission recommendation, doc SEC (2009) 983, final with the second Commission recommendation, doc SEC (2010) 1145 final.

[51] Council Decision on the participation of the EU in negotiations on a legally binding instrument on mercury etc, Council doc 16632/10.

[52] See presently Art 218(9) TFEU. This provision was first inserted in the Treaty at Amsterdam.

[53] Personal participatory observation by the author.

[54] Council Decision 2012/17/EU of 14 December 2012 establishing the position to be taken by the European Union within the relevant instances of the World Trade Organization on the accession of Russia to the WTO, OJ [2012] L6/6.

the Commission will coordinate the negotiations on the spot more or less in line with the Commission proposal.[55] One may argue that the well-known *PFOS* case, apart from censuring Sweden for its unilateral action of placing this substance (perfluorooctane sulfonate) on the list of the Persistent Organic Pollutants' (POP) Convention, at the same time provided a certain protection for the procedure of Article 218(9).[56] If even the (temporarily) negative outcome of the discussion in the Council after a proposal from the Commission pursuant to that Article has the power to trigger Sweden's obligation of Union loyalty, both the Commission and the Council have an interest in taking the procedure of Article 218(9) very seriously and executing it in good faith.

(ii) Conclusion

The prerogative of the Council alone to conclude treaties, although after the Lisbon Treaty subject to prior approval of the European Parliament, has been strongly defended by the Court in *France v Commission*.[57] When the Commission purported to conclude an agreement with the US Federal Trade Commission and the US Department of Justice about administrative coordination and exchange of information in the field of competition law enforcement, the Court applied the attributed powers doctrine strictly. Although the Commission believed that the agreement was non-binding and that moreover it could be implemented entirely within the powers relating to competition and the budget that the EC Treaty granted to the Commission, the Court simply pointed out that the terms of the agreement showed that it was binding and that nowhere in the Treaty was the Commission granted the power to conclude international agreements.[58] What Member States often allowed their departments of government to do, the European Commission could not do, since it could only derive its powers from the Treaty. The internal powers of the Commission in the field of competition could not 'alter the allocation of powers between the Community institutions with regard to the conclusion of international agreements'.[59]

A decade later the Commission took great care that the Guidelines on Regulatory Cooperation and Transparency, which it negotiated with the US in the framework of the Transatlantic Economic Partnership, were clearly non-binding under international law. However, in a new case brought by France the Court stipulated that the non-binding character was not in itself sufficient to confer on the Commission the power to adopt such instruments on its own.[60] It was only in the special circumstances of the case that the Court could accept that the

---

[55] This way of acting is comparable but less serious than the clash over mercury related above.
[56] Case C-246/07 *Commission v Sweden* [2010] ECR I-3317, paras 73ff.
[57] Case C-327/91 *France v Commission* [1994] ECR I-3641.
[58] ibid, paras 33–37.
[59] ibid, paras 40–41.
[60] Case C-233/02 *France v Commission* [2004] ECR I-2759, para 40.

Commission had approved a non-binding arrangement with a third country.[61] The Court remarked that, during the negotiations with the US, the Commission and the Council had observed the rules for such negotiations, which moreover took place in constant contact with the Committee on Trade Policy. Once again, even where non-binding instruments in international law are concerned, the Court upholds the relevant negotiation procedures, ensuring a balance between the Commission and the Council.

(iii) Suspension

As we have seen above, there was a case of suspension of an international agreement, even before the relevant provision had been inserted into (then) Article 300 EC Treaty at Amsterdam, namely the immediate suspension of the Cooperation Agreement with the former Yugoslavia upon the outbreak of the civil war in that country.[62] In that case the suspension was done by way of a Council Regulation on a proposal of the Commission[63] and the Court concentrated entirely on the question of the review of the Council's act in the light of customary international law. In fact, there could be no question of validity under Community law, since the agreement had been concluded in the same way in which it was suspended, namely by Council Regulation on the basis of a proposal from the Commission.[64] There was thus *parallellisme des formes* between the two acts. It is all the more remarkable that the final denunciation of the Cooperation Agreement was done by Council Decision, after a Commission proposal and with the assent of the European Parliament.[65]

(iv) Termination

This brings us to the termination of treaties. Here the Court has had no opportunity at all to express itself, whilst the Treaty, even after Lisbon, remains entirely silent on this topic. The crucial issue is the same everywhere in different constitutional systems: must the European Parliament have a say in termination? Should the doctrine of *actus contrarius* apply, which in the past, for instance, excluded the European Parliament from participation in such an act in the domain of the common commercial policy, but now, after Lisbon, no longer would? Or should political flexibility and decisiveness count most of all and hence the Commission (proposal) and Council (decision) do this together, just as in the case of suspension? With the added argument that obligations are dissolved not undertaken which reduces the need to include the European Parliament in the chain of

---

[61] ibid, paras 41–44.
[62] See Case C-162/96 *Racke* (n 44).
[63] See Council Regulation No 3300/91 [1991] OJ L315/1.
[64] See Council Regulation No 314/83 [1983] OJ L41/1.
[65] See Council Decision 91/602/EEC [1991] OJ L325/23.

decision-making. The practice of the Member States is disparate, as is that of the Union.[66] It is obvious that the Court sooner or later will have to cut a Gordian knot on this issue.

(v) Preference for Parliament?

Reverting for a moment to the question of the reduced role in foreign policy and external relations of the parliaments of Member States and of the European Parliament, it was mentioned above that, especially in environmental protection, the Court gave a preference to those legal bases which guaranteed the highest political legitimacy, ie the best position for the European Parliament in the decision-making making procedure, at least if there is a possible double legal basis.[67]

However, when analysing the case law of the Court on the legal basis in the external aspects of EU environmental policy, the outcome seems to be determined more than anything else by the famous 'objective criteria' that the Court always invokes, when being asked to rule on the appropriate legal basis of Community legislation. Given that the European Parliament had no say in the adoption of international trade agreements until the entry into force of the Lisbon Treaty, one would expect a clear preference for environmental legal bases over the legal basis of the common commercial policy. Such a trend is not evident if one analyses the case law before Lisbon. The Court decided in favour of a commercial policy basis in the so-called *Chernobyl* case in 1990.[68] Ten years later it favoured the environmental legal basis on its Opinion on the Cartagena Protocol.[69] Shortly thereafter the Court plumped for the commercial policy basis in respect of the Energy Star Agreement between the EU and the US on a label for energy-efficient fridges and dishwashers.[70] In a case concerning the Rotterdam Convention a few years later, the Court decided on a double legal basis, environmental and trade.[71]

Later, in the *ECOWAS* case, where the Court was called upon to determine the borderline between the CFSP and the Community development policy in the framework of the Convention of Cotonou—in relation to a programme for enticing people to turn in their small arms and light weapons left over from the civil wars in West Africa—the Court came to the conclusion that the programme fell under both policies. It was only due to the way the relevant article in the TEU at the time protected the Community method over the CFSP intergovernmental approach that the Court felt compelled to annul the CFSP measure as 'ultra

---

[66] See PJ Kuijper, JA Wouters, F Hoffmeister, G De Baere and T Ramopoulos (eds), *The Law of EU External Relations, Texts, Cases and Materials* (Oxford, Oxford University Press, 2013) ch 3.8.

[67] Case C-300/89 *Commission v Council* (*Titanium dioxide*) (n 46).

[68] Case 62/88 *Greece v Council* (*Chernobyl*) [1990] ECR I-1527.

[69] Opinion 2/00 *Cartagena Protocol* [2001] ECR I-9713.

[70] Case C-2801/01 *Commission v Council* (*Energy Star*) [2002] ECR I-12049.

[71] Case C-178/03 *Commission v Council* (*Rotterdam Convention*) [2006] ECR I-107. On this sequence of cases, see also Kuijper, Wouters et al (eds), *The Law of EU External Relations* (n 66) ch 10.

vires'.[72] Thus in this case the Commission was preferred as the executive over the Council in development policy and potentially there was greater influence of the European Parliament.

The well-known *PNR* case also speaks against the proposition that the Court decides its legal bases cases in the field of external relations with a special preference for democratic legitimisation of external policies of the EU and to the contrary decides such cases on the basis of the facts and the arguments in every individual case.[73] The Court ruled that the agreement with the USA on the transfer of passenger name records should have been concluded on the basis of the third pillar, since the objective lay within the domain of combating terrorism. Thus it excluded the European Parliament's power to co-conclude the agreement and largely its own competence to rule on the agreement in the near future.

(vi) The Court's Own Position

It has already been noted above that the Court in the matter of the direct effect of certain international agreements has been modest in leaving leeway to the Commission as executive power and the Council as co- legislative power (together with the European Parliament). The same is also true in the field of certain autonomous actions in the field of trade policy, such as anti-dumping and countervailing duties and safeguard measures. In respect of all such cases the Court has granted considerable discretion to the Commission and the Council in the same way as it does so in other, internal, decisions requiring difficult policy choices based on complicated economic factors.[74]

However, it would seem that when the Court's own position as exclusive applier and interpreter of EU law is at issue, the Court is far less tolerant of any deviation from the straight and narrow application of Article 344 TFEU.[75] In such cases, including cases on the validity of international agreements decided after the signature or conclusion of the agreement, the Court is anything but self-effacing in the interest of the freedom of manoeuver of the coordinate institutions of Union government in the field of external relations. It does not hesitate to leave the Commission and the Council in a difficult position on the international scene, having to renegotiate and reconclude the international agreement in question. On the other hand, the Court has been careful in respecting the rule of the law of treaties that says that the obligations from a treaty persist in international law, even when the internal act of approval is declared wanting from a constitutional

[72] Case 91/05 *Commission v Council (ECOWAS)* [2008] ECR I-3651.
[73] Joined Cases C-317 and 318/04 *Parliament v Council and Commission (Passenger Name Records, PNR)* [2006] ECR I- 4721.
[74] E Vermulst and F Graafsma, *WTO Disputes; Anti-dumping, Subsidies and Safeguards* (London, CMP Publishing, 2002).
[75] See Opinion 1/76 Laying-up Fund for the Rhine, Opinion 1/91 EEA I, Opinion 1/92 ILO Convention, Opinion 1/03 Lugano Convention and Case C-91/05 *Commission v Ireland (MOX-plant)*, Opinion 1/09 Patents dispute settlement. See further ch 3 by de Witte in this volume.

point of view.[76] In that respect the Court has given the other institutions time and opportunity to correct their mistakes by preserving the effects of the quashed acts and has thus attempted to reduce the international embarrassment of the other institutions as much as possible.[77]

V. SOME MODEST CONCLUSIONS

At the beginning of this analysis two questions were asked. The first one was whether the same tendency existed in the Union as in the Member States to grant pride of place in the field of foreign policy to the executive power. An initially affirmative, but evolutionary, answer should be given to that question. The initial constitutional structure of the European Economic Community (EEC) hardly knew a democratically legitimised legislative power and thus it was inherently excluded from the external relations domain. The Court itself only slowly started getting involved in cases relating to external relations of the EEC in the 1970s. Moreover the picture is complicated by the fact that the different powers (for instance. executive and legislative powers) in the EU were (and are) sometimes allocated to the same institution by the treaties, more so than in national constitutions or constitutional custom.

The EC/EU went through a similar development of the foreign policy sector as its Member States, eg increased technocratic and specialist knowledge was necessary to conceive and carry out foreign policy. The consequence of that was a broader interest from civil society in the field of foreign policy than was traditionally the case, when elitist Foreign Affairs Councils and similar institutions were the favoured interlocutors of Foreign Ministries. Consequently foreign policy underwent a wave of democratisation. What happened as a political development in Member States was translated into changes to the treaties at the level of the Community and later the Union. The technocratic development was reflected in the creation of the HR and its EEAS and in giving the HR a coordinating role in conceiving and executing the Union's external action. Democratisation in the meantime had been taking shape step by step through successive treaty changes granting more and more legislative power to the European Parliament in the field, culminating in letting it into the common commercial policy after Lisbon.

How has the Court given shape to its role in this development and how has it maintained or altered the allocation of powers in the external relations field? That was the second question evoked at the beginning. A brief analysis led us to the conclusion that, given the peculiar distribution of powers over the different major institutions, it was better to maintain the Court's terminology of the 'balance between the Institutions'.

---

[76] Art 27 Vienna Convention on the Law of Treaties 1969.
[77] Eg Joined Cases C-317 and 318/04 *Parliament v Council and Commission* (n 73), paras 71–74.

In so-called 'interpretation cases', especially those on direct effect of international agreements, the Court has always been mindful of applying conditions to direct effect that respected in particular the rights of the legislative power that had approved the agreement, whether it was the Council or later also the European Parliament. In some cases the Court developed the interpretative criteria of object and purpose of an international agreement to such a point that it arrived at the conclusion that some specific treaties were inherently incapable of being invoked before Union jurisdictions and courts of the Member States. Again an important motivating force behind this approach seems to have been a concern to leave the terrain open to the legislative and executive powers (whichever institution was exercising these in the Union constitutional scheme at any one time) to find solutions for important international conflicts and not to pre-empt that solution by applying the doctrine of direct effect.

In 'ultra vires' and 'legal basis' cases the Court seems primarily to have been keen to protect the proper Community or Union procedures and the role of the different institutions in them, including its own position. There is no indication that the Court has been particularly favouring the European Parliament in order to ensure the democratic legitimisation of EU external action, in contrast to the field of internal environmental policy, where this was the case at least for a certain time. In some cases concerning EU external relations the Court has attached great importance to upholding the EU judicial system with itself at its pinnacle and has not tolerated any adaptation to international realities, which the institutions negotiating and concluding such agreements deemed reasonable. On the other hand there is at least one very strong example in which the Court decided that its own and the European Parliament's rights had to cede before the evidence that a particular treaty did not come under the 'community method'.

In short, the Court of Justice in the field of external relations has been quite sensitive with regard to the balance between the institutions and the maintenance of the Community method and procedures. It has broadly done so with moderation and good judgment, except perhaps where its own powers are concerned.

7

The Potential for Inter-Institutional Conflicts before the Court of Justice: Impact of the Lisbon Treaty

PETER VAN ELSUWEGE

I. INTRODUCTION

THE *AETR* CASE of 1970 was the first of a long list of inter-institutional conflicts before the Court of Justice (hereafter also referred to as 'the Court').[1] Such conflicts are of constitutional significance for two main reasons. First, they directly concern the division of powers within a legal system that is based on the principle of conferral. Typically, inter-institutional conflicts concern questions about the appropriate choice of legal basis for European Union (hereafter referred to as 'the EU' or 'the Union') (external) action as well as the scope and nature of the EU's competences to conclude international agreements or adopt unilateral measures. Second, the outcome of inter-institutional conflicts has far-reaching repercussions for the EU decision-making process and the institutional balance within the Union. Decisions about the competent institution to conduct international negotiations, the applicable voting rules in the Council and the extent of the European Parliament's involvement in the procedure for concluding an international agreement are crucial in the EU's constitutional system of checks and balances.

The abundance of inter-institutional conflicts in the field of EU external relations cannot be disconnected from the inherent complexity of the Union's primary legal framework.[2] The blurred division between different sectoral policies each having their own specific objectives and procedural requirements as well as the very complex and detailed rules defining the nature of the horizontal and vertical division of competences offer a plethora of opportunities for turf

---

[1] Case 22/70 *Commission v Council (AETR)* [1971] ECR 263.
[2] B de Witte, 'Too Much Constitutional Law in the European Union's Foreign Relations?' in M Cremona and B de Witte (eds), *EU Foreign Relations Law. Constitutional Fundamentals* (Oxford, Hart Publishing, 2008) 6.

battles between the major institutional actors ultimately to be decided by the judges in Luxembourg. Whereas the settlement of inter-institutional disputes before the Court of Justice appears logical in a Union that is based on the rule of law, such internal power struggles are often perceived as detrimental to the efficiency of the EU's external action and the EU's image as a credible international partner.[3]

In an attempt to counterbalance the often negative consequences of inter-institutional competence competition, the Treaty of Lisbon has introduced new instruments and mechanisms. The formal abolition of the pillar structure, the reshuffling of the EU's external competences and institutional innovations such as the President of the European Council, the High Representative of the Union for Foreign Affairs and Security Policy ('High Representative') and the European External Action Service (EEAS), all aim to improve the coherence and consistency of the Union's activities at the international level. Moreover, the Treaty of Lisbon has elevated the duties of loyal or sincere cooperation and consistency as key constitutional principles of the Union.[4]

Despite the laudable ambitions of the Lisbon Treaty reform, it would be a huge overstatement to suggest that all problems of competence delimitation have been solved. First, the Lisbon catalogue of competences, including a division between exclusive, shared, complementary, supportive, coordinating and supplementary as well as *sui generis* competences is not necessarily helpful in determining the precise scope for EU external action.[5] Second, the Common Foreign and Security Policy (CFSP) remains 'subject to specific rules and procedures'.[6] The division between CFSP and other EU policies is crucial for the determination of the appropriate decision-making procedures and, therefore, entails a huge potential for inter-institutional conflicts. Third, the Treaty of Lisbon significantly changed the balance between the major institutional actors and created new challenges for inter-institutional cooperation.

The aim of this chapter is to analyse the impact of the Lisbon Treaty innovations for the potential for inter-institutional conflicts before the Court of Justice. Specific attention is devoted to the Court's case law regarding the choice of legal basis for EU external action (section II) and the procedure for the conclusion of international agreements (section III). A final section (section IV) is devoted to the role of the Court in preventing inter-institutional conflicts.

---

[3] ibid, 11.

[4] P Van Elsuwege and H Merket, 'The Role of the Court of Justice in Ensuring the Unity of the EU's External Representation' in S Blockmans and R Wessel (eds), *Principles and Practices of EU External Representation*, CLEER Working Papers 2012/5, 37.

[5] Arts 2–6 TFEU. I Govaere, 'Multi-faceted Single Legal Personality and a Hidden Horizontal Pillar: EU External Relations Post-Lisbon' (2010–2011) 13 *Cambridge Yearbook of European Legal Studies* 94.

[6] Art 24(1) TEU.

II. CONFLICTS ABOUT THE CHOICE OF THE APPROPRIATE LEGAL BASIS

A. The Centre of Gravity Test in the Post-Lisbon Constellation

Inter-institutional conflicts before the Court of Justice often relate to the choice of the appropriate legal basis for EU external action. As pointed out in Opinion 2/2000, this choice has 'constitutional significance'.[7] It determines whether the Union has a competence to act and which decision-making procedures have to be followed. Accordingly, Court judgments about the correct legal basis ensure compliance with the principle that both the Union (Article 7 TFEU) and the institutions (Article 13(2) TFEU) act within the limits of their powers.

Pursuant to the Court's settled case law, decisions about the choice of legal basis cannot be settled on the basis of the institutions' own preferences or existing practice but must be determined on the basis of 'objective factors which are amenable to judicial review'.[8] Traditionally, the Court applies a so-called 'centre of gravity test'. Based upon an examination of the aim and content of the measure in question, the 'leading objective' dictates which single legal basis will be controlling. In other words, the dominant objective 'absorbs' the possible other substantive legal bases which are pursuing objectives of a subsidiary or ancillary nature.[9] In case of an inextricable link between two objectives without one being incidental to the other, recourse to a dual legal basis can exceptionally provide a way out on the condition that procedures laid down for the respective legal bases are not incompatible and do not undermine the rights of the European Parliament.[10]

The application of the centre of gravity test is not always a straightforward exercise, particularly in the field of EU external relations. International agreements frequently bring together a wide range of objectives in a single framework and in such a context the decision about the correct legal basis is always somewhat unpredictable and often depends on the exact formulation of the preamble or the first provisions of the agreement.[11] The Court's case law defining the borderline between the EU's external trade and environmental policies forms a perfect illustration of this problem.[12]

---

[7] Opinion 2/00 *Cartagena Protocol* [2001] ECR I-9713, para 5.

[8] See eg: Case C-300/89 *Commission v Council (Titanium dioxide)* [1991] ECR I-2867, para 10; Case C-176/03 *Commission v Council* [2005] ECR I-7879, para 45; Case C-440/05 *Commission v Council* [2007] ECR I-9097, para 61.

[9] Case C-268/94 *Portugal v Council* [1996] ECR I-6177. On the 'absorption doctrine' in the EU's external relations practice, see: M Maresceau, 'Bilateral Agreements Concluded by the European Community' (2004) 309 *The Hague Academy of International Law Recueil des Cours* 156–58.

[10] Case C-300/89 *Commission v Council (Titanium dioxide)* (n 8), paras 17–21; Case C-94/03, *Commission v Council* [2006] ECR I-1, para 52; Case C-178/03 *Commission v Parliament and Council* [2006] ECR I-107, para 57.

[11] M Klammert, 'Conflicts of Legal Basis: No Legality and No Basis but a Bright Future under the Lisbon Treaty?' (2010) 35 *EL Rev* 497.

[12] P Koutrakos, 'Legal Basis and Delimitation of Competence in EU External Relations' in M Cremona and B de Witte (eds), *EU Foreign Relations Law. Constitutional Fundamentals* (Oxford, Hart Publishing, 2008) 176–80.

Arguably, the uncertainties surrounding the application of a centre of gravity test in deciding on the correct legal basis in the field of EU external relations only have aggravated with the Treaty of Lisbon. Of particular significance is the introduction of a single set of external action objectives, listed in Article 21 TEU. Inspired by an attempt to increase the coherence of the EU's external activities, those objectives horizontally apply to all external Union policies and the external aspects of its other policies. At first sight, this makes differentiation between legal bases even more difficult than before.[13]

Nevertheless, the implications of this innovation must not be overestimated. The inclusion of a horizontal list of external action objectives in Article 21 TEU does not absolve the institutions from respecting the principle of conferral as expressed in the specific legal bases mentioned in the treaties.[14] Except for the CFSP, those specific legal bases generally include more detailed policy objectives. Hence, the application of a traditional centre of gravity test appears particularly difficult to distinguish between CFSP and non-CFSP external action. Moreover, the old delimitation rule that priority should be given to the non-CFSP legal basis whenever possible no longer applies.[15] Pursuant to Article 40 TEU, a new balance between CFSP and non-CFSP external action has been established: measures adopted in the field of CFSP shall not affect the application of the procedures and the extent of the powers of the institutions as laid down under the other Treaty provisions and vice versa. In contrast to ex Article 47 TEU, the 'mutual non-affectation clause' of Article 40 TEU is more than a delimitation rule between 'integrated but separate legal orders'.[16] Rather, it is the expression of the fundamental constitutional principle of institutional balance within the unitary legal order of the EU.

Whereas the formulation of Article 40 TEU appears logical after the abolition of the pillar structure and in light of the ambition to reinvigorate the CFSP as an important part of the EU's external action, it creates significant challenges for the Court of Justice.[17] It is, for instance, not very clear how the Court can delineate between CFSP and non-CFSP external action in the absence of specific

---

[13] M Cremona, 'Defining Competence in EU External Relations: Lessons From the Treaty Reform Process' in A Dashwood and M Maresceau (eds), *Law and Practice of EU External Relations* (Cambridge, Cambridge University Press, 2008) 42.

[14] A Dashwood, 'Conflicts of Competence in Responding to Global Emergencies' in A Antoniadis, R Schütze and E Spaventa (eds), *The European Union and Global Emergencies. A Law and Policy Analysis* (Oxford, Hart Publishing, 2011) 35.

[15] Ex Art 47 EU as interpreted in Case C-91/05 *Commission v Council* [2008] ECR I-3651, paras 58–62. For comments, see eg P Van Elsuwege, 'On the Boundaries between the European Union's First Pillar and Second Pillar: A Comment on the ECOWAS judgment of the European Court of Justice' (2008) 15 *Columbia Journal of European Law* 531–48.

[16] Joint Cases C-402/05 P and C-415/05 P, *Kadi and Al Barakaat v Council and Commission* ECR [2008] I-6351, para 202. On ex Art 47 TEU, see: A Dashwood, 'Article 47 TEU and the Relationship between First and Second Pillar Competences' in A Dashwood and M Maresceau (eds), *Law and Practice of EU External Relations* (Cambridge, Cambridge University Press, 2008) 70–103.

[17] P Van Elsuwege, 'EU External Action after the Collapse of the Pillar Structure: In Search of a New Balance between Delimitation and Consistency' (2010) 47 *CML Rev* 1002.

CFSP objectives. Nevertheless, the Court's interpretation of this borderline has significant institutional implications because the adoption of CFSP decisions is a matter for the Council alone, without any direct involvement of the European Parliament and the Commission, whereas measures falling within the sphere of non-CFSP external action generally require the agreement of both the Council and the European Parliament after an initiative of the Commission under the ordinary legislative procedure.

Hence, due to the ill-defined nature of CFSP competences and objectives, the specific institutional requirements for CFSP decision-making and the mutual non-affectation clause of Article 40 TEU, the delimitation between CFSP and non-CFSP external action is expected to become a major battlefield for inter-institutional conflicts in the post-Lisbon era (section II(B)) whereas the scope for inter-institutional litigation on the horizontal division of non-CFSP competences is reduced due to the generalised use of the ordinary legislative procedure under the TFEU(section II(C)).

B. The Blurred Borderline between CFSP and Non-CFSP External Action as a Major Source of Inter-Institutional Tensions

Pre-Lisbon, the Commission acted as the defender of the Community method against potential encroachment on the part of intergovernmental decision-making under the second or third pillar. This resulted in a number of Commission versus Council cases concerning the interpretation of ex Article 47 TEU.[18] Post-Lisbon, the dual function of the High Representative, acting as Vice-President within the Commission and head of the CFSP within the Council, decreases the likelihood that the Commission will initiate court cases against the Council in order to safeguard TFEU competences from CFSP influences.[19] Instead, this role is increasingly picked up by the European Parliament, which is basically excluded from CFSP decision-making.[20] It appears no coincidence that the first post-Lisbon inter-institutional conflict before the Court of Justice was initiated by the European Parliament against the Council and Commission precisely on the difficult borderline between the internal and external aspects of the EU's security policy.[21]

---

[18] Case C-170/96 *Commission v Council* [1998] ECR I-2763; Case C-176/03 *Commission v Council* [2005] ECR I-7879; Case C-440/05 *Commission v Council* [2007] I-9097; Case C-91/05 *Commission v Council* [2008] ECR I-3651.

[19] Govaere, 'Multi-faceted Single Legal Personality' (n 5) 108.

[20] In his Opinion to Case C-130/10 (n 21), Advocate General Bot argues that 'the Parliament's role in the sphere of CFSP is by no means negligible' (para 71). However, it seems a huge overstatement to suggest that the obligations incumbent on the High Representative to consult the European Parliament under Art 36 TEU compensate the lack of an ordinary legislative procedure in CFSP matters.

[21] Action brought on 11 March 2010—Case C-130/10 *European Parliament v Council*.

The case concerned the adoption of restrictive measures against individuals or non-State entities. In contrast to the pre-Lisbon situation, where, in the absence of a specific legal basis, recourse to a combination of Articles 60, 301 and 308 of the EC Treaty provided a pragmatic solution, the Treaty of Lisbon now explicitly foresees in a legal basis for the adoption of so-called 'smart sanctions' in Articles 75 TFEU and 215(2) TFEU. Both provisions have a different aim and function within the legal framework of the EU. Article 75 TFEU allows for the adoption of measures necessary to achieve the objectives of the Area of Freedom, Security and Justice (AFSJ), as regards preventing and combating terrorism and related activities. Article 215 TFEU, on the other hand, belongs to Part V of the TFEU on the Union's external action and allows for the implementation of CFSP decisions. Of particular importance are the procedural differences for the adoption of restrictive measures under the respective provisions. With regard to Article 215(2) TFEU, a unanimously adopted CFSP decision is implemented by a qualified majority in the Council on a joint proposal from the High Representative and the Commission. The European Parliament only has to be informed about the adopted measures. The situation is different under Article 75 TFEU where the Council and the European Parliament act in accordance with the ordinary legislative procedure, without a prior CFSP decision.

The legal complexities resulting from the ambiguous relationship between Articles 75 and 215(2) TFEU became obvious in the context of amendments to Regulation 881/2002/EC imposing restrictive measures directed against certain persons and entities associated with Usama bin Laden, the Al-Qaida network and the Taliban. Following the entry into force of the Treaty of Lisbon, the Commission announced that the amendments were to be adopted under the single legal basis of Article 215(2) TFEU implying that the European Parliament was no longer to be consulted on the adoption of sanctions that relate to individuals.[22] Immediately, the Committee on Legal Affairs of the European Parliament contested this course of events and suggested Article 75 TFEU as the proper legal basis for the proposed regulation 'since the objective is preventing and combating terrorism and related activities by non-State entities'.[23]

On 19 June 2012, the Grand Chamber of the Court of Justice delivered its long-awaited judgment and provided the first insights on the legal relationship between CFSP and non-CFSP external action in the post-Lisbon era.[24] A crucial question,

---

[22] Communication from the Commission to the European Parliament and the Council, 'Consequences of the entry into force of the Treaty of Lisbon for ongoing inter-institutional decision-making procedures', COM (2009) 665 final, 2 December 2009.

[23] European Parliament Committee on Legal Affairs, Opinion on the legal basis of the proposal for a Council Regulation amending Regulation (EC) No 881/2002 imposing certain specific restrictive measures directed against certain persons and entities associated with Usama bin Laden, the Al-Qaida network and the Taliban, JURI_AL(2009)430917, 8.

[24] Case C-130/10 *European Parliament v Council*, judgment of 19 July 2012, nyr. For comments, see: G De Baere, 'Reflections on the Choice of Legal Basis in EU External Relations after the Court's Judgment in the *Legal Basis for Restrictive Measures* Case' (2012–2013) 15 *Cambridge Yearbook of European Legal Studies* 537–62.

of course, concerned the possibility to adopt restrictive measures on the basis of a joint, AFSJ and CFSP, legal basis. Proceeding from the interconnection between terrorism and security and between the domestic and international aspects of security threats coming from persons linked with Usama bin Laden, Al-Qaida and the Taliban, it could well be argued that the envisaged measures pursue both the objectives of the AFSJ and of the CFSP.[25] The Court, however, quickly ruled out such an option for procedural reasons. Combining the ordinary legislative procedure under Article 75 TFEU, requiring qualified majority voting in the Council and full participation of the European Parliament, with the CFSP requirements under Article 215(2) TFEU, involving a prior unanimous Council decision and only a right of information for the European Parliament, is considered to be procedurally incompatible.[26]

By excluding a combination of Articles 75 and 215(2) TFEU, the Court explicitly rejected a potential compromise solution involving unanimity in the Council with a role for the European Parliament in the decision-making process. It is noteworthy that such a solution has been accepted in another context. In *International Fund for Ireland,* the Court acknowledged the combination of ex Article 159 EC (175 TFEU), requiring qualified majority voting in the Council and co-decision of the European Parliament, and ex Article 308 EC (352(1) TFEU), implying unanimity in the Council and consultation of the Parliament.[27] In this case, the Court simply ignored the rule established in *Titanium dioxide* that two legal bases cannot be combined as a result of procedural incompatibilities. Apparently, the interest of preserving the horizontal and vertical 'checks and balances' by granting a veto right to the Member States in the Council whilst recognising the decision-making powers of the European Parliament turned out to be more important than formal procedural requirements.[28] Be that as it may, the Court's firm confirmation in Case C-130/10 that the approach spelled out in *Titanium dioxide* 'is still valid after the entry into force of the Treaty of Lisbon, in the context of the ordinary legislative procedure' plays down all speculations about a fundamental revision in the case law on the choice of legal basis.[29]

In determining the choice between Articles 75 and 215 TFEU for the adoption of Regulation 1286/2009, the Court attached a lot of importance to the link between the pre- and post-Lisbon procedure for the adoption of restrictive measures against individuals. Just as former Articles 60 and 301 EC, Article 215 TFEU provides a bridge between CFSP and non-CFSP external action. Such a

---

[25] P Van Elsuwege, 'The Adoption of "Targeted Sanctions" and the Potential for Inter-institutional Litigation after Lisbon' (2011) 7 *Journal for Contemporary European Research* 496.

[26] Case C-130/10 *European Parliament v Council* (n 24), paras 45–48.

[27] Case C-166/07 *European Parliament v Council* [2009] ECR I-7135, with case note of T Corthaut, 'Institutional Pragmatism or Constitutional Mayhem?' (2011) 48 *CML Rev* 1271–96.

[28] K Lenaerts, 'EU Federalism in 3-D' in E Cloots, G De Baere and S Sottiaux (eds), *Federalism in the European Union* (Oxford, Oxford University Press, 2012) 30–31.

[29] Case C-130/10 *European Parliament v Council* (n 24), para 46.

link is absent in Article 75 TFEU.[30] In the case at stake, the fact that the contested regulation constituted one of the instruments by which the EU put into effect UN Security Council Resolution 1390 (2002) intended to preserve international peace and security formed a crucial consideration in the finding that the measures essentially concerned the CFSP.[31] Moreover, the adopted restrictive measures were targeted at persons and entities designated by the UN Sanctions Committee and the EU only reproduced the list adopted at the UN level.

Significantly, the Court did not accept the reasoning that preference should always be given to the decision-making procedure which maximises the participation of the European Parliament. As already argued by Advocate General Maduro in another context, such an approach 'would be tantamount to altering the institutional and democratic balance laid down by the Treaty'.[32] Of course, participation by the European Parliament in the legislative process is a reflection of democratic legitimacy at EU level but 'it is the result of the choice made by the framers of the Treaty of Lisbon [to confer] a more limited role on the Parliament with regard to the Union's action under the CFSP'.[33] This is an important consideration. It appears to suggest that, more than formal procedural incompatibilities, the clear intention of the Treaty drafters to keep CFSP separate from other EU external policies is a crucial argument against the use of a dual legal basis. Even though the Court's judgment remains silent on Article 40 TEU, it implicitly reflects the principle that the implementation of non-CFSP policies shall not affect the application of the procedures and the extent of the powers of the institutions in the field of CFSP.

The Court also rejected the argument that Article 75 TFEU should nevertheless prevail since it includes more specific provisions on terrorism and the freezing of funds (*lex specialis*), whereas Article 215 TFEU more generally refers to all types of restrictive measures (*lex generalis*) and also measures against third countries.[34] Rather, both provisions are regarded as part of complementary EU policies pursuing different objectives applying in different contexts. Article 215(2) TFEU applies in the context of the CFSP aiming at the strengthening of international peace and security, whereas the scope of Article 75 TFEU is limited to the adoption of autonomous EU sanctions, independent of any initiative falling within the sphere of CFSP.

This basic division between CFSP sanctions based on Article 215 (2) TFEU and AFSJ sanctions under Article 75 TFEU cannot conceal the continued existence of certain grey zones. For instance, it remains unclear what this means for the implementation of the EU's autonomous sanctions policy. The latter is based on

---

[30]   ibid (n 24), para 59.
[31]   ibid (n 24), para 67.
[32]   Opinion of Advocate General Maduro in Case C-411/06 *Commission v European Parliament and Council* [2009] ECR I-7585 at para 6, fn 5.
[33]   Case C-130/10 *European Parliament v Council* (n 24), para 82.
[34]   ibid (n 24), para 66.

Common Position 2001/931/CFSP, which gives effect to UN Security Council Resolution 1373 (2001) laying out a general call to freeze funds that could be used to finance terrorist activities. It is noteworthy that in the pre-Lisbon period all amendments to original Common Position 2001/931/CFSP were based on the cross-pillar legal basis of ex Articles 15 and 34 TEU reflecting the link with a UN Security Council Resolution on the one hand, and the need for information exchange and mutual assistance in criminal investigations among EU Member States, on the other hand.[35] In the post-Lisbon period, such amendments are consistently based on a single CFSP instrument (Article 29 TEU).[36] Hence, the question arises whether the adoption of sanctions against terrorist groups and persons which have not been listed at the level of the UN Sanction Committee and which essentially constitute a threat to the internal security of the Union can legitimately be adopted under this legal basis. To give one example, Council Decision 2012/333/CFSP of 25 June 2012 inter alia refers to the 'Hofstadgroep' and several of its members.[37] This organisation is a 'home-grown terrorist network in the Netherlands', responsible for a number of violent confrontations with the local authorities and the murder of Dutch artist Theo Van Gogh.[38] It appears that the implementation of sanctions against such persons falls within the scope of Article 75 TFEU. Otherwise, it is hard to see how Article 75 TFEU can have any effect in practice.

Another open question concerns the implications of the Court's findings in Case C-130/10 for the conclusion of international agreements involving both CFSP and non-CFSP elements.[39] In contrast to the separate procedures for the adoption of autonomous acts in either CFSP or other EU policies, there is a unified procedure for international agreements under Article 218 TFEU. However, the application of Article 218 TFEU is not without problems. Depending on the subject of the agreement, different procedural rules apply for the negotiation and for the conclusion of the agreement. Where the agreement envisaged relates *exclusively or principally* to the CFSP, the High Representative and not the Commission shall submit recommendations to the Council. The latter will take into account the subject of the agreement for the nomination of the EU negotiator. Where agreements *exclusively* relate to the CFSP, the European Parliament is not involved in the concluding procedure. Hence, in order to determine the precise procedural

---

[35] Common Position 2002/340/CFSP, OJ [2002] L116/75; Common Position 2003/482/CFSP, OJ [2003] L160/100; Common Position 2004/309/CFSP, OJ [2004] L99/61; Common Position 2005/427/CFSP, OJ [2005] L144/54; Common Position 2006/231/CFSP, OJ [2006] L82/60; Common Position 2007/871/CFSP, OJ [2007] L340/109; Common Position 2008/586/CFSP, OJ [2008] L188/71.

[36] Council Decision 2011/70/CFSP, OJ [2011] L28/57; Council Decision 2012/333/CFSP, OJ [2012] L165/72.

[37] OJ [2012] L165/72.

[38] The 'Hofstadgroep' at: www.transnationalterrorism.eu/tekst/publications/Hofstadgroep.pdf.

[39] See, for instance, Council Decision 2012/308/CFSP on the accession of the European Union to the Treaty of Amity and Cooperation in Southeast Asia [2012] OJ L154/1, which is based on a joint legal basis of Arts 31(1) and 37 TEU and Arts 209, 212, and 218(6)(a) and (8), second subparagraph, TFEU.

requirements for the negotiation and conclusion of an agreement, a centre of gravity test seems unavoidable. Of course, the question remains how the Court can deal with this issue given the lack of clearly distinguishable CFSP objectives.

The delimitation between CFSP and non-CFSP policies is at stake in the pending case on the procedure for the conclusion of an agreement between the EU and the Republic of Mauritius on the conditions of transfer of suspected pirates and associated seized property from the EU-led naval force to the Republic of Mauritius and on the conditions of suspected pirates after transfer.[40] According to the European Parliament, this agreement does not relate exclusively to CFSP but also to judicial cooperation in criminal matters, police cooperation and development cooperation. In the European Parliament's view, even an incidental presence of one of those non-CFSP components is sufficient to require its consent for the conclusion of the agreement.[41]

As observed by Advocate General Bot, such a strict interpretation of Article 218(6) TFEU would imply the European Parliament's involvement for the adoption of nearly all international agreements. In light of the consistency requirement of Article 21(3) TEU, it is indeed 'rare that an agreement concluded in the field of CFSP does not concern other policies, at least indirectly'.[42] Deriving from an indirect link with a non-CFSP policy a requirement to involve the European Parliament in the procedure for the conclusion of the agreement would be 'contrary to the wish of the authors of the treaties'. According to the Advocate General, Article 218(6) TFEU only aims to establish a symmetry between the procedure for adopting measures internally and externally. Hence, only for international agreements which are not solely based on a substantive CFSP legal basis, the involvement of the European Parliament is indispensable. Any other interpretation 'would affect the institutional balance established by the Treaty of Lisbon, which envisages a limited role for the Parliament in defining and implementing the CFSP, whether through unilateral measures or international agreements'.[43]

Of course, this interpretation does not solve the difficulties surrounding the application of a centre of gravity test for the definition of the substantive legal basis. The solution offered by Advocate General Bot in Case C-130/10 to apply a pre-Lisbon understanding of CFSP objectives[44] is difficult to reconcile with the horizontal application of Article 21 TEU and the aim of the Lisbon Treaty to ensure more coherence in the EU's external action. It is, therefore, no surprise that the Court adopted a more diplomatic position. Without attaching Article 21(2)(c) exclusively to CFSP, it simply observed that terrorism constitutes a threat to

---

[40] Case C-658/11 *European Parliament v Council*—action brought on 21 December 2011.

[41] Opinion of Advocate General Bot in Case C-658/11 *European Parliament v Council* (ibid), paras 15–16.

[42] ibid, para 22.

[43] ibid, para 31.

[44] Opinion of Advocate General Bot in Case C-130/10 *European Parliament v Council* (n 24), para 63.

peace and international security and, therefore falls within the scope of CFSP.[45] However, as illustrated in the *Philippines border management project* and *ECOWAS* cases, measures with an impact on the preservation of peace and security are not automatically reserved for the CFSP domain.[46] As a result, any attempt to establish a fixed boundary between areas of activity such as development cooperation and CFSP is almost by definition an artificial endeavour prone to inter-institutional litigation. This has not changed with the Treaty of Lisbon. The inherent interconnection between different EU policies as reflected in Article 21 TEU, on the one hand, and the separation of CFSP as a special external policy area shielded from parliamentary involvement, on the other hand, almost naturally leads to conflicts between the European Parliament and the Council.

In the absence of any clear guidelines on the delimitation between CFSP and non-CFSP competences, a case-by-case analysis appears to be the only option.[47] This almost necessarily comes at the detriment of legal certainty and may result in bitter inter-institutional disputes undermining the credibility of the EU as an actor at the international level.

C. The Reduced Potential for Inter-Institutional Conflicts in the Field of Non-CFSP External Action

With the Treaty of Lisbon the ordinary legislative procedure has become the standard decision-making procedure for all areas of non-CFSP external action (common commercial policy (CCP), development cooperation, technical assistance with third countries, humanitarian aid) and for most internal policy areas with external implications. Taking into account that the existence of different decision-making requirements for closely related or even partly overlapping policies provides a fertile ground for inter-institutional litigation, the standardisation of the ordinary legislative procedure reduces the scope for inter-institutional conflicts before the Court. Of course, this observation only concerns disputes about the horizontal division of competences.

From the perspective of the vertical division of competences, it remains important whether or not a measure is adopted under a legal basis providing exclusive Union competence. Hence, the Court will be asked to adjudicate on the precise scope of the CCP and its relationship with other, non-exclusive, bases for Union competence.[48] Also the ambiguous codification of the implied powers doctrine raises questions about the exact limits of the EU's exclusive competences and it

---

[45] ibid (n 24), para 62.

[46] Case C-403/05 *European Parliament v Commission (Philippines border management project)* [2007] ECR I-9045, para 57 and Case C-91/05 *Commission v Council (ECOWAS)* [2008] ECR I-3651, para 65.

[47] De Baere, 'Reflections on the Choice of Legal Basis in EU External Relations' (n 24).

[48] M Cremona, 'Balancing Union and Member State Interests: Opinion 1/08, Choice of Legal Base and the Common Commercial Policy after the Treaty of Lisbon' (2012) 35 *EL Rev* 690.

will be for the Court to create some clarity.[49] Significantly, in contrast to disputes about the horizontal delimitation between CFSP and non-CFSP competences, where the European Parliament seems to replace the Commission as the initiator of inter-institutional court cases (*cf* above), post-Lisbon practice reveals that issues about the vertical delimitation of competences still place the Commission, as the defender of a broad exclusive Union competence, in opposition to the Council, as the defender of Member State interests.[50]

A comparison between the Nice and Lisbon Treaty rules confirms that there are fewer incentives for inter-institutional litigation on the horizontal division of non-CFSP powers. For instance, there is less likelihood that the European Parliament will start a procedure against the Council regarding the choice of legal basis for the adoption of a decision including both cooperation with developing and other third countries.[51] Under the Nice Treaty rules, a neat division between the scope of the EU's development cooperation and technical cooperation with third countries was much more important given the different role of the European Parliament in the decision-making process.[52]

In the same vein, the further fragmentation of the EU's external policies due to the introduction of a new, separate legal basis for humanitarian aid does not necessarily increase the scope for inter-institutional conflicts. Even though the borderline between Article 214 TFEU on humanitarian assistance, which focuses on 'ad hoc assistance and relief and protection for people in third countries who are victims of natural and man-made disasters' and other Treaty provisions dealing with structural development assistance (Article 208 TFEU), economic, financial and technical cooperation with third countries (Article 212 TFEU) or civil protection (Article 196 TFEU) may be difficult to draw in practice, the generalised use of the ordinary legislative procedure reduces the likelihood of inter-institutional conflicts on the horizontal division of those competences. It is true that in the field of humanitarian aid, the ordinary legislative procedure is only necessary to define a *framework* within which the EU's humanitarian aid policy shall be implemented, whereas this procedure is required for the adoption of *implementation* measures in the context of the EU's development and general cooperation

---

[49] Art 3(2) TFEU and Art 261(1) TFEU. P Koutrakos, 'Primary Law and Policy in EU External Relations—Moving Away from the Big Picture' (2008) 33 *EL Rev* 683.

[50] Case C-114/12 *Commission v Council*, action brought on 1 March 2012, on the participation of the EU and its Member States in negotiations for a Convention of the Council of Europe on the protection of the rights of broadcasting organisations; Case C-137/12 *Commission v Council*, action brought on 14 March 2012, on the signing on behalf of the Union of the European Convention on the legal protection of services.

[51] For a pre-Lisbon example, see Case C-155/07 *European Parliament v Council* [2008] ECR I-8103.

[52] Under the Nice Treaty rules, the European Parliament was attributed the right of co-decision in the field of development cooperation (ex Art 179 EC) and only a right of consultation for economic, technical and financial cooperation with third countries (ex Art 181a EC). Under the Treaty of Lisbon, both legal bases (Arts 209 and 212 TFEU) require the ordinary legislative procedure.

policy.[53] Hence, the implementation of individual humanitarian aid operations is possible without involvement of the European Parliament. In theory, this may lead to conflicts as to the choice of legal basis because the European Parliament may prefer to use either Article 209 or 212 TFEU instead of Article 214 TFEU. However, in practice this is not a very likely scenario taking into account that any amendment of the implementation procedure requires the involvement of the European Parliament.[54]

A noticeable exception to the standard use of the ordinary legislative procedure for non-CFSP external action is Article 213 TFEU on urgent financial assistance to third countries. Such measures can be adopted by the Council on the basis of qualified majority voting on a proposal from the Commission without any involvement from the European Parliament. The introduction of Article 213 TFEU must be regarded in the light of the EU's Macro-Financial Assistance (MFA) granted to third countries dealing with short-term balance of payments or budget difficulties. In the pre-Lisbon context, decisions granting MFA were adopted on the legal basis of ex Article 308 EC (now 352 TFEU) because Declaration 10 attached to the Treaty of Nice explicitly excluded balance of payment aid from the scope of ex Article 181a EC (now Article 212 TFEU) on economic, financial and technical cooperation with third countries. With the entry into force of the Lisbon Treaty, this exception no longer applies meaning that MFA decisions can be legally adopted following the ordinary legislative procedure as foreseen in Article 212 TFEU. In situations of 'urgent financial assistance', Article 213 TFEU allows for the adoption of MFA decisions without involvement of the European Parliament. Hence, there is a potential overlap between the scope of application of Articles 212 and 213 TFEU, particularly because the definition of what precisely constitutes 'urgent financial assistance' is far from evident.

The granting of MFA is by its very nature an exceptional instrument, mobilised on a case-by-case basis to help the recipient third country deal with pressing financial needs. In such circumstances, it is important to act quickly. In other words, there may be good arguments to use Article 213 TFEU as the regular legal basis for the adoption of MFA decisions. However, such a practice would risk creating inter-institutional tensions with the European Parliament which, for obvious procedural reasons, opposes the application of Article 213 TFEU in this respect.[55] Significantly, the legal services of both the Council and the Commission seemed to understand the sensitivities surrounding the use of Article 213 TFEU

[53] Compare Art 209(1) TFEU; Art 212(2) TFEU and Art 214(3) TFEU.

[54] Dashwood, 'Conflicts of Competence in Responding to Global Emergencies' (n 14) 39. On Article 214 TFEU, see also: P Van Elsuwege and J Orbie, 'The EU's Humanitarian Aid Policy after Lisbon: Implications of a New Treaty Basis' in I Govaere and S Poli (eds), *EU Management of Global Emergencies. Legal Framework for Combating Threats and Crises* (Boston-Leiden, Martinus Nijhoff, 2014) 20–45.

[55] D Gauci, 'The European Parliament and EU External Aid: Measures of Response to Emergency Situations' in A Antoniadis, R Schütze and E Spaventa (eds), *The European Union and Global Emergencies. A Law and Policy Analysis* (Oxford, Hart Publishing, 2011) 295.

and quickly confirmed that this legal basis could only be used in 'truly exceptional circumstances'.[56] As a matter of fact, all MFA decisions post-Lisbon have been adopted in accordance with the ordinary legislative procedure as foreseen under Article 212 TFEU.[57] Whereas this practice at least avoids problems with the European Parliament, the lengthy decision-making process is generally recognised as problematic.[58] In an attempt to deal with this issue, the Commission has proposed the adoption of a framework regulation laying down general provisions for MFA to third countries.[59] This regulation, to be adopted jointly by the Council and the Parliament, would allow the Commission to adopt operational decisions on granting MFA as part of its implementing powers under Article 291 TFEU. The objective is to speed up the decision-making process while respecting the interest of the European Parliament to co-define the general rules and criteria governing MFA decisions.

The formula of adopting a framework regulation in combination with swift operational decisions by the Commission after the submission of the proposal to a Committee of Member States may be regarded as a good practice example of pragmatic inter-institutional co-operation. Nevertheless, the adoption of the framework decision is not without problems. In particular, the institutions disagree on the applicable comitology procedures in relation to MFA decisions. The Commission and the European Parliament propose the 'advisory procedure', which gives the Member States a possibility to adopt an opinion by simple majority and then the Commission decides 'taking the utmost account' of the Member States' opinion.[60] The Council, on the other hand, insists on the 'examination procedure', which is much more constraining on the Commission in the sense that no decision can be adopted when the Member State Committee delivers a negative opinion.[61] A practical consequence of this disagreement is that the approval of the Commission's proposal of January 2011 to grant MFA, amounting to EUR 46 million, to Georgia as a follow-up to commitments made at the International Donor's Conference of October 2008 was blocked until August 2013.[62] As observed by the Commission, it is indeed 'regrettable that this delay is taking place despite the fact

---

[56] Commission Staff Working Document accompanying the proposal for a framework regulation on macro-financial assistance, SEC (2011) 865 final, 4 July 2011, 9.

[57] Report from the Commission on the implementation of macro-financial assistance to third countries in 2011, COM (2012) 339 final, 28 June 2012, 2.

[58] M Emerson, 'EU Micro-Financial Assistance: A Critical Assessment', Study for the European Parliament's Committee on International Trade, PE 433.868, at www.europarl.europa.eu/committees/en/studies.html.

[59] Proposal for a Regulation of the European Parliament and of the Council laying down general provision for Macro-Financial Assistance to third countries, COM (2011) 396 final, 4 July 2011.

[60] Art 4 of Regulation (EU) 182/2011 of the European Parliament and of the Council of 16 February 2011 laying down the rules and general principles concerning mechanisms for control by Member States of the Commission's exercise of implementing powers OJ [2011] L55/13.

[61] Under the examination procedure, the Member State committee acts by qualified majority, see Art 5 of Regulation 182/2011.

[62] Proposal for a decision of the European Parliament and of the Council providing further macro-financial assistance to Georgia, COM (2010) 804 final, 13 January 2011.

that the two co-legislators agree on the substance of the proposal'.[63] Ultimately, a compromise solution was found. Where the assistance is equal to or below EUR 90 million, the Commission will act in accordance with the advisory procedure. For assistance above EUR 90 million, the examination procedure applies.[64]

Finally, the proposed framework regulation does not fully exclude potential inter-institutional conflicts. The Commission proposal explicitly provides that 'the adoption of a general regulation for macro-economic assistance [...] is without prejudice to the provisions of Article 213 TFEU, governing urgent financial assistance to third countries, and of the related prerogatives of the Council'.[65] It is noteworthy that the European Parliament deleted this sentence in the first reading, illustrating once again its aversion of this legal basis for the adoption of MFA decisions.[66] Any attempt by the Commission and the Council to follow the emergency procedure laid down in Article 213 TFEU may, at least theoretically, lead to inter-institutional litigation.

III. CONFLICTS ABOUT THE PROCEDURE FOR THE CONCLUSION OF INTERNATIONAL AGREEMENTS

In addition to disputes about the choice of legal basis, the procedure for the negotiation and conclusion of international agreements as laid down in Article 218 TFEU is subject to inter-institutional tensions. In particular, the involvement of the European Parliament (section III(A)) and the practice of concluding mixed agreements (section III(B)) requires further clarification from the Court.

A. European Parliament v Council: Interpretation of the Right of Consent

The Lisbon Treaty considerably increased the external action powers of the European Parliament. Of key importance is the extension of the European Parliament's consent powers under Article 218(6) TFEU and the right to be 'immediately and fully informed at all stages of the procedure' for the conclusion of international agreements of the EU under Article 218(10) TFEU.

From a strict legal point of view, the consent procedure appears to suggest that the European Parliament only has a right to say 'yes' or 'no' after the end of the

---

[63] Communication from the Commission to the European Parliament pursuant to Article 294 (6) TFEU concerning the position of the Council at first reading on the adoption of a decision of the European Parliament and of the Council providing further macro-financial assistance to Georgia, COM (2012) 219 final, Brussels, 11 May 2012, p 3.

[64] Joint Declaration by the European Parliament and the Council adopted together with the decision providing for macro-financial assistance to Georgia OJ [2013] L218/18.

[65] COM (2011) 396, recital 5.

[66] Report on the Proposal for a Regulation of the European Parliament and of the Council laying down general provisions for macro-financial assistance to third countries, A7-0157/2012, 3 May 2012.

negotiations without any possibility to intervene in the negotiating procedure. The latter is a task for the Commission, or the High Representative where the agreement envisaged relates exclusively or principally to the CFSP, following the negotiating directives adopted by the Council.[67] In political terms, however, it makes sense that the European Parliament is somehow involved from the very beginning of the negotiations.[68] This may avoid unpleasant surprises at the end of the procedure, when the European Parliament simply refuses to give its consent to a deal that has been carefully negotiated with (a) third partner(s). The European Parliament's rejection of the SWIFT draft agreement with the US[69] and its refusal to accept the Anti-Counterfeiting Trade Agreement (ACTA),[70] serve as examples of such a practice. To say the least, this is not very instrumental to increase the EU's credibility as a reliable actor at the international stage.

In the European Parliament's view, the right to be 'immediately' and 'fully' informed at all stages of the procedure, laid down in Article 218(10) TFEU, entails an obligation for the Council to provide access to the negotiating directives (mandate) without any restrictions.[71] The Council, on the other hand, is not very keen to provide this information, particularly when it concerns classified information relating to CFSP issues.[72] The Commission, on the other hand, has been much more receptive to the European Parliament's concerns. Under the terms of the 2010 framework agreement on relations between the European Parliament and the Commission, 'Parliament shall be immediately and fully informed at all stages of the negotiation and conclusion of international agreements, *including the definition of negotiating directives*'.[73] In this respect, the Commission promises to provide the European Parliament 'all relevant information that it also provides to the Council', and to 'take due account of Parliament's comments throughout the

---

[67] Art 218(3)–(4) TFEU.

[68] R Passos, 'The European Union's External Relations a Year after Lisbon: A First Evaluation from the European Parliament' in P Koutrakos (ed) *The European Union's External Relations a Year after Lisbon*, CLEER Working Papers 2011/3, 51.

[69] European Parliament legislative resolution of 11 February 2010 on the proposal for a Council decision on the conclusion of the Agreement between the European Union and the United States of America on the processing and transfer of Financial Messaging Data from the European Union to the United States for purposes of the Terrorist Finance Tracking Program OJ [2010] C341 E/100.

[70] European Parliament legislative resolution of 4 July 2012 on the draft Council decision on the conclusion of the Anti-Counterfeiting Trade Agreement between the European Union and its Member States, Australia, Canada, Japan, the Republic of Korea, the United Mexican States, the Kingdom of Morocco, New Zealand, the Republic of Singapore, the Swiss Confederation and the United States of America, P7_TA(2012)0287.

[71] Passos, 'The European Union's External Relations a Year after Lisbon' (n 68) 52.

[72] Access to sensitive information of the Council in the field of security and defence policy is based on an inter-institutional agreement of 20 November 2002 (OJ [2002] C298/1) and implies that only the President of the European Parliament and a special committee of four MEPs 'may ask to consult the documents in question on the premises of the Council'. With regard to access to classified information on matters other than those in the area of CFSP, the Council and the European Parliament concluded a separate inter-institutional agreement at the end of 2012 allowing for the consultation of sensitive documents in a secure reading room of the European Parliament and under strict conditions (2012/2069(ACI); procedure completed, awaiting publication in the OJ).

[73] OJ [2010] L304/50, para 23 (emphasis added).

negotiations'.[74] While recognising that 'Members of the European Parliament may not participate directly in these negotiations', the Commission shall facilitate their participation as observers in all relevant meetings, under its responsibility before and after the negotiating sessions.[75] According to the Council, such arrangements have the effect of modifying the institutional balance set out in the treaties since they aim to accord the European Parliament prerogatives which are not provided for in Article 218 TFEU.[76] In a formal statement, the Council therefore warned to 'submit to the Court of Justice any act or action of the European Parliament or of the Commission performed in application of the provisions of the Framework Agreement that would have an effect contrary to the interests of the Council and the prerogatives conferred upon it by the Treaties'.[77] This threat of the Council is remarkable because, in contrast to the Commission and the European Parliament, it has no tradition to initiate Court cases on inter-institutional conflicts.

The controversy surrounding the deal between the European Parliament and the Commission clearly illustrates the tension between the objective of increased transparency and democratic accountability of the EU's external action, on the one hand, and the interest to ensure that international negotiations with third countries can proceed in a secret, diplomatic atmosphere, on the other hand.[78] Arguably, the procedure laid down in Article 218 TFEU aims to find a balance between both positions. It may well be that, politically speaking, the European Parliament's request to be fully involved in the determination of the negotiating directive is a logical corollary of its right of consent,[79] but respect for the institutional division of competences requires that the role of the Parliament in the procedure for the negotiation and conclusion of international agreements is not unlimited.

B. Commission v Council on the Conclusion of Mixed Agreements

Respect for the principle of institutional balance is also a key argument in a pending row between the Commission and the Council regarding the procedure for the conclusion of mixed agreements.[80] In essence, the Commission contests the

---

[74] Annex III to the framework agreement between the European Parliament and the Commission OJ [2010] L304/61.

[75] OJ [2010] L304/50, para 25.

[76] Council of the EU, doc.15018/10, 18 October 2010.

[77] Council of the EU, doc. 15172/10, 21 October 2010, 17.

[78] Of particular significance in this respect is the pending appeal case between MEP Sophie in 't Veld and the Council regarding access to an internal document of the Council's legal service about the legal basis of an international agreement. In first instance, the General Court held that the Council could not deny access to this document with the exception of those elements concerning the specific content of the envisaged agreement or the negotiating directives. Case T-529/09 *Sophie in 't Veld v Council*, judgment of 4 May 2012, nyr; Case C-350/12 P, pending.

[79] Passos, 'The European Union's External Relations a Year after Lisbon (n 68) 68.

[80] Case C-28/12, *Commission v Council*, pending (regarding the signing and provisional application of the accession of Iceland and Norway to the Air Transport Agreement with the United States) and Case C-114/12, *Commission v* Council, pending (regarding the participation of the EU and its Member

Council's practice to adopt a 'hybrid' act consisting concurrently of a decision of the Council and of the Representatives of Governments of the Member States meeting within the Council. In the Council's view such a procedure reflects the mixed nature of the agreement, including provisions relating to the Union's and the Member States' competences. Following the same logic, the Council is of the opinion that the Member States have to be involved in the adoption of Union positions within the Joint Committee established under this agreement as far as matters not belonging to the EU's exclusive competences are concerned. The Commission, on the other hand, argues that the involvement of the Member States violates the treaties because the adoption of a 'hybrid act' on the signature of the agreement undermines the qualified majority rule set out in the first sub-paragraph of Article 218(8) TFEU and Article 218(9) TFEU and does not grant any competences to the Member States in establishing positions within bodies set up by an international agreement. Moreover, the Commission is of the opinion that the Council has violated the principle of sincere cooperation laid down in Article 13(2) TEU since the practice of adopting 'hybrid acts' circumvents the procedural rules laid down in Article 218(2) and (5) TFEU.

As long as the Court of Justice has not clarified the exact implications of Article 218 TFEU for the conclusion of mixed agreements, the EU's external action is subject to legal uncertainties, which may be difficult to understand for third parties. For instance, the signature of a long-awaited aviation agreement between the EU and Moldova has been delayed by about three months following the dispute between the Commission and the Council regarding the involvement of the Member States' representatives in the adoption process. Contrary to the Commission's proposal, the Council ultimately decided to follow the 'hybrid procedure' and amended the rules on the establishment of Union positions within the Joint Committee set up by this agreement.[81] In response, the Commission issued a formal statement added to the Council minutes on the conclusion of the agreement, in which it expresses the view that the Council's actions are contrary to the treaties and reserves its right to bring the matter before the Court of Justice.[82]

Even when institutional conflicts do not lead to litigation, the negative impact for the EU's image as an effective external actor is at stake. A typical example is the saga surrounding the EU's participation in the negotiations for a global legally binding instrument on mercury.[83] Also in this context, the Commission opposed the Council's preference for the 'hybrid' procedure and simply decided to withdraw its recommendation to open negotiations under Article 218(3) TFEU.[84]

States in negotiations for a Convention of the Council of Europe on the protection of the rights of broadcasting organisations.

[81] Council of the EU, doc. 10453/12, 1 June 2012.
[82] ibid.
[83] See G De Baere, 'Mercury Rising: The European Union and the International Negotiations for a Globally Binding Instrument on Mercury' (2012) 37 *EL Rev* 640–55.
[84] Council of the EU, doc 10564/10, 4 June 2010.

Despite some last-minute practical arrangements, the EU's performance at the first round of international negotiations was not very glorious. In the absence of a formal Council decision appointing the EU's negotiating team, the Commission, on behalf of the EU, and the Spanish Presidency, on behalf of the Member States, could only issue some general statements and try to explain the internal stalemate to the other participants.[85]

IV. THE PREVENTION OF INTER-INSTITUTIONAL CONFLICTS: WHAT ROLE FOR THE COURT?

Taking into account the often detrimental implications of inter-institutional power struggles for the EU's performance on the international stage, it is worthwhile to consider how such situations can be prevented and what role can be played by the Court of Justice in this respect. Of particular significance is the well-known duty of cooperation. The latter is a constitutional principle, derived from the treaty provision on loyal or sincere cooperation (Article 4(3) TEU) and essentially developed in the context of mixed agreements.[86] It presupposes that Member States, while exercising their retained competences, refrain from taking actions which could compromise the effectiveness of EU provisions.[87] This implies, for instance, a duty to inform and consult the relevant institutions prior to instituting dispute-settlement proceedings.[88] Simultaneously, it entails a commitment for the EU institutions to cooperate with the Member States, including in areas of exclusive powers,[89] and applies to the dialogue between institutions.[90] In this context, it is noteworthy that Article 13(2) TEU now explicitly provides that 'the institutions shall practice mutual sincere cooperation'. In other words, the principle of sincere cooperation equally applies to inter-institutional relations as to the relationship between the EU and its Member States. However, in practice, the principle essentially restrains the scope of unilateral Member State action. This may be related to the active role of the Commission in bringing Member States to the Court for infringement of their Treaty obligations under Article 258 TFEU.[91] Nevertheless, the introduction of Article 13(2) TEU may help to rebalance this situation. It is noteworthy that in the pending cases on the adoption of 'hybrid acts' in the Council and in the discussion on the role of the European

---

[85] De Baere, 'Mercury Rising' (n 83) 650–51.

[86] See C Hillion, 'Mixity and Coherence in EU External Relations: The Significance of the Duty of Cooperation', CLEER Working Papers 2009/2. E Neframi, 'The Duty of Loyalty: Rethinking its Scope through its Application in the Field of EU External Relations' (2010) 47 *CML Rev* 331–37.

[87] Case C-124/94 *Centro-Com* [1997] ECR I-81, paras 25–27; Case C-205/06 *Commission v Austria* [2009] ECR I-1301; Case C-249/06 *Commission v Sweden* [2009] ECR I-1335; Case C-246/07 *Commission v Sweden* [2010] ECR I-3317.

[88] Case C-459/03 *Commission v Ireland* [2006] ECR I-14635, para 179.

[89] Case C-45/07 *Commission v Greece* [2009] ECR I-701, para 25.

[90] Case C-65/93 *European Parliament v Council* [1995] ECR I-643, para 23.

[91] Van Elsuwege and Merket, 'The Role of the Court of Justice' (n 4) 52.

Parliament in the procedure for concluding international agreements, Article 13(2) TEU is used as a major argument.[92]

In addition to the duty of cooperation, the Treaty of Lisbon significantly strengthened the duty of consistency as a key constitutional principle of the EU legal order and as a central thread of the EU's external action.[93] For the first time, this principle falls within the jurisdiction of the Court of Justice. The amalgam of actors and policies over which consistency is to be ensured, may render this new judicial competence particularly challenging. The question arises therefore how the Court will make use of this extended jurisdiction. Despite the considerable weight it attaches to the principle, the Lisbon Treaty does not give us many hints in this regard. Arguably, the Court may develop various guidelines leading to substantive and procedural obligations for the institutions comparable to the obligations for the Member States under the duty of cooperation.[94]

Finally, when discussing the role of the Court in preventing inter-institutional conflicts to negatively affect the practice of EU external action, the specific procedure of Article 218(11) TFEU cannot be ignored.[95] Already in Opinion 1/75, the Court underlined that the objective is 'to forestall complications which would result from legal disputes concerning the compatibility with the Treaty of international agreements binding upon the Community'.[96] It is well established that the initiation of this procedure does not have suspensory effect. As expressed in Opinion 3/94, such an effect is not deemed necessary because the Member State or institution which has requested the Court's opinion may bring an action for annulment of the Council's decision to conclude the agreement.[97] This is of course true, but the Court adopts a very narrow approach if it only considers the issue from the perspective of judicial protection of institutional prerogatives. Taking into account the wider implications for the coherence and effectiveness of the EU's external action, it may well be argued that concluding an agreement after a request for an opinion has been initiated fails to respect the duty of cooperation.[98] It remains to be seen to what extent the revised treaty rules on sincere cooperation and consistency will have an impact on the Court's reasoning on this issue. Anyhow, recent practice regarding the forced denunciation of the initial passenger name record (PNR) agreement and

---

[92] Pending Cases C-28/12 *Commission v Council* and C-114/12 *Commission v Council* (n 80).

[93] M Cremona, 'Coherence in European Union Foreign Relations Law' in P Koutrakos (ed), *European Foreign Policy: Legal and Political Perspectives* (Cheltenham, Edward Elgar, 2011) 75.

[94] C Hillion and R Wessel, 'Competence Distribution in EU External Relations after ECOWAS: Clarification or Continued Fuzziness?' (2009) 46 *CML Rev* 581.

[95] For comments, see S Adam, *La procédure d'avis devant la Cour de justice de l'Union européenne* (Brussels, Bruylant, 2011).

[96] Opinion 1/75 *Local Cost Standard* [1975] ECR 1355.

[97] Opinion 3/94 *Framework Agreement on Bananas* [1995] ECR I-4577, paras 20–22.

[98] This has been argued by the European Parliament in Joint Cases C-317/04 and C-318/04 *European Parliament v Council* (PNR) [2006] ECR I-4721 but the Court did not address this issue in its judgment as it decided to annul the contested Council decision on other grounds. In his Opinion, Advocate General Leger dismissed the argument with a reference to the Court's reasoning in Opinion 3/94.

the abrupt termination of the procedure for the conclusion of the ACTA reveals the added value of such a preventive procedure. In both occasions, awaiting the Opinion of the Court after the procedure of Article 218(11) TFEU had been initiated could have avoided problems with partner countries.[99]

V. CONCLUSION

Despite all intentions of the Lisbon Treaty reform, inter-institutional conflicts on competence delimitation appear unavoidable in the complex legal framework of the EU. In particular, the division between CFSP and non-CFSP external action remains a major source of tension. The separate rules and procedures for CFSP almost naturally place the Council, as the dominant actor in CFSP matters, against the European Parliament, which virtually has no role to play in this field. The absence of specific CFSP objectives and the lack of a viable alternative to the centre of gravity test place the Court of Justice for a nearly impossible task. An incremental case-by-case approach seems to be the only option but it is doubtful whether this will diminish the appetite for legal basis disputes. Anyhow, it will take some time to settle the dust with regard to the implications of the Lisbon Treaty for the EU's institutional balance. All institutional actors jealously defend their newly acquired powers and it is not illogical that this creates inter-institutional tensions. The row about the procedure for the conclusion of international agreements, uncertainties about the exact scope of the EU's exclusive competences and discussions about the EU's external representation result from the often ambiguous new Treaty provisions.

Achievement of the Lisbon Treaty objective to improve the coherence and consistency of the EU's external action largely depends upon the political goodwill of all institutional actors. The conclusion of inter-institutional agreements, the adoption of framework regulations or policy initiatives establishing a procedural framework for pragmatic cooperation may help to avoid 'tiresome disputes between the Union institutions about allocation of competence'.[100] The need for pragmatism does not affect the key role of the Court of Justice in developing the law of EU external relations. Also after Lisbon, its role as constitutional adjudicator is crucial for the delineation of areas covered by CFSP and non-CFSP external action, for clarifying the scope and nature of the EU's external competences and

---

[99] With regard to the initial PNR agreement, a request for an opinion of the Court had been initiated by the European Parliament on 21 April 2004 (see Joint Cases Case C-317/04 and C-318/04 (n 98), para 39). With regard to the ACTA, a request for an opinion of the Court had been initiated by the Commission on 10 May 2012 (http://trade.ec.europa.eu/doclib/docs/2012/may/tradoc_149464.doc.pdf). The European Parliament decided to withdraw its request on 9 July 2004 following the decision of the Council to conclude the PNR agreement. The Commission decided to withdraw its request on 20 December 2012 following the negative vote in the European Parliament (n 70).

[100] G De Baere and P Koutrakos, 'The Interactions between the Legislature and the Judiciary in EU External Relations' in P Sypris (ed), *The Judiciary, the Legislature and the EU Internal Market* (Cambridge, Cambridge University Press, 2012) 271.

for defining the role of the institutions in the practice of concluding international agreements with third countries. The reinforced duties of cooperation and consistency provide the Court with new instruments to fully play its role as an honest broker in inter-institutional relations.

Part III

External Relations, the Court and the Union Legal Order

8

General Principles in the Development of EU External Relations Law

ANNE THIES

I. INTRODUCTION

THE EUROPEAN COURT of Justice ('ECJ') (hereafter also referred to as 'the Court') has contributed to the development of European law by establishing general principles of EU law to 'supplement and refine the Treaties'.[1] When establishing those principles, the Court has referred to the legal traditions of the Member States, the special nature of the European legal order, and international law, in particular the European Convention on Human Rights for the development of European Union (hereafter referred to as 'the EU' or 'the Union') fundamental rights in the form of EU general principles.[2] Throughout the process of European legal integration, general principles of EU law have played an important role in dealing with the impact and hierarchy of EU law norms in the EU and its Member States' legal orders,[3] and the organisation of the EU and its Member States' exercise of competence.[4] At the same time, the ECJ relied on general principles to provide a foundation for fundamental rights in the EU legal order.[5] The ECJ has therefore contributed to the constitutionalisation of the EU internal legal order by establishing rules on: (a) how to address conflicts

---

[1] T Tridimas, *The General Principles of EU Law* 2nd edn (Oxford, Oxford University Press, 2006) 4.

[2] Case 4/73 *Nold v Commission* [1974] ECR 491, 502f; Cases C-46 and C-48/93 *Brasserie du Pêcheur v Germany* and *the Queen v Secretary of State for Transport, ex p Factortame Ltd* [1996] ECR I-1029, paras 27, 41; see also Opinion of Advocate General Léger in Case C-353/99 P *Council v Hautala* [2001] ECR I-9565, paras 66ff; Tridimas, *The General Principles of EU Law* (n 1) 5ff, 23ff, 25ff.

[3] See eg: Case 26/62 *Van Gend en Loos* [1963] ECR 1 (principle of direct effect); Case 6/64 *Costa v Enel* [1964] ECR 585 (principle of supremacy).

[4] See eg: Case C-70/88 *Parliament v Council* [1990] ECR I-2041, paras 21ff (principle of institutional balance); Case C-426/93 *Germany v Council* [1995] ECR I-3723, paras 42ff (principle of proportionality); Cases C-36/97 and C-37/97, *Hilmar Kellinghusen* [1998] ECR I-6337, para 30 (principle of sincere cooperation); Case C-260/04 *Commission v Italy* [2007] ECR I-7083, paras 24ff (principle of transparency).

[5] See for an overview of the development of EU fundamental rights with reference to case law and scholarship, Tridimas, *The General Principles of EU Law* (n 1) 298ff.

between different layers of EU and Member State law ('interpretative principles');[6] (b) how to exercise conferred EU, or retained Member State competence in the interest of shared objectives ('organisational principles'); and (c) the conditions for lawfulness of EU and Member State conduct ('benchmark principles'), in particular regarding the protection of individuals.

This chapter claims that the judicial application and development of all three categories of principles introduced above have posed particular challenges for the ECJ in the context of the EU and its Member States' external action for three main reasons. First, an additional layer of law (ie international law) becomes more relevant when dealing with the EU and its Member States' conduct on the international stage, and that additional layer often needs to be accommodated in one way or another by European courts.[7] Second, the EU and its Member States' external relations involve non-EU actors (ie other states and international organisations) that possibly have an interest in the enforcement of the EU and/or its Member States' international legal obligations, or are affected by the organisation of the EU and its Member States' inter-/action on the international stage. And, third, the EU and its Member States' external action often pursues policy objectives that are not only established *within* the EU legal order but shaped by interests of a group of states/actors *outside* the EU, or even the international community as a whole. This makes it more difficult for EU courts to identify the applicable benchmark of lawfulness of the EU and its Member States' conduct, and to ensure an appropriate protection of individual rights. As will be shown in this chapter, all three aspects of the external dimension of EU external relations law ((1) relevance of international law, (2) involvement of non-EU actors and (3) possibly external objectives) have already required the ECJ to redefine the scope of existing EU general principles (eg in the *FIAMM, Kadi, Open Skies* cases). Moreover, the ECJ's judicial activity on the reach and implications of EU principles has already had serious repercussions for the EU Member States' scope for manoeuvre as individual subjects of the international legal order (eg *PFOS*).

The entry into force of the Lisbon Treaty has arguably brought some further clarification to the vertical and horizontal division of external competences,[8]

---

[6] See B de Witte, 'Institutional Principles in Judicial Development of the EU Legal Order' in F Snyder (ed), *The Europeanisation of Law: The Legal Effects of European Integration* (Oxford, Hart Publishing, 2000) 83–100, 88, for a discussion of the principles of primacy and direct effect as principles of interpretation.

[7] While international law might be relevant also in the EU internal legal order with regard to the relationship between the EU and its Member States, as well as with regard to substantive rules of the EU and its Member States shaped by international law, it is suggested here that the implications of international law obligations of the EU and/or its Member States are more significant where the EU and its Member States act outside established EU internal fora and interact with non-EU actors.

[8] Such clarification had been politically envisaged by the Member States in the Laeken Declaration of 2001; see 'Laeken Declaration on the Future of the European Union', adopted during the Belgian presidency, 14–15 December 2001, p 21f, section II A; at http://ec.europa.eu/governance/impact/background/docs/laeken_concl_en.pdf.

See for EU competences in general Arts 2 to 6 TFEU, for explicit EU external competences Arts 4(4), 209(2), 211, 212(3), 214(1), 216(1) TFEU, and for the broad EU competence in common foreign

and testified the Member States' commitment to strengthen the role of the EU as a global actor.[9] However, the EU treaties are not conclusive with regard to the *exercise* of external competences by the EU and/or its Member States.[10] While the Lisbon Treaty confirmed the existence of certain 'organisational'[11] and 'benchmark principles',[12] it remains unclear how exactly the strengthened role of the EU relates to the Member States' own capacity to act on the international stage. At the same time, the increased involvement of the EU in global governance and its obligations under international treaty regimes have raised further questions regarding the reach of EU fundamental rights, inter alia in the form of general principles of EU law.[13] These developments have raised questions regarding the potential role of the ECJ in further constitutionalising—through the development of general principles—the legal framework in which the EU institutions and Member States take action on the international plane, both with regard to their internal coordination of external policies or action, and the external representation and conduct of the EU and its Member States in the international fora.[14] While the jurisdiction of the ECJ regarding the balancing of fundamental rights

and security policy in principle Art 24 TEU. See for retained Member State competence for external action, for example, Arts 191(4), 212(3), 219(4) TFEU; the Member States have also declared the retention of their powers 'in relation to the formulation and conduct of [their] foreign policy, [their] national diplomatic service, relations with third countries and participation in international organisations, including [their] membership of the Security Council of the United Nations' upon the adoption of the Lisbon Treaty (Declaration #14). See for further discussion in this book: P Van Elsuwege, 'The Potential for Inter-Institutional Conflicts before the Court of Justice: Impact of the Lisbon Treaty' (ch 7); PJ Kuijper, 'The Case Law of the Court of Justice of the EU and the Allocation of External Relations Powers. Whither the Traditional Role of the Executive in EU Foreign Relations' (ch 6); and E Neframi 'Vertical Division of Competences and the Objectives of the European Union's External Action' (ch 5).

[9] Arts 3(5) (referring to the EU's 'relations with the wider world' and its commitment to international law), 21 TEU (eg the 'Union shall seek to develop relations and build partnerships with third countries, and international, regional or global organisations', 'promote multilateral solutions to common problems, in particular in the framework of the United Nations' and 'shall work for a high degree of cooperation in all fields of international relations' in order to, inter alia, 'promote an international system based on stronger multilateral cooperation and good global governance'), 27 TEU ('The High Representative shall represent the Union for matters relating to the common foreign and security policy. He shall conduct political dialogue with third parties on the Union's behalf and shall express the Union's position in international organisations and at international conferences').

[10] M Cremona, Case Comment on Case C-246/07 *Commission v Sweden* (*PFOS*) (2011) 48 *CML Rev* 1639–66 (on uncertainties regarding the duty of cooperation in the context of mixed agreements); P Van Elsuwege, 'EU External Action after the Collapse of the Pillar Structure: In Search of a New Balance between Delimitation and Consistency' (2010) 47 *CML Rev* 987–1019.

[11] See eg Art 4(3) TEU (mutual principle of sincere cooperation), Art 24(3) TEU (loyalty in the area of the Common Foreign and Security Policy (CFSP)).

[12] For the principles for the protection of fundamental rights, see Art 6(1) TEU and the Charter of Fundamental Rights of the European Union.

[13] See for a study of the impact of global legal pluralism on individuals' rights, remedies and responsibilities in areas such as human rights, trade law and criminal law the special issue by T Isiksel and A Thies (eds), 'Changing Subjects: Rights, Remedies and Responsibilities of Individuals under Global Legal Pluralism' (2013) 2 *Global Constitutionalism* 151–344.

[14] On the role of the ECJ in delivering Opinions with regard to the compatibility of envisaged international agreements with the EU Treaties, see G De Baere, *Constitutional Principles of EU External Relations Law* (Oxford, Oxford University Press, 2008) 93ff.

with national and international interests (eg security) has arguably been enlarged through the recognition of the Charter having the 'same legal value as the Treaties' (Article 6(1) TEU), the Court's capacity to contribute to the legalisation of the Common Foreign and Security Policy (CFSP) remains limited.[15]

Since the entry into force of the Treaty of Lisbon, scholars have started to analyse the implications of the Treaty changes for, inter alia, the delimitation of different external competences,[16] the 'principles and practices of EU external representation'[17] and the 'legal dimension' of the 'EU's role in global governance'.[18] In accordance with the theme of this book, this chapter focuses on the judicial contribution of the ECJ to the development of EU law on such issues from an EU constitutional law perspective. The present analysis starts from the premise that the ECJ's judicial activity not only involves the interpretation of EU Treaty provisions but also the application, development and creation of principles of EU law.[19]

The purpose of this chapter is two-fold. First, it aims to shed light on the ECJ's approach towards the applicability and scope of EU general principles in cases with an external dimension. In the interest of identifying the particular challenges the ECJ is facing when accommodating the foreign affairs dimension in its (established) constitutional jurisprudence, the chapter focuses on selected EU law principles, which were subject to recent decisions regarding the EU and/ or its Member States' *external* action but find their origins in the *internal* EU legal order: the principle of direct effect, fundamental rights, and the principles of effectiveness and sincere cooperation.[20] The second aim of the chapter is to highlight some systemic challenges the ECJ faces when further developing EU law principles entailing legal constraints on the EU and its Member States on the global stage, balancing the protection of individual rights against political room for manoeuvre and the effectiveness of the EU as an international actor.

The following part (section II) introduces the already mentioned three categories of EU law principles, which the ECJ has developed predominantly for the EU's internal legal order as part of its judicial contribution to the process of European integration over the last five decades. It briefly looks at the 'interpretative' principle of direct effect and its significance in the context of external relations law

---

[15] Art 24(1) TEU; Art 275 TFEU. See for further discussion in this book, C Hillion, 'A Powerless Court? The European Court of Justice and the Common Foreign and Security Policy' (ch 4).

[16] Van Elsuwege, 'EU External Action after the Collapse of the Pillar Structure' (n 10).

[17] S Blockmans and RA Wessels (eds), *Principles and Practices of EU External Representation*, CLEER Working Papers 2012/5, at www.asser.nl/upload/documents/20120911T102448-cleer2012-5book_web.pdf.

[18] S Blockmans, B van Vooren and J Wouters (eds), *The Legal Dimension of Global Governance: What Role for the EU?* (Oxford, Oxford University Press, 2013).

[19] On the role and process of legalisation of foreign policy, see ME Smith, 'Diplomacy by Decree: The Legalization of EU Foreign Policy' (2001) 39 *Journal of Common Market Studies* 79–104.

[20] For a discussion of external relations specific principles of pre-emption and coherence of EU external policy, see eg R Schütze, 'Supremacy without Pre-emption? The Very Slowly Emergent Community Doctrine of Community Pre-emption' (1996) 43 *CML Rev* 1023–48; I Bosse-Platière, *L'article 3 du traité UE: Recherche sur une exigence de cohérence de l'action extérieure de l'Union européenne* (Brussels, Bruylant, 2009).

(section II(A)), analyses recent case law on the reach and adaptation of established 'benchmark principles' for the protection of individuals in the ECJ's review of EU and/or EU Member States' conduct with an external dimension (section II(B)), and evaluates the ECJ's approach towards the organisational principles of effectiveness and sincere cooperation that shape the Member States' retained external scope for manoeuvre (section II(C)). Subsequently, the chapter concludes with highlighting some particular challenges the ECJ faces when 'contribut[ing] to the creation and development of a common constitutional space'[21] which frames the EU and its Member States' external policy-making as well as their action and interaction on the global stage (section III).

II. CATEGORIES OF EU LAW PRINCIPLES AND EU FOREIGN AFFAIRS

The ECJ has identified, developed and applied general principles as unwritten law of the EU. The following paragraphs distinguish between interpretative principles of EU law (section II(A)), benchmark principles that have added obligations imposed on the EU and the EU Member States in the form of self-standing norms of EU law for the protection of individuals (section II(B)), and organisational principles (section II(C)). At the same time, the principles' relevance for external relations law is analysed, taking account of some examples of their judicial adaptation in the context of external relations law.

A. EU Law Principles as Tool for Interpretation

The ECJ has recognised interpretative principles concerning the effect and ranking of EU law within the Member States' domestic legal systems (eg the principles of direct effect and supremacy).[22] The establishment of such principles has not entailed the creation of self-standing legal norms under EU law. Instead, interpretative principles have an ancillary purpose in that they ensure the effectiveness of existing norms of EU law as well as the EU legal order as a whole. In the context of EU external relations law, interpretative principles can be relevant with regard to (1) the interpretation of *EU* law and its implications for the EU Member States' external action and national legal orders, and (2) the interpretation of *international* law binding on the EU and/or its Member States. The following paragraphs will only briefly revisit the judicial adaptation of interpretative principles in the context of external action, given that *EU* law needs to be interpreted with the aim to ensure its effectiveness also in that context, and the ECJ's approach regarding

---

[21] K Lenaerts and JA Gutiérrez-Fons, 'The Role of General Principles of EU Law' in A Arnull, C Barnard, M Dougan and E Spaventa (eds), *A Constitutional Order of States? Essays in EU Law in Honour of Alan Dashwood* (Oxford, Hart Publishing, 2011) 179–97.

[22] See n 3.

the implications of *international* law obligations for EU external action and the ECJ's own judicial review have been addressed elsewhere in this book.[23]

The applicability and implications of principles on the interpretation of *EU law* remain unchanged in the context of external relations law: where Member States' external action entails or leads to the adoption of national law that conflicts with EU law, the latter's effect and ranking in the multi-layered EU legal order are assessed with the help of established EU principles. In the same way as in the EU internal context, interpretative principles ensure the effectiveness of EU law, which Member States might have derogated from—possibly by committing to,[24] or implementing[25] their own international legal obligations. Where Member States' measures of that kind are in conflict with their obligations under EU law, EU law prevails and can possibly be relied on directly before national courts to challenge the national measures in question. At the same time, where the EU's conclusion of international treaties is followed by the adoption of EU legislative measures, their effect and ranking in the EU legal order is equivalent to other EU law, provided it has been adopted within the framework of the EU legal order in the form of EU law.[26] The EU law principles concerning the effect and ranking of (internal) EU law will therefore not be considered further in this chapter.[27]

Yet, the above conclusion regarding the applicability of interpretative principles regarding EU law in the context of external relations law does not concern the interpretation and immediate implications of *international* law for the EU and its Member States' legal orders. While international treaties concluded by the EU are binding on the EU under international law and upon the EU institutions and the Member States on the basis of Article 216(2) TFEU,[28] the ECJ has developed additional tools for assessing the effect of international law on the EU and the national legal orders.[29] These judicial tools have been applied to assess the extent to which rules of international law can serve as a benchmark for the lawfulness of EU and

[23] See for a discussion of the ECJ's approach to the effect of international law, PJ Kuijper, 'The Case Law of the Court of Justice of the EU and the Allocation of External Relations Powers. Whither the Traditional Role of the Executive in EU Foreign Relations?' (ch 6).

[24] Case C-476/98 *Commission v Germany* [2002] ECR I-9855, paras 144ff (freedom of establishment: non-discrimination obligation).

[25] Case C-205/06 *Commission v Austria* [2009] ECR I-1301; Case C-249/06, *Commission v Sweden* [2009] ECR I-1335 (obligation to take steps to eliminate incompatibilities with EU law that were established in agreements prior to accession to the EU).

[26] Art 288 f TFEU.

[27] What needs to be distinguished, of course, are the implications of 'non-legislative' EU conduct for the Member States' (unilateral) external action. This question does not concern the interpretation of EU law, but the effects of certain procedures, discussions or negotiations within the EU internal legal order for the external scope for manoeuvre of the Member States. See for discussion of the principles of effectiveness, loyalty and unity below, section II(C).

[28] See Case 181/73 *Haegeman v Belgium* [1974] ECR 449, para 5, where the Court held that an agreement was an 'integral part' of the EU legal order.

[29] See also M Cremona's contribution to this book, 'A Reticent Court? Policy Objectives and the Court of Justice' (ch 2), in which she distinguishes between the interpretation of Union agreements, direct effect of international agreements and effect of international law more generally; nn 65–67 (with reference to case law).

Member State conduct, and they have thereby also defined the scope of the Court's own judicial review. For instance, the ECJ has established a two-step test regarding the direct effect of international treaty obligations in the EU legal order, assessing the nature of the international agreement as well as the wording of the enforced Treaty provision.[30] On that basis, the ECJ has regularly acknowledged direct effect of the EU's international obligations within the legal orders of the *Member States*, in particular where it arguably led to an expansion of the applicability of EU law in substance (as embedded in international treaty obligation).[31] Yet, the Court has exercised significant judicial self-restraint by denying direct effect of international legal obligations imposed on the *Union*, respecting the EU institutions' scope for manoeuvre on the international plane.[32] At the same time, the ECJ has recognised its obligation to interpret EU law in accordance with international legal obligations where possible.[33]

B. EU Law Principles as Benchmark for Lawfulness

In addition to the recognition of principles and tools that help assess the effect and ranking of EU and international law, the ECJ has established general principles for the protection, or at least the benefit of individuals (eg fundamental rights, the principle of protection of legitimate expectations).[34] Several of these principles have by now been codified.[35]

---

[30] For a detailed discussion of the 'two-pronged test', which questions (1) whether the agreement as a whole allows for directly effective rights and obligations, and (2) whether invoked provisions are sufficiently clear and precise to be applied by the Court, see A Peters, 'The Position of International Law within the European Community Legal Order' (1997) 40 *German Yearbook of International Law* 9–77, 53ff. See also eg Case C-308/06 *International Association of Independent Tanker Owners (Intertanko) v Secretary of State for Transport* [2008] ECR I-4057, para 45.

[31] Case 17/81 *Pabst* [1982] ECR 1331, para 27; Case C-416/96 *El-Yassini* [1999] ECR-1209 (EEC-Morocco Agreement/non-discrimination of workers); Case C-63/99 *Głoszczuk* [2001] ECR I-6369; Case C-235/99 *Kondova* [2001] ECR I-6427; Case C-257/99 *Barkoci and Malik* [2001] ECR I-6557; Case C-268/99 *Jany* [2001] ECR I-8615; Case C-162/00 *Pokrzeptowicz-Meyer* [2002] ECR I-1049— all concerning the 'Europe Agreements' with Hungary, Poland, Romania, Bulgaria, Slovakia, Czech Republic, Latvia, Lithuania, Estonia and Slovenia. Case C-265/03 *Simutenkov* [2005] ECR I-2579 (EC Russia Partnership Agreement of 1997).

[32] Case C-149/96 *Portugal v Council* [1999] ECR I-8395, para 46; Cases C-120 and 121/06 P *FIAMM and Others* [2008] ECR I-6513, paras 116ff. See also PJ Kuijper and M Cremona's contributions to this book.

[33] A Peters, 'The Position of International Law within the European Community Legal Order' (1997) 40 *German Yearbook of International Law* 9–77, 71, with reference to case law. See also J Wouters, J Odermatt and T Ramopoulos' contribution to this book, 'Worlds Apart? Comparing the Approaches of the European Court of Justice and the EU Legislature to International Law' (ch 13).

[34] Tridimas, *The General Principles of EU Law* (n 1) 242ff (legal certainty and protection of legitimate expectations), 298ff (fundamental rights). P Craig and G de Búrca, *EU Law—Text, Cases, and Materials* 5th edn (Oxford, Oxford University Press, 2011) 109, stating that general principles can be used 'as a ground for invalidation if a particular legislative, delegated, or implementing act contravenes these principles'.

[35] See in particular the Charter of Fundamental Rights of the EU, which has the 'same legal value as the Treaties' (Art 6(1) TEU).

With the recognition of principles for the protection of individuals, the Court has established EU law in the form of unwritten 'self-standing' legal norms that can be applied in principle as a benchmark when assessing the lawfulness of *EU* conduct.[36] More difficult to assess, however, has been the extent to which *Member State* conduct can be challenged on the ground of EU general principles. The ECJ has held that Member States are bound by EU general principles when they implement[37] or derogate[38] from EU law, or where Member State measures 'fall within the scope of [EU] law'.[39] Where Member States take action that neither falls within an area regulated by EU law, nor affects EU legislation, it seems difficult to argue that they need to comply with EU general principles.[40]

What then are the implications of what have been called here EU benchmark principles for the EU and its Member States' *external* action, and hence the constitutional framework in which such action is taken? At first sight, there seems to be no reason why EU benchmark principles concerning the lawful exercise of conferred or retained competence should not play a comparable role in the external as well as the domestic context. The rule of law requires compliance with EU general principles,[41] and the EU and its Member States are committed to the protection of human rights not only with regard to the EU internal legal order.[42] Yet, in the context of its 'foreign affairs jurisprudence' the ECJ has taken account of additional factors that shape the scope of EU principles as legal constraints of the EU institutions' conduct as well as the Member States.

In the light of recent jurisprudence of the ECJ, the following analysis will focus on the fundamental rights constraints imposed on the EU (institutions) and Member

---

[36] Tridimas, *The General Principles of EU Law* (n 1) 36.

[37] Joined Cases 201 and 202/85 *Marthe Klensch and Others v Secrétaire d'Etat à l'Agriculture et à la Viticulture* [1986] ECR 3477, 3508, para 10; Case 5/88 *Wachauf v Bundesamt für Ernährung und Forstwirtschaft* [1989] ECR 2609, para 19; and Joined Cases C-20 and 64/00 *Booker Aquacultur and Hydro Seafood* [2003] ECR I-7411, paras 65ff, 92 (EU fundamental rights); Case C-279/09 *DEB Deutsche Energiehandels- und Beratungsgesellschaft mbH v Bundesrepublik Deutschland* [2010] ECR I-13849, para 30 (access to a court); Order of 14 December 2011 in Joined Cases C-483/11 and C-484/11 *Boncea and Others*, judgment of 14 December 2011, nyr, para 29.

[38] Case C-260/89 *Elliniki Radiophonia Tiléorassi AE and Panellinia Omospondia Syllogon Prossopikou v Dimotiki Etairia Pliroforissis and Sotirios Kouvelas and Nicolaos Avdellas and Others (ERT v DEP)* [1991] ECR I-2925, 2959, para 43; Case C-368/95 *Vereinigte Familiapress Zeitungsverlags—und Vertriebs GmbH v Bauer Verlag* [1997] ECR I-3689, 3717, para 24; Case C-71/02 *Herbert Karner Industrie-Auktionen GmbH v Troostwijk GmbH* [2004] ECR I-3025, paras 48ff.

[39] Case C-260/89 *ERT* [1991] ECR I-2925, para 42; Case C-159/90 *Grogan* [1991] ECR I-4685, para 31. See for further discussion, Tridimas, *The General Principles of EU Law* (n 1) 36ff.

[40] See also Tridimas, *The General Principles of EU Law* (n 1) 40ff, with case law examples. For a denial of admissibility because of a lacking connection between national legislation and EU law, see Case C-27/11 *Vinkov*, judgment of 7 June 2012, nyr, para 59.

[41] A Reinisch, 'Entschädigung für die unbeteiligten "Opfer" des Hormon- und Bananenstreites' (2000) *Europäische Zeitschrift für Wirtschaftsrecht* 42, 44. See also Case T-315/01 *Kadi v Council and Commission* [2005] ECR II-3649, paras 209ff. For the different issue of the EU as a promoter and 'exporter' of the rule of law, see L Pech, 'The Rule of Law as a Guiding Principle of the European Union's External Action', CLEER Working Papers 2012/3, 1–56, at www.asser.nl/upload/documents/2102012_33322cleer2012-3web.pdf.

[42] See eg Art 21(1), (2)(b) TEU.

States. In order to assess the reach of EU and Member State fundamental rights obligations under existing principles of EU law, it seems important to distinguish between different dimensions of foreign policy-making: (i) the internal formulation, coordination and implementation of EU and Member State external policy and action; (ii) the EU and its Member States' external representation and interaction with non-EU actors; and (iii) EU Member States' unilateral external action on the global stage.

(i) The Internal Dimension of EU Foreign Affairs

With regard to the internal dimension of EU foreign affairs, the legal context for action seems in principle to be similar to the one for EU domestic affairs: the EU institutions need to comply with principles for the protection of individuals when adopting legislative measures, policies, strategies or positions regarding EU foreign affairs. Arguably this is also true with regard to the EU's Common Foreign and Security Policy (CFSP): even though the ECJ's jurisdiction to review EU conduct in that area is limited, it has been authorised to review the 'legality of decisions providing for restrictive measures against natural or legal persons adopted by the Council'.[43] Whatever the precise reach of this jurisdiction, it is suggested here that in the light of the EU's nature as a law-bound entity, which derives its powers from the Member States, and its Member States' interest in the EU's compliance with the rule of law, the reach of general principles in substance should be assessed independently from the scope of the ECJ's jurisdiction.

The ECJ has reviewed EU legislative measures, which implemented the EU Member States' international legal obligations, in the light of general principles.[44] Moreover, the Court alluded to the EU's possible obligation to provide compensation on the basis of EU general principles to individuals, who suffer from the consequences of a continued breach by the EU of an EU international legal obligation.[45] The Court has thus acknowledged the *applicability* of EU general principles for the protection of individuals also where their enforcement might hinder the effective implementation of external policies,[46] or increase the 'costs' of foreign affairs undertaken in the public interest.[47]

---

[43] Art 24(1) TEU; Art 275 TFEU. See for detailed discussion, C Hillion, 'A Powerless Court? The European Court of Justice and the Common Foreign and Security Policy' (ch 4).

[44] Joined Cases C-402/05 P and C-415/05 P *Yassin Abdullah Kadi and Al Barakaat International Foundation v Council* [2008] ECR I-6351, paras 326, 281ff. Confirmed in Joined Cases C-584/10 P, C-593/10 P and C-595/10 P *Commission and Others v Kadi*, judgment of 18 July 2013, nyr, paras 66, 67, 97ff.

[45] Cases C-120 and 121/06 P *FIAMM* (n 32), paras 180ff, 184 (concerning the EU's upholding of challenged EU legislation in breach of WTO law in the absence of a compensation mechanism for caused retaliation).

[46] Eg The annulment of EU legislation implementing UN sanctions without effect for the Member States' international legal obligations on the same issue), see n 44.

[47] Eg The obligation to provide financial compensation in exchange for pursuing international trade disputes in the EU's general interest, which negatively affect individuals), see n 45.

What deserves further attention, however, is the extent to which the ECJ recognises the international dimension or context of the contested EU conduct/measure to be shaping the *scope* of protection under EU general principles that are invoked by applicants before the Court. In the assessment of EU legislation, which had been adopted on the basis of UN Security Council resolutions, the ECJ took account of the 'importance of the aims pursued' when identifying the scope of protection of the EU fundamental right to property (in the form of a general principle[48]) in *Kadi I*.[49] Also in the context of the internal market, the ECJ has held that the right to property does 'not constitute [an] absolute prerogative, but must be viewed in relation to [its] social function' and that restrictions, 'particularly in the context of a common organisation of the market', can be justified, 'provided that [they] in fact correspond to objectives of general interest pursued by the Community and that they do not constitute, with regard to the aim pursued, a disproportionate and intolerable interference which infringes upon the very substance of the rights guaranteed'.[50]

What distinguishes the situation in *Kadi I* from a purely internal situation is that 'important aims' were not only not related to the common organisation of the market, but also set neither by the EU nor its Member States. The 'security objective' pursued but the UN Security Council and Sanctions Committee was of an international nature and adopted by the EU on the basis of correlating international obligations of its Member States as members of the UN.[51] Nonetheless, the ECJ reiterated that the EU courts had to 'ensure the review, in principle the full review, of the lawfulness of all Union acts in the light of the fundamental rights'.[52] Even though the Court did not question the validity of the UN's security objectives, the restriction of Kadi's right to property was considered unlawful due to the way in which the pertinent EU legislation had been applied to him, ie without giving him 'a reasonable opportunity of putting his case to the competent authorities'.[53] In *Kadi II*, the ECJ confirmed that EU authorities—in order to

---

[48] According to (now) Art 6(3) TEU, '[f]undamental rights, as guaranteed by the European Convention for the Protection of Human Rights and Fundamental Freedoms and as they result from the constitutional traditions common to the Member States, shall constitute general principles of the Union's law'.

[49] Joined Cases C-402/05 P and C-415/05 P *Yassin Abdullah Kadi and Al Barakaat International Foundation v Council* [2008] ECR I-6351, paras 361ff. See also Case C-84/95 *Bosphorus* [1996] ECR I-3953, paras 22ff.

[50] Case C-295/03 P *Alessandrini and Others v Commission* [2005] ECR I-5673, para 86, with reference to further case law.

[51] Joined Cases C-584/10 P, C-593/10 P and C-595/10 P *Commission and Others v Kadi*, judgment of 18 July 2013, nyr, paras 106ff.

[52] Joined Cases C-402/05 P and C-415/05 P *Yassin Abdullah Kadi and Al Barakaat International Foundation v Council* [2008] ECR I-6351, paras 326. See also Joined Cases C-584/10 P, C-593/10 P and C-595/10 P *Commission and Others v Kadi* (n 51), para 97.

[53] Joined Cases C-402/05 P and C-415/05 P *Yassin Abdullah Kadi and Al Barakaat International Foundation v Council* (ibid), paras 367ff. See for a detailed review of EU legislation in the light of EU fundamental rights also Joined Cases C-584/10 P, C-593/10 P and C-595/10 P *Commission and Others v Kadi* (n 51), paras 97ff, 112.

justify measures constraining fundamental rights—had to disclose evidence relied on to the individual concerned, to assess the allegations made by the Sanctions Committee, and to establish that the reasons relied on are well founded.[54] While the ECJ admitted that 'overriding considerations to do with the security of the European Union or of its Member States or with the conduct of their international relations related information may preclude the disclosure of some information or some evidence to the person concerned', it held that 'the secrecy or confidentiality of that information or evidence [was] no valid objection' to its own judicial review in the interest of effective judicial protection.[55]

The question of the extent to which the ECJ takes, or should take account of the international dimension of contested EU conduct also arose in the context of international trade disputes and their consequences for individual traders. The EU's infringement of the law of the World Trade Organization (WTO) had triggered retaliation imposed by other WTO members, which allegedly damaged 'retaliation victims', who claimed compensation from the EU.[56] According to the ECJ, the political flexibility of the EU institutions on the international stage had to be maintained in the general EU interest, which could justify constraints of individual rights resulting from the consequences of international trade disputes.[57] Interestingly, the ECJ took no account of the fact that the general EU interest had been pursued through a continuous breach by the EU of international law—which had been identified by the Dispute Settlement Body of the WTO. This is remarkable given the EU's commitment to the rule of law.[58]

(ii) The External Dimension of EU Foreign Affairs

Turning to the external dimension of foreign affairs, there seems to have been no case in which the Court reviewed the legality of *EU* conduct on the international plane (such as the exercise of powers in international organisations, operational action, or the actual negotiation in the context of treaty-making or international disputes). At first sight, this might not be surprising, as the EU representative is meant to express views, or exercise powers in the international fora in a way that has previously been defined through the EU's internal mechanisms and comply with EU principles. It is thus primarily the underlying internal measure that might be subject to review where need be, or—once considered in compliance with EU

---

[54] Joined Cases C-584/10 P, C-593/10 P and C-595/10 P *Commission and Others v Kadi* (n 51) paras 111, 114, 119, 121, 163.

[55] ibid (n 51), para 125.

[56] See for a study of grounds for compensation relied on by retaliation victims and related case-law, A Thies, *International Trade Disputes and EU Liability* (Cambridge, Cambridge University Press, 2013).

[57] Cases C-120 and 121/06 *FIAMM* (n 32), para 186.

[58] See for more detailed discussion, also of the discretion granted under the WTO Dispute Settlement Understanding to accept retaliation while upholding a breach of WTO law, A Thies, 'EU Membership of the WTO: International Trade Disputes and Judicial Protection of Individuals by EU Courts' in T Isiksel and A Thies (eds), 'Changing Subjects: Rights, Remedies and Responsibilities of Individuals under Global Legal Pluralism' (2013) 2 *Global Constitutionalism* 237–61, 256.

principles—serve itself as a benchmark for subsequent action.[59] However, in the context of the implementation of external policies, the obligations to protect fundamental rights might become relevant in the future. For instance, individual rights might be affected by the EU's operational action in the context of the CFSP. It should be added, however, that the ECJ's jurisdiction under Article 275 TFEU is limited to the review of acts, which are subject to annulment actions,[60] and would not as such apply to (for example) an action for damages.[61]

(iii) Member States' External Action

Defining the obligations resulting from principles for the protection of individuals for Member States' (unilateral) external action remains more challenging. As stated above, Member States are in principle bound to comply with EU general principles when they implement or derogate from EU law.[62] The ECJ has also recognised Member States' obligations under EU general principles where contested Member State conduct was considered to fall within the 'scope of application' of EU law.[63] It does not seem to be entirely clear yet what implications this case law has for Member States' external action on the international stage, which fall within their retained exclusive or shared competence. Can EU Member States still act outside the scope of application of EU law when acting as separate entities of the international order on the basis of retained competence?

In *Centro-Com*, the ECJ held that Member States must exercise their retained competence 'in a manner consistent with [EU] law'.[64] The Court found 'that the Member States cannot treat national measures whose effect is to prevent or restrict the export of certain products as falling outside the scope of the common commercial policy on the ground that they have foreign and security objectives'.[65] While this might now be established case law with regard to the reach of EU law

[59] In Case C-25/94 *Commission v Council (FAO)* [1996] ECR I-1469, para 49, the ECJ considered the arrangement between the Council and the Commission regarding their participation and voting rights in the UN Food and Agriculture Organization (FAO) to represent 'fulfilment of [the] duty of cooperation between the Community and the Member States in the FAO', and 'that the two institutions intended to enter into a binding commitment towards each other'. The contested Council decision, which indicated to the FAO that the draft agreement fell within shared competence and that the Member States had the right to vote, was considered by the ECJ to be in breach of the arrangement.
[60] Art 263 TFEU.
[61] See for further discussion in this book, C Hillion, 'A Powerless Court? The European Court of Justice and the Common Foreign and Security Policy' (ch 4).
[62] See nn 37, 38.
[63] See n 39.
[64] Case C-124/95 *The Queen, ex p Centro-Com v HM Treasury and Bank of England* [1997] ECR I-81, para 25, with reference to Joined Cases 6/69 and 11/69 *Commission v France* [1969] ECR 523, para 17; Case 57/86 *Greece v Commission* [1988] ECR 2855, para 9; Case 127/87 *Commission v Greece* [1988] ECR 3333, para 7, and Case C-221/89 *Factortame and Others* [1991] ECR I-3905, para 14. All of these cases concerned the Member States' obligation to comply with Treaty obligations.
[65] Case C-124/95 *The Queen, ex parte Centro-Com v HM Treasury and Bank of England* (n 64), para 26.

in particular policy areas covered by Treaty provisions, the reach of fundamental rights in the form of general principles remains more controversial. Even though the ECJ has ruled on the Member States' obligation to comply with the principle of non-discrimination between EU nationals when concluding international agreements, it is pointed out here that the invoked principle had been codified in the EU Treaty as part of the EU law on the freedom of establishment.[66] The Member States' external action therefore fell within the application of EU law on that basis.

Given the capacity of fundamental rights obligations to constrain Member States' scope for manoeuvre, the reach of those rights has been limited explicitly in the Charter of Fundamental Rights to when the Member States 'are implementing Union law'.[67] To extend the reach of fundamental rights and the ECJ's jurisdiction to review *any* Member State conduct on the international stage, would risk contradicting this provision. The implications of EU general principles will thus have to be assessed on a case-by-case basis where contested Member State external conduct can be linked to the scope of application of EU law.[68] Where such link cannot be established, the standards and enforcement of rights will continue to be defined by the national legal orders, the European Convention for the Protection of Human Rights and Fundamental Freedoms (ECHR), and the case law of the European Court of Human Rights. Yet, the actual constraints imposed on Member States in the interest of the protection of rights should in substance be comparable to those that could be enforced on the basis of EU general principles and the Charter, which find their origin in the national legal orders and the ECHR.[69]

C. The Principle of Effectiveness, Loyalty Obligations and Unity in International Representation

As mentioned in the introduction, the ECJ has also developed organisational principles that have provided a legal framework for both the relations between different EU institutions and those between the EU and its Member States as separate entities within and outside the EU legal framework.[70] In the light of recent case law, this section focuses on the ECJ's application of the principles of effectiveness and sincere cooperation, and their judicial adaptation in the context of external relations law. It

---

[66] Case C-476/98 *Commission v Germany* (*Open Skies Agreement*) [2002] ECR I- 9855, paras 144ff, para 153 (non-discrimination principle/freedom of establishment).

[67] According to Art 51(1) of the Charter, '[the provisions of this Charter are addressed to the institutions and bodies of the Union with due regard for the principle of subsidiarity and to the *Member States only when they are implementing Union law*. They shall therefore respect the rights, observe the principles and promote the application thereof in accordance with their respective powers' (emphasis added).

[68] See examples in nn 64–66.

[69] See for the claim that the ECJ makes selective use of the case law of the ECtHR, Bruno de Witte's contribution to this book, n 1 (ch 3), with reference to B de Witte, 'The Use of the ECHR and Convention Case Law by the European Court of Justice' in P Popelier, C Van de Heyning and P Van Nuffel (eds), *Human Rights Protection in the European Legal Order: The Interaction between the European and the National Courts* (Antwerp, Intersentia, 2011) 17.

[70] See n 4.

begins with (i) outlining the meaning of the principle of effectiveness for the overall process of European integration by highlighting some related legal obligations imposed on the EU Member States in the *internal* EU legal order.[71] Subsequently, the discussion (ii) turns to the reach of the principles of effectiveness and sincere cooperation in external action, introducing the Court's approach towards Member States' obligations under Article 4(3) TEU[72] to refrain from unilateral external action and what it called for the first time 'principle of unity in the international representation of the Union and its Member States'.[73] It is argued that the precise scope of these principles in the context of external action continues to constitute a particular constitutional challenge for the ECJ, as they affect significantly the Member States' scope for manoeuvre as distinct subjects of the *international* legal order.

(i) The Effectiveness of EU law: Member States' Obligations in the Internal EU Legal Order

The principle of effectiveness of EU law has been recognised by the ECJ since the early days of European integration.[74] Scholars have analysed the principle's implications for EU Member States, often focusing on correlating obligations imposed on national courts[75]—including the provision of remedies for individuals[76]—and on the national administration[77] in the interest of the effectiveness of EU law.

---

[71] See for a detailed discussion of the ECJ's formula relating to the applicability of EU law where States exercise retained powers, L Azoulai, 'The "Retained Powers" Formula in the Case Law of the European Court of Justice: EU Law as Total Law?' 4 *European Journal of Legal Studies* (2011) 192–219.

[72] Art 4(3) TEU states that '[p]ursuant to the principle of sincere cooperation, the Union and the Member States shall, in full mutual respect, assist each other in carrying out tasks which flow from the Treaties. The Member States shall take any appropriate measure, general or particular, to ensure fulfilment of the obligations arising out of the Treaties or resulting from the acts of the institutions of the Union. The Member States shall facilitate the achievement of the Union's tasks and refrain from any measure which could jeopardise the attainment of the Union's objectives'.

[73] Case C-246/07 *Commission v Sweden* (*PFOS*) [2010] ECR I-3317, para 104.

[74] See already Case 26/62 *Van Gend en Loos* [1963] ECR 3, at 13, where the Court refers to the 'effective supervision' (of EU law) by individuals (in addition to the Commission and the Member States) before confirming direct effect of Treaty provisions. Joined Cases C-46 and C-48/93 *Brasserie de Pêcheur* and *Factortame Ltd* [1996] ECR I-1029, para 95; see recently eg: Case C-565/11 *Mariana Irimie*, judgment of 18 April 2013, nyr, para 26; Case C-191/12, *Alakor Gabonatermelő*, judgment of 16 May 2013, nyr, para 27; already in 1978, the Court had referred to the 'effectiveness of obligations undertaken unconditionally and irrevocably by member states pursuant to the treaty' reflecting 'the very foundations of the Community' when recognising a national court's obligation to set aside national law conflicting with (now) EU law, see Case 106/77 *Simmenthal* [1978] ECR 629, paras 18, 20, 22–23.

[75] A Biondi, 'The European Court of Justice and Certain National Procedural Limitations: Not such a Tough Relationship' (1999) 36 *CML Rev* 1271–87, 1277ff; M Ross, 'Effectiveness in the European Legal Order(s): Beyond Supremacy to Constitutional Proportionality?' (2006) 31 *EL Rev* 476–98, 477.

[76] J Lonbay and A Biondi (eds), *Remedies for Breach of EC law* (Chichester, Wiley & Sons, 1997); T Tridimas, 'Enforcing Community Rights in National Courts: Some recent Developments' in DA O'Keeffe and A Bavasso (eds), *Judicial Review in European Union Law: Liber Amicorum in Honour of Lord Slynn* (Alphen aan den Rijn, Kluwer, 2000), 465–79.

[77] C Harlow, 'Codification of EC Administrative Procedures? Fitting the Foot to the Show or the Shoe to the Foot' (1996) 2 *European Law Journal* 3–25.

Effectiveness has been considered to be 'emerging as the driver of constitutional evolution'.[78] The nature of effectiveness as well as the '[EU] legal and institutional preconditions [of the effectiveness of EU law]'[79] in the context of European integration have been analysed, and the principle of effectiveness' 'role as a guarantee for the functioning and coherence of the [internal] Community legal order [has been conceptualised]'.[80] While the principle resulted in Member State obligations that could sometimes be enforced before national courts,[81] the task of ensuring the overall effectiveness of EU law has been seen to lie primarily with the European Commission and the ECJ.[82]

(ii) EU Effectiveness on the International Stage?

In recent years, the EU's role, standing and impact as a global actor has increasingly become the focus of scholarly attention.[83] The Lisbon Treaty has fostered the EU's visibility and importance as a global actor, and the international community and media continue to formulate expectations regarding its responsibilities in the light of global challenges and crises. The notion of 'effectiveness' in the context of foreign affairs has been endorsed by the Member States in the EU treaties, applied by the ECJ's Advocates General, and analysed by scholars from different disciplines through a variety of lenses such as: the EU's external policy-making and 'outputs',[84] the exercise of Union competence,[85] the role and impact of newly

---

[78] Ross, 'Effectiveness in the European Legal Order(s)' (n 75) 477.

[79] F Snyder, 'The Effectiveness of European Community Law: Institutions, Processes, Tools and Techniques' (1993) 56 *MLR* 19–54.

[80] M Accetto and S Zleptnig, 'The Principle of Effectiveness: Rethinking Its Role in Community Law' (2005) 11 *European Public Law* 375–403.

[81] See eg F Jacobs, 'Enforcing Community Rights and Obligations in National Courts: Striking the Balance' in Lonbay and Biondi (eds), *Remedies for Breach of EC Law* (n 76) 25–36.

[82] Snyder, 'The Effectiveness of European Community Law' (n 79).

[83] C Bretherton and J Vogler, *The European Union as Global Actor* 2nd edn (Abingdon, Routledge, 2006); M Cremona, 'The Union as a Global Actor: Roles, Models and Identity' (2004) 41 *CML Rev* 553–73, C Hill and M Smith (eds), *International Relations and the European Union* 2nd edn (Oxford, Oxford University Press, 2011); P Koutrakos, *EU International Relations Law* (Oxford, Hart Publishing, 2006); E Cannizzaro (ed), *The European Union as an Actor in International Relations* (Alphen aan den Rijn, Kluwer, 2002).

[84] Art 13(1) TEU (institutional framework that, inter alia, ensures consistency, effectiveness and continuity of its policies and actions); Art 24(3) TEU (Member States 'shall refrain from any action which is contrary to the interests of the Union or likely to impair its effectiveness as a cohesive force in international relations'); Art 26(2) subparagraph 2 TEU (obligation on Council and the High Representative to ensure the unity, consistency and effectiveness of (external) action by the Union); Art 28(5) TEU (implementation should not interfere with the effectiveness of decisions on operational action); Art 45(1) TEU (effectiveness of military expenditure); Protocol (No 23) on external relations of the Member States with regard to the crossing of external borders (effectiveness of external border controls); L Aggestam, 'Introduction: Ethical Power Europe?' (2008) 84 *International Affairs* 1–11. See also KE Smith, 'The EU in the World: Future Research Agendas', LSE European Foreign Policy Unit Working Paper 2008/1, 23.

[85] Case C-246/07 *Commission v Sweden (PFOS)* (n 73), Opinion of Advocate General Maduro, para 38.

introduced institutions, such as the External Action Service,[86] the upholding and promotion of EU values 'in its relations with the wider world',[87] the achieving of the EU treaties' objectives,[88] and the 'broader influence in the international system',[89] including the international representation of the EU and its Member States' interests in international organisations.[90] While the quest for 'effectiveness' brings to mind prior developments of European integration, the ECJ has not yet fully accommodated the particular characteristics of the 'system of external action', in which Member States and the EU institutions continue to co-exist, and which supposedly enables the EU institutions to exercise their role effectively while respecting Member States sovereignty.[91] How does a bigger role for the EU relate to its Member States' powers as subject of the international (legal) order? What is, or could be the constitutional basis for the ECJ to acknowledge Member State obligations in the interest of 'EU effectiveness' in the context of foreign affairs? To what extent can the established principle of the effectiveness of *EU law* be of use where the EU's international role and impact is measured in the light of the successful adoption of common positions, efficient negotiation processes, representation of EU interests and objectives, or the improvement of multilateral

---

[86]   R Balfour and H Ojanen, 'Does the European External Action Service Represent a Model for the Challenges of Global Diplomacy?', 1117 IAI Working Papers (2011); M Emerson et al, *Upgrading the EU's Role as Global Actor: Institutions, Law and the Restructuring of European Diplomacy* (Brussels, Centre for European Policy Studies, 2011); L Erkelens and S Blockmans, 'Setting up the European External Action Service: An Institutional Act of Balance', CLEER Working Papers 2012/1; S Vanhoonacker and K Pomorska, 'The European External Action Service and Agenda-setting in European Foreign Policy' (2013) 20 *Journal of European Public Policy* 1332, DOI: 10.1080/13501763.2012.758446.

[87]   Arts and 3(5) TEU; see with regard to, inter alia, the processes 'through which values are both imported and exported from the EU legal order', M Cremona, 'Values in EU Foreign Policy' in P Koutrakos and M Shaw (eds), *Beyond the Established Orders—Policy Interconnections between the EU and the Rest of the World* (Oxford, Hart Publishing, 2011) 275–315, 313.

[88]   KE Smith, *European Union Foreign Policy in a Changing World* 2nd edn (Polity Press, Cambridge 2008) 237; M Cremona, 'Defining Competence in EU External Relations: Lessons from the Treaty Reform Process' in A Dashwood and M Maresceau (eds), *Law and Practice of EU External Relations* (Cambridge, Cambridge University Press, 2008) 34–69, 51ff (with reference to Opinion 1/03 on the Competence of the Community to conclude the new Lugano Convention on jurisdiction and the recognition and enforcement of judgments in civil and commercial matter [2006] ECR I-1145, and implied powers).

[89]   Smith, 'The EU in the World: Future Research Agendas' (n 84) 10, with reference to C Hill and M Smith, 'Acting for Europe: Reassessing the European Union's Place in International Relations' in C Hill and M Smith (eds), *International Relations and the European Union* (Oxford, Oxford University Press, 2005) 404–46.

[90]   With regard to negotiations in the context of the WTO, see eg: Case C-13/07 *Commission v Council* (*Vietnam Accession to the WTO*), nyr, Opinion of Advocate General Kokott of 26 March 2009, para 72; on the EU's influence at the UN on human rights issues, see eg: KE Smith 'Speaking with One Voice? European Union Co-ordination on Human Rights Issues at the United Nations' (2006) 44 *Journal of Common Market Studies* 113–37; see also D Mahnke and S Gstöhl (eds), *European Union Diplomacy—Coherence, Unity and Effectiveness* (Berne, Peter Lang, 2012).

[91]   JHH Weiler, 'The External Legal Relations of Non-Unitary Actors: Mixity and the Federal Principle' in JHH Weiler, *The Constitution of Europe* (Cambridge, Cambridge University Press, 1999) 130–87; RA Wessel, 'The Multilevel Constitution of European Foreign Relations' in N Tsagourias (ed), *Transnational Constitutionalism: International and European Perspectives* (Cambridge, Cambridge University Press, 2007) 160–206.

systems? Can other EU principles serve to increase the EU's effectiveness, and/ or limit the Member States' individual scope for manoeuvre on the international stage? How can the EU's interest in speaking with one voice be balanced with the Member States' sovereign interests? How can the EU constitutional framework at the intersection of supranational and intergovernmental mechanisms be made functional and sustainable?

It would go beyond the scope of this chapter to deal with all of these questions. What is important for the present chapter, however, is that the ECJ has already employed EU principles in order to acknowledge or substantiate far-reaching legal constraints on the Member States in the context of mixed external action. It is claimed here that in particular in its recent decision in the *PFOS* case, brought by the Commission against Sweden, the ECJ further developed the reach of EU principles in the interest of an overall EU effectiveness on the international stage.[92] Sweden was considered to be in breach of its EU law obligations for taking unilateral external action in the context of the Stockholm Convention, despite in principle having retained competence to act in the area of environmental policy.[93] Even though the ECJ did not refer explicitly to the need to ensure the EU's 'effectiveness', effectiveness considerations seem to have been underlying the Court's conclusions on the Member State's loyalty obligations under Article 4(3) TEU[94] and its reference to the principle of unity in international representation as well as the EU's negotiating power on the international stage.[95] How does the ECJ's approach to the reach of Article 4(3) TEU relate to the principle of effectiveness of EU law? And, how does the 'principle of unity' relate to the ECJ's case law on the principle of effectiveness and/or other EU principles?

---

[92] Case C-246/07 *Commission v Sweden* (*PFOS*) (n 73).

[93] See for analysis of the case eg Cremona, Case Comment on C-246/07 *Commission v Sweden* (*PFOS*) (n 10); G De Baere, "'O, Where is Faith? O, Where is Loyalty?" Some Thoughts on the Duty of Loyal Co-operation and the Union's External Environmental Competences in the Light of the PFOS Case' (2012) 36 *EL Rev* 405–19; A Thies, 'The *PFOS* Decision of the ECJ: The Member States' Obligation to Refrain from Unilateral Action in Areas of Shared Competence' in J Díez-Hochleitner, C Martínez Capdevila and I Blázquez Navarro (eds), *Recent Trends in the Case Law of the Court of Justice of the EU (2008–2011)* (Madrid, La Ley, 2012) 703–728; A Thies, 'Le devoir de coopération loyale dans le cadre de l'action extérieure' in E Neframi (ed), *Objectifs & compétences dans l'Union européenne* (Brussels, Bruylant, 2012) 315–40.

[94] See n 72.

[95] Case C-246/07 *Commission v Sweden* (*PFOS*) (n 73), para 104: 'Such a situation is likely to compromise the principle of unity in the international representation of the Union and its Member States and weaken their negotiating power with regard to the other parties to the Convention concerned'. Casolari refers in this context to a 'strengthening [of] the external representation of the [EU]' as the ECJ's notion of 'loyalty' is 'essentially represented by negative obligations imposed upon Member States, which prevent them from acting if their action risks undermining the capacity of the EU as an international actor', see F Casolari, 'The Principle of Loyal Co-operation: A "Master Key" for EU external representation?' in S Blockmans and RA Wessels (eds), *Principles and Practices of EU External Representation*, CLEER Working Papers 2012/5, at www.asser.nl/upload/documents/20120911T102448-cleer2012-5book_web.pdf, 11–36, 19.

As outlined above, the principle of effectiveness has been the basis for a variety of different Member State obligations.[96] The ECJ has recognised the principles of supremacy and direct effect on the basis of what is now Article 4(3) TEU in order to ensure the effectiveness of the European legal order.[97] By doing so, the Court has emphasised the need 'to ensure fulfilment' of Treaty obligations.[98] Also in the context of external relations law, the ECJ has referred to Article 4(3) TEU when establishing Member States' obligations resulting from the EU's 'concerted action' initiated by a legally binding Council decision.[99] Interestingly, however, in the *PFOS* case the ECJ based Sweden's obligation to refrain from unilateral action on a 'strategy, which although not a formally adopted decision may—as in this case—nonetheless carry implications for the Member States'.[100] The additional reference of the Court to what it then called for the first time 'the *principle* of unity in the international representation of the Union and its Member States' (emphasis added)[101] has raised questions concerning the legal foundation and nature of such principle as well as its implications for Member States' international scope for manoeuvre in areas of shared competence. A requirement of 'unity' does not exist in the *internal* EU legal order. Member States might be pre-empted from exercising shared competence once the EU has done so,[102] and they can be overruled in the context of established voting mechanisms.[103] However, Member

---

[96] See nn 74ff.
[97] Case 26/62 *Van Gend en Loos* (n 74); Case 6/64 *Costa v Enel* [1964] ECR 585. See for further discussion, J Temple Lang, 'The Most Important "General Principle" of Community Law' in U Bernitz, J Nergelius and C Cardner (eds), *General Principles of EC Law in a Process of Development* (Alphen aan den Rijn, Kluwer, 2008) 75–113, 76.
[98] Art 4(3) subparagraph 2 TEU. See also de Witte, 'Institutional Principles in Judicial Development of the EU Legal Order' (n 6) 88.
[99] According to Art 4(3) TEU, Member States need to comply with Treaty obligations as well as obligations from institutional acts (eg legally binding instruments under Art 288 TFEU and implemented international agreements, Art 216(2) TFEU). See for Council decision authorising the Commission to negotiate international treaty, eg: Case C-433/03 *Commission v Germany* [2005] ECR I-6985, para 66; Case C-266/03 *Commission v Luxembourg* [2005] ECR I-4805, para 60.
[100] Cremona, Case Comment on Case C-246/07 *Commission v Sweden* (PFOS) (n 10) 1640. See Case C-246/07 *Commission v Sweden* (PFOS) (n 73), paras 77ff, 89ff.
[101] Case C-246/07 *Commission v Sweden* (PFOS) (ibid) (n 73), para 104; see also para 73 (with reference to prior decisions, in which the Court referred not to the 'principle' but to the 'requirement' of unity in the international representation of the Community. Also in the context of mixed agreements, the Court had stressed already in Case C-25/94 *Commission v Council* (FAO) (n 59), para 48, that it was essential to ensure close cooperation between the institutions and the Member States, both in the process of negotiation and conclusion and in the fulfilment of the commitments entered into; according to the Court 'that obligation to cooperate flows from the requirement of unity in the international representation of the Community' (with reference to Ruling 1/78 [1978] ECR 2151, paras 34–36, Opinion 2/91 on the conclusion of Convention N° 170 of the International Labour Organization concerning safety in the use of chemicals at work [1993] ECR I-1061, para 36, and Opinion 1/94 on the Competence of the Community to conclude international agreements concerning services and the protection of intellectual property [1994] ECR I-5267, para 108.
[102] See Schütze, 'Supremacy without Pre-emption?' (n 20).
[103] See for a definition of a qualified majority, Art 16(3) and (4) TEU and Art 238 TFEU.

States cannot be required to 'remain silent'[104] in the *internal* EU decision-making process, in which they participate as equal members with regard to both internal and external policy. So where does the principle of unity come from, and/or what is its constitutional basis?

As argued elsewhere, further judicial reasoning would have been useful to bring more clarity with regard to the question of whether 'the principle of unity' can be considered a new principle of EU law that ensures the effectiveness of EU 'institutional acts' (Article 4(3) subparagraph 2 TEU)—and thus constitutes a further dimension of the principle of effectiveness of EU law—or a self-standing EU objective, the attainment of which Member States should not 'jeopardise' (Article 4(3) subparagraph 3 TEU).[105] It seems difficult to acknowledge an overall obligation of Member States to adapt their external action to what the EU institutions do, or intend to do, merely on the basis of unity, without providing further justification for the existence of such principle of unity and its interrelationship with the allocation of competence.[106] It seems more convincing to establish a clearer set of criteria, according to which EU institutional acts can have constraining implications for the Member States' international scope of manoeuvre in areas of shared competence.

The ECJ focused in its reasoning in *PFOS* on the existence of an 'EU strategy' at the time that Sweden had taken unilateral action.[107] It is suggested here that the Court has thus further developed the EU principle of effectiveness in that it has recognised an EU strategy as EU institutional action, with which Member States should not interfere. The respect for such strategy/institutional action was thus required to ensure the effectiveness of the EU legal order. This is confirmed also by the Court's reference to the consequences that Sweden's action could have for the EU through the 'adoption of international legal rules', which are binding on all parties to the Convention.[108] It is because of the implications of Sweden's unilateral action on the legal order of the EU that Sweden needs to refrain from such action. To put it differently, the ECJ seems to consider crucial that the EU law-making activities envisaged under the EU strategy (including the envisaged

---

[104] A Delgado Casteleiro and J Larik, 'The Duty to Remain Silent: Limitless Loyalty in EU External Relations?' (2011) 36 *EL Rev* 524–41.

[105] Thies, 'The *PFOS* Decision of the ECJ' (n 93) 703–28, 721ff.

[106] In his Opinion of 1 October 2009 in Case C-246/07,*Commission v Sweden* (*PFOS*) (n 73), para 37, Advocate General Maduro considered the unity of international representation of the (then) European Community and its Member States not to have 'an independent value' but 'merely an expression of the duty of loyal cooperation under [then] Article 10 EC'; he stated that '[t]he question whether such unity is required by the duty of loyal cooperation can be resolved only by analysing the obligations laid down in a specific agreement'. See, however, E Neframi, 'The Duty of Loyalty: Rethinking its Scope through its Application in the Field of EU External Relations' (2010) 47 *CML Rev* 323–59, 353f, who considered the (then-called) *requirement* of unity to be an autonomous external action objective, which is 'not an explicitly provided objective, but one deriving from the objective of the assertion of the EU identity on the international scene', which could be jeopardised by unilateral and diverging international action of the EU and the Member States.

[107] See n 100.

[108] Case C-246/07 *Commission v Sweden* (*PFOS*) (n 73), paras 100ff.

sequence of domestic and external law-making activities in the field)[109] will be
'effective', and that this would not be guaranteed, if a Member State's unilateral
action creates legally binding obligations also for the EU that conflict with the
EU's own law-making activities. Even though the ECJ recognised that Sweden
had retained in principle shared competence in the field of environment,[110] its
reasoning arguably resonates with the principle of pre-emption,[111] as the EU's
capacity to adopt law in the future is protected. It is claimed here, however, that
the basis for Sweden's obligations under Article 4 (3) TEU was the existing legislative *strategy* and not particular legislation to be adopted in the foreseeable future.

For reasons of completeness it should be added that not only the Member
States but also the EU is requested to 'assist [the Member States] in carrying out
tasks which flow from the Treaties' (see Article 4(3) subparagraph 1 TEU). As
suggested by Casolari, 'the duty of loyalty and the good faith principle impose
over the EU institutions an obligation to interpret EU secondary law in the light
of the wording and purpose of the Member States' international engagements
they implement',[112] which the ECJ has recognised in *Intertanko*.[113] Yet, it should
be noted that the reach of this suggestion is limited to scenarios in which the
EU is implementing Member State obligations but the field is not one for which
competence has been fully transferred to the EU.[114] In *Commission v Greece*, the
ECJ recognised that loyalty obligations might arise for the EU institutions under
what is now Article 4(3) TEU, but that an infringement of those obligations would
not authorise Member States to take 'corrective or protective measures designed
to obviate' such infringement.[115]

It remains to be seen how the ECJ is going to develop inter-institutional loyalty
obligations, which it has recognised in principle when referring to an 'inter-
institutional dialogue' that is subject to 'mutual duties of sincere cooperation'.[116]
In the *PNR* case,[117] this issue was raised: The Council had concluded an agreement with the US on passenger name records of air passengers even though the
European Parliament had already asked for a Court Opinion on the compatibility
of the agreement with the EU Treaties.[118] The European Parliament brought an

[109] On the choice of law-making venues, see B de Witte and A Thies, 'Why Choose Europe? The
Place of the European Union in the Architecture of International Legal Cooperation' in S Blockmans,
B Van Vooren and J Wouters (eds), *The Legal Dimension of Global Governance: What Role for the EU?*
(Oxford, Oxford University Press, 2013) 23–38.

[110] Case C-246/07 *Commission v Sweden (PFOS)* (n 73), para 72.

[111] See Schütze, 'Supremacy without Pre-emption?' (n 20).

[112] Casolari, 'The Principle of Loyal Co-operation' (n 95) 11–36, 31.

[113] Case C-308/06 *The Queen, on the application of International Association of Independent Tanker
Owners (Intertanko) and Others v Secretary of State for Transport* [2008] ECR I-4057, paras 50, 52.

[114] See for an example above at n 44ff regarding the EU legislation implementing Member State UN
obligations under the UN sanctions regime.

[115] Case C-45/07 *Commission v Greece* [2009] ECR I-701, paras 25, 26.

[116] Case 204/86 *Greece v Council* [1988] ECR 5323, para 16; Case C-65/93 *Parliament v Council*
[1995] ECR I-643, para 23.

[117] Case C-317/04 *Parliament v Council (PNR)* [2006] ECR I-4721.

[118] Art 218(11) TFEU.

action against the Council, relying, inter alia, on the 'principle of cooperation in good faith'.[119] The Advocate General argued that the Council's conclusion of the agreement was not a breach of the principle of loyal cooperation on the ground that the Opinion procedure does not have suspensory effect and is not designed to defend the institutions' prerogatives.[120] However, the ECJ did not need to address the principle in its decision after having annulled the decision for a lack of legal base.[121] In 2012, the Commission brought an action against the Council before the ECJ, in which it has challenged a Council Decision on the signing, on behalf of the Union, of agreements relating to air transport. The Commission has claimed, inter alia, that 'the Council [by co-signing a Decision together with Member State Representatives] infringed the objectives set out in the Treaties and the principle of sincere cooperation laid down in Article 13 (2) TEU.[122] The Council—it argues—should have exercised its powers so as not to circumvent the institutional framework of the Union and the Union procedures set out in Article 218 TFEU and should have done so in conformity with the objectives set out in the Treaties.'[123] This case is still pending.

III. CONSTITUTIONAL CHALLENGES AND CONCLUDING REMARKS

While other contributions to this book have evaluated the ECJ's approach towards the accommodation of EU institutions' *political* agenda and scope for manoeuvre in the context of external relations,[124] this chapter has analysed the Court's approach towards the implications of established EU *legal* principles in the context of foreign affairs for both the EU Member States and the EU as a whole. The chapter has thereby focused on EU law principles that had previously been developed in the context of the internal EU legal order: the principle of direct effect, EU fundamental rights and the principle of effectiveness. These EU principles were recognised or established by the ECJ in the interest of the effectiveness of EU law, the autonomy of the EU legal order—comprising not only states but also individuals—and the functioning of the internal market. However, the context of foreign affairs has required the ECJ to accommodate the international (legal) context of external action and interaction of the EU and its Member States on the international plane. At the same time, the ECJ has increasingly been asked to define the reach of principles for the protection of individuals against the background of

---

[119] Case C-317/04 *Parliament v Council (PNR)* (n 117), para 62.

[120] ibid (n 117), paras 277ff.

[121] ibid (n 117), para 70.

[122] According to Art 13(2) TEU, '[e]ach institution shall act within the limits of the powers conferred on it in the Treaties, and in conformity with the procedures, conditions and objectives set out in them. The institutions shall practice mutual sincere cooperation'.

[123] Case C-28/12 *European Commission v Council*, action brought on 18 January 2012, [2012] OJ C73/23.

[124] M Cremona, 'A Reticent Court? Policy Objectives and the Court of Justice' (ch 2).

political objectives pursued on the international plane when assessing the lawfulness of EU or Member State external conduct. This has raised constitutional questions regarding the extent to which international political interests, international legal obligations, or the interest in political flexibility and international scope for manoeuvre can justify the restrictions of individual rights protected by EU law. Distinguishing between interpretative, benchmark and organisational principles, this chapter has provided some examples of how the ECJ has so far managed to accommodate the special nature of EU and its Member States' foreign affairs in its case law on the applicability and scope of general principles without reinventing its judicial techniques.

When dealing with the EU interpretative principle of direct effect to determine the implications of the EU's international treaty obligations, the ECJ has taken account of the legal context in which international treaties are concluded—including the intention and degree of discretion of contracting parties to create rights and obligations for themselves rather than creating enforceable rights for individuals—as well as the actual content and addressees of the legal obligations.[125] The ECJ has thus linked the principle of direct effect closely to the degree of political discretion enjoyed by the EU as subject of the international legal order as well as the Court's own role as constitutional court of the EU and respect for the EU institutions' scope for manoeuvre. Whereas the Court could relate the principle of direct effect in internal matters to the effectiveness of EU law and the overall EU legal order, the Court has been more reluctant to interfere with the EU's executive powers exercised on the international stage by acknowledging direct effect of international law.[126]

The ECJ has confirmed the applicability of EU general principles as a benchmark for lawful—at least from an EU law perspective—EU external action, while acknowledging that the international dimension of contested EU conduct can justify restrictions of fundamental rights and/or the scope of judicial control. The Court has thereby recognised the particular nature of international law as well as the international legal context of external action as shaping the scope of general principles and the Court's own judicial review.[127] EU fundamental rights in the form of general principles also serve as a benchmark for the lawfulness of EU Member State external conduct, as long as such conduct falls within the scope of application of EU law.[128]

While the ECJ seems to have found a functioning formula regarding the principle of direct effect of international law and has started to accommodate the international context in its fundamental rights jurisprudence, the reach and adaptation of EU organisational principles in the context of external relations law would benefit from further judicial clarification. The ECJ's recent application

---

[125] See discussion at nn 29ff.
[126] See also M Cremona and PJ Kuijper's contributions to this book.
[127] See discussion at nn 48ff.
[128] See discussion at nn 62ff.

of the principle of loyalty in its *PFOS* decision has caused criticism regarding its far-reaching consequences for the Member States' international scope for manoeuvre on the international stage.[129] It has been suggested here, however, that the ECJ has not actually added a new EU law principle by referring to the 'principle of unity in international representation of the EU' but has further developed the principle of effectiveness in the light of an existing EU strategy regarding external action that Member States should not interfere with through unilateral action.[130]

The last part of this chapter outlines some (further) systemic challenges that the ECJ faces when contributing to the legal framework for the EU and its Member States' foreign affairs.[131] More specifically, it highlights the limits to the ECJ's capacity to further develop EU principles shaping the scope for manoeuvre and interaction of the EU and its Member States on the international plane. For this purpose, it takes as a starting point the ECJ's jurisdictional basis and the legal/judicial context, in which the ECJ has established and developed EU principles for the internal legal order. At the same time, it identifies additional challenges posed by the international (legal) context of EU foreign affairs.

First, the process of legal integration in the context of external action is not embedded in a recognised framework of Treaty objectives in the same way as the process of legal integration has been with regard to the internal market.[132] The EU Member States' focus might be shifting from the functioning of the internal market to the role and impact of the EU in the world, but current political struggles and disagreements (eg as manifested in the context of the establishment of the External Action Service) indicate that this is not an easy process. While the ECJ referred to the effectiveness of the autonomous EU legal order in order to develop principles such as the principles of supremacy and direct effect (ie justifying the need for the full effect of EU law and its prevailing nature in the interest of the creation and functioning of the internal market),[133] it seems more difficult to

---

[129] See eg: Delgado Casteleiro and J Larik, 'The Duty to Remain Silent' (n 104); J Heliskoski, 'The Obligation of Member States to Foresee, in the Conclusion and Application of their International Agreements, Eventual Future Measures of the European Union' in A Arnull, C Barnard, M Dougan and E Spaventa (eds), *A Constitutional Order of States? Essays in EU Law in Honour of Alan Dashwood* (Oxford, Hart Publishing, 2011), 545–64, 561, 562; see also P Eeckhout, *EU External Relations Law* 2nd edn (Oxford, Oxford University Press, 2011) 254, who has questioned whether the Court could not have analysed *PFOS* within the paradigm of *AETR*-type exclusive implied powers rather than loyalty obligations.

[130] See discussion above at nn 107ff.

[131] For a recent detailed study of the legal restraints to the ECJ's judicial lawmaking in general, see T Horsley, 'Reflections on the Role of the Court of Justice of the European Union as the Motor of European Integration: Legal Limits to Judicial Lawmaking' (2013) 50 *CML Rev* 931–64.

[132] See M Cremona in this book, who refers to the treaties' 'progressive objectives which help to define a policy direction or strategy, rather than end-goals'.

[133] Case 26/62, *Van Gend en Loos* (n 3); Case 6/64, *Costa v Enel* (n 3). See for further discussion, J Temple Lang, 'The Most Important "General Principle" of Community Law' in U Bernitz, J Nergelius and C Cardner (eds), *General Principles of EC Law in a Process of Development* (Alphen aan den Rijn, Kluwer, 2008) 75–113, 76.

identify a point of reference for the ECJ's recognition of principles that shape the EU as a global actor, beyond a clearly expressed transfer of powers by the Member States under the EU treaties.

The second challenge concerns the implications of other sources of law for the recognition of EU principles. When developing general principles within the domestic EU context, the ECJ has referred to, for example, international human right treaties and the common traditions of the Member States (ie introducing a benchmark for EU action which already existed for the Member States). This technique can also be applied in the context of external relations law where national and international law possibly contain rules concerning the interaction between states and other actors of the international legal order. For example, national law and practice of the EU Member States as well as public international law could serve as a source of inspiration for the ECJ to develop EU rules on diplomatic exchange, coordination and cooperation. What makes the introduction, application, reach and enforceability of EU principles more difficult in the context of foreign affairs, however, is that interaction and law-making on the international stage involve non-EU actors, which might not be willing to accept organisational principles stemming from the EU courts that affect their existing or future links with individual EU Member States and the EU.

A third challenge for the development of general principles in the context of external relations law is the fact that the ECJ's jurisdiction is limited with regard to matters of CFSP.[134] Yet, as argued above, the lack of judicial control does not modify the scope of application of EU general principles. Moreover, it is in the exceptional cases that the ECJ exercises jurisdiction that general principles seem to be most relevant: (a) where EU conduct restricts individuals; and (b) where a case is about the delimitation of competences. The ECJ will therefore continue to shape the scope of general principles for the protection of individuals also in the context of CFSP, as well as further define the existence and exercise of competences, not least because in practice EU and Member States' action on the international plane might need to address both CFSP and non-CFSP matters in combined action. It is claimed here that despite the ECJ's limited jurisdiction in CFSP matters, the Court will need to do justice to its role as EU constitutional court by contributing to the establishment of a sustainable legal framework for the EU and its Member States action, and interaction with non-EU states on the international plane. In order to do so successfully, the Court will need to apply legal parameters that go beyond the mere protection of the EU's autonomous legal order in the field of EU external relations law.[135]

---

[134] See n 43. See for further discussion in this book, C Hillion, 'A Powerless Court? The European Court of Justice and the Common Foreign and Security Policy' (ch 4).

[135] See for a discussion of the 'mutual non-affection clause' under Art 40 TEU and its implications for existing case law and rules on the delimitation of competences, Van Elsuwege, 'EU External Action After the Collapse of the Pillar Structure' (n 10) 1002ff. See for a discussion of the scope of 'principled parallelism between the constitutional regime for external and internal policies', D Thym, 'Foreign

Fourthly, the process of legal integration in the context of external relations law is different from the internal EU law context also for its lack of judicial dialogue. Even though the ECJ might have established EU principles in the first place, the EU Member States' national courts' recognition and application of constitutional EU law principles, such as the principle of supremacy, has been crucial for the crystallisation, development and reach of such principles.[136] The context of external relations law provides far less scope for judicial dialogue between the ECJ and national courts. It is unlikely that actions will be brought before national courts that concern the existence or exercise of external competence, or other rules concerning the interplay between the EU institutions and the Member States.

The ECJ therefore remains the main constitutional court dealing with issues of the EU's role as a global actor, its interrelationship with the Member States in this respect, and the reach of principles for the protection of individuals in the context of EU and—at least to some extent—its Member States' foreign affairs. This constitutes a particular challenge, given the Member States' sensitivity regarding external relations and activities, which they emphasised again in the context of the Lisbon Treaty.[137] The ECJ thus needs to take its role, and the balancing between Member States' retained sovereignty and EU interests, seriously in order to contribute to the further development of a sustainable constitutional framework for external action. Only principles that are rooted in a shared legal order can provide the stability required for the coordination and interaction between the EU institutions and Member States on the international stage.

Affairs' in A von Bogdandy and J Bast (eds), *Principles of European Constitutional Law* 2nd edn (Oxford and Munich, Hart Publishing and Verlag CH Beck, 2010) 309–43, 316, 343.

[136] See for the legitimacy of general principles (developed by the ECJ) in the EU as a 'union of law' (integrated municipal legal order, polity of citizens, judiciary) more generally, S Besson, 'General Principles in International Law—Whose Principles?' in S Besson and P Pichonnaz (eds), *Les principes en droit européen—Principles in European Law* (Geneva, Zurich, Basel, Schulthess Médias Juridiques SA, 2011) 19–64, 52.

[137] See n 8; see also B de Witte, 'The European Union as an International Legal Experiment' in G de Búrca and JHH Weiler (eds), *The Worlds of European Constitutionalism* (Cambridge, Cambridge University Press, 2012) 19–56.

9

The Many Visions of Europe: Insights from the Reasoning of the European Court of Justice in External Relations Law

LOÏC AZOULAI

I. THE BANALITY OF EU EXTERNAL RELATIONS LAW REASONING

INTEREST IS GROWING in the modes of reasoning employed by the European Court of Justice (hereafter referred to as 'the Court').[1] Questions of how the Court justifies its decision, the kinds of arguments it uses and methods of interpretation it relies on have been the subject of number of recent insightful studies.[2] These works have generally been concerned with the operation of internal European Union law. Nonetheless much of their findings can be applied with equal validity to the field of external relations law. In fact the legal argumentation and judicial methodology used in the case law on the competence of the European Union (hereafter referred to as 'the EU' or 'the Union') and its Member States to assume international commitments and their participation in international organisations does not appear to display any real specificity.

From the seminal judgment in the *AETR* case to more recent opinions, the main justification invoked by the Court for asserting the external competence of the Union or for imposing restraints on the external action of the Member States has been instrumental in nature and has related to 'the unity of the common market and the uniform application of Community law' and the need 'to preserve

---

[1] J Bengoetxea is a pioneer in this field: see *The Legal Reasoning of the European Court of Justice* (Oxford, Clarendon Press, 1993).

[2] See recently G Conway, *The Limits of Legal Reasoning and the European Court of Justice* (New York, Cambridge University Press, 2012); G Beck, *The Legal Reasoning of the Court of Justice of the EU* (Oxford, Hart Publishing, 2012); S Sankari, *European Court of Justice Legal Reasoning in Context* (Groningen, European Law Publishing, 2013).

the full *effectiveness of EU law*.[3] The Court placed heavy reliance on the rationale of the *'effet utile'* of EU law.[4] This takes the form of a teleological argument where emphasis is put on the potential negative consequences of the alternatives to its decision for the effectiveness of EU law. In short, it states that if the Member States were permitted to act without restrictions or, in cases requiring exclusivity, concurrently to the Union, the Union's legislation would be compromised.[5] Echoes of this technique are found in the internal sphere. Indeed, the structure of the Court's most successful argument in relation to internal matters is much the same.[6] This is no surprise since when dealing with external powers, the Court bases its decisions on the effectiveness of the *internal objectives* of the Union. The Court's external law reasoning is clearly focused on EU internal law.[7] Unilateral Member State action would have negative consequences not only by undermining the strength of the Union's negotiation position, but more importantly by unduly binding it in the internal sphere and jeopardising the attainment of its objectives.[8] The rationale of effectiveness is used to draw a link between internal objectives and external powers. Admittedly, this justification is rather poor. If the only question is the effectiveness of EU internal law and ultimately of the integration project, the meaning of this project and therefore the reason for establishing the link is never clearly stated.

These arguments may quite easily be presented in a more attractive way as a problem of representation. The idea of representation is already present in the Opinion of Advocate General Dutheillet de Lamothe in the *AETR* case where he terms it as a matter of 'a certain Community "ethic"': whenever a specific subject-matter has been transferred to the Community level as the result of the adoption of a regulation, the Community should be considered as the best placed actor to negotiate and enter into agreements with third countries, to the exclusion of

---

[3] Case 22/70 *Commission v Council (AETR)* [1971] ECR 263, para 31; Opinion 1/03 on the competence of the Community to conclude the new Lugano Convention on jurisdiction and the recognition and enforcement of judgments in civil and commercial matters [2006] ECR I-1145, paras 122 and 128. See also Opinion 1/09 on the creation of a unified patent litigation system [2011] OJ C211/29, para 82.

[4] On the *effet utile* principle in this context, see A Dashwood and J Heliskoski, 'The Classic Authorities Revisited' in A Dashwood and C Hillion, *The General Law of E.C. External Relations* (London, Sweet & Maxwell, 2000) 3.

[5] Opinion 2/91 on ILO Convention n° 170 [1993] ECR I-1061, para 11.

[6] See the classic statements of the Court in Case 6/64 *Costa v ENEL* [1964], ECR 585, at 594 where it held that '[t]he executive force of Community law cannot vary from one State to another in deference to subsequent domestic laws, without jeopardising the attainment of the objectives of the Treaty' and in Case C-106/77 *Simmenthal* [1978] ECR 629, para 18: any recognition of the authority of national legislative measures incompatible with EU law 'would amount to a corresponding denial of the effectiveness of obligations undertaken unconditionally'.

[7] For confirmation and nuances, see M Cremona, 'EU External Relations: Unity and Conferral of Powers' in L Azoulai (ed), *The Question of Competence in the European Union* (Oxford, Oxford University Press, 2014).

[8] Case C-246/07 *Commission v Sweden (PFOS)* [2010] ECR I-3317, paras 101 and 102.

the Member States acting individually or collectively.[9] Translated into political language, the common interests involved are better 'represented' both internally by Community rules and externally by Community institutions.[10] It follows that it makes no sense to share external competence in areas that fall within the ambit of Community law. Accordingly the Community alone is capable of concluding such agreements. Although he acknowledged the weight of these considerations, the Advocate General went on to reject them on a practical level: 'it would be impossible to confer such an effect to all Community regulations (…). The Ministers would resist the adoption of regulations which would result in the loss, in cases not provided for by the Treaty, of their authority in international matters'. Moreover, 'not even the representative of the Commission' dared assert this. Nonetheless this is exactly the approach adopted by the Court in its judgment. It stated that the Community was entirely empowered to conclude the European Agreement concerning the work of crews of vehicles engaged in international road transport with third countries thereby excluding the possibility of concurrent powers on the part of Member States. Its implicit reference to the common interests of the Member states as adequately captured by European Community (EC) rules is familiar in the internal sphere where it is presented as a problem of the scope of application of EU law. The argument that 'the common concern of Member states' should prevent them from adopting unilateral measures, lead to the applicability of EC rules and the involvement of Community institutions, including in areas of Member States' reserved powers, can be found in *Commission v France* of 1969.[11] It is, however, different as to its effects. The objective is not to dismiss any Member State's action but to prevent the adoption of measures prohibited by the EU Treaties. Yet, in both cases, the same constitutional vision is at stake. An idea of the Union that is something greater than the sum of its individual members is reflected in this argument. However this vision remains implicit; it is not clearly elaborated by the Court.[12]

The same kind of parallel can be drawn regarding judicial methodology. As in internal matters, the Court relies to a large extent on judicial formulas and it can be found repeating, often out of context, a number of expressions or linguistic arrangements developed in prior judgments.[13] The resulting judicial decisions are

---

[9] Opinion of Advocate General Dutheillet de Lamothe in Case 22/70 *Commission v Council* (*AETR*) (n 3), at 291–92.

[10] The reference to EU internal measures admits some exceptions where the subject matter at issue involves third countries: see Opinion 1/94 on the competence of the Community to conclude international agreements concerning services and the protection of intellectual property [1994] ECR I-5267, para 85.

[11] Case 6/69 and 11/69 *Commission v France* [1969] ECR 525.

[12] Consider, by contrast, the Opinion of the US Supreme Court by Justice Marshall in *McCulloch v Maryland* 17 US 316 (1819) where the same kind of assumption is present.

[13] See further L Azoulai, 'La fabrication de la jurisprudence communautaire' in P MBongo and A Vauchez (eds), *Dans la fabrique du droit européen. Scènes, acteurs et publics de la Cour de justice des Communautés européennes* (Brussels, Bruylant, 2009) 153; 'The Retained Powers Formula in the Case Law of the European Court of Justice: EU Law as Total Law?' (2011) 4 *European Journal of Legal Studies* 192.

most frequently the result of a combination of different strands of reasoning and judicial formulas patched together. This is certainly an efficient way to proceed and one which brings some security in a process of judicial-making where factors of uncertainty abound: the instability in the composition of the Court, the costs of deliberation in a system of collegiate deliberation, the multiplicity of languages involved, the diversity and technical character of the subject matters, the variety of interlocutors and enforcement bodies. In the external field, this may also be a way for a non-specialised court to cope with the complexities and uncertainties of the international realities. Nonetheless this formulaic approach may be to the detriment of clarity and consistency as illustrated by the example of the 'Brown Bear judgment'.

Delivered by the Court in March 2011, the *Brown Bear* case concerned the direct effect of Article 9(3) of the Aarhus Convention on access to information, public participation in decision-making and access to justice in environmental matters.[14] The Convention was concluded in the form of a mixed agreement by the Union and its Member States. The Court ruled that the provision in question did not have direct effect in European law. However, prior to arriving at its substantive conclusion, the Court first had to determine if it had jurisdiction to decide on this point or, to put it differently, whether the dispute felt within the scope of EU law. In the course of its reasoning the Court invokes two slightly different concepts and strands of reasoning. First, the definition of the scope of EU law depends on the question of whether the Union has exercised its powers 'in the particular field into which Article 9(3) of the Aarhus Convention falls' by having implemented it through the adoption of legislation.[15] However two paragraphs later it changes tack and refers to the case law that holds that an issue is part of EU law 'where that issue is regulated in agreements concluded by the European Union and the Member States and it concerns a field in large measure covered by it'.[16] The latter reference sounds familiar. The concept of 'a field in large measure covered by EU law' is directly drawn from Opinion 2/91 where it was used as an extension of the *AETR* test in order to determine whether an exclusive competence has been established for the Union.[17] Here it is used for another purpose, namely to establish the jurisdiction of the Court. This conceptual move is not unprecedented. In previous cases, the Court relied on this formula to justify its jurisdiction to assess Member States' compliance with the provisions of a mixed agreement, even if the provisions at issue have not been the subject of Union legislation.[18] The justification for this is uncertain. It may be argued that the Union has a special interest to require Member States' compliance to the parts of the

---

[14] Case C-240/09 *Lesoochranárske zoskupenie VLK* [2011] ECR I-1255.
[15] ibid, para 34.
[16] ibid, para 36.
[17] Opinion 2/91 on ILO Convention n° 170 [1993] ECR I-1061, para 25.
[18] Case C-13/00 *Commission v Ireland* [2002] ECR I-2943, paras 16–18; Case C-239/03 *Commission v France* [2004], paras 29–31.

agreement which concern areas where a substantive body of EU law exists.[19] It is different, however, when it comes to the issue of direct effect of international provisions adopted in areas not specifically regulated by Union law. The justification cannot be the same. In this case, the issue of direct effect was traditionally considered by the Court to fall within the scope of national law.[20] In the *Brown Bear* case, the Court decided to depart from its settled case law by simply extending the formula originally fashioned in relation to the Union's exclusive competence. It is a strategic move. By shifting from the field covered by Article 9 to the field 'in large measure covered' by EU law, the Grand Chamber further expanded its jurisdiction on this matter, thereby pre-empting national courts' jurisdiction. It follows from this judgment that, to establish the jurisdiction of the Court to rule on the direct effect of a provision which is part of a mixed agreement, the existence of a shared competence and the reference to unspecific EU rules relating to the dispute constitute sufficient grounds.[21] Arguably, this result would have deserved more than a combination of formulas found in the case law.

In terms of legal argumentation and judicial methodology, the external relations case law is no different from other areas of the Court's jurisprudence. To find some originality, a further step needs to be made by exploring the assumptions underpinning the Court's reasoning.[22] Specific features of this field may have compelled the Court to make them visible. The first one is procedural. Under Article 218(11) TFEU, the Court has advisory jurisdiction to rule on the compatibility of envisaged agreements between the Union and third countries or international organisations with the treaties. The abstract and preventive nature of its control may have encouraged the Court to articulate a vision of the Union aimed at securing its position vis-à-vis its Members and partners. At the substantive level, the involvement of third countries and the pressing claims of the Member States to retain their 'external sovereignty' have rendered more tangible the existential vulnerability of the Community/Union. Against the backdrop of the Member States' concern about a loss of authority,[23] the Court seems to have internalised a concern about a potential loss of authority of the Community/ Union. The idea that unrestricted external action of the Member States could

---

[19] CWA Timmermans, 'The Court of Justice and Mixed Agreements' in A Rosas, E Levits and Y Bot (eds), *The Court of Justice and the Construction of Europe: Analyses and Perspectives on Sixty Years of Case-Law* (The Hague, Asser Press, 2013) 659.

[20] Case C-300/98 and C-392/98 *Parfums Christian Dior* [2000] ECR I-11307; Case C-431/05 *Merck Genéricos* [2007] ECR I-7001.

[21] In that case, the Habitats Directive which, as noted by JH Jans, 'does not have any provision at all on matters relating to access to justice' (JH Jans, 'Who is the Referee? Access to Justice in a Globalised Legal Order' (2011) 4 *Review of European Administrative Law* 85).

[22] This may explain the approach adopted by R Holdgaard in *External Relations Law of the European Community. Legal Reasoning and Legal Discourses* (Alphen aan den Rijn, Kluwer International Law, 2008). This work focuses on what it calls 'legal discourses' defined as socio-linguistic structures of meaning containing a certain representation of reality, certain assumptions about the world, and a set of values (p 8).

[23] See Opinion of Advocate General Dutheillet de Lamothe (n 9).

undermine the authority, powers and functions of the Union is present, explicitly or implicitly, throughout the caselaw.

II. REASONING 'POWER'

Costa v ENEL is well known for asserting the existence of a new legal order. EC law was conceptualised as an autonomous legal order, a set of norms which takes effect independently of national and international law and draws authority exclusively from the Treaty and its constitutional values. A few years later, in the *AETR* case, the Court established the existence of a new form of European power. This is not a form of pure factual power. Instead, by the Court's reference to a capacity to act through the establishment of contractual links with third countries, law is presented as the main instrument of the Union's power in the external sphere.

The focus on the notion of power may be identified in the first few lines of the argumentation. A distinction is made between the capacity and the authority of the Community.[24] The latter term is a bad translation of the term '*compétence*' found in the original French version of the judgment. 'Compétence' denotes both powers and jurisdiction (the scope of powers). From a traditional perspective, one would have expected that the Community's competence is established first on the basis of the substantive provisions related to the transport policy.[25] This could have been confirmed on the basis of teleological (the objectives of the Treaty), systemic (the whole scheme of the Treaty) and even organic (legal personality) arguments. However, contrary to what is usually assumed, the traditional teleological argument is not dominant in the decision.[26] The systemic argument, whilst important, comes as a second-order type of reason: to determine the competence in a particular case, 'regard must be had to the whole scheme of the Treaty no less than its substantive provisions'.[27] Instead the Court began with the recognition of a general capacity to act which is derived from the grant of legal personality to the Community.[28] This reference to the legal personality of the Community is not original and borrows from international law.[29] But placing this reference at the forefront of the judgment is meaningful and reflects the importance given

[24] Case 22/70 *Commission v Council (AETR)* (n 3), paras 14–15.
[25] D Simon, 'Les relations extérieures de la CEE à la lumière de l'arrêt de la Cour de justice des Communautés "Commission contre conseil" (AETR)' in *La Communauté économique européenne dans les relations internationales*, Centre Universitaire de Nancy 1972, at 64.
[26] See, however, T Tridimas and P Eeckhout, 'The External Competence of the Community and the Case-Law of the Court of Justice: Principle versus Pragmatism' (1994) 14 *Yearbook of European Law* 143.
[27] Case 22/70 *Commission v Council (AETR)* (n 3), para 14.
[28] ibid (n 3), para 13.
[29] Advisory Opinion of the International Court of Justice of 11 April 1949, Reparation for Injuries Suffered in the Service of the United Nations. The Court states that 'The Charter ... by giving the Organisation legal capacity and privileges ... [and] practice [have] confirmed this character of the [UN] Organization, which occupies a position in certain respect in detachment from its Members ...' (178–79).

the notions of capacity and autonomy. Indeed concern regarding 'the surrender of the independence of action of the Community in its external relations'—in the French version: '*l'abandon de l'autonomie d'action de la Communauté dans ses rapports extérieurs*'—overshadows the whole conceptual framework constructed by the Court in this field.[30]

The concept of autonomy put forward in this context differs from the concept of autonomy famously developed in the internal sphere. The EEC Treaty, declared the Court, has created a substantive 'body of law', a 'new legal order', its 'own legal system' and this law stemming from the Treaty is 'an independent source of law'—'*un droit issu d'une source autonome*'. This is generally understood as meaning that the EC/EU law locates its source of validity within itself and is endowed with its own force. This rather sophisticated affirmation of 'constitutional' authority has proved to be very demanding and, in some respects, self-deceiving. Autonomy, in the external context, means something rather more basic. It simply refers to independence of action, not a new concept in the Court's jurisprudence. Ironically it is inspired by the part of the *Costa v ENEL* decision that serves as a premise to the fashioning of an independent legal system: 'By creating a Community of unlimited duration, *having its own institutions, its own personality, its own legal capacity and capacity of representation on the international plane and, more particularly, real powers stemming from a limitation of sovereignty or a transfer of powers from the states to the Community*, the Member States have limited their sovereign rights, albeit within limited fields, and have thus created a body of law which binds both their nationals and themselves'. Returning to the basics of legal integration, the Court articulates a vision of the Community/Union as a distinct external actor enjoying its own capacity to act. As a matter of fact, this vision has been quite successful, allowing the Union to be active in many areas of international law-making.[31]

This conceptualisation in terms of power carries with it two features peculiar to this area of EU law. The first characteristic of a power is that it is liable to affect external situations and may, in turn, be affected by them. 'Affect' is a recurring concept in the case law. As from 1977, the Court acknowledges that by responding to 'the problems resulting from requirements inherent in the external relations of the Community', the autonomy of the Community may be affected.[32] An international agreement may empower or disempower the Union. In recent Opinions, the Court has made clear that 'an international agreement entered into by the Union ... may affect the powers of the Union institutions, without, however, being regarded as incompatible with the Treaty'.[33] It recognised that the

---

[30] Opinion 1/76 on the draft agreement establishing a European laying-up fund for inland waterway wessels [1977] ECR 741, para 12.

[31] See P Eeckhout, *EU External Relations Law* 2nd edn (Oxford, Oxford University Press, 2011).

[32] Opinion 1/76 on the draft agreement establishing a European laying-up fund for inland waterway wessels (n 30), para 12.

[33] Opinion 1/92 on the draft agreement between the Community, on the one hand, and the countries of the European Free Trade Association, on the other, relating to the creation of the European

capacity to conclude international agreements may entail the power to submit to the decisions of an external court.[34] It went so far as to say that this might affect the powers of the Commission[35] or even its own judicial powers.[36] Accordingly the main question that presents itself in this area is to what extent may the power of the Union be externally affected without compromising its independence of action and altering its internal structure. The Court accepts that, in the general capacity conferred on the Union, there is not only a capacity to act but also a capacity to be affected by international law and transnational realities. What is decisive is that this 'does not alter the essential character of the powers conferred on the Union institutions'.[37]

A second feature concerns the temporal dimension of the exercise of power. Time is an important parameter of action. In the area of external relations one must pay attention to the prospects for future action. This holds true for the Union itself[38] as well as for the Member States acting in the external sphere.[39] Quite simply entering into international agreements may involve some restraints on the future exercise of powers by the Union, both externally and internally. Therefore, the important thing for the Court to consider is whether what is done now, at a certain point in time, is not 'likely progressively to undo the work of the Community, irreversibly'.[40] A freedom of action for the Union should always be preserved. This concerns not only the future negotiating power of the Union and of its Member States but also the internal dimension, the progress of EU harmonisation. As a result, when confronted with a question of the nature of the Union's competence[41] or with the existence of an incompatibility between a Member State's agreement and Member States' obligations under EU law,[42] the Court

Economic Area [1992] ECR I-2821, paras 32 and 41; Opinion 1/00 on the proposed agreement between the European Community and non-Member States on the establishment of a European Common Aviation Area [2002] ECR I-3498, para 20.

[34] Opinion 1/91 on the draft agreement between the Community, on the one hand, and the countries of the European Free Trade Association, on the other, relating to the creation of the European Economic Area [1991] ECR 6079, para 40. [1991] ECR I-6079, para 40.

[35] Opinion 1/92 (n 33), para 41.

[36] Opinion 1/09 (n 3), para 76.

[37] Opinion 1/00 (n 33), para 20. This is a variation on the expression found in Opinion 1/76 (n 30), para 12, mentioning 'the alteration of essential elements of the Community structure as regards both the prerogatives of the institutions and the position of the Member States *vis-à-vis* one another'.

[38] See Holdgaard, *External Relations Law of the European Community* (n 22) 88.

[39] See J Heliskoski, 'The Obligation of Member States to Foresee, in the Conclusion and Application of Their International Agreements, Eventual Future Measures of the European Union' in A Arnull, C Barnard, M Dougan and E Spaventa (eds), *A Constitutional Order of States? Essays in EU Law in Honour of Alan Dashwood* (Oxford, Hart Publishing, 2011) 545.

[40] Opinion 1/76 (n 30), para 14; the French expression has a stronger connotation: the risk would be to '*désintégrer* [disintegrate] *progressivement l'oeuvre communautaire de manière irréversible*'.

[41] Opinion 1/03 (n 3), para 126; Opinion 2/91 (n 5), para 25.

[42] As regards pre-accession bilateral investments agreements, see Case C-205/06 *Commission v Austria* [2009] ECR I-1301; Case C-249/06 *Commission v Sweden* [2009] ECR I-1335; Case C-118/07 *Commission v Finland* [2009] ECR I-10889. As regards post-accession agreements, see Case C-246/07 *Commission v Sweden (PFOS)* (n 7).

insists on the 'need to take into account not only the current state of EU law but also its future development, insofar as that is foreseeable'.[43] Not only the integrity of the existing *acquis*, but the possibility of future action must be preserved.

The two-fold dimension of affect and prospect is absent from the traditional conceptualisation of the EU legal order resulting from the internal perspective. On the one hand, the Court has been principally concerned with guaranteeing the integrity of the EU legal order. To be sure this legal order is not a hermetically sealed legal system; the Court has shown openness to a selection of external demands concerning in particular the protection of fundamental rights.[44] However, this does not call into question the formal indifference of the EU legal order towards external constitutional arrangements. This is a structural principle that has been consistently maintained.[45] On the other hand, time does not matter in the construction of the EU legal order. It is autonomous; it has not and is not supposed to 'become autonomous'.[46]

III. AN INSTITUTIONAL PHENOMENON

The seminal definition of power put forward in the *AETR* case is of a peculiar nature. It is not a pure factual power; it is not a pure legal power either. Law is seen as an instrument of power, not part of its definition. In essence what emerges from the Court's reasoning is an institutional phenomenon which manifests itself through a common structure and scope of action.

In the judgment the most common term is 'common'. The repetition of the term associated with different substantive notions (policy, rules, action, institutions) is even more striking in the original French language version of the decision. The existence of a common policy envisaged by the Treaty and the promulgation of EC common rules should lead the Member States to act within the framework of the common institutions. Paragraph 22 does not read: 'when Community rules are adopted for the attainment of the objectives of the Treaty, the Member States cannot, *outside the framework of the Community institutions*, assume obligations which might affect those rules', as in the translation. The original French formulation states: 'les Etats membres ne peuvent, *hors du cadre des institutions communes*, prendre des engagements ...'. A more accurate English translation would read: 'outside of the framework of the *common* institutions'. By translating 'institutions communes' with '*Community institutions*', the translator certainly made a linguistic mistake but one that may have been legally sound.[47] What the Court actually meant is that it is the Council as a Community institution which should conclude

---

[43] Opinion 1/03 (n 3), para 126; Opinion 2/91 (n 5), para 25.
[44] D Chalmers, 'Judicial Preferences and the Community Legal Order' (1997) *MLR* 164.
[45] See recently Case C-409/06 *Winner Wetten* [2010] ECR I-8015, para 61.
[46] R Barents, *The Autonomy of Community* Law (Alphen aan den Rijn, Kluwer International Law, 2004) at 255.
[47] As noted by Simon, 'Les relations extérieures' (n 25) 55.

the agreement.[48] In that case, it is the Community itself that is responsible for this action and not the joint Member States acting through common organs.

The ambiguity of the original version may very well have been deliberate. We may call it a 'consistent ambiguity'. By use of this formulation the Court achieves a two-fold effect. First, it borrows and slightly alters an expression used in competing theories in order to underline the difference with its own position. It is a rejoinder to the notion of 'common organs' advocated by authors who adopt the contractual theory of international organisations especially as developed by Anzilotti.[49] According to this theory, international organisations are constructed as common organs in the hands of a group of States who use them to further their interests. Instead the Court understands the system of the Treaty as the Community acting both internally and externally through its own institutional channels, in light of its own ends and promoting the common interests of all its Members. The Court opposes and substitutes an institutional view for the contractual view.[50] Rhetorically the 'common institutions' refer to the Community institutions as opposed to common organs. Second, this formulation points to the possibility that the Community institutions may be precluded from acting in the international sphere. This is the case, for instance, when the Community is not allowed to become a member of an international organisation dealing with matters that fall within the ambit of Community law. In such a case the Court's reference means that even when the Member States act outside the institutional framework of the Community they must be prepared to act jointly within a 'common framework' and accordingly be bound by requirements of solidarity.[51]

In Opinion 1/76, the Court explicitly refers to the need to uphold the 'internal constitution of the Community' by which it means 'the powers of the institutions and the relationships between the Member States within the context of the Community'. This is another characteristic of the external relations law perspective. The Constitution of Europe does not lie in a set of substantive principles and values, the so-called 'Union of law'.[52] It lies in the institutional machinery of the Community and in the mutual obligations that are attached to the status of membership. This is where we see a form of 'Institutionalism'. The Community

[48] On the characterisation of the Council as a distinct Community institution in the internal sphere, see Case 38/69 *Commission v Italy* [1970] ECR 48, para 10.
[49] D Anzilotti, *Cours de droit international*, vol 1 (Paris, Sirey, 1929). See recently on this doctrine, E Lagrange, *La représentation institutionnelle dans l'ordre international. Une contribution à la théorie de la personnalité morale des organisations internationales* (Alphen aan den Rijn, Kluwer Law International, 2002). For a revitalisation of the doctrine in the current international context, including the European one, C Santulli, 'Retour à la théorie de l'organe commun' (2012) 116 *Revue Générale de Droit International Public* 565.
[50] See for a general defence of this position, P Pescatore, *The Law of Integration. Emergence of a New Phenomenon in International Relations, Based on the Experience of the European Communities* (Leiden, Sijthoof, 1974).
[51] Case 22/70 *Commission v Council (AETR)* (n 3), paras 77–78; Opinion 1/76 (n 30), para 12; Case C-45/07 *Commission v Greece* [2009] ECR I-701, para 31.
[52] See recently Cases C-584/10 P, C-593/10 P and C-595/10 P *Kadi II*, judgment of 18 July 2013, nyr, para 66.

is dignified as an institutional project carrying out common interests that are concurrently or alternatively defended by the Community institutions and by the Member States bound together.

A second pivotal theme which emerges from the reasoning of the Court is the idea that the 'sphere of application' of EU law must be protected. In *AETR*, the main justification for asserting the exclusive competence of the Community is the necessity not to affect the 'scope' of the EC rules adopted in the internal sphere. The Court refers even more broadly to the necessity to protect 'the whole sphere of application of the Community legal system'. EC/EU law is thought of in terms of a vast 'sphere' or 'area' composed of sub-areas. These areas are covered by EU common rules or (if less frequently) correspond to the objectives of the Treaty.[53] We may call this approach 'Area-lism'. This is not to say that the Court is not attentive to the current economic and political realities on the international stage. The reference to the international context is an important yardstick in the delimitation of the EU's competence, in particular as regards the common commercial policy.[54] Arealism is not anti-realism. However, as far as the determination of the existence and the nature of the competence are concerned, it is maintained that the grant of external powers, if not provided by the treaties, directly follows from the delineation of EU legal areas, an approach that is now enshrined in the Lisbon Treaty.[55]

Piet Eeckhout aptly remarks that 'the Court could easily have adopted a different approach', one more traditionally based on the rule of primacy of EC rules over the international obligations of the Member States.[56] However, instead of approaching the dispute as a conflict of norms, the Court chose to frame it as an issue of competences. Thus presented, the problem is not so much a question of a hierarchy of norms of different origins but one of coincidence or proximity in the scope of action of the Community in different spheres. The determination of the Community competence relies on a comparison between the areas covered by EU law internally and by the envisaged agreement. Far-reaching consequences ensue. As was made clear in the *Open Skies* cases, the Member States may not enter into international commitments when these commitments fall within an area largely covered by EU rules—an area of exclusive competence—'even if there is no

[53] Opinion 2/91 (n 5), para 10; Opinion 1/03 (n 3), para 119.

[54] As demonstrated in Opinion 1/78 on the International Agreement on Natural Rubber [1979] ECR 2894, paras 43–44. Paradoxically, the rather formal and even legalistic approach adopted by the Court in Opinion 1/94 (n 10), paras 42–46 may be seen as another instance of realism whereby the Court shows awareness to the political context and the reluctance of the Member States to enlarge the scope of the exclusive competence of the EU in commercial matters.

[55] See Arts 216(1) TFEU and 3(2) TFEU. The rather problematic interaction between these provisions, especially in view of the settled case law, has been pointed out by M Cremona, 'Defining Competence in EU External Relations: Lessons from the Treaty Reform Process' in M Maresceau and A Dashwood (eds), *Law and Practice of EU External Relations* (Cambridge, Cambridge University Press, 2008) 34.

[56] P Eeckhout, 'Bold Constitutionalism and Beyond' in M Poiares Maduro and L Azoulai (eds), *The Past and Future of EU Law. The Classics of EU Law Revisited on the 50th Anniversary of the Rome Treaty* (Oxford, Hart Publishing, 2010) at 219.

contradiction between those commitments and the common rules'.[57] This goes far beyond the application of the rule of primacy of EU law. It amounts to a complete pre-emption of national legislative powers.

Admittedly, such a conception is hard to maintain in the context of an increasing body of EU legislation. Indeed, it may lead to a total deprivation of Member States' external powers. As demonstrated by M Cremona, there has been an evolution in thinking about EC/EU external competence since the *AETR* line of cases.[58] The method of comparison has been refined to give a more limited role to the Union's exclusive competence. In the *Lugano* case, the Court requires that 'a specific analysis' be carried out and clarifies that an 'area' consists not only of the scope of the rules in question as they appear 'in the current state of [EU] law' but also of the 'nature and content' of these rules and their 'future development'.[59] Nonetheless the approach in terms of an *internal area* to be protected holds true. It is part of the strategy of protecting a common structural core. Both institutionalism and arealism are inward-looking. In the Court's vision the Union should only engage in international relations on the condition that a particular structure, defined as an institutional fact and as a certain scope of action, is safeguarded.

IV. TWO FORMS OF INSTITUTIONALISM

The classic authorities of the 1970s set out the vision and themes that were to dominate the Court's external relations case law until the present day. This vision is based on a 'basic idea of what is, constitutionally speaking, "*une certaine idée de l'Europe*"', and is meant to rebut competing visions that tend to reduce the Union to a contractual arrangement.[60] It postulates the absolute precedence of the Union's institutional framework in the conduct of external action within the ambit of EU law. This is justified firstly by a concern about the consistency and credibility of the EU in the international arena.[61] It is crucial that the EU 'seeks to function and to represent itself to the outside world as a unified system' even in areas of shared competence.[62] Moreover, by requiring the involvement of the supranational organs with their own independent authority in international negotiations, the Court assumes that the 'common interests' will be properly defended.[63] But there

---

[57] Opinion 2/91 (n 5), paras 25–26; Case C-467/98 *Commission v Denmark (Open Skies)* [2002] ECR I-9528, para 82.

[58] Cremona, 'EU External Relations: Unity and Conferral of Powers' (n 8).

[59] Opinion 1/03 (n 3), para 126.

[60] P Pescatore, 'Some Thoughts on the Allocation of Power in the External Relations Field' in CWA Timmermans, *Division of Powers between the European Communities and their Member States in the Field of External Relations* (Alphen aan den Rijn, Kluwer 1981) at 75.

[61] In Opinion 1/75 on the power of the Community to conclude the OECD Understanding on a Local Cost Standard [1975] ECR 1355, the Court refers to 'the necessity of ensuring that international transactions to which the Communities are party should have as uniform a character as possible' (at 1365).

[62] Opinion of Advocate General Tesauro in Case C-53/96 *Hermès* [1998] ECR I-3603, para. 21.

[63] Case C-467/98 *Commission v Denmark* [2002] ECR I-9528, para 79.

is more than this. Ultimately, this involvement is meant to reflect the existence of something termed the 'work of the Community' (*l'oeuvre communautaire*).[64] There is a special mixture of idealism and pragmatism in this reference. The 'Community *oeuvre*' is what enables the Member States to be bound together—a project of work to be achieved in common. It is the end, and at the same time the process through which that end, will be realised. Furthermore it points to the proper institutional mechanisms through which it shall be attained.

The phraseology of the Court seems to find its source in the theory of institution developed by the French public lawyer Maurice Hauriou in the first part of the twentieth century.[65] Not by chance, one of the Court's most prominent members was a self-declared reader of Hauriou.[66] Hauriou defines an institution as 'an idea of a work [une idée d'oeuvre] that is realized and endures juridically in a social context; for the realization of this idea, a power is organized that equips it with organs; on the other hand, among the members of the group interested in the realisation of the idea, manifestations of communion occur that are directed by the organs of the power and regulated by procedures'.[67] Replace the 'idea of a work' with the Community system, the 'power' with the Community's institutional framework and the 'members of the group' with the Member States in the above extract and Hauriou's institution strangely resembles the way the Court portrayed the Community immersed in the outside world.

In the initial phase, the Court actually called for 'manifestations of communion'. How to ensure that the common cause is defended? The response is simple: by substituting a Community action for the unilateral action of the Member States. The Court assumed that the Community institutions alone were capable of representing the entirety of the Community. Thus, in *AETR*, it established the existence of Community competence at the same time as its exclusivity. This approach may explain the long-standing difficulty of the Court in making a clear distinction between the issue of the existence and the issue of the nature of the Union's competence.[68] In other early cases, whilst admitting the legitimacy of the participation of the Member States, the Court strongly suggested an

---

[64] Opinion 1/76 (n 30), para 14.

[65] For an introduction to Hauriou's's work and a translation of some if his writings in English, see A Broderick (ed), *The French Institutionalists. Maurice Hauriou, Georges Renard, Joseph T. Delos* (Cambridge, MA, Harvard University Press, 1970).

[66] Pierre Pescatore, an influential member of the Court of Justice at the time of the bold judicial pronouncements on external relations, conceives EC law as the realisation of an '*idée d'oeuvre commune*' that is supposedly manifest in the founding Treaties (see Pescatore, *The Law of Integration* (n 50). The impact of Hauriou's work on Pescatore's legal conceptions is evidenced in P Pescatore, *La philosophie du droit au tournant du millénaire. Etat des problèmes, essais de solution* (Brussels, Bruylant, 2009).

[67] M Hauriou, 'La théorie de l'institution et de la fondation' (1925) in M Hauriou, *Aux sources du droit. Le pouvoir, l'ordre et la liberté* (Paris, Librairie Bloud & Gay, 1933), reed. Centre de Philosophie politique et juridique, Université de Caen, 1986, p 96; translated into English in Broderick, *The French Institutionalists* (n 65) at 99.

[68] See, for an articulation of the distinction, P Eeckhout, 'Exclusive External Competences: Constructing the EU as an International Actor' in A Rosas, E Levits and Y Bot (eds), *The Court of*

integration of their individual interests into the framework of a common action and a transfer of their external powers to the institutions of the Community.[69] The normative justification for this stance is to be found in Opinion 1/75 where the Court established the exclusive nature of the common commercial policy. The Court claimed that the defence of common interests 'within which the particular interests of the Member States must endeavour to adapt to each other' is better expressed and better served by the Community institutions, using the specific decision-making procedures and the legal instruments provided by the treaties. This will not only ensure that action is taken 'on behalf of the whole of the Community' but also that the 'mutual trust within the Community' is protected.[70] However the possibility always exists that the Community institutions are unable or unwilling to act. In such a case, the Member States are allowed to participate in the international negotiations but they are 'bound (...) to act jointly in the defence of the interests of the Community'.[71] This means that they will act 'in the interest and on behalf of the Community in accordance with their obligations under Article 5 of the Treaty'.[72] In other words they are made 'trustees of the common interest'.[73]

The Court was certainly aware of the degree to which this conception was distancing itself from the intergovernmental view of integration but also from the largely accepted vision of the Community as a pluralist entity, as a 'constitutional order of states'.[74] It may have believed that this was the only way to ensure durable foundations for a real Community at this historical moment. Or to put it more pointedly with R Post, this conception was justified by the need to safeguard the formation of an internal political space.[75] In later cases, the Court broke explicitly with this integrative version of institutionalism and accepted that exclusivity is the exception and that the shared exercise of external competence the rule.

Justice and the Construction of Europe: Analyses and Perspectives on Sixty Years of Case-Law (The Hague, Asser Press, 2013), 613.

[69] In Opinion 1/76 (n 30), the Court stated that 'the participation of [the] Member States, though justified (...), has however produced results (...) which are incompatible with the requirements implied by the very concepts of the Community and its common policy' (para 8). See also Opinion 1/78 (n 54), the Court considers that the participation of the Member States in the agreement together with the Community may be envisaged. In that case, however, the Court suggests an agreement with the Community with regard to the arrangements envisaged as an alternative to their parallel participation (para 62).

[70] Opinion 1/75 (n 61), at 1364.

[71] Case 22/70 *Commission v Council (AETR)* (n 3), para 77. See, however, the apparently more pragmatic approach adopted by the Court in Opinion 1/78 (n 54).

[72] ibid (n 54), para 90.

[73] M Cremona, 'Member States as Trustees of the Union Interest: Participating in International Agreements on Behalf of the European Union' in A Arnull, C Barnard, M Dougan and E Spaventa (eds), *A Constitutional Order of States? Essays in EU Law in Honour of Alan Dashwood* (Oxford, Hart Publishing, 2011) 435.

[74] See A Dashwood, 'The Relationship between the Member States and the European Union/ European Community' (2004) 41 *CML Rev* 355.

[75] R Post, 'Constructing the European Polity: ERTA and the *Open Skies* Judgments' in M Poiares Maduro and L Azoulai (eds), *The Past and Future of EU Law* (Oxford, Hart Publishing, 2010).

Moreover, it has notoriously facilitated the use of mixed agreements.[76] However this did not imply the end of institutionalism and the necessity of defending the powers of the Union's institutions is still present within the Court. The increasing overlap of the Union's and the Member States' external competences has rather blurred the distinction between Union action and Member States action. In such a context attention is focused on the need to organise the 'close association' of European institutions and nationals organs.[77] To ensure the cohesion of the Union, the Court relies on procedures of cooperation rather than on exclusive powers. The fact of mutual membership and the ensuing obligations of loyalty take precedence over the legal personality of the Union and the strict defence of its institutional structure. An associative form of institutionalism takes over. It may be that it better suits post-foundational periods and perhaps also the current context of political discontent with the idea of ever-increasing and exclusionary Union competence.

Associative institutionalism manifests itself through rules of conduct imposed on Member States as well as on European institutions. In particular, a duty of close and loyal cooperation applies to the Union and the Member States exercising their powers in areas of exclusive or shared Union competence.[78] This procedural framework amounts to a form of discipline that requires Member States to adopt a 'common attitude' as is demonstrated by the reasoning of the Court in the *PFOS* case.[79] In this case, the Court ruled that in an area of shared competence, in the absence of a formal decision of the Council to act externally, the Member States were still bound by the 'concerted common strategy within the Council'. A strategy that demonstrates an intention not to act for the time being was a sufficient basis to consider that a common framework had been put in place and triggered an obligation on the part of the Member States to abstain from action. In this context, even though the legal nature of the common position was not entirely clear, an individual course of action was seen by the Court as a deliberate act of 'dissociation' from the common framework and deemed to be a breach of former Article 10 EC (Article 4(3) TFEU).

Despite this shift from 'integrative' to 'associative' institutionalism, a structural concern remains. It may be found in the Court's repeated expression that respect for 'the autonomy of the Community/EU legal order' must be assured.[80] This expression

---

[76] Timmermans, 'The Court of Justice and Mixed Agreements' (n 19) 659.

[77] Opinion 2/91 (n 5), para 36. See also Opinion 1/94 (n 10), para 108.

[78] See C Hillion, 'Mixity and Coherence in EU External Relations: The Significance of the "Duty of Cooperation"' in C Hillion and P Koutrakos (eds), *Mixed Agreements Revisited* (Oxford, Hart Publishing, 2010) 87; M Cremona, 'Defending the Community Interest: the Duties of Cooperation and Compliance' in M Cremona and B de Witte (eds), *EU Foreign Relations Law. Constitutional Fundamentals* (Oxford, Hart Publishing, 2008) 125.

[79] Case C-246/07 *Commission v Sweden* (*PFOS*) (n 7). The notion of 'common attitude' is to be found in Case C-205/06 *Commission v Austria* [2009] ECR I-1301, para 44.

[80] Opinion 1/91 (n 34), para 35.

typically pertains to the 'internal dimension of European constitutionalism'.[81] In the external relations case law, it does not stand on its own but is put forward in connection with a reference to the 'federal order of competences' enshrined in the system.[82] The whole sequence reads: 'the allocation of responsibilities defined in the treaties and, hence, the autonomy of the EU legal order' must be protected.[83] What is worthy of protection is a set of institutional relations: the relations between the Union and the Member States' competences and prerogatives,[84] the mutual relations between the Member States,[85] the relations between the Court itself and the national courts.[86] Instead of a concern for the specific prerogatives of the Union's institutions, the Court now concentrates on the role of the EU institutions in relation to the main institutional players involved—what it calls the 'essential character' of the powers conferred on the Union's institutions.[87] From the external relations law standpoint, the essence of the system lies in its relational dimension. As a consequence, the Court rejects any introduction of external mechanisms that would disrupt this system.[88] That the Union may be affected by international agreements and that this is the unavoidable consequence of its engagement in international relationships is one thing. Accepting an 'alteration of the essential elements of the [Union] structure'[89] is an altogether different matter. Not by chance the Court itself is situated at the core of this structure. It presents itself as the regulator of the division of powers between the Union and the Member States, the mediator between the Member States within the ambit of EU law, the authentic interpreter of EU law and the privileged interlocutor of the Member States' courts. It plays a central role in the system the essence of which it strives to protect. Hence the characterisation of the Court as a 'selfish Court'.[90]

---

[81] The expression is borrowed from D Halberstam, 'Local, Global and Plural Constitutionalism: Europe Meets the World' in G de Búrca and JHH Weiler, *The Worlds of European Constitutionalism* (Cambridge, Cambridge University Press, 2012) at 186.

[82] For a doctrinal elaboration of this reference, A von Bogdandy and J Bast, 'The Federal Order of Competences' in A von Bogdandy and J Bast (eds), *Principles of European Constitutional Law* (Oxford, Hart Publishing; München, Beck, 2011) 276; R Schütze, 'The European Community's Federal Order of Competences—A Retrospective Analysis' in M Dougan and S Currie (eds), *50 Years of the European Treaties—Looking Back and Thinking Forwards* (Oxford and Portland, Hart Publishing, 2009) 63.

[83] Opinion 1/91 (n 34), para 35. The original French expression refers to 'l'ordre des compétences défini par les traités'.

[84] ibid (n 34), para 34.

[85] Opinion 1/76 (n 30), paras 10–12.

[86] Opinion 1/09 (n 3), paras 82–85.

[87] Opinion 1/92 (n 33), para 41; Opinion 1/00 (n 33), para 20; Opinion 1/09 (n 3), para 75.

[88] It may be noted that this approach has been transposed by the Court to deal with internal issues regarding the compatibility with EU law of obligations imposed on the European institutions by the law of the UN or by an international treaty concluded between some Member States outside the EU legal framework: see respectively, Joined Cases C-402/05 P and C-415/05 P *Kadi I* [2008] ECR I-6351, para 282 and Case C-370/12 *Pringle*, judgment of 27 November 2012, nyr, para 158.

[89] Opinion 1/76 (n 30), para 12.

[90] See the chapter by B de Witte (ch 3), this volume.

V. A CHALLENGE TO THE COURT'S VISION?

In fashioning a distinct European power, the Court has constructed a vision that has proved difficult to live up to. The Member States of the EU have long since deviated from the institutional route suggested in *AETR*. Aware of their high degree of interdependence but sometimes reluctant to use the constraining means of the Union, they have developed alternative mechanisms of cooperation, thereby creating an original sphere of joint action, a true political space outside the Union's institutional framework.[91] It seems that this sphere has now gained scope and intrudes on the Union's own competence or even exclusivity.[92] Indeed it is not uncommon to see the Member States conducting external relations in areas where, according to the treaties, the Union is supposed to make use of its own powers. Conversely, we see the Member States entrusting the Union's institutions with a power of international negotiation in areas where they are supposed to act on their own behalf. To be sure these phenomena reflect a change in the European political landscape and raise fresh legal issues that have yet to be brought before the Court.[93]

As we have seen, the Court's reasoning in the field of external relations offers two options in response to this evolution. One possible response would be a return to an integrative version of institutionalism. The role given to the Member States in a context of presumed centralisation would be contested, whilst the role given to the European institutions in areas of supposed national autonomy could be justified in the name of the uniformity required. Presumably, there are voices within the Court to defend at least the former outcome.[94] An alternative strategy would be to rely on associative institutionalism. The institutional mechanisms agreed in practice between the European institutions and the Member States regarding the allocation of their respective responsibilities and their cooperation, even if not strictly speaking compliant with the treaties, would be confirmed. The Court would take the initiative and develop the basic procedural framework set out in relation to mixed agreements.

There is however a third option available. Confronted with new shocks, surrounded by a deep and widespread concern about the efficiency and the legitimacy of the Union's actions both internally and externally, the Court might be inclined to break with the idea that the involvement of the Union's institutions in compliance with the complex of procedures provided for in the treaties is the best means of promoting common interests and representing the peoples of the

---

[91] For a reconstruction and justification of this development, see recently L van Middelaar, *The Passage to Europe. How a Continent became a Union* (New Haven and London, Yale University Press, 2013).

[92] See the case brought recently by the Commission before the Court: Case C-114/12 *Commission v Council* [2012] OJ C138/09 pending.

[93] On these points, Cremona, 'EU External Relations: Unity and Conferral of Powers' (n 58).

[94] A strict position of this type has been endorsed by Advocate General Kokott in her Opinion in Case C-13/07 *Commission v Council* (2009; case withdrawn), paras 83–84.

Member States. This would not mean a total eclipse of EU law and responsibilities. The EU presence would basically amount to the creation of substantive
conditions on the conduct of the Member States' individual or joint action. This
might even entail a certain unconventional involvement of the Union's institutions which would be entrusted with the task of coordinating the action of the
Member States. This was the approach adopted by the Court in the recent *Pringle*
case in relation to the Treaty establishing the European Stability Mechanism
between some of the Member States.[95] In this case, the collective action of the
Member States was deemed to promote the 'general interest of the Union' (in the
form of the objective to protect 'the financial stability of the euro area as a whole')
and the EU institutions acting outside the EU legal framework were presented
as mere instruments to foster this goal.[96] To be sure, this approach was dictated
by the exceptional context of the economic crisis. But even outside such special
circumstances, what is at stake is a withdrawal from institutionalism as it has been
understood up to now in the case law. The focus is on the independence of action
of the Member States rather than on the independence of action of the Union.

In the external field, the Court's current concern is to articulate a 'principle of
unity in the representation of the Union *and* its Member States'.[97] This potentially
means a lot. It entails bold constitutional commitments from both parties. One
the one hand, the EU's institutions must accept and deal with the existence of two
legitimate subjects of representation in the external field, the Member States and
their people alongside the EU. The European public interest encompasses both
Member States' and the EU's interests. On the other hand, the Member States
must accept that common action within the EU institutional framework is to be
preferred to unilateral or joint action outside the EU framework. The EU machinery is to be seen as a laboratory for the reshaping and approximation of national
and European preferences.

The question is whether the Court will be able to solve the conundrum of
providing for the unity of a non-unitary polity and to do it is within the institutionalist paradigm—or by renouncing to it. In the first case, a re-elaboration of
the institutionalist paradigm is required. In the latter case, this would mean a shift
in the foundations of the EU external power.

[95] Case C-370/12 *Pringle*, judgment of 27 November 2012, nyr.
[96] On the legitimacy of the use of EU institutions outside the EU legal framework, see P Craig,
'*Pringle* and the Use of EU Institutions Outside the EU Legal Framework: Foundations, Procedure and
Substance' (2013) 9 *Euro Constitutional Law Review* 263.
[97] Case C-246/07 *Commission v Sweden* (*PFOS*) (n 7), para 104.

10

The Court of Justice's Participation in Judicial Discourse: Theory and Practice

CHRISTINA ECKES[1]

I. INTRODUCTION

JUDGES ARGUE WITHIN a legal frame of reference. They identify and interpret this frame and read factual situations before them in the light of it. By interpreting the law and the facts coherently with the relevant legal frame of reference they aim to objectively justify their decisions. This may sound naïve and often be much less heroic in practice. However, the core value of separation of powers and of independent judicial review is widely accepted, including the added value of the judiciary's attempts to objectify what is 'just' outside of the political power struggle. Judicial discourse, it is here argued, could help the judiciary to continue to offer this objectifying value in a pluricontextual setting,[2] where the internal and the external become increasingly interlocked because policy making is increasingly externalised, rights relevant decisions are taken by the executive outside the domestic constitutional framework, and an increasing number of players claim authority, including ultimate authority, to govern a legal situation.[3]

The chapter hopes to contribute to the thinking about the role of the judiciary in a pluricontextual setting and turns to the European Union (hereafter referred to as 'the EU' or 'the Union') for inspiration. Within the EU the relationship between EU law, on the one hand, and the Member States collectively and individually on

[1] I would like to thank Dennis van Berkel and Stephan Hollenberg for their comments on earlier drafts and Robbert-Jan Winters for his research assistance. All remaining errors are of course my own. This chapter loosely draws on my earlier work published as: C Eckes, 'EU Accession to the ECHR: Between Autonomy and Adaptation' (2013) 76 *MLR* 254 and 'European Union Legal Methods— Moving Away From Integration' in U Neergaard and R Nielsen (eds), *European Legal Method—Towards a New European Legal Realism?* (Copenhagen, DJØF Publishing, 2013).
[2] Throughout the text the term legal 'context' is chosen rather than 'level' or 'order', since the different contexts are not layered because they do not relate hierarchically to each other and public international law (PIL) is not organised to a degree that would justify calling it an order.
[3] For a more detailed distinction between the different phenomena, see N Barber, *The Constitutional State* (Oxford, Oxford University Press, 2010) ch 9.

the other, is characterised by an ongoing pulling and pushing of law and politics.[4] Both the Court of Justice of the European Union (CJEU) and Member States' courts have long functioned in this setting. The Union legal order is a compound constitutionalised construction with interlocking claims of ultimate authority. This chapter considers what could be learned from interaction between different judiciaries within the EU legal order for the CJEU's approach to external claims of authority.

Traditionally, the phenomenon that courts refer to decisions of other jurisdictions is called 'judicial dialogue'.[5] This chapter however uses the term 'discourse', which, from Latin *discursus*, refers more loosely to 'running to and from' rather than to the purposeful directed exchange that 'dialogue' seems to evoke. This appears appropriate since judicial interaction ranges from 'ignoring' or 'appearing to have considered' to 'taking into account' or 'making references'.[6] Furthermore, with the participation of an ever-increasing number of international judicial bodies, as well as an increasing number of highest courts within the EU,[7] the interaction has moved from a dialogue to 'a round table discussion' or a 'multilogue'.[8]

The chapter is structured as follows. Section II lays out the theoretical grounding of the value and necessity of judicial reasoning. It then makes the argument that both within the EU and beyond the boundaries of the EU legal order, the same philosophical arguments and theories require not only an inward looking judicial reasoning but also a discourse with other judicial bodies. Section III looks consequently into the practice of judicial interaction between the CJEU and the courts of the Member States (internal discourse) and then to the interaction between the CJEU and international judicial bodies (external discourse). This sets the scene for section IV, which addresses the core questions of this chapter: What lessons can the CJEU learn from the internal European judicial discourse that can be transferred to the external discourse with international courts and tribunals? What considerations should guide the CJEU's external relations case law in the described pluricontextual setting?

---

[4] For an excellent analysis, see L van Middelaar, *De passage naar Europa—Geschiedenis van een begin* (Groningen, Historische Uitgeverij, 2009).

[5] See, for example: A Rosas, 'The European Court of Justice in Context: Forms and Patterns of Judicial Dialogue' (2007) 1 *European Journal of Legal Studies* 1; C Baudenbacher, 'The EFTA Court, the ECJ, and the Latter's Advocates General—a Tale of Judicial Dialogue' in A Arnull, P Eeckhout, and T Tridimas (eds), *Continuity and Change in EU Law* (Oxford, Oxford University Press, 2008); H Lambert, 'Transnational Judicial Dialogue, Harmonization and the Common European Asylum System' (2009) 58 *ICLQ* 519.

[6] Bruno de Witte questioned whether we can speak of a conversation between judges/courts: B de Witte, 'The Closest Thing to a Constitutional Conversation in Europe: The Semi-Permanent Treaty Revision Process' in P Beaumont, C Lyons and N Walker (eds), *Convergence and Divergence in European Public Law* (Oxford, Hart Publishing, 2002).

[7] See on the participation of the courts of the newer Member States, W Sadurski, '"Solange, Chapter 3": Constitutional Courts in Central Europe—Democracy—European Union' (2006) *EUI Working Paper* no 40.

[8] The latter term is used by: M Cartabia, 'Europe and Rights: Taking Dialogue Seriously' (2009) 5 *European Competition Law Review* 5.

II. THE VALUE OF JUDICIAL DISCOURSE

Legal reasoning is commonly and appropriately supported by coherence theories.[9] Coherence theories require that any proposition that is to be justified (judicial decision) harmoniously relates to other propositions that find reasonable support (recognised claims of judicial authority; authoritative norms). Justification of a judicial decision takes place in the world of legal propositions in a legal, mind-dependent context rather than reality. The aim is to 'objectify' the decision of what is just or unjust and to communicate in a legal context with others about the supporting reasons.[10] If we accept the justifying value of placing judicial decisions within a coherent relationship with norms that are recognised as authoritative it is logical that all *relevant* norms would have to be considered. The latter requires an interpretation of law as a meaningful whole and a decision on which norms are relevant. In a pluricontextual setting, this includes external claims of (ultimate) authority that compete with internal claims of ultimate authority. As a consequence, the reference framework will have to be determined by recognising or rejecting these external claims. *Ultimate* authority is only claimed where the external authority supposes that no internal recognition of the specific proposition is necessary for its validity inside the domestic legal context. EU law for instance claims ultimate authority within national legal orders. Even if originally recognition by national authorities was necessary, individual provisions of EU law now become part of the national legal context without requiring specific recognition. However, direct practical effect, eg of the decisions of international expert bodies, is different from claiming ultimate authority.

External claims of authority multiply in the pluricontextual setting. Across an ever-wider range of policy areas, an ever-wider range of actors engages in cross-border activities. These cross-border activities produce an increasingly dense net of rules with an ever greater impact not only on national legal orders and on the EU, but also on individuals.[11] Multiple claims of authority over the same factual situation exist that somehow recognise each other and that find expression in multiple norms potentially applicable to that situation. 'Somehow recognise' means that an internal actor has confirmed the relevance of the external claim of authority, including in the past. Continuous recognition can result in an expectation to recognise and in an interlocking of legal spheres. While these interlocking

---

[9] See eg: M Moore, 'The Semantics of Judging' (1981) 54 *Southern California Law Review* 151. This does not exclude that a coherence approach to legal reasoning will sometimes result in morally arbitrary decisions: see KK Kress, 'Legal Reasoning and Coherence Theories: Dworkin's Rights Thesis, Retroactivity and the Linear Order of Decisions' (1984) 72 *California Law Review* 369.

[10] See on this point, A Sen, *The Idea of Justice* (Cambridge, MA, The Belknap Press of Harvard University Press, 2009) ch 1.

[11] See for literature on decisions of international organisations, JE Alvarez, *International Organizations as Law-Makers* (Oxford, Oxford University Press, 2006). On the regulatory impact of international law, see S Cassese, 'Administrative Law without the State? The Challenge of Global Regulation' (2005) 37 *International Law and Politics* 663.

processes of different legal spheres aspiring to exercise ultimate authority can be witnessed internationally, they are particularly strong in the EU. As Anne-Marie Slaughter puts it: 'The world is not likely to replicate [the European] experience in terms of actual political and economic integration monitored by coercive supranational institutions. But to the extent that the European way of law uses international law to transform and buttress domestic political institutions, it is a model for how international law can function, and in our view, will and must function to address twenty-first century international challenges'.[12] Classic contemporary examples under international law are: the standards of the *Codex Alimentarius* Commission, which have gained formal weight through the Sanitary and Phytosanitary Measures (SPS) Agreement;[13] the rulemaking, both formal and informal, in international organisations such as the World Health Organization (WHO)[14] or the International Civil Aviation Organization (ICAO); sanctions of the UN Security Council;[15] and standards of international regulatory associations such as the Basel Committee for Banking Supervision[16] or the Financial Action Task Force on Money Laundering (FATF).[17] Furthermore, there is a growing amount and intensity of rulemaking by private actors that directly impacts on domestic law.[18] Examples that came to fame more recently are debt security rating agencies, such as Moody's and Standard & Poor's (S&P).[19] Additionally, international law becomes increasingly judicialised and domestic courts are increasingly and actively referring to each other's judicial decisions, as well as to international law.[20] However, most international examples are claims of authority and even

---

[12] AM Slaughter and W Burke-White, 'The Future of International Law is Domestic (or, the European Way of Law)' (2006) 47 *Harvard International Law Journal* 327, 352.

[13] T Büthe, 'The Law and Politics of International Delegation: The Globalization of Health and Safety Standards: Delegation of Regulatory Authority in the SPS Agreement of the 1994 Agreement Establishing the World Trade Organization' (2008) 71 *Law & Contemporary Problems* 219.

[14] F Snyder, *The EU, the WTO and China: Legal Pluralism and International Trade Regulation* (Oxford, Hart Publishing, 2010) 22.

[15] Counter-terrorist sanctions against individuals resemble individual decisions rather than 'rules' but they certainly have a great and direct impact on the rights of individuals and domestic legal orders: C Eckes, *EU Counter-Terrorist Policies and Fundamental Rights—The Case of Individual Sanctions* (Oxford, Oxford University Press, 2009).

[16] GRD Underhill and X Zhang, 'Setting the Rules: Private Power, Political Underpinnings, and Legitimacy in Global Monetary and Financial Governance' (2008) 84 *International Affairs* 535.

[17] JT Gathii, 'The Financial Action Task Force and Global Administrative Law' (2010) *Journal of the Professional Lawyer* 197 (see for a draft version: Albany Law School Research Paper no 10-10, available on the SSRN website, at http://www.ssrn.com/en/).

[18] For examples and analysis of this phenomenon, see T Büthe and W Mattli, *The New Global Rulers: The Privatization of Regulation in the World Economy* (Princeton, Princeton University Press, 2011).

[19] Other examples are ICANN—Internet Cooperation of Assigned Names and Numbers; the International Standards Organization (ISO); and the International Accounting Standards Committee (IASC).

[20] AM Slaughter, 'A Global Community of Courts' (2003) 44 *Harvard International Law Journal* 191 and AM Slaughter, 'A Typology of Transjudicial Communication' (1994) 29 *University of Richmond Law Review* 99. See similarly, E Benvenisti and GW Downs, 'National Courts, Domestic Democracy, and the Evolution of International Law' (2009) 20 *European Journal of International Law* 59.

ultimate expertise, but they do not claim to govern in the internal legal context without further recognition.[21] Yet, the practical effect can at times be very similar. The WHO for instance determines the existence of public emergencies and makes specific recommendations for appropriate measures that states comply with without further implementing legislation. The developments are far from homogeneous but one general tendency is that international claims of authority shift from considering the will of sovereign state subjects as the ultimate benchmark of legality to focussing on the impact on individuals.[22]

Pluricontextuality makes it necessary to consider the applicability of authority external to the domestic legal setting. Typically, it is the task of the judiciary to discover and determine the internal relevance of external authoritative claims. The judiciary does so by relying on internal constitutional principles and norms; however, these are often far from narrowly prescriptive and do not clearly determine the relevance of any particular international claim.[23] The judiciary from different constitutional orders is required to make sense of the interlocking, the same norms (with different grounds for recognition), and de facto interdependence between legal contexts. This does not entail that the different judiciaries come to the same conclusions. Justice that can be achieved through judicial review is necessarily system bound. It is the just outcome within an artificially limited normative structure that serves as a practical tool to determine justice. The justice delivered by domestic courts necessarily does not at all times approach a standard of universal justice.[24] Where the frame of reference includes external claims of authority the normative structure can change through sustained recognition by courts, political players and citizens. Courts are creatures of their system, be it a state or be it the EU: changes in the domestic system and the frame of reference influence the exercise of their powers and potentially even their entire role within this system. Both legal reasoning and judicial discourse are tools to achieve coherence with accepted, albeit limited, standards of justice and to make some standard of justice possible in practice. Judicial discourse is a tool to allow for limited interaction between judiciaries rooted in different system. While it does not necessarily lead to harmonisation, it extends normative claims beyond the domestic legal context and can contribute to controlling the external exercise of political power, as well as to a cross-border exchange on the legitimacy of specific claims of authority.[25]

---

[21] See, however, how voluntary standards can become internationally binding and develop normativity that can make them part of the frame of reference: R Howse, 'A New Device for Creating International Legal Normativity: The WTO Technical Barriers to Trade Agreement and "International Standards"' in C Joerges and EU Petersmann (eds), *Constitutionalism, Multilevel Trade Governance and International Economic Law* (Oxford, Hart Publishing, 2011).

[22] R Teitle and R Howse, 'Cross-Judging: Tribunalization in a Fragmented but Interconnected Global Order' (2009) *International Law and Politics* 959.

[23] The German Constitution (Grundgesetz (GG)) did introduce a provision on EU law only after the Treaty of Maastricht, see Art 23 GG. See also Art 59 II GG for the status of international law.

[24] T Nagel, 'The Problem of Global Justice' (2005) 33 *Philosophy and Public Affairs* 113.

[25] Teitle and Howse, 'Cross-Judging' (n 22).

In the pluricontextual setting, recognition of external claims by courts is unavoidably part of the legal reasoning since it includes determining the frame of reference in which a decision must be coherently placed. Judicial discourse is then the necessary next step to contribute to coherence in a compound pluricontextual setting where the global, the regional, and the local directly interlink. Under the separation of powers doctrine, the judiciary has a duty towards the individual to counterbalance the other powers and to maintain the authority necessary to settle disputes that are brought before it. A network of mutually recognised judicial claims could contribute to counterbalancing the emerging network of executive power. Limits could emerge in a discursive fashion. As states lose part of their autonomy as a result of the growing network of external norms and factual constraints, their actions cannot be judged coherently without taking into account these external norms. Under these circumstances, courts are no longer able to effectively and coherently fulfil their task in the state structure without taking account of the claims of external judicial bodies. Only the latter can effectively control the validity of the claims made by the political actors of their own legal order, including in the international context. Indeed in the pluricontextual setting, the monolithic state is subdivided into its different bodies and entities which then cooperate outside and, some would argue, above the state structure.[26] Judicial discourse offers a combination of domestically rooted and constitutionally legitimised jurisprudence with an external reach. A 'network of judges' could make a contribution to construe and control the pluricontextual legal reality.[27]

III. JUDICIAL DISCOURSE AND THE COURT OF JUSTICE

A. Inside the EU Legal Order: Discourse Practice in a Pluricontextual Setting

Cross-jurisdictional judicial discourse is long established within the EU. The focus here is the communicative and restraining function of judicial discourse through judgments. The underlying question is what lessons, if any, could be learned from the internal EU discourse for a broader international judicial discourse.

(i) Under the Preliminary Ruling Procedure

The internal discourse between the CJEU and national courts has a direct institutionalised dimension: the preliminary ruling procedure (Article 267 TFEU). National courts ask questions and enforce the CJEU's replies in the national legal order. A recent example of a broad judicial discourse, where a number of the

---

[26] J Habermas, *Zur Verfassung Europas—Ein Essay* (Berlin, Suhrkamp, 2011).
[27] AM Slaughter, *A New World Order* (Princeton, Princeton University Press, 2004) ch 2 describes both the existing judicial discourse with a focus on the US and the Commonwealth and speaks of 'judicial networks'.

highest national courts and the CJEU are considering the same factual situations and legal norms, is the judicial consideration of legal instruments adopted to mitigate the Eurocrisis. In 2012, the German Constitutional Court (GCC) gave two rulings concerning the Treaty Establishing the European Stability Mechanism (ESM): first in an intergovernmental dispute (June 2012)[28] and then in a challenge of its compliance with German constitutional law (September 2012).[29] The Estonian and Irish Supreme Courts ruled on the constitutionality of the ESM under their respective law.[30] Furthermore, while the Irish High Court had earlier declined to refer to the CJEU,[31] the Irish Supreme Court made a reference to the CJEU. The questions raised before the different national courts and the CJEU concern the same legal instrument and raise parallel issues, including whether the agreed Treaty amendments entailed an increase in Union competences (since in this case the simplified amendment procedure cannot be used); whether it involved the treaties or the general principles of Union law, such as the Union's exclusive competences in monetary policy, the functions of the Union institutions, and the principle of sincere cooperation;[32] whether the budget autonomy of national parliaments was infringed, whether the ESM limited unduly the autonomy of the constitutional legislator, and whether the ESM undermined the democracy principle and crossed the line to a federal state.[33] It is artificial to hide behind a strict dualist reading and argue that each court only considers domestic law (ratification and implementation measures in the case of national courts or the ESM Treaty in the case of the CJEU) and unrealistic to assume that the courts do not take notice of each other's decisions. It was the Irish Supreme Court that framed the preliminary questions on the legality of the ESM and that influenced in this way the debate. The GCC by contrast had for more than 50 years avoided entering into this very direct discourse that would necessarily entail formal recognition of a relationship with the CJEU, in which the latter gives guidance to the former in questions of EU law. The UK House of Lords, now the Supreme Court, has entered into a direct discourse with CJEU many times. Recently, even the Italian Constitutional Court has started referring preliminary questions

---

[28] BVerfG, 2 BvE 4/11, ruling of 19 June 2012, Absatz-Nr. (1–172). English Press Release available at http://www.bundesverfassungsgericht.de/en/press/bvg12-042en.html.

[29] BVerfG, 2 BvR 1390/12, 2 BvR 1421/12, 2 BvR 1438/12, 2 BvR 1439/12, 2 BvR 1440/12, 2 BvE 6/12, ruling of 12 September 2012, Absatz-Nr. (1–248). Available in English at http://www.bundesverfassungsgericht. de/en/decisions/rs20120912_2bvr139012en.html.

[30] Supreme Court of Estonia, no 3-4-1-6-12, decision of 12 July 2012, available in English at http:// www.riigikohus.ee/?id=1347; Irish Supreme Court, *Thomas Pringle v The Government of Ireland, Ireland and the Attorney General* [2012] IESC 47, focused on the lawfulness of using the simplified revision procedure in Art 48(6) TFEU to add a paragraph 3 to Art 136 TFEU and on the lawfulness of the alleged 'vague and open-ended amendment that enables the granting of financial assistance without limitations or restrictions as provided for in the Union Treaties' (argument of the appellant).

[31] See summary in *Pringle v Ireland* (ibid).

[32] See questions referred under the expedited reference procedure (Art 104a of the Court's Rules of Procedure) in *Pringle v Ireland* (n 30).

[33] BVerfG (n 29).

to the CJEU.[34] The Polish Constitutional Tribunal has at least accepted direct communication with the CJEU through the preliminary reference procedure as a possibility.[35] Only as recently as February 2014, the GCC also changed its increasingly isolated stand and made a reference to the CJEU (*OMT* case).[36] Prima facie, this may have made constitutional complaints to the GCC more attractive from the perspective of the individual who wants to rely on their rights under EU law. Yet the *OMT* case should not necessarily be read as the beginning of a broader practice. It is a very particular case concerning the ECB's announced Outright Monetary Transactions (OMT) bond buying scheme. Firstly, any decision in this case entails direct and exceptionally far-reaching economic consequences for the Eurozone. Secondly in the *OMT* case, the GCC is confronted for the first time with a direct challenge of an act of a EU institution. The closest so far has been the case of *Honeywell* in 2010,[37] where the GCC was in essence asked to rule on the constitutionality of a decision of the CJEU. In this case, the GCC in principle accepted that it would check whether the CJEU had overstepped its mandate. However, it showed great deference to the EU judiciary and reduced that control to whether there was a manifest violation. And highly relevant for the present discussion, the GCC also made clear in *Honeywell* that it would not rule on whether an act of the (other) EU institutions goes beyond their mandate without giving the CJEU the opportunity, in a preliminary ruling, to give its interpretation of the matter. This is precisely what it did in the *OMT* case four years later.

The GCC enjoys a unique position as a constitutional court that is exceptionally powerful[38] and popular[39] within a big and influential Member State. If one understands EU law and German law as two juxtaposed legal contexts, rather than as interlocked in a way that excludes taking an exclusively national perspective, one could argue that a reference would limit the GCC's near-absolute judicial powers within the national legal context. Hence, from an internal perspective, based on an artificial conceptual separation of the two legal contexts, the GCC's choice of refusing for more than 50 years to refer to the CJEU was a strategy to preserve its own powers. In the 'Euro Bailout case', an earlier high-profile missed opportunity of the GCC to refer a question to the CJEU,[40] the Court faced a great

---

[34] Italian Constitutional Court, decision no. 103 of 2008, available at www.corteconstituzionale.it.

[35] Polish Constitutional Tribunal, decision of 11 May 2005, K 18/04, para 18.

[36] BVerfG, *OMT*, 2 BvR 2728/13, 2 BvR 2729/13, 2 BvR 2730/13, 2 BvR 2731/13, 2 BvE 13/13, ruling of 14 January 2014, nyr.

[37] BVerfG, *Honeywell*, 2 BvR 2661/06, ruling of 6 July 2010, Absatz-Nr. (1–116).

[38] Its decisions take the exceptional force of ordinary laws in the national legal hierarchy, see Art 93 and 94 GG, in particular Art 94(2).

[39] See a Frankfurter Allgemeine Zeitung article on an opinion poll conducted by the respected Allensbach Institute finding inter alia that 80 percent of interviewees welcomed Karlsruhe's ability to overrule parliamentary decisions. Available at http://www.faz.net/aktuell/politik/inland/bundesverfassungsgericht-das-bollwerk-11863396.html. See also comments by Armin von Bogdandy, stating: '(The GCC) give[s] a voice to those parts of the population that don't have an influence […] It is largely successful. The court enjoys very high public reputation'. Available at http://www.ft.com/cms/s/0/78df7420-dfa5-11e1-9bb7-00144feab49a.html#axzz2HIhzmibt.

[40] BVerfG, 2 BvR 987/10, ruling of 7 September 2011, Absatz-Nr. (1–142).

amount of international criticism. Some argued that it might face marginalisation as a consequence of its continuous boycott of the preliminary ruling procedure.[41] Furthermore in the *OMT* case, the GCC did not make a reference to the CJEU without making a clear statement how it sees the case—clearer than what is usual in this context. Indeed, it gave a number of reasons why it assumed that the OMT scheme exceeded the ECB's monetary policy mandate and thus infringed the sovereignty of the Member States, as well as that it violates the prohibition of monetary financing, which is one of the key pillars of the architecture of the European Monetary Union (EMU). However, the GCC pointed the CJEU at the same time to a back door by indicating that a restrictive interpretation of the scheme could potentially achieve conformity with EU law. The GCC hence entered into a direct conversation with the CJEU but with a clear stand and a demand to be treated as an equal. The preliminary ruling procedure only works as part of a relationship of trust and cooperation between the judiciaries of the different legal contexts. The CJEU 'for the most part, has been careful to understand its position as a *Primus Inter Pares*—as playing its role in a cooperative, non-hierarchical, judicial process involving "European" courts [...]'.[42] Lower national courts may by requesting preliminary rulings 'be good Europeans, extend the reach of the rule-of-law to cover the obligations their states have assumed within the European Union and, last but certainly not least, enjoy a huge judicial empowerment boost'.[43] The preliminary ruling procedure thereby creates a win-win situation. It empowers (lower) national courts, extends the reach of their control and has the great advantage of the 'compliance pull associated with domestic courts'.[44] This has allowed the CJEU to give influential constitutional rulings under a procedure, which is meant to ensure that the application and enforcement in detail is left to the national court and is part of a system that is aimed to ensure cultural and legal diversity. Indeed, the CJEU's case law distilling general principles of EU law from the 'constitutional traditions common to the Member States'[45] presupposes that the traditions of the Member States are different from the outset and that they remain diverse. It does not impose one set of uniform European values. The costs of breaking with the legal recognition of claims of EU law are extraordinarily high and for lower national courts this would also mean breaking with the broader continuous recognition of EU law by national law. This gives the CJEU extraordinary compliance pull. Perhaps originally there was no 'compelling reason' to subscribe to the CJEU's vision of the EU as an integration organisation[46]—neither for national

---

[41] Cartabia, 'Europe and Rights' (n 8) at 29. See also: JHH Weiler, 'Judicial Ego' (2011) 9 *International Journal of Constitutional Law* 1, arguing that 'on matters of European law its [the GCC's] reputation has gone from bad to worse and at present its credibility on Europe is in the dog house'.

[42] Weiler, 'Judicial Ego' (ibid).

[43] ibid (n 41).

[44] ibid (n 41) at 1.

[45] Later codified, see Art 6(3) TEU.

[46] N MacCormick, *Questioning Sovereignty* (Oxford, Oxford University Press, 1999) 104.

courts nor for national Governments. The interlocking of legal spheres, furthered by the CJEU's case law, has created this compelling reason.

(ii) Without a Formal Mechanism

As is well explored in literature, national courts and the CJEU have also entered long ago into a judicial discourse outside of the preliminary ruling procedure. The most articulate discourse has taken place between the CJEU and the GCC, including the early rulings in *Solange I*, *Solange II*, and the *Maastricht Treaty* ruling, as well as the more recent rulings in *Lisbon Treaty* (2009) and *Honeywell* (2010).[47] The relationship between the two courts is characterised by a mix of exercising judicial pressure and respect for political reality.

The GCC has flagged up different issues of concern, including human rights protection (*Solange I* and *II*), ultra vires control (*Maastricht Treaty*), and an *identity* review (*Lisbon Treaty*). Additionally in the above-mentioned case of *Honeywell,* the GCC accepted to rule on whether the CJEU had acted ultra vires. Yet, it took a 'remarkably restrictive approach to *ultra vires* review' and followed in this 'a similar path as in its famous *Solange* jurisprudence with regard to fundamental rights review'.[48] The GCC explained its decision to reject the constitutional complaint against the CJEU's decision by stating that the CJEU is 'not precluded from refining the law by means of methodically bound case-law'.[49] This might be a surprise in light of the poor reasoning that the CJEU offered in the contested case, *Mangold*,[50] for introducing a general principle of non-discrimination on the grounds of age, which came to many as a surprise.[51] Nonetheless, the case demonstrates national courts' respect for methodologically sound legal reasoning in principle. While legal reasoning of course is not free of the political, legal

---

[47] *Solange I*, BVerfGE 37, 271, 2 BvL 52/71, ruling of 29 May 1974; *Solange II*, BVerfGE 73, 339, 2 BvR 197/83, ruling of 22 October 1986; *Maastricht Treaty*, BVerfGE 89, 155, 2 BvR 2134, 2159/92, ruling of 12 October 1993; *Lisbon Treaty*, 2 BvE 2/08, ruling of 30 June 2009. *Honeywell* (n 37).

[48] M Payandeh, 'Constitutional Review of EU law after *Honeywell*: Contextualizing the Relationship between the German Constitutional Court and the EU Court of Justice' (2011) 48 *CML Rev* 9. See similarly, M Kumm, 'Constitutionalism and the Moral Point of Constitutional Pluralism: Institutional Civil Disobedience and Conscientious Objection' in J Dickson and P Eleftheriadis (eds), *Philosophical Foundations of EU Law* (Oxford, Oxford University Press, 2012).

[49] BVerfG, *Honeywell* (n 37), at para 62: 'Dem Gerichtshof ist auch Rechtsfortbildung im Wege methodisch gebundener Rechtsprechung nicht verwehrt'. Similarly the GCC ruled that national courts had an obligation to consider the ECHR and rulings of the ECtHR in a methodologically sound manner. See BVerfG, 2 BvR 2307/06, ruling of 4 February 2010, Absatz-Nr. (1–27)), nyr, available at http://www.bverfg.de/entscheidungen/rk20100204_2bvr230706.html.

[50] *Mangold*, BVerfGE 126, 286, 2 BvR 2661/06, ruling of 6 July 2010.

[51] See eg: R Herzog, 'Stoppt den Europaischen Gerichtshof', *Frankfurter Allgemeine Zeitung*, 8 September 2008; S Krebbert, 'The Social Rights Approach of the European Court of Justice to Enforce European Employment Law' (2006) 27 *Comparative Labor Law & Policy Journal* 377, 382–92; K Riesenhuber, 'Annotation on Mangold Judgment' (2007) 3 *European Review of Contract Law* 62, 67–68. On the weak methodology, see U Preis, 'Verbot der Altersdiskriminierung als Gemeinschaftsgrundrecht' (2006) 23 *Neue Zeitschrift für Arbeitsrecht* 401, 405 which notes: 'The ECJ is walking on thin ice. [...] A legal argument can hardly be weaker'.

reasoning can allow stepping away from immediate political pressures and give courts an authority different from policy makers (see above). Legal reasoning has allowed for a parallel discussion that complements and restrains the political debate in the specific compound context of EU law. Indeed, what the internal EU discourse demonstrates is that courts can draw lines for the political, but that they must be sufficiently aware of political realities. At the same time, if law is used to disguise the political it loses its independent judgment and ultimately credibility.

This is the background of Joseph Weiler's accusation that the GCC has 'cried Wolf too many times to be taken seriously',[52] which continues to be very relevant in the context of the judicial review of instruments adopted to mitigate the Eurocrises. In 2009, the GCC indicated specifically that 'fundamental fiscal decisions on revenue and expenditure' must be taken in the national context. In 2011, the GCC ruled that 'the amount of the guarantees given' in the Greece aid and Euro rescue package did not exceed 'the limit of budget capacity to such an extent that budget autonomy would virtually be rendered completely ineffective'[53] and that it cannot step into the shoes of the national legislator. The 'lines drawn in the sand'[54] that the *Lisbon Treaty* judgment placed around the national expenditure, appear to have been erased by the tides of the financial markets. In 2012, the heads of states and governments of 25 Member States took a further step of interlocking by signing a Treaty on Stability, Coordination and Governance in the Economic and Monetary Union (Fiscal Compact) that requires its signatories to introduce the agreed budget deficit rules in national law through 'provisions of binding force and permanent character, preferably constitutional, or otherwise guaranteed to be fully respected and adhered to throughout the national budgetary processes'.[55] As a result the authority of the EU and of the national (constitutional) legislator are so closely interlocked that they blur from the perspective of the individual. The Fiscal Compact was concluded by national governments, ratified by national parliaments. It is an intergovernmental treaty adopted outside the EU legal context but so closely interwoven with the EU law, in particular the fiscal provisions of the EU treaties, that it can easily be mistaken for EU law. In light of the complex political and economic situation, the GCC understandably demonstrated great respect for the political powers (internal legislator). It may also have recognised that rulings on EU issues are no longer a matter of EU power versus national sovereignty but that the two contexts are so closely interlocked that they set together the background for an ongoing struggle between law and politics.

The CJEU's rulings also frequently contain statements of principle that are in practice highly flexibly interpreted, including by the CJEU itself. Illustrative

---

[52] Weiler, 'Judicial Ego,' (n 41).

[53] BVerfG (n 40).

[54] MacCormick, *Questioning Sovereignty* (n 46) at 100 with regard to the Maastricht decision.

[55] Art 3(2). The German Constitution does already contain a clause on budgetary discipline, see Art 109 GG.

examples are the CJEU's flexible approach to finding a legal basis[56] and its broad human rights approach without paying much attention to the specific boundaries of EU law in its rulings on rights of transsexuals[57] and citizenship.[58] Hence, both the GCC and the CJEU can at times be accused of making constitutional asser-tions but finding practical solutions that later undermine these vocal assertions. This is part of their discourse: both make principled statements about existing *legal* limits of EU competences but when it comes to the test of political real-ity they are willing to extend these limits. Even before the German Constitution introduced a special provision on EU law in 1992, the GCC accepted that EU law ranks higher than later adopted ordinary national laws—arguably without any basis in the national constitution but rather influenced by the (constitutional character of) EU law itself and of the decisions of the CJEU.[59] Similarly, the GCC's *Solange* doctrine recognised the authority of EU law and accepted it as different from international law—again before the special position of EU law was codified in the Germany Constitution.

The disagreement about how tensions between international, national and EU law should be reconciled is not new. Nor are situations where different courts rule on identical or at least very similar factual situations that involve the same norms. However, in certain policy fields a new intensity of overlapping judicial review has been reached, including beyond the boundaries of the EU. An example is counter-terrorist sanctions against individuals implementing UN Security Council Resolutions. A large number of judicial bodies have been called on to rule on the legality of these measures, including the CJEU, the Court of First Instance/the General Court, the European Court of Human Rights (ECtHR), the UK Supreme Court, the Swiss Supreme Court, and the Canadian Federal Court.[60] The different

---

[56] See on the pre-Lisbon legal basis for counter-terrorist sanctions, C Eckes, 'Judicial Review of European Anti-Terrorism Measures—The Yusuf and Kadi judgments of the Court of First Instance' (2008) 14 *European Law Journal* 74. See also on the EU tobacco legislation, M Kumm, 'Constitutionalising Subsidiarity in Integrated Markets: The Case of Tobacco Regulation in the European Union' (2006) 12 *European Law Journal* 503, 516–17. For a wider survey of the CJEU's case law after *Tobacco Advertising I*, see S Weatherill, 'The Limits of Legislative Harmonization Ten Years after Tobacco Advertising: How the Court's Case Law has Become a 'Drafting Guide'" (2011) 12 *German Law Journal* 828.

[57] Case C-117/01 *KB v National Health Service Pensions Agency and Others* [2004] ECR I-541; Case C-423/04 *Richards v Secretary of State for Work and Pensions* [2006] ECR I-3585.

[58] Eg Case C-256/11 *Dereci et al v Bundesministerium für Inneres*, judgment of 15 November 2011, nyr.

[59] BVerfGE 22, 293 (1967) and BVerfGE 31, 145 (1971).

[60] ECtHR, *Case of Nada v Switzerland* Application no 10593/08 (2012); UK Supreme Court, *Her Majesty's Treasury (Respondent) v Mohammed Jabar Ahmed and others (FC) (Appellants); Her Majesty's Treasury (Respondent) v Mohammed al-Ghabra (FC) (Appellant); R (on the application of Hani El Sayed Sabaei Youssef) (Respondent) v Her Majesty's Treasury (Appellant)* [2010] UKSC 2; on appeal from: [2008] EWCA Civ 1187. Views of the Human Rights Committee, *Nabil Sayadi and Patricia Vinck against Belgium* [2008], concerning communication no 1472/2006; Court of Justice, Joined Cases C-584, 593 & 595/10 P, *Kadi II*, judgment of 18 July 2013, nyr; General Court, Case T-85/09 *Yassin Abdullah Kadi v Commission (Kadi II)* [2010] ECR I-5177; Court of Justice, Case C-402/05 P and C-415/05 P *Kadi v Council (Kadi I)* [2008] ECR I-6351; CFI, T-315/01 *Yassin Abdullah Kadi v Council and Commission* [2005] ECR II-3649; Federal Court of Canada, *Abousfian Abdelrazik v The Minister of Foreign Affairs and the Attorney General of Canada* [2009] FC 580.

courts have considered each other's decisions to different degrees. In its high-profile ruling on sanctions in the case of *Nada*,[61] the ECtHR engaged intensively with the previous sanctions decision of other courts.[62] In its *Ahmed* ruling of 2010, the UK Supreme Court by contrast largely ignored the previous *Kadi* ruling of the CJEU and also disregarded the existing EU law governing the legal situations of the applicants—ignoring in fact the 'legal limits on the sovereignty of the UK Parliament [...] entailed by membership of the EU'.[63] The judicial discourse will continue: the CJEU is now asked to rule for the second time on the legality of UN counter-terrorist sanctions.[64] And even from the 'internal perspective' of the same legal order, there is no longer normative agreement on how the different claims of authority relate to each other.[65] In truly interlocked legal contexts, the *one* correct solution can no longer be found by simply looking harder. The internal legal context has been modified and the validity of internal norms depends (at least de facto) on external norms and vice versa.

In the past, both national courts and the CJEU have regularly argued from a systemic perspective of national law versus EU law and vice versa. However, the understanding might be growing that in legal contexts that are so deeply interlocked this systemic juxtaposition is misrepresenting not only political but also legal reality. This is to some extent also a result of judicial interaction. The internal European judicial discourse, including the judicial discourse outside of the preliminary ruling procedure, has contributed as much to the enforcement of the principle of supremacy as it has contributed to the delimitation of EU powers. The latter is often the focus of the analysis of the discourse between the CJEU and the GCC. The GCC has not only threatened to impose limits, but also vested EU law with authority by giving it a special position not recognised by the German Constitution at the time and by adapting its own principled statements to politics. It would be wrong to conclude that the GCC has not been listened to, only because it entered into the direct institutionalised discourse only in 2014. Its rulings concerning EU law extensively engage with the existence and nature of EU law. They aim to establish an intellectual authority and attract much attention beyond the national legal context. It is questionable whether the UK Supreme

---

[61] ECtHR, *Case of Nada* (ibid).

[62] See for a detailed analysis, C Eckes and S Hollenberg, 'Reconciling Different Legal Spheres in Theory and Practice: Pluralism and Constitutionalism in the Cases of Al-Jedda, Ahmed and Nada', (2013) 20 *Maastricht Journal of European and Comparative Law* 220.

[63] F Jacobs, *The Sovereignty of Law—The European Way* (Cambridge, Cambridge University Press, 2007) 7.

[64] The hearing in the appeal against the *Kadi II* decision of the General Court took place on 16 October 2012.

[65] The most prominent example is the diametrically opposed decisions of the CJEU and the CFI in the *Kadi* case (n 59). However, equally interesting on this point is a comparison of the attitude of the First and the Second senate of the GCC. While the former appears more open towards EU law, the latter is in principle responsible for European affairs. In its data retention decision, the First Senate barely mentions the Lisbon Treaty decision of the Second Senate. See BVerfG, 1 BvR 256/08, 1 BvR 263/08, 1 BvR 586/08, ruling of 2 March 2010, Absatz-Nr. (1–345).

Court's choice to ignore EU law has placed it in a more credible position in the internal European discourse.

B. The Court of Justice Taking Part in the External Discourse

Besides the judicial discourse within the EU, the CJEU is also increasingly involved in an external discourse. It takes account of and refers to the decisions of external judicial bodies, most prominently the ECtHR. It further gives rulings in cases concerning issues that are overlapping with the issues raised in other judicial bodies, such as the European Free Trade Association States (EFTA) Court and the WTO Dispute Mechanism.

(i) European Court of Human Rights

The Strasbourg and the Luxembourg Court take note of each other's rulings—this has already been observed 20 years ago.[66] A significant ruling in the early years was the *Marckx* case.[67] The ECtHR relied on a completely new doctrine of temporary limitation of the effects of judicial ruling by referring to the CJEU's ruling in the *Defrenne* case,[68] in which the CJEU for the first time limited the retroactive effect of its own ruling. The CJEU did not rely on the 'common traditions of the Member States' in this case since the retroactive limitation of the effect of judicial rulings was largely unknown.[69]

In the other direction, as is well known, the Lisbon Treaty has made EU accession to the European Convention on Human Rights (ECHR) a legal obligation.[70] Pre-accession, the EU is not itself directly bound by the Convention, either under international law or EU law. However, the ECHR and its interpretation by the ECtHR have played a great role in the EU's constitutionalisation. In many landmark cases, the CJEU uses both general principles of EU law and the ECHR and the ECtHR's case law to support its argument[71] and the EU treaties and the EU Charter of Fundamental Rights all include references to the ECHR.[72] In more recent years,

---

[66] J Polakiewicz and V Jacob-Foltzer, 'The European Human Rights Convention in Domestic Law: The Impact of the Strasbourg Case-Law in States Where Direct Effect is Given to the Convention—Part 2' (1991) 12 *Human Rights Law Journal* 125, 142.

[67] *Marckx v Belgium* (1979) Series A no 31.

[68] Case C-43/75 *Defrenne v Sabena* [1979] ECR 455.

[69] F Jacobs, 'Judicial Dialogue and the Cross-Fertilization of Legal Systems: the European Court of Justice' (2003) 38 *Texas International Law Journal* 547: Austria, which was not a Member State until 20 years later, applied this doctrine.

[70] Art 218(8) TFEU.

[71] Case C-60/00 *Carpenter* [2002] ECR I-6279; Case C-112/00 *Schmidberger* [2003] ECR I-5659.

[72] See Art 6(2) and (3) TEU, Art 218(6)(a)(ii) and (8) TFEU; Arts 1 and 2 of Protocol 8 and Protocol 24. Arts 52(3) and 53 of the Charter of Fundamental Rights.

the EU Charter of Fundamental Rights has grown in importance[73] and the CJEU has dropped its earlier 'general principles' or 'source of inspiration' approach, and has started to refer directly to ECHR provisions.[74] The EU Charter—after much discussion[75]—also specifically refers to the case law of the ECtHR, albeit in its Preamble, not in the main text.[76] The CJEU has ruled in *JMcB v LE* that where rights in the Charter correspond to rights in the ECHR, the CJEU should follow the case law of the ECtHR.[77] The CJEU has made significantly more references to the ECHR in the years 2010, 2011 and 2012 than in the previous three years.[78] By contrast with the internal discourse discussed above, the CJEU has not taken a systemic perspective in the interaction with the ECHR and the case law of the ECtHR, but rather considered individuals the ultimate point of reference. This becomes apparent in recent cases on citizenship and migration, in which the CJEU relies particularly often on Convention rights.[79] Furthermore, EU law is regularly used in the arguments before the ECtHR[80] and the ECtHR has repeatedly given judgments that are directly relevant for the EU.[81] In line with its mandate, the ECtHR does so by relating all considered law to the position of the individual. In light of Article 6(3) TEU in particular, it would be contrary to EU law to disregard the Convention. At the same time, there is an important legal difference between 'giving due account to' and being legally bound by the provisions of the ECHR, as authoritatively interpreted by the ECtHR. This was demonstrated most impressively by the CJEU's *Kadi* ruling.[82] Even though before 2008 the Court had in settled case law given due account to UN Security Council

---

[73] See eg: Joined Cases C-92/09 *Volker and Markus Schecke GbR* and C-93/09 *Hartmut Eifert v Land Essen* [2010] ECR I-000. See also, N O'Meara, '"A More Secure Europe of Rights?" The European Court of Human Rights, the Court of Justice of the European Union and EU Accession to the ECHR' (2011) 12 *German Law Journal* 10, 1813–32 at 1819.

[74] Case C-413/99 *Baumbast* [2002] ECR I-7091, 72; Case C-60/00 *Carpenter* (n 70) at 41–42; Case C-200/02 *Kunqian Catherine Zhu Chen* [2004] ECR I-9925, 16.

[75] L Scheek, 'Diplomatic Intrusions, Dialogues, and Fragile Equilibria: The European Court as a Constitutional Actor of the EU' in J Christoffersen and MR Madsen (eds), *The European court of Human Rights between Law and Politics* (Oxford, Oxford University Press, 2011) 172.

[76] Art 52(3) of the Charter of Fundamental Rights.

[77] Case C-400/10 PPU *JMcB v LE* [2010] ECR I-8965, 53. S Douglas-Scott interprets 'correspond' as 'the same' or 'identical', see: S Douglas-Scott, 'The European Union and Human Rights after the Treaty of Lisbon' (2011) 11 *Human Rights Law Review* 4, 655–66. This seems to be an overly strict reading. Indeed, the explanations to the Charter offer a list of 'corresponding rights'. This appears to offer a good interpretation of the scope of the CJEU's ruling.

[78] In 2010, 2011 and 2012, 90 judgments of the CJEU and AG opinions refer to the ECHR. In the three previous years (2007–09), 68 judgments and opinions made a reference to the Convention.

[79] In the years 2010 to 2012, the Court referred to the ECHR in nine judgments concerning Area of Freedom, Security and Justice (AFSJ) matters and in four judgments concerning citizenship, including landmark cases such as Case C-34/09 *Ruiz Zambrano*, judgment of 8 March 2011, nyr. In the same period, the ECHR was used in 13 Advocate General Opinions on cases concerning AFSJ matters, nine opinions concerning citizenship and three opinions concerning equal treatment. See also: Eckes, 'EU Accession to the ECHR: Between Autonomy and Adaptation' (n 1).

[80] In 2012 only, the EU was brought up 51 times in rulings of the ECtHR, including 15 times by the parties and 18 times by the court (including separate opinions).

[81] See Eckes, 'EU Accession' (n 78) 254–85.

[82] Cases C-402/05 P and C-415/05 P *Kadi* (n 59).

Resolutions,[83] it chose to rely on the fact that the EU is not a member of the UN and is therefore not directly bound by its Charter or its Security Council Resolutions.[84]

After the EU's accession to the ECHR,[85] the ECHR will be directly binding on the EU and judicial discourse between the CJEU and the ECtHR will become institutionalised with the establishment of the prior involvement option under the co-respondent mechanism.[86] The co-respondent mechanism will 'allow the EU to become a co-respondent to proceedings instituted against one or more of its Member States and, similarly, to allow the EU Member States to become co-respondents to proceedings instituted against the EU'.[87] If the CJEU was not previously involved in a case, in which the EU becomes a co-respondent, the ECtHR may stay the proceedings and give the CJEU the opportunity to scrutinise compliance with the Convention. Similar arrangements have earlier been made under the second Agreement on the European Economic Area[88] and under the Agreements Establishing the European Common Aviation Area.[89] It places the CJEU in the privileged position of being asked for an interpretation before the ECtHR gives its ruling. The Court's opinion is likely to have an impact on the legal discourse in Strasbourg. It might even frame the further discussion, since parties are invited to submit their observations after the CJEU has given its opinion on the case.[90] They will most likely engage with the CJEU's views. At present, the CJEU does so by holding the case law of the ECtHR at arm's length. This might no longer be possible after accession. The CJEU would for the first time be at the receiving end of a formalised judicial discourse.

---

[83] See eg: Case C-84/95 *Bosphorus* [1996] ECR I-3953 and Case C-124/95 *Centro-Com* [1997] ECR I-81.

[84] Cases C-402/05 P and C-415/05 P *Kadi* (n 59) at 294: 'special importance' not 'binding force'.

[85] See on the EU's accession also, J Heliskoski, 'The Arrangement Governing the Relationship between the ECtHR and the CJEU in the Draft Treaty on the Accession to the ECHR' in this volume (ch 12).

[86] This is what has been agreed in the Draft Agreement on the Accession of the European Union to the European Convention on Human Rights, CDDH-UE(2011)16.

[87] ibid, para 29.

[88] Accepted by the Court of Justice in Opinion 1/92 *Re Second Draft EEA Agreement* [1992] ECR I-2821. See Arts 105(3) and 111(3) of the EEA Agreement.

Art 105(3): 'If the EEA Joint Committee within two months after a difference in the case law of the two Courts has been brought before it, has not succeeded to preserve the homogeneous interpretation of the Agreement, the procedures laid down in Article 111 may be applied'.

Art 109(5): 'In case of disagreement between these two bodies [EFTA Surveillance Authority and EU Commission] with regard to the action to be taken in relation to a complaint or with regard to the result of the examination, either of the bodies may refer the matter to the EEA Joint Committee which shall deal with it in accordance with Article 111'.

Art 111(3): 'If a dispute concerns the interpretation of provisions of this Agreement, which are identical in substance to corresponding rules of the Treaty establishing the European Economic Community and the Treaty establishing the European Coal and Steel Community and to acts adopted in application of these two Treaties and if the dispute has not been settled within three months after it has been brought before the EEA Joint Committee, the Contracting Parties to the dispute may agree to request the Court of Justice of the European Communities to give a ruling on the interpretation of the relevant rules'.

[89] Opinion 1/00 *Proposed Agreement between the European Commission and non-Member States on the Establishment of a European Common Aviation Area* [2002] ECR I-3493.

[90] Art 3(6) of the Accession Agreement.

(ii) EFTA Court

Less frequently discussed is the discourse between the EFTA Court and the CJEU. The European Economic Area (EEA) Agreement sets out that the interpretation and application of EU law and EEA law must be carried out 'in full deference to the independence of courts'.[91] Yet, it is an unequal institutionalised judicial discourse. The EFTA Court is bound by the case law of the CJEU preceding the conclusion of the EEA Agreement[92] and must take account of the CJEU's case law subsequent to 2 May 1992.[93] In practice, this has not made a difference.[94] The EFTA Court refers to the CJEU's case law in all its advisory opinions and in all its judgments.[95] It has further frequently adopted both the CJEU's reasoning and principles of EU law. The CJEU is not bound by the interpretation of the EFTA Court but has referred to and been influenced by its case law.[96] This is a rare honour in light of the fact that otherwise the Court only refers to the ECtHR. It even remains controversial whether it may be justified to interpret the EEA and the EU law differently.[97] Daniele Galo argues that the EEA Agreement should be construed as aiming to ensure at all times uniform interpretation between the two legal regimes.[98] The argument is that homogeneity is the purpose of the EEA Agreement, notwithstanding constitutional differences between EU law and the EEA Agreement. Francis Jacobs argues that differences in context and objectives of EU law and the EEA Agreement could justify a different interpretation. This finds support in the case law of the CJEU.[99]

It is fair to conclude that the relationship between the CJEU and the EFTA Court is very particular, because of its institutionalisation and also because of the choice to make it unequal—not only because of political importance but also as a matter of law. This has allowed the CJEU to recognise the authority of the EFTA Court without being threatened.

(iii) WTO Dispute Mechanism

The WTO has an exceptionally well-developed dispute settlement mechanism and produces (quasi-)judicial decisions that do not require consent and that are subject to an enforcement mechanism (trade sanctions). As is well known

[91] Recital 15 of the Preamble and Art 106 of the EEA Agreement.

[92] Art 6 EEA Agreement.

[93] Art 3(2) of the Agreement between the EFTA States on the Establishment of a Surveillance Authority and a Court of Justice (ESA/Court Agreement).

[94] Baudenbacher (n 5) at 204–13.

[95] D Galo, 'From Autonomy to Full Deference in the Relationship between the EFTA Court and the ECJ: The Case of the International Exhaustion of the Rights Conferred by a Trademark', *EUI Working Papers* RSCAS 2010/78.

[96] Jacobs, 'Judicial Dialogue' (n 68); Galo (ibid).

[97] In favour: Jacobs, 'Judicial Dialogue' (n 68) 552–53. Against: Galo (n 94).

[98] Galo (n 94) at 2 referring to: Preamble, paras 4 and 15; Arts 1, 6, 106, 107 and 111 of the EEA Agreement, as well as Art 3 of the ESA/Court Agreement.

[99] See in particular Opinion 1/91 *EEA Agreement* [1991] ECR I-6079.

and possibly discussed too extensively,[100] the CJEU does not give direct effect to decisions of the WTO dispute mechanism. This means that these decisions cannot directly be used as yardstick against which acts of the EU institutions can be reviewed. On appeal in the case of *Biret*,[101] the CJEU indicated in passing that the question of whether WTO dispute decisions enjoyed direct effect could be examined separately from general WTO law. This gave rise to speculation of whether the WTO dispute decision could enjoy direct effect. However, in the case of *Van Parys*,[102] the Court closed this avenue and made clear that the nature of the dispute settlement mechanism did not justify conferring direct effect on WTO dispute decisions. It later confirmed this line in the case of *FIAMM*.[103]

The Court's rejection of direct effect of decisions of the WTO dispute settlement mechanism is based on several strands of argument. The first focuses on the nature of the WTO dispute settlement mechanism. Both in *Van Parys* and in *FIAMM* the Court emphasised the fact that WTO dispute resolution relied on negotiation between the parties. It focused on the temporary measures of compensation and suspension of concessions. The second strand traces the effect of the WTO dispute decision back to the effect of WTO law as such. In *FIAMM*, the Court explained that WTO dispute decisions do not have direct effect because they apply WTO law which does not have direct effect either.[104] Thirdly and this is a motivation that the Court does not make explicit, the Court might want to avoid acting in the place of or even against the legislator.[105] It should be added that this is not to say that WTO law does not play a role in disputes before the CJEU. The Court routinely interprets secondary EU law consistently with WTO law[106] and with rulings of the WTO Appellate Body.[107] It might even have entered into what Marco Bronckers called 'a muted dialogue'.[108] Decisions exist in which

---

[100] See eg E Paasivirta and PJ Kuijper, 'Does One Size Fit All? The European Community and the Responsibility of International Organizations' (2005) 36 *Netherlands Yearbook of International Law* 169. They emphasise that WTO law and decisions of the dispute settlement bodies are the exception that confirm the rule that international agreements do form part of the EU legal order and can have direct effect. More recently also decisions of the UN Convention on the Law of the Sea (UNCLOS) Tribunal, see Case C-308/06 *Intertanko* [2008] ECR I-4057.

[101] Case C-93/02 P *Biret International v Council* [2003] ECR I-10497.

[102] Case C-377/02 *Van Parys* [2005] ECR I-1465. See on the same issue and with the same outcome in more detail, Opinion of Advocate General Léger in Case C-351/04 *IKEA Wholesale* [2007] ECR I-7723, para 77 f.

[103] Cases C-120/06 P and C-121/06 P *FIAMM v Council and Commission* [2008] ECR I-6513.

[104] ibid.

[105] See PJ Kuijper and F Hoffmeister, 'WTO Influence on EU Law—Too Close for Comfort?' in R Wessel and S Blockmans (eds), *Between Autonomy and Dependence: The EU Legal Order Under the Influence of International Organizations* (The Hague, TMC Asser Press, 2013)

[106] See eg Case C-70/94 *Werner v Germany* [1995] ECR I-3189, para 23 and Case C-83/94 *Leifer and Others* [1995] ECR I-3231, para 24; but see also for an example where the Court did not take recourse to the technique of consistent interpretation: *Ikea Wholesale* (n 101). See in more detail about the attitude of the CJEU to giving effect to WTO dispute decisions, Kuijper and Hoffmeister, 'WTO Influence on EU Law' (ibid).

[107] See eg Case C-310/06 *FTS International v Belastingdienst –Duane West* [2007] ECR I-6749.

[108] M Bronckers, 'From "Direct Effect" to "Muted Dialogue": Recent Developments in the European Courts' Case Law on the WTO And Beyond' in M Bulterman, L Hancher, A McDonnell

the panel or Appellate Body took a position on the allocation of responsibility on the basis of the division of competences or tasks between the EU and its Member States under EU law.[109] In cases that could have been problematic, the Appellate Body has displayed considerable deference towards the EU. In the case of *Selected Customs Matters*, for instance, the Appellate Body was essentially invited to declare that the entire EU customs system was not sufficiently coherent.[110] However, it chose not to enter into this argument.

The concept of 'direct effect' and its understanding both with regard to EU law and with regard to international law should be seen in the light of the relations and discourse between different judicial bodies. By not giving direct effect to the decisions of the WTO dispute mechanism, the CJEU equally found a way to hold these decisions at arm's length. It can give effect to them and consider them without having to submit to their authority.

IV. WHAT LESSONS CAN BE TAKEN FROM THE INTERNAL EU DISCOURSE?

The Court has gained, during the past 50+ years, considerable experience in interacting with Member States' courts and in giving rulings that translate into different linguistic and conceptual universes. In areas falling within the scope of EU law, the case law of the CJEU serves as a 'co-operation tool' to frame the discussion in a linguistically accessible way. Suggestions have been made that international law could be used to a similar purpose[111] and that the International Court of Justice (ICJ) and the ECtHR should equally be equipped with the possibility of giving preliminary rulings.[112] With regard to the latter the first formalised direct discourse will be introduced between the CJEU and the ECtHR in the prior involvement procedure after EU accession. This raises the broader question: What could be learned from the inner EU experience for a wider judicial discourse?

The first main observation is that differences prevail between the judicial discourse within the EU and the external judicial discourse. In the former the CJEU has expressed a claim of *ultimate* authority for all matters of EU law, which

---

and H Sevenster (eds), *Views of European Law From the Mountain* (Alphen aan den Rijn, Kluwer Law International, 2009).

[109] See eg *European Communities—Customs Classification of Certain Computer Equipment*, Panel Report (adopted 5 February 1998) WT/DS62/R, WT/DS67/R, WT/DS68/R.

[110] Cases: *European Communities—Selected Customs Matters*, Request for Consultation by the US (21 September 2004) WT/D315/1; *European Communities—Selected Customs Matters*, Panel Report (adopted 16 June 2006) WT/DS 315/R, see paras 2.2–2.31; *European Communities—Selected Customs Matters*, AB Report (adopted 13 November 2006) WT/D315/AB/R, see para 69.

[111] Suggesting that this could also be the role of international law: E Benvenisti and GW Downs, 'National Courts, Domestic Democracy, and the Evolution of International Law' (2009) 20 *European Journal of International Law* 59, 66.

[112] See two of the past presidents of the ICJ at: R Higgins, 'The ICJ, the ECJ and the Integrity of International Law' (2003) 52 *ICLQ* 1, 17–20 and Opinion of Advocate General Warner in Case C-130/75 *Prais v Council* [1979] ECR 1589.

reaches—in different degrees of intensity—across the full range of policy fields. The effect of EU law within the national legal order does not usually depend on recognition or implementation of the particular EU command. The CJEU is at the centre of a pluricontextual compound legal system that is built through and on internal judicial discourse. It does not stand in a straight hierarchical line at the peak of an appeal system, but is used to being greatly dependent on the support of national courts. Indeed, the internal EU judicial discourse is part and parcel of the systemic purpose of 'creating an ever closer union among the peoples of Europe',[113] which has grown into a Union of fate and even if the ultimate threat of disobedience and even withdrawal from the Union continues to exist even after decades of interlocking between the EU and the national legal orders.[114] Furthermore, within the EU the continuous joint decision-taking and ever so close interaction between national players has created an institutionalised European political discourse, which may not be matched by a popular European political discourse, but which contributes nonetheless to the creation and continuation of this community of fate. While withdrawal may remain a *political* option, albeit at high political costs, interlocking through continuous recognition makes disobedience *legally* very difficult to justify for any individual national court. In the interlocked legal context of the EU, disobeying EU law would require lower national courts to also disobey national law and the authority of the higher national courts. For all courts, including the highest national courts, it entails disobeying national practice and disappointing created expectation.

By contrast, the purpose of an external discourse cannot be to work towards an ever closer Union. Indeed, the external discourse does not serve a joint systemic purpose. No external claim of authority is at the same time as comprehensive and ultimate as the claim of EU law within the national legal order. External claims of authority may be ultimate in the sense that they claim to set the highest applicable norm on a particular issue (eg UN Security Council Resolutions), but they do not claim ultimate authority on a broad range of issues immediately determining the lives of individuals, as does EU law. External claims remain limited to particular issues or areas and more often declare an ultimate expert judgment without direct legal authority within the domestic legal order. Hence, even though similarities can be indicated in the way, in which individual claims penetrate and in practice change the national legal context without specific confirmation by national legal authority in the particular case, the nature of the claim of ultimate authority of EU law is different from all phenomena in the international sphere. It is constitutional in nature because it claims ultimate authority over how to govern the political community. This has consequences for the judicial discourse. Externally the CJEU would neither be able to make a claim of ultimate authority. Even in

---

[113] Art 1(2) TEU.

[114] Great Britain has spoken more frankly about this option in recent years than many years before that (see eg the title story of the *Economist* of 8 December 2012).

the case of the EFTA Court, which follows the CJEU on all occasions, one cannot speak of ultimate authority.

Taking too much inspiration from the CJEU's authoritative participation in the internal discourse would most likely result in an overstretching of the CJEU's external authority. Only in a cooperative and interlocked system, where the distinction between external and internal claims of authority is at times impossible to draw, influence from the outside can be as effective as it is within the EU. Purely external control always entails a danger that the judicial body overstretches its authority and loses support within the other legal and judicial context. The described level of interlocking between the European and the national context, which is a result of both the CJEU's claim of *ultimate* authority and the fact that power is exercised by the same persons in both contexts, does no longer allow neatly juxtaposing the two contexts in legal analysis. Any such juxtaposition is overly conceptually simplified. This is different from the external EU context. EU law is not to any similar degree interwoven with the international legal context. Even in the case of the ECHR, where it is largely assumed that membership is an unwritten requirement for EU accession and from which much inspiration is drawn for the interpretation of EU law, in particular the Charter, the interlocking has been softened by the CJEU's arm's-length approach. Until accession the validity of EU law depends on compliance with the CJEU's interpretation of the ECHR. This is a rejection of the ultimate authority of the ECtHR in matters of human rights. Similarly, the CJEU has kept WTO law and the authority of the WTO dispute mechanism at distance with its decision not to grant direct effect.

A parallel between the judicial discourses within the EU legal order and outside is that they are both characterised by a power struggle between law and politics. Judicial decisions that cannot always be explained in purely legal terms restrain political actors, as well as the judiciary in a different legal context. A fundamental difference is the understanding of sovereignty in practice. States, including both the political actors and the national judiciaries, have accepted the limitation of their autonomy or sovereignty, if you will, in practice. EU law has managed to restrain Member States as a whole, and national actors, including the courts, individually. It attained a level of sovereignty within the national legal context that is not matched outside. To borrow the words of AG Jacobs this constitutes 'sovereignty of [EU] law',[115] which empowers courts in the ongoing struggle between law and politics. The CJEU does not have the same authority over external judicial bodies, nor do they have the same authority over the CJEU as national courts, whose recognition and support is particularly important in a constitutionalised system, with little tolerance for non-compliance. However, there are parallels between the internal and the external. One is the complexity of considerations underlying a decision in the balance between legal reasoning

---

[115] F Jacobs, *The Sovereignty of Law. The European Way* (Cambridge, Cambridge University Press, 2007).

and political considerations. It is not always possible to make a transparent *legal* argument. It might be simply impossible to legally reconcile different claims of ultimate authority with reference to some consistent legal framework. From the perspective of the individual citizen, both claims of ultimate authority have increasingly come into play alongside each other, usually demanding compliance with the same rules. The EU has installed its own claim of authority inside the national legal orders by evolution rather than revolution. No break has occurred and the old national political powers continue to rule alongside and within the EU sphere. Parallel developments can be witnessed in the international sphere. The test case is when the two claims conflict.

The CJEU is used to reconciling not only the views of different national courts but also to deal with executive power being exercised in the different contexts by either the same actors or at least in close interaction between the different contexts. The CJEU cannot be accused of being partisan for any individual Member State, European integration itself and the effectiveness of EU law has been the single most important concern of the CJEU. This might also explain why the CJEU avoids referring to case law of the Constitutional Courts of the EU Member States. It usually refers to the abstract of 'constitutional traditions common to the Member States' without specifically naming any. It does not endorse particular claims of authority more than others. The GCC by contrast, regularly refers to judgments of the CJEU[116]—in 2011 more often than to the case law of the ECtHR.[117] Outside of a constitutionalised framework, inclusion of external claims of authority and recognition of the authority of specific external judicial bodies is necessary to strengthen their relevance and allows extending authority beyond the domestic legal context. Outside, the CJEU rightly takes a discriminative approach towards external claims of authority.

The CJEU is further in a particular position, different from national courts interacting with external legal contexts. *Kadi* exemplifies the first particular difficulty of the CJEU in the external judicial discourse. The internal and the external discourse are connected at a deeper level. On the one hand, the CJEU may have additional difficulties to require obedience from national courts if it does not accept the authority of the UN Security Council (not a court!). On the other, had the CJEU accepted the UN Security Council's claim for absolute authority within the EU legal order, the GCC might have reconsidered its de facto acceptance that fundamental rights are sufficiently protected within the EU.[118] Secondly, the CJEU's position is different because the political organs of its own constitutional order (the EU institutions) are largely excluded from the decision-making process in most international organisations and under most international conventions by the simple fact that most international organisations and conventions allow only

---

[116] Sixteen references in 2011.

[117] ECtHR: 11 times in 2011.

[118] C Eckes, 'Protecting Supremacy from External Influences: A Precondition for a European Constitutional Legal Order?' (2012) 18 *European Law Journal* 230.

states to join. The UN, the Council of Europe, and the International Monitory Fund (IMF) are examples of powerful international organisations that the EU cannot join because of the provisions of their founding treaties.[119] The ECHR is the most prominent example where this is currently changing.[120] The exception is the WTO. This may explain why the CJEU defers to the EU political forces in the case of WTO dispute settlement decisions. At the same time within the EU legal order, Member States, rather than the EU political institutions, are at least in principle in the position to include more specific provisions in the EU treaties on how international law and the decisions of international courts and tribunals should be received.

On a more detailed level, a possible conclusion from the internal judicial discourse may be that there is a difference between influencing the specific substantive content of external claims of authority and reining in the exercise of power by the external institution. Within the informal internal EU discourse, national courts have exercised pressure and plausibly threatened disobedience not only to the EU actors but also to national political actors, who cannot control their own judiciaries. They mainly aimed to reign in the exercise of power and exclude ultra vires acts. To cooperate in a strictly organised constitutional structure, such as the preliminary ruling procedure, is a strong form of recognition. It allows debate on substance,[121] while interaction and mutual influence are institutionalised, usually with clear consequences for the exercise of power. The GCC's reference may optimistically be read as a recognition that trench warfare, ie pushing integration (CJEU) and defending national sovereignty (GCC), is ill suited to control the exercise of executive power in the context of the financial and economic crisis. It may be a step towards the next level of maturity of the European judicial network, in which institutionalised recognition trickles down through the domestic system and influences formal political acceptance and ultimately acceptance by individuals. Depending on the institutionalised interaction courts are in a stronger position to influence the substantive focus of the discussion.

V. CONCLUSION

The times of self-contained jurisdictions are over. Legal spheres interlock with no reasonably articulated theoretical framework. This entails new configurations of compound executive power stretching across jurisdictions. It evokes a Schmittian view in several respects. Carl Schmitt's analysis of the general debility

---

[119] Art 4(1) of the UN Charter: 'peace-loving states'; Art 4 of the Council of Europe Statute: 'European state'; Art II s 2 of the Agreement of the International Monetary Fund: 'other countries'.
[120] Protocol 14.
[121] Specific legal concepts, such as proportionality and legal certainty have been introduced into English law: F Jacobs, 'Judicial Dialogue' (n 68) at 549.

of legislatures and judges in the modern administrative state[122] applies not only to the exceptional times of war but may become a permanent phenomenon in a pluricontextual setting. It is most visible in the current economic and financial crises in the EU context. The practices of a 'strong' executive are unprecedented: instruments, practices and (even) institutions have emerged in Europe with extensive powers over national constitutions and institutions, particularly on national budgets, banking supervision and financial stability.[123] When introduced into the national constitution, they are recognised by the domestic legal system. Yet, these external rules are not stable but develop separately from the domestic legal order and are rooted in their separate claim of ultimate authority. At the same time, European and international executive power is composed of (components of) national executive power and thus they are inextricably linked in a manner that at times defies attempts to hold individual or collective actors to account separately, either legally or politically.

Judicial discourse can make a contribution to counterbalancing and controlling the executive in the increasingly pluricontextual setting, where norms interlock in a non-hierarchical manner. To formulate the issue within the state-centric linguistic framework of international law: judicial discourse is necessary to address problems resulting from the inter-state origin of intra-state norms of international and European law. This chapter concluded that the internal EU discourse can only contribute to reflections on the external discourse at an abstract level. Fundamental differences will continue to require a very different approach of the CJEU to the internal and the external. This is an indirect confirmation of the fact that the legal spheres within the EU are more closely interlocked than the EU legal sphere with any of the discussed external ones.

What can be learned from the internal EU discourse is that in a struggle of power in the space between law and politics legal ambiguity can be a conscious choice to avoid political confrontation. The CJEU, as well as the Member States' courts, have long experience in respecting the political while at the same time exercising judicial pressure. While many criticise the CJEU and also the GCC for ultimately bowing to politics, both have had great influence on reigning in the political forces in the EU context. At the same time in the external sphere, law is necessarily in a weaker position in relation to politics. Lower constitutionalisation requires more cautious legal attempts to exercise any control of the external context. External control largely depends on recognition, and within the EU national recognition by courts, political actors and individuals of the EU's claim of authority has led to an autonomous sovereignty of EU law within the national legal order. While all courts, national as well as international, start from a perspective

---

[122] C Schmitt, *Legalität und Legitimität* 7th edn (Berlin, Duncker & Humblot, 1998); see also: WE Scheuerman, *Between the Norm and the Exception: The Frankfurt School and the Rule of Law* (Cambridge, MA, MIT Press, 1994).

[123] N Moloney, 'The European Securities and Market Authority and Institutional Design for the EU Financial Markets—a Tale of Two Competences: Part (1) Rule-Making' (2011) 12 *European Business Organization Law Review* 41.

of judicial autarchy and tend to be self-referential,[124] the national courts of the Member States have grown into their role as European courts. The CJEU has successfully convinced national courts to 'include validity-in-E[U]-law as a criterion of validity domestically'.[125]

Conceptual borrowing is a second characteristic of the internal EU discourse that could inspire and arguably has inspired the external discourse in the case of the ECHR. The CJEU has succeeded in translating national constitutional rights into the EU context. These rights, read through the CJEU's filter, have had a great effect on the development of the EU legal order. This has fostered recognition and mutual influence within the EU. Judicial discourse practices are a core element of the development of EU public law. Even though judicial systems deliver justice contingent on their own legal and constitutional context, repeated recognition of external claims of authority can change the conception of justice at a deep level. Legal systems are artificial normative constructions that develop dynamically. External norms can simply become part of the internal legal system, including their practice of claiming of ultimate authority. It becomes part of how citizens (and lawyers) understand the law. The motivation of compliance might become pluricontextual too. Citizens comply with EU law because their state says so, but increasingly citizens, in particular those who rely on their free movement rights, also recognise the Union's authority and respect rules because the Union says so. As long as the two sources of authority point in the same direction, no decision of loyalty needs to be taken. Contradictory claims of ultimate authority do not need to result in contradictory rules for citizens. This is similar in the external sphere. The most illustrative example might be the EFTA Court, which borrows the CJEU's interpretation for identical legal concepts under the EFTA Agreement.

Finally, while the CJEU and national courts have often relied on a systemic legal reasoning, which is unsuited for the external judicial discourse, EU law itself also makes the individual the ultimate point of reference. In an environment where ultimate political authority remains ambiguous, the individual has served as a point of reference for actors from different legal contexts. The direct link between EU law, including rulings of the CJEU, and individuals is one of the particularities of EU law. The Court relies not only on support and recognition by national judges but also on the recognition (use in national disputes) by individuals. For the external discourse this might be more difficult, since by their nature, external relations have less often a direct impact on the rights of individuals. They often concern question of division of power rather than straight forwardly questions of individual justice. One sign of this is the fact that many fundamental decisions in the area of EU external relations were taken as enforcement actions rather than preliminary rulings. However, examples are increasing in which external claims of authority affect individuals. This is a chance for a move away from a systemic approach to an approach that reasons from the position of the individual legal subject.

---

[124] See for international courts, CPR Romano, 'Deciphering the Grammar of the International Jurisprudential Dialogue' (2009) 41 *International Law and Politics* 755, 758.
[125] MacCormick, *Questioning Sovereignty* (n 46) at 115.

Part IV

The Court and the International Legal System

11

The Kadi Case—Constitutional Core Values and International Law— Finding the Balance?[1]

JULIANE KOKOTT AND CHRISTOPH SOBOTTA

I. INTRODUCTION

T HE *KADI* CASE[2] is perhaps the most visible and interesting case of the Court of Justice of the European Union (hereafter referred to as 'the CJEU' or 'the Court') for external relations in recent years. The Court essentially had to decide whether a UN Security Council resolution should enjoy primacy over the law of the European Union (hereafter referred to as 'the EU' or 'the Union'). We all know that the Court did not allow for this primacy.

This judgment and the Court's reasoning have provoked severe criticism. The Court's dualist approach was described as unfaithful to its traditional fidelity to public international law[3] and inserting itself in the tradition of nationalism.[4] However, we would underline the opening that the Court indicated which would allow for precedence of Security Council measures, if sufficient safeguards for human rights were created. Most interestingly, it seems that the Security Council

---

[1] An earlier version of this text was published in (2012) 23(4) *European Journal of International Law* 1015, at http://ejil.oxfordjournals.org/content/23/4/1015.full.pdf. See also the comments by: N Yang, at http://www.ejiltalk.org/comment-on-kokottsobotta-the-kadi-case-constitutional-core-values-and-international-law-finding-the-balance/; A Tzanakopoulos, at http://www.ejiltalk.org/kadi-and-the-solange-argument-in-international-law-2/; as well as the reply by the present authors, at http://www.ejiltalk.org/the-kadi-case-response-by-juliane-kokott-and-christoph-sobotta/.

[2] Cases C-402/05 P and C-415/05 *P Kadi and Al Barakaat International Foundation v Council and Commission (Kadi I)* [2008] ECR I–6351.

[3] G de Búrca, 'The European Court of Justice and the International Legal Order After *Kadi*' (2010) 51 *Harvard International Law Journal* 1, at 44ff.

[4] B Fassbender, 'Triepel in Luxemburg. Die dualistische Sicht des Verhältnisses zwischen Europa- und Völkerrecht in der "Kadi-Rechtsprechung" des EuGH als Problem des Selbstverständnisses der Europäischen Union' (2010) *Die Öffentliche Verwaltung* 333, at 340. See also C Tomuschat, 'The Kadi Case: What Relationship is there between the Universal Legal Order under the Auspices of the United Nations and the EU Legal Order?' (2009) 28 *Yearbook of European Law* 654, at 658ff and 663; E Cannizzaro, 'Security Council Resolutions and EC Fundamental Rights: Some Remarks on the ECJ Decision in the Kadi Case' (2009) 28 *Yearbook of European Law* 593, at 597ff.

has recently risen to the challenge by introducing a strong review mechanism. Though this mechanism cannot exclude all possible conflicts between EU law and UN law, it can significantly reduce the risk of divergent decisions.

After a short overview of the General Court's (GC's) reasoning in the first instance judgment and of the judgment on appeal, we will show how far the Court's approach should be characterised as dualist, or rather as a variation of the so-called '*Solange*' concept. This concept was developed by the German Constitutional Court and also applied by the European Court of Human Rights. Against this background, we will address the review mechanism introduced by the Security Council after *Kadi*.

II. THE *KADI* JUDGMENT

The basic facts of the *Kadi* case are as follows. In the UN Security Council, Kadi was identified as a possible supporter of Al-Qaida. Therefore, he was singled out for sanctions, in particular for an assets freeze. The EU transposed this UN sanction by a regulation which Kadi then attacked before the EU courts. At first instance, the GC refused to review the EU regulation because this would amount to a review of the measure of the Security Council. Nevertheless, the GC examined whether the Security Council had respected *ius cogens*, in particular certain fundamental rights. But the GC did not find an infringement of this standard.

In its judgment on appeal, the CJEU pursued a different path. It reviewed the lawfulness of the EU regulation transposing the resolution.[5] Its central argument was that the protection of fundamental rights forms part of the very foundations of the Union legal order.[6] Accordingly, *all* Union measures must be compatible with fundamental rights.[7] The Court reasoned that this does not amount to a review of the lawfulness of the Security Council measures. The review of lawfulness would apply only to the Union act that gives effect to the international agreement at issue and not to the latter as such.[8]

Having established that, the review for compliance with fundamental rights was a relatively simple task. The claimant had not been informed of the grounds for his inclusion in the list of individuals and entities subject to the sanctions. Therefore he had not been able to seek judicial review of these grounds, and consequently his right to be heard as well as his right to effective judicial review[9] and the right to property[10] had been infringed.

---

[5] *Kadi I* (n 2), at paras 290ff.
[6] ibid (n 2), at paras 303ff.
[7] ibid (n 2), at paras 281ff.
[8] ibid (n 2), at para 286.
[9] ibid (n 2), at paras 384ff.
[10] ibid (n 2), at paras 368ff, referring to the judgment in *Jokela/Finland* App no 28856/95 (ECtHR, 21 May 2002), para 45 and the cited case law, as well as para 55.

III. DUALIST BUT READY TO COMPROMISE?

In contrast to the judgment of the GC,[11] the judgment of the CJEU in *Kadi* has been associated with a dualist conception of the interplay between the international and the Union legal order. It is seen as underscoring and defending the autonomy of EU law.[12] On this point, the Court followed Advocate General Poiares Maduro's Opinion[13] holding that 'obligations imposed by an international agreement cannot have the effect of prejudicing the constitutional principles of the EC Treaty'.[14] However, deriving from this a general hostility towards public international law would be unjust. It would disregard the complex argument the Court developed and ignore the nuanced signals it sent.

In particular, it should be recalled that at the outset it was not clear whether the EU, not being a member of the UN, was bound at all by UN Security Council measures. Although the EU did not assume the powers of its Member States in the UN system, as it did with regard to the General Agreement on Tariffs and Trade (GATT),[15] the Court nevertheless considered that the EU must respect the undertakings given in the context of the UN and take due account of the resolution.[16]

The choice of a somewhat dualist approach in this particular context has to be understood as a reaction to a specific situation that may occur in multi-level systems. In such systems it is possible that the level of protection of fundamental rights guaranteed by a higher level does not attain the level of protection the lower level has developed and considers indispensable. Refusing to accept

---

[11] See Tomuschat, 'The Kadi Case' (n 4) at 657.

[12] See eg de Búrca, 'The European Court of Justice and the International Legal Order After *Kadi*' (n 3) at 2; Fassbender (n 4) at 333; and R Pavoni, 'Freedom to Choose the Legal Means for Implementing UN Security Council Resolutions and the ECJ *Kadi* Judgment: A Misplaced Argument Hindering the Enforcement of International Law in the EC' (2009) 28 *Yearbook of European Law* 627, at 630. Critical of still using this terminology are A von Bogdandy, 'Let's Hunt Zombies', *ESIL Newsletter* 2, Guest Editorial, September 2009 and HG Krenzler and O Landwehr, '"A New Legal Order of International Law": On the Relationship Between Public International Law and European Union Law After *Kadi*' in U Fastenrath et al (eds), *From Bilateralism to Community Interest. Essays in Honour of Judge Bruno Simma* (Oxford, Oxford University Press, 2011) at 1004, 1022.

[13] Advocate General Poiares Maduro stated, 'The relationship between international law and the Community legal order is governed by the Community legal order itself, and international law can permeate that legal order only under the conditions set by the constitutional principles of the Community': *Kadi I* (n 2), at para 24.

[14] *Kadi I* (n 2), at para 285; for further evidence of the Court's rather dualistic approach *cf* de Búrca, 'The European Court of Justice and the International Legal Order After *Kadi*' (n 3) at 24.

[15] The GATT has been the only instance where the Court has accepted a legal succession (see Cases 21–24/72 *International Fruit Company and Others* [1972] ECR 1219, at paras 10–18) though it might have been possible to apply this concept to the ECtHR as well: see for this point G Ress, 'Die EMRK und das Europäische Gemeinschaftsrecht. Überlegungen zu den Beziehungen zwischen den Europäischen Gemeinschaften und der Europäischen Menschenrechtskonvention' (1999) 4 *ZEuS* 471; C Sobotta, 'Sources of Fundamental Rights 'in A Weber (ed), *Fundamental Rights in Europe and North America* (Dordrecht, Kluwer, 2000) at 83, 88ff; see also J Kokott, 'Die Institution des Generalanwalts im Wandel: Auswirkungen der Rechtsprechung des EGMR zu ähnlichen Organen der Rechtspflege in den Mitgliedstaaten' in J Bröhmer (ed), *Internationale Gemeinschaft und Menschenrechte. Festschrift für Georg Ress* (Neuwied, Carl Heymanns Verlag, 2005) at 577, 593ff.

[16] *Kadi I* (n 2), at paras 292ff.

the primacy of the higher level can be a proper means of responding to this deficiency. The insufficient protection of fundamental rights at UN level[17] therefore required the adoption of a dualist conception of the interplay of EU law and international law.[18]

The Court found itself in a comparable situation in the 1970s, its counterpart at that time being the German Bundesverfassungsgericht. The latter considered the level of fundamental rights protection available at EU level to be lower than at national level. This was only natural in view of the historical stage of development of the European Economic Community and of the CJEU at the time. The Bundesverfassungsgericht therefore decided to reserve to itself the right to review Union action for its conformity with national fundamental rights as long as there was insufficient protection at EU level.[19] This is the so-called *Solange I* decision, derived from the German for 'as long as'. Twelve years later, taking account of the positive development of EU fundamental rights protection, the Bundesverfassungsgericht declared that it no longer needed to perform this review, as long as the EU kept to its elevated standard of protection. This is referred to as its *Solange II* decision.[20]

The European Court of Human Rights (ECtHR) followed comparable reasoning in its *Bosphorus* decision where it chose to abstain from exercising control with regard to EU acts.[21] Quite remarkably, it chose to pursue a different path when it declared itself incompetent to review UN Security Council measures. There that Court decided to deny its competence without keeping the safety net of a '*Solange* caveat'.[22] Some commentators criticised this decision severely.[23]

In his opinion on *Kadi* Advocate General Maduro had pointed out the possibility of adopting a *Solange*-type solution.[24] The Court was more prudent but has left the door open for such an approach.[25] It examined fairly extensively the argument presented by the Commission that the Court must not intervene since Mr Kadi

---

[17] But see M Scheinin, 'Is the ECJ Ruling in Kadi Incompatible with International Law?' (2009) 28 *Yearbook of European Law* 637ff, who argues that the targeted sanctions regime of the Security Council infringes the human rights guaranteed at the level of the UN.

[18] In that sense, see also Tomuschat, 'The Kadi Case' (n 4) at 660.

[19] BVerfGE 37, 271 *Solange I*, ruling of 29 May 1974.

[20] BVerfGE 73, 339 *Solange II*, ruling of 22 October 1986.

[21] *Bosphorus/Ireland* App no 45036/98 (ECtHR, 30 June 2005); see on that aspect of this case, A Haratsch, 'Die Solange-Rechtsprechung des Europäischen Gerichtshofs für Menschenrechte' (2006) *Zeitschrift für ausländisches öffentliches Recht und Völkerrecht* 927.

[22] *Behrami and Behrami v France; Saramati v France, Germany and Norway* App nos 71412/01 and 78166/01 (ECtHR, 2 May 2007). But see also *Al-Jedda/United Kingdom* App no 27021/08 (ECtHR, 7 July 2011), § 102, and *Nada/Switzerland* App no 10593/08 (ECtHR, 12 September 2012), §§ 171, 176 and 212.

[23] See eg Milanović and Papić, 'As Bad as It Gets: The European Court of Human Rights' Behrami and Saramati Decision and General International Law' (2009) 58 *ICLQ* 267.

[24] Opinion of Advocate General Poiares Maduro in *Kadi I* (n 2), at para 54.

[25] See in this regard also, A Rosas, 'Counter-Terrorism and the Rule of Law: Issues of Judicial Control' in AM Salinas de Frías, K Samuel and N White (eds), *Counter-Terrorism, International Law and Practice* (Oxford, Oxford University Press, 2012) at 83, 109ff; Cannizzaro, 'Security Council Resolutions and EC Fundamental Rights' (n 4) at 596.

had had, through the re-examination procedure before the Sanctions Committee, an acceptable opportunity to be heard within the UN legal system. The Court responded that such an immunity from EU jurisdiction 'appears unjustified, for clearly *that* re-examination procedure does not offer the guarantees of judicial protection'.[26] By referring solely to the procedure in question in the proceedings, the Court implied that the position could be different with regard to procedures that do offer the guarantees of judicial protection.[27]

This proves that the Court did not follow a strictly dualist approach in its judgment. In that case there would have been no reason to discuss the argument as to an alleged *Solange II* situation in substance. Pointing to the autonomy of the Union legal order and the competence of the CJEU within that legal order to review the validity of EU acts would have sufficed to exclude, as a matter of principle, the mere possibility of a *Solange II* approach.[28]

The Court's decision not, at least for the time being, to accord precedence to Security Council measures is understandable, if not indispensable in regard to another *Solange* relationship; that between EU Member States' legal orders and the Union legal order. Should the EU convey the impression of sacrificing basic constitutional guarantees by accepting the general primacy of Security Council measures, Member States, in particular their constitutional courts, would probably feel tempted to take safeguarding these guarantees into their own hands. From an international perspective this would be even worse: It would not only question the primacy of public international law within the EU legal order but also call into question the primacy of EU law over national law.[29] This would undermine the whole concept of integration through law. Also from this perspective *Kadi* could hardly have been decided differently.

---

[26] *Kadi I* (n 2), at para 322 (emphasis added).

[27] See in that sense also, P Eeckhout, 'Kadi and Al Barakaat: Luxembourg is not Texas—or Washington DC', *European Journal of International Law: Talk!*, 25 February 2009, at http://www.ejiltalk.org/kadi-and-al-barakaat-luxembourg-is-not-texas-or-washington-dc/; P De Sena and MC Vitucci, 'The European Courts and the Security Council: Between Dédoublement Fonctionnel and Balancing of Values' (2009) 20 *European Journal of International Law* 193, at 224; for a different opinion, see de Búrca, 'The European Court of Justice and the International Legal Order After *Kadi*' (n 3) at 25 and 44; D Halberstam and E Stein, 'The United Nations, the European Union, and the King of Sweden: Economic Sanctions and Individual rights in a Plural World Order' (2009) 46 *CML Rev* 13, at 60ff, PJ Kuijper and L Boisson de Chazournes, 'Mr. Kadi and Mrs. Prost: Is the UN Ombudsperson Going to Find Herself Between a Rock and a Hard Place?' in I Govaere and H Rieter (eds), *Evolving Principles of International Law. Studies in Honour of Karel C. Wellens* (The Hague, Martinus Nijhoff, 2012) 71, n 19.

[28] See in this sense, K Ziegler, 'Strengthening the Rule of Law but Fragmenting International Law: The *Kadi* Decision of the ECJ from the Perspective of Human Rights' (2009) 9 *Human Rights Law Review* 288, at 300ff.

[29] See JW van Rossem, 'Interaction between EU Law and International Law in the Light of Intertanko and Kadi: the Dilemma of Norms Binding the Member States but not the Community' (2009) 40 *Netherlands Yearbook of International Law* 183, at 197; Halberstam and Stein, 'The United Nations, the European Union, and the King of Sweden' (n 27) at 63.

IV. SUBSEQUENT DEVELOPMENTS AT THE SECURITY
COUNCIL—IS IT TIME FOR *SOLANGE II*?

To envisage a *Solange II* relationship between the EU and the Security Council, the judicial protection at the UN level has to improve substantially in comparison to the situation examined by the Court in *Kadi*. As there have been improvements, the question is whether they could be sufficient.

The Security Council began, in 2008, by introducing the narrative summary. It is provided and published for every listing, summarising the main reasons for an inclusion in the list.[30]

This mechanism was applied in the *Kadi II* case. Before the Commission again froze the assets of Mr Kadi, he was given the opportunity to comment on the narrative summary provided by the Security Council.[31] The Court accepted the summary as an important starting point provided that reasons given in it were sufficiently detailed and specific to allow for a defence and judicial control.[32] However, taking into account the submissions of the plaintiff, the Court verified whether at least one of these reasons could be deemed sufficient to support the sanction and whether it was substantiated.[33] Four of the five reasons given in the summary were considered to be sufficiently detailed and specific, but they were either not sufficiently proven or not sufficiently serious to justify the listing of Mr Kadi.

Meanwhile, in 2009, the Security Council created the office of an independent Ombudsperson. In 2010, Kimberly Prost, a former judge at the International Criminal Tribunal for the former Yugoslavia, was appointed to this position. Her task is to process requests of individuals or entities to be to be deleted from the list. The Ombudsperson does not decide on her own; rather she collects data, communicates with petitioners, and drafts reports to the Sanctions Committee. If the request is refused, the Ombudsperson informs the petitioner of the reasons for refusal, provided that they are not confidential.[34]

Initially, only the Sanctions Committee was competent to decide on a possible removal from the list. During this stage, the Committee had to decide unanimously to delist a petitioner. Consequently, any individual state could prevent a removal from the list in spite of the position of the Ombudsperson. It should be noted that the GC, in an obiter dictum to the *Kadi II* case, did not consider these improvements sufficient.[35]

---

[30] Point 13 of Security Council Resolution 1822 (2008) of 30 June 2008; the narrative summaries are published at http://www.un.org/sc/committees/1267/narrative.shtml.

[31] Third recital of Commission Regulation (EC) No 1190/2008 of 28 November 2008 amending for the 101st time Council Regulation (EC) No 881/2002, OJ [2008] L322/25).

[32] Cases C-584/10 P, C-593/10 P and C-595/10 P *Commission v Kadi* (*Kadi II*), EU:C:2013:518, paras 118 and 141ff.

[33] ibid, at paras 119 and 151ff.

[34] Points 20ff of Security Council Resolution 1904 (2009) of 17 December 2009 and its Annex II.

[35] Case T–85/09 *Kadi v Commission* [2010] ECR II-5177, at para 128. AJ Kirschner, 'Security Council Resolution 1904 (2009): A Significant Step in the Evolution of the Al-Qaida and Taliban

However, in June 2011, the Security Council strengthened the Ombudsperson's powers significantly.[36] Since then, a recommendation to delist in principle becomes effective if it is not rejected by *consensus* in the Sanctions Committee within 60 days. In the absence of consensus, this outcome can be avoided only if a Committee member requests referral to the Security Council. This means that delisting will require the votes of nine out of the 15 members of the Security Council and can be blocked by the veto of any of the five permanent members.[37] As the Security Council usually publishes its deliberations, opposition to a recommendation of the Ombudsperson could engage the political responsibility of the state in question. It might even open the way to judicial remedies before the courts of that state.

This amended procedure responds to some extent to a number of concerns voiced by the Court, especially regarding the grounds for listing. Though a listing may still in part be based on confidential information, why a person is or stays listed no longer remains completely secret.[38] Additionally, petitioners now can themselves or through their chosen representatives assert their rights before the Ombudsperson.[39]

Moreover, the Ombudsperson seeks to guarantee fair proceedings and transparent standards to analyse information on the individuals concerned consistently and objectively.[40] The yardstick for the examination is 'whether there is sufficient information to provide a reasonable and credible basis for the listing'.[41]

Her track record for the first 49 cases is impressive: Until 6 August 2013, in 28 cases the applicants were delisted, among them Mr Kadi, in only three cases the delisting was denied, in another case the request for delisting was withdrawn. Seventeen more cases are currently under investigation or already with the Committee.[42]

It is not inconceivable that the independent recommendations of the Ombudsperson may amount to a quasi-judicial role that could provide a counter-balance to the diplomatic nature of the proceedings within the Sanctions Committee.[43] Already her

---

Sanctions Regime?' (2010) 70 *ZaöRV* 585, at 604ff is also critical in that respect. Rosas, 'Counter-Terrorism and the Rule of Law' (n 25), agrees with this assessment; at 109 he characterises this stage of the mechanism as half-hearted. But see also Kuijper and Boisson de Chazournes, 'Mr. Kadi and Mrs. Prost' (n 27) at 85 and 87.

[36] Points 22 and 23 of Security Council Resolution 1989 (2011) of 17 June 2012. Nevertheless, it should also be noted that sanctioned persons related to the Taliban were at the same time completely removed from the remit of the Ombudsperson.

[37] The former Special Rapporteur of the Human Rights Council on human rights and counter terrorism, Martin Scheinin, considered this an important weakness of the new rules: see http://www. ohchr.org/en/NewsEvents/Pages/DisplayNews.aspx?NewsID=11191&LangID=E.

[38] *Cf Kadi I* (n 2), at para 325.

[39] *Cf Kadi I* (n 2), at para 324.

[40] Points 23 and 25 of the Report of the Office of the Ombudsperson pursuant to Security Council Resolution 1904 (2009), UN Doc S/2011/29 of 24 January 2011.

[41] See http://www.un.org/en/sc/ombudsperson/approach.shtml.

[42] See http://www.un.org/en/sc/ombudsperson/status.shtml.

[43] See in this regard also, Tomuschat, 'The Kadi Case' (n 4) at 661ff, who believes that an essentially diplomatic procedure can still be tailored in a way to provide sufficient legal protection.

recommendations have politically and practically acquired some binding effect on the Sanctions Committee, making derogation difficult.

However, her role has not attained the quality of a court of law,[44] in particular because the Committee or the Security Council can reserve the final decision for itself. In the latter case any of the permanent members can prevent a delisting without having to provide reasons. Moreover, as her recommendations to the Sanctions Committee are not accessible, it cannot be assessed whether the Ombudsperson applies clear legal standards, equivalent to the fundamental rights guaranteed within the EU. Finally, the Court highlights as the most important shortcoming that the person concerned cannot obtain rehabilitation by way of judicial finding that he was wrongly put on the list.[45]

V. EXHAUSTION OF 'LOCAL' REMEDIES

Nevertheless, this procedure could give rise to another type of *Solange* relationship, reducing the risk of conflict between UN sanctions and EU judicial protection significantly. This could be achieved if the action in the EU courts was necessarily preceded by an unsuccessful petition to the Ombudsperson.[46] A petition would enable the UN Ombudsperson, being closer to the case, to work towards a resolution of the problem at the source.[47] Cases without sufficient grounds for a listing should be resolved by her review. And they should be resolved much faster than in the EU courts: The completed reviews took between six and 13 months. Mr Kadi, on the other hand, has spent more than 10 years before the EU courts.

Even if such a review does not result in a delisting, it generates information on the reasons for the listing. The Ombudsperson will collect all the available information and allow the petitioner to comment, at least on the non-confidential parts. She and the Committee will evaluate this information and provide the petitioner with a reasoned decision. In the context of a subsequent judicial procedure the EU courts could require the applicant to submit the communication he had with the Ombudsperson, in particular any reasons provided for maintaining the listing. The EU courts could use this information to examine the case. If the UN institutions decide rationally to maintain the listing, it should be possible to confirm their decisions most of the time.

---

[44] On the necessary attributes of a Court, see *Kadi I* (n 2), at paras 323–25, and also *Chahal v UK* App no 22414/93 (ECtHR, 15 November 1996) at 131.

[45] *Kadi II* (n 32), at para 134. Anticipated by ML Fremuth, 'Ein Prozess …: Zum Ausgleich zwischen der effektiven Bekämpfung des Terrorismus und der Beachtung der Menschenrechte in der Sanktionspraxis des Sicherheitsrates' (2012) *Die öffentliche Verwaltung* 81, at 87ff.

[46] Scheinin (n 37), demands additional measures to strengthen the Ombudsperson before this can be expected.

[47] Such reasoning also underlies the local remedies rule in international human rights law and the law of diplomatic protection.

Problems are likely to arise if the listing cannot be justified exclusively on the basis of disclosed information, but also depends on confidential evidence. Up to now, such information is not even submitted to the EU Courts because it is not foreseen to keep it from the plaintiff. However, in the *Kadi II* case the Court addressed this issue. First of all, it found that it is for the EU courts to determine whether the reasons to keep information confidential are well founded.[48] Where such reasons exist, an appropriate balance needs to struck between the requirements attached to the right to effective judicial protection, in particular respect for the principle of an adversarial process, and those flowing from the security of the EU or its Member States or the conduct of their international relations.[49] Disclosure of a summary outlining the information's content or that of the evidence in question could be means of striking such a balance.[50] In any event, the Court will also need to assess whether the complete or partial failure to disclose evidence affects its probative value.[51] It remains to be seen how this method is applied in practice, and in particular, whether it may allow to uphold a listing that is based exclusively or to a decisive degree on evidence that cannot be disclosed.[52] According to the ECtHR the requirements of a fair trial do not allow to base detention on such evidence.[53]

The question remains how a requirement for a preliminary review by the Ombudsperson can be introduced into the judicial procedure of the EU courts. At first view a requirement to exhaust remedies provided by another legal system, in this case the UN, is counterintuitive under EU law. The right to bring an action before the EU courts is provided for in the Treaties and it is also an expression of the fundamental right to effective judicial protection, enshrined in Article 47 of the EU Charter of Fundamental Rights. Therefore, it is doubtful whether even the legislator could require applicants to exhaust the UN review procedure before addressing the EU courts.

Nevertheless, some inspiration may be found in the case law of the GC on similar sanctions that the EU imposes because competent Member State authorities have identified the persons or associations in question. In these cases it must be assessed whether the EU decision to introduce or maintain a sanction is justified. In this regard, the GC restricts the scope of substantial judicial review until Member States' remedies are exhausted. Because the sanctions are based on Member States' decisions, the EU institutions should afford precedence to matters

[48] *Kadi II* (n 32), at para 126.
[49] ibid (n 32), at para 128.
[50] ibid (n 32), at para 129.
[51] ibid.
[52] The US standard can be seen in the decision of the US District Court for the District of Columbia of 19 March 2012 in *Kadi v Geithner,* available at https://ecf.dcd.uscourts.gov/cgi-bin/show_public_doc?2009cv0108-56.
[53] *A v UK* App no 3455/05 (ECtHR, 19 February 2009) at 220.

of internal procedure when assessing the need to maintain a sanction.[54] This case law is based on the principle of loyal cooperation between EU institutions and Member States.[55]

UN sanctions could be treated similarly. It could be considered that the EU acts appropriately, if it waits for the result of a review by the Ombudsperson before re-examining whether sanctions should be maintained. Although the EU principle of loyal cooperation as such does not apply to relations with the Security Council, the Court has already recognised similar obligations in the *Kadi I* case. There, it found that the EU must respect the undertakings given in the context of the UN and take due account of the resolution.[56] This finding is based on the treaties: According to Articles 3(5) and 21(1) TEU, the EU respects the principles of the UN Charter. Additionally, Article 220 TFEU requires that the Union establishes all appropriate forms of cooperation with the organs of the UN.

Moreover, this solution would be another expression of the well-established local remedies rule in international human rights law and the law of diplomatic protection. This rule has already inspired the Court in another context, namely with regard to accession to the European Convention on Human Rights and Fundamental Freedoms. In a discussion paper, the CJEU stressed that the ECtHR should not decide on the conformity of an act of the Union with the Convention without the CJEU first having had an opportunity to give a definitive ruling on the point.[57] Accordingly, the draft accession agreement includes provisions that would allow such a ruling.[58]

The local remedies rule activates the self-healing forces of the system concerned. It also helps to prepare the case for judicial review on another level because it promotes the assessment of the relevant facts and the development of legal reasoning before the judicial or, in this case, quasi-judicial institution near to the source of the controversy. This is a reasonable application of the principle of subsidiarity. Obviously, the analogous application advanced here would add a new aspect to this concept: exhaustion of international rather than local remedies!

---

[54] Case T–348/07 *Al-Aqsa v Council II* [2010] ECR II-4575, at para 161, and the case law cited therein. The judgment on appeal, Cases C-539/10 P and C-550/10 P *Al-Aqsa v Council*, EU:C:2012:711, implies that the absence of local remedies does not pose a problem.

[55] *Al-Aqsa v Council II* (n 54), at paras 80 and 163, and the case law cited therein.

[56] *Kadi I* (n 2), at paras 292ff.

[57] Discussion document of the CJEU on certain aspects of the accession of the EU to the ECHR Luxembourg, 5 May 2010, available at: http://curia.europa.eu/jcms/upload/docs/application/pdf/2010-05/convention_en_2010-05-21_12-10-16_272.pdf. See also the Joint communication from Presidents Costa and Skouris of 24 January 2011, available at http://curia.europa.eu/jcms/upload/docs/application/pdf/2011-02/cedh_cjue_english.pdf, point 2.

[58] See Art 3(6) of the Draft legal instruments on the accession of the EU to the ECHR of 10 June 2013, 47+1(2013)008rev2, and point 65ff of the explanatory report to the draft agreement, available at http://www.coe.int/t/dghl/standardsetting/hrpolicy/Accession/Meeting_reports/47_1(2013)008rev2_EN.pdf. On this provision, see C Ladenburger, 'European Union Institutional Report' in J Laffranque (ed), *The Protection of Fundamental Rights Post-Lisbon*, Reports of the XXV FIDE Congress Tallinn 2012, vol 1 (Tallinn, Tartu University Press, 2012) 141, at 206ff. See further J Heliskoski, ch 12 in this volume.

At first view the CJEU was very dismissive of the review procedure of the Security Council in the *Kadi II* case. It declared that despite the improvements added, in particular after the second listing of Kadi, the procedures at the Security Council do not provide the guarantee of effective judicial protection.[59] However, this does not exclude reliance on the existing Security Council remedies, as far as they go, to improve the handling of such cases by the EU Courts. Moreover, this finding relied on a judgment of the ECtHR[60] that concerned the situation in 2007, not the current state of affairs. Most importantly, the current review procedure was only introduced and refined while the case was already pending in Luxembourg. It should also be borne in mind that the Court has not yet taken a position on the case law of the GC with regard to Member States' remedies.

VI. CONCLUSIONS

Observers should recognise that the Court's willingness to strike a balance between effective judicial protection and the legitimate interest in safeguarding confidential information constitutes an important step towards reconciliation with the international measures to combat terrorism. However, more could be done by requiring the exhaustion of the review mechanism. This would not only improve international relations but could also help to strengthen the mechanism. Regardless of possible substantial improvements, its most obvious weakness is that it is limited to Al-Qaida sanctions. None of the other individual sanctions regimes, eg of the Taliban,[61] Somalia,[62] Côte d'Ivoire,[63] or Congo,[64] come under the competence of the Ombudsperson. However, actions against such sanctions can be introduced in the EU courts.[65]

Finding a proper balance between constitutional core values and effective international measures against terrorism is not easy. However, the developments following the *Kadi* case demonstrate the intention of the relevant actors to find a workable balance. Already the current system is a huge improvement on the initial mechanism. Therefore, we are optimistic that the balance will be found.

---

[59] *Kadi II* (n 32), at para 133.

[60] *Nada/Switzerland* (n 22), at para 211.

[61] Resolution 1988 (2011). When the review mechanism was strengthened by Resolution 1989 (2011), the Taliban sanctions were split off from the Al-Qaida sanctions and excluded from the remit of the Ombudsperson. However, even before this split the Ombudsperson received no petition from any person or organisation on this part of the list.

[62] Resolution 1844 (2008).

[63] Resolution 1572 (2004).

[64] Resolution 1596 (2005).

[65] *Cf* Cases C-478/11 P to C-482/11 P *Gbagbo and Others v Council*, EU:C:2013:258. However, this appeal only raised the question whether the GC was correct to consider the action out of time. It seems that most other individual sanctions cases currently pending in the GC do not concern sanctions mandated directly by the Security Council.

12

The Arrangement Governing the Relationship between the ECtHR and the CJEU in the Draft Treaty on the Accession of the EU to the ECHR

JONI HELISKOSKI[1]

I. INTRODUCTION, BACKGROUND AND PURPOSES

IN THE FIELD of external relations of the European Union (hereafter referred to as 'the EU' or 'the Union'), the project aiming at the accession of the EU to the European Convention on Human Rights (hereafter referred to as 'the ECHR or 'the Convention') is a well-known one and hardly needs any general introduction. The present contribution therefore has a specific objective, focusing on one, particularly delicate, aspect of the project: the organisation of the relationship between the Court of Justice of the European Union (hereafter referred to as 'the CJEU' or 'the Court of Justice') and the European Court of Human Rights (ECtHR) in the context of the EU's accession to the Convention. While that issue has also been explored in the past—at least since the Commission's 1979 memorandum on the question of accession of the Communities to the ECHR[2]—questions of an entirely novel character have arisen in the negotiations on accession of the EU to the ECHR that started in 2010 and were finalised with a draft agreement on the accession of the EU to the ECHR (hereafter 'the Draft Agreement')[3] in April 2013. As regards the relationship between the two courts in

---

[1] While the author is an official of the Ministry for Foreign Affairs, Helsinki, the views expressed are personal.

[2] Accession of the Communities to the European Convention on Human Rights: Commission Memorandum, Bulletin of the European Communities, Supplement 2/79, COM (79) 210 final. See also Opinion 2/94 *Accession by the Community to the European Convention for the Protection of Human Rights and Fundamental Freedoms* [1996] ECR I-1759.

[3] The text of the Draft Agreement as well as the other instruments on the accession are reproduced in Appendices I to V Council of Europe document 47+1(2013)008 rev2 (10 June 2013). The document concerned, as well as the other public documents of the Council of Europe Steering Committee for Human Rights relating to the accession negotiations, are available at: http://www.coe.

particular, attention should be drawn to Article 3(6) of the Draft Agreement that
reads as follows:

> In proceedings to which the European Union is co-respondent, if the Court of Justice of
> the European Union has not yet assessed the compatibility with the Convention rights
> at issue of the provision of European Union law as under paragraph 2 of this Article,
> sufficient time shall be afforded for the Court of Justice of the European Union to make
> such an assessment, and thereafter for the parties to make observations to the Court. The
> European Union shall ensure that such assessment is made quickly so that the proceed-
> ings before the Court are not unduly delayed. The provisions of this paragraph shall not
> affect the powers of the Court.

The provision envisages a special kind of an arrangement whereby the CJEU may
participate in proceedings of the ECtHR before the decision of the latter is rendered. Nothing of its kind has ever been contemplated, or at least not formally
proposed, during the decades in which the accession of the Union to the European
Convention has been on the agenda. The mechanism, commonly (albeit rather mis-
leadingly) known as one of 'prior involvement', is therefore an entirely novel one.

As will emerge in the following, the background of the mechanism is equally
exceptional; it was neither the EU Commission nor the EU Member States nor
the Council of Europe, but the CJEU that came up with the suggestion that such
a mechanism was not only desirable but also legally necessary so as to ensure the
compatibility of the accession with EU law. Before a closer analysis of the mechanism, it is appropriate briefly to describe, by way of an introduction, the background leading to the proposal for the mechanism, with the year 2002 as the point
of departure.

For the EU, the authority for the current negotiations of accession derives from
Article 6(2), of the Treaty of European Union (TEU), the drafting history of which
goes back to 2002 when the Convention on the Future of Europe, under the auspices of a Working Group 'Incorporation of the Charter/Accession to the ECHR'
chaired by Mr Antonio Vitorino, began to consider the issue. In 2002, the Steering

---

int/t/dghl/standardsetting/hrpolicy/Accession/Working_documents_en.asp. For recent commentary
on the negotiations and earlier versions of the Draft Agreement, see J-P Jacque, 'The Accession of
the European Union to the European Convention on Human Rights and Fundamental Freedoms'
(2011) 48 *CML Rev* 995; T Lock, 'Walking on a Tightrope: The Draft ECHR Accession Agreement
and the Autonomy of the EU Legal Order' (2011) 48 *CML Rev* 1023; J Polakiewicz, 'The European
Union's Accession to the European Convention on Human Rights—A Report on Work in Rapid
Progress' in W Meng et al (eds), *Europäische Integration und Globalisierung* (Baden-Baden, Nomos,
2011) 375; J Králová, 'Comments on the Draft Agreement on the Accession of the European Union
to the Convention for the Protection of Human Rights and Fundamental Freedoms' (2011) 2 *Czech
Yearbook of Public & Private International Law* 127; and X Groussot, T Lock and L Pech, 'EU Accession
to the European Convention on Human Rights: A Legal Assessment of the Draft Accession Agreement
of 14th October 2011', Foundation Robert Schuman Policy Paper, available at: http://www.robert-
schuman.eu/doc/questions_europe/qe-218-en.pdf. See also the General Report (by LFM Besselink)
and the Institutional Report (by C Ladenburger) for the 2012 FIDE Session, 'The Protection of
Fundamental Rights Post-Lisbon: The Interaction between the Charter of Fundamental Rights of the
European Union, the European Convention on Human Rights and National Constitutions', available
at http://www.fide2012.eu/General+and+EU+Reports/id/217/.

Committee for Human Rights (hereafter referred to as 'the CDDH') also published a 'Study of Technical and Legal Issues of a Possible EC/EU Accession to the European Convention of Human Rights'.[4] The position of the CJEU in regard to an eventual accession to the ECHR was considered within the framework of both of these exercises.

It may now be concluded that in neither of those contexts the Union's accession to the ECHR was considered to pose any particular problems or to require special arrangements in terms of the position of the CJEU under EU law. While the CDDH Study included no mention of the issue,[5] the documentation of the Convention's Working Group shows that extensive attention was devoted to the matter. Initially, the Secretariat of the Convention issued a discussion paper[6] addressing, inter alia, the question of the modalities and consequences of possible accession of the Union to the ECHR. Recalling the principal arguments for and against the accession, the paper identified as the main argument against the accession the threat posed to the principle of the autonomy of Union law, including the position of the CJEU as the sole arbiter of that law.[7] To counter that argument it was pointed out that the ECtHR would have no power to reverse or declare invalid the instruments of the contracting parties or judgments by their supreme courts, but could only establish violations of the Convention. The practical consequences of the judgments of the ECtHR for the domestic legal systems remained within the competence of the institutions of the contracting parties.[8] In the end, it was clearly the latter position that prevailed in the Working Group. After having received concurring statements by experts,[9] the Group concluded in its Final Report that:

> ... the principle of autonomy [of Union law] does not place any legal obstacle to accession by the Union to the ECHR. After accession, the Court of Justice would remain the sole supreme arbiter of questions of Union law and of the validity of Union acts; the European Court on Human Rights could not be regarded as a superior Court but rather as a specialised court exercising external control over the international law obligations of the Union resulting from accession to the ECHR. The position of the Court of Justice would be analogous to that of national constitutional or supreme courts in relation to the Strasbourg Court at present.[10]

---

[4] Council of Europe document DG-II (2002)006 (28 June 2002).

[5] The only issue mentioned in regard to the position of the CJEU was the need for a special procedure enabling the CJEU to request an interpretation of the ECHR from the ECtHR. See CDDH Study (ibid), paras 75–77.

[6] CONV 116/02 (18 June 2002).

[7] ibid, p 18.

[8] ibid, p 20.

[9] Notably by Judges Skouris (WD document No 19) and Fischbach (CONV 295/02) as well as by Mr Schoo, Director-General at the Legal Service of the European Parliament, and Mr Petit, Director-General at the Legal Service of the Commission (WD No 13).

[10] CONV 354/02 (22 October 2002) p 12.

The view that the autonomy of Union law and the position of the Court of Justice would not be undermined by accession also prevailed in the Convention's plenary.[11] Consequently, an obligation for the Union to 'seek accession' to the ECHR was included in Article 7(2) of the Draft Treaty establishing a Constitution for Europe, the sole precondition being that the accession should not 'affect the Union's competences' as defined in the Constitution.[12] On this question the Convention text was also maintained by the Inter-governmental Conference during the Italian Presidency in the second half of 2003, including the legal and technical review of the text by the Working Party of IGC Legal Experts. It was only during the Irish Presidency in the spring 2004 when this approach appeared to be qualified to some extent. For the meeting of 'Focal Points' of the Conference, the Presidency proposed a new draft Protocol relating to Article I-7(2), 'designed to meet the concerns of some delegations'.[13] According to the draft Protocol, the agreement relating to the accession of the Union to the ECHR should 'take into account ... the specific characteristics of the Union and Union law'[14] and 'not affect the competences of the Union and the powers of its institutions'.[15]An accompanying draft Declaration, requiring, inter alia, the introduction of '[a] system ... for liaison between the Court of Justice and the European Court of Human Rights in order to avoid, as far as possible, any discrepancies in case law',[16] was also proposed. The substance of both the draft Protocol and the draft Declaration was subsequently included in the Treaty establishing a Constitution for Europe and carried over to the Treaty of Lisbon.[17]

Following the entry into force of the Lisbon Treaty, the Commission submitted to the Council, on 17 March 2010, a recommendation for a Council Decision authorising the Commission to negotiate the Accession Agreement of the EU to the ECHR. The following day, in an audition on 'institutional aspects' of the EU's accession to the ECHR organised by the Committee on Constitutional Affairs (AFCO) of the European Parliament, Mr CWA Timmermans, at the time Judge at the CJEU, made an intervention in which he strongly pleaded for a mechanism ensuring the prior involvement of the CJEU in proceedings where the ECtHR was to assess the Union's compliance with the Convention.[18] It appeared 'unacceptable'

---

[11] For the discussion on the Final Report of the Working Group, see the Summary report of the plenary session, Brussels, 28 and 29 October 2002, CONV 378/02 (31 October 2002). See also the Summary report on the plenary session, Brussels, 27 and 28 February 2003, CONV 601/03 (11 March 2003) and the Summary report of the additional plenary session, Brussels, 26 March 2003, CONV 674/03 (8 April 2003).

[12] CONV 850/03 (18 July 2003).

[13] CIG 73/04 PRESID 16 (29 April 2004) pp 112–13.

[14] ibid.

[15] CIG 79/04 PRESID (10 June 2004).

[16] CIG 76/04 PRESID 18 (13 May 2004) p 48.

[17] See Protocol (No 8) relating to Art 6(2) of the TEU on the Accession of the Union to the European Convention on the Protection of Human Rights and Fundamental Freedoms and Declaration (No 2) on Art 6(2) of the TEU.

[18] Available at http://www.europarl.europa.eu/document/activities/cont/201003/20100324ATT712 35/20100324ATT71235EN.pdf.

to him that the Strasbourg Court could condemn the Union for a violation of fundamental rights when the CJEU had not had an opportunity to pronounce on the question in the first place (for example, when no reference for a preliminary ruling under Article 267 of the Treaty on the Functioning of the European Union (TFEU) had been made). While the mechanism proposed by Judge Timmermans was different from the one now included in Article 3(6) of the Draft Agreement, his intervention before the AFCO none-the-less marked the 'inauguration' of the idea of prior involvement of the CJEU in the context of the accession negotiations.

While Judge Timmermans had appeared before the AFCO in his personal capacity, his main arguments were put forward and reiterated in a 'discussion document' published by the CJEU in May 2010.[19] In the document concerned, the CJEU effectively established the creation of a mechanism of prior involvement as a condition for the compatibility of the accession with EU law, by stating that:

> [I]n the context of preparing for accession, the Union must make sure, as regards acts of the Union which are susceptible to being the subject of applications to the European Court of Human Rights, that external review by the Convention institutions can be preceded by effective internal review by the courts of the Member States and/or of the Union.[20]
>
> [...]
>
> Consequently, ... a mechanism must be available which is capable of ensuring that the question of the validity of a Union act can be brought effectively before the Court of Justice before the European Court of Human Rights rules on the compatibility of that act with the Convention.[21]

The question of the means of guaranteeing the prior involvement of the CJEU in cases where that court has not been able to pronounce on the compatibility of an EU act with fundamental rights was then taken up by the Union as one of the central issues in the accession negotiations launched between the EU Commission and experts from the CDDH in July 2010. In January 2011, Presidents Costa and Skouris issued a Joint Communication on the matter, stressing the need for a procedure that would ensure that the CJEU may carry out an internal review before the ECHR carries out external review.[22] The following month, a first draft article establishing such a procedure was to be found in Article 4(3) of the first Draft Agreement on the accession published by the CDDH.[23]

The purpose of this chapter is to provide for an analysis of the relationship between the ECtHR and the CJEU in the light of the Draft Agreement in general and the mechanism of prior involvement included in Article 3(6) thereof in

---

[19] Available at http://curia.europa.eu/jcms/upload/docs/application/pdf/2010-05/convention_en_2010-05-21_12-10-16_272.pdf.

[20] ibid, p 3.

[21] ibid, p 5.

[22] Available at http://curia.europa.eu/jcms/upload/docs/application/pdf/2011-02/cedh_cjue_english.pdf.

[23] Document CDDH-UE(2011)04 (25 February 2011).

particular. The analysis will be based upon the text of the Draft Agreement and other instruments on accession as presented in the final report of the negotiators of the 47 Council of Europe Member States and the EU (the so-called hoc group '47+1') to the CDDH in April 2013. It was highlighted by members of the ad hoc group that the completion of internal procedures would be required before final adoption of the accession instruments. The representative of the EU indicated in particular that an opinion (pursuant to Article 218(11) TFEU) of the CJEU on the compatibility of the Draft Agreement with EU treaties would be sought and that the Council would thereafter have to adopt unanimously the decision authorising the signature of the Agreement on behalf of the EU.[24] A request for an opinion (Opinion 2/13) was submitted to the CJEU by the Commission on 4 July 2013.

The structure of the chapter is as follows. The paper first explains the material and procedural conditions for the application of the proposed mechanism of prior involvement (section II). This is followed by an analysis of the rationale and foundations of the mechanism (section III). The chapter then discusses the implications of the mechanism from the perspective of the Convention system in general and the applicant before the ECtHR in particular (section IV). In this respect, it will however have to be acknowledged that a number of issues are left to the phase of implementation of the Draft Agreement and, therefore, no definitive conclusion may be drawn at this stage. Finally, an overall assessment is made of the mechanism of prior involvement (section V).

II. THE MATERIAL AND PROCEDURAL CONDITIONS FOR
THE PRIOR INVOLVEMENT OF THE CJEU

A. Preliminary Observations

The mechanism of the prior involvement is set out in Article 3(6) of the Draft Agreement on the Accession of the EU to the ECHR, the title of the provision being the 'Co-respondent mechanism'. Article 3 of the Draft Agreement amends Article 36 of the Convention ('Third party intervention') the title of which will be amended to read 'Third party intervention and co-respondent'. The scope of application of the mechanism of prior involvement is indeed intrinsically linked with the scope of application of the other new arrangement, the so-called 'co-respondent mechanism'.

The material conditions for the application of the mechanism of prior involvement are set out in the first sentence of Article 3(6) as follows:

> In proceedings to which the European Union is co-respondent, if the Court of Justice of the European Union has not yet assessed the compatibility with the Convention rights at issue of the provision of European Union law as under paragraph 2 of this Article,

---

[24] Document 47+1(2013)008 rev2 (n 3), para 8.

sufficient time shall be afforded for the Court of Justice of the European Union to make such an assessment ....

The remainder of the first sentence and the second sentence of Article 3(6) then lay down the modalities of the application of the mechanism as follows:

> ... then sufficient time shall be afforded for the Court of Justice of the European Union to make such an assessment and thereafter for the parties to make observations to the Court. The European Union shall ensure that such assessment is made quickly so that the proceedings before the Court are not unduly delayed.

The final sentence of Article 3(6) provides that '[t]he provisions of this paragraph shall not affect the powers of the Court'.

It is appropriate to explain briefly the material conditions for (or, the scope of) application of the mechanism as well as the principal procedural aspects of the Article 3(6) of the Draft Agreement.

B. The Material Conditions of Prior Involvement of the CJEU

There are two basic material conditions for the prior involvement of the CJEU under the proposed mechanism. The first is the existence, before the ECtHR, of 'proceedings to which the European Union is co-respondent', the second being the fact of the CJEU 'not [having] assessed the compatibility with the Convention rights at issue of the provision of European Union law as under paragraph 2 of this Article'. The first condition is a rather straight forward one, while the meaning of the second one may turn out to be more complicated.

(i) 'Proceedings to which the European Union is Co-respondent'

The key to the understanding of the first condition is Article 3(2) of the Draft Agreement that defines the conditions for the Union to be entitled to join, as a co-respondent, in proceedings instituted against one of more of its Member States. The provision concerned reads follows:

> Where an application is directed against one or more member States of the European Union, the European Union may become a co-respondent to the proceedings in respect of an alleged violation notified by the Court if it appears that such allegation calls into question the compatibility with the rights at issue defined in the Convention or in the protocols to which the European Union has acceded of a provision of European Union law, including decisions taken under the Treaty on European Union and under the Treaty on the Functioning of the European Union, notably where that violation could have been avoided only by disregarding an obligation under European Union law.

The right of the EU to become a co-respondent is therefore governed by the following conditions.

Firstly, there must be 'an application ... directed against one or more Member States of the European Union'. In principle, the co-respondent mechanism applies to 'applications' both under Article 33 ('Inter-State cases', to be renamed 'Inter-Party cases') and under Article 34 ('Individual applications'), as there is no explicit indication of the limitation of the application of the mechanism to individual application only.[25] Such an interpretation is also supported by Protocol (No 8) relating to Article 6(2) of the TEU on the Accession of the Union to the European Convention where reference is made to 'the mechanisms necessary to ensure that *proceedings by non-Member States and individual applications* are correctly addressed to Member States and/or the Union as appropriate'.[26] In practice, the mechanism would of course apply to individual applications in an overwhelming majority of cases, given the much smaller number of inter-party cases.

Secondly, the alleged violation must have been 'notified by the Court' to one or more Member States. The co-respondent mechanism will therefore not alter the current practice under which the ECtHR makes a preliminary assessment of an application, with the result that many manifestly ill-founded or otherwise inadmissible applications are not communicated.[27] In particular, it is not the aim of the mechanism to 're-direct' applications that are incompatible *ratione personae*, that is, where the applicant has erroneously directed the application against the Union in respect of an alleged violation attributable to Member States and vice versa. The scope of the mechanism is therefore more narrow than what was envisaged in Protocol No 8, since the latter refers to mechanisms 'necessary to ensure that proceedings by non-Member States and individual applications are correctly addressed to Member States and/or the Union as appropriate'.[28]

Thirdly, the alleged violation must prima facie call into question the compatibility with the Convention rights at issue 'of a provision of European Union law …, notably where that violation could have been avoided only by disregarding

---

[25] The new para 4 to be inserted into Art 36 of the Convention simply refers 'proceedings' and Art 3(2) and (3) of the Draft Agreement to 'an application'. Had the intention been to limit the application of the mechanism to individual applications, it would have been appropriate to spell out the limitation in Art 36 of the Convention and/or in Art 3 of the Draft Agreement. In the preparatory documentation the scope of application of the mechanism is not explicitly discussed. But see the Draft Explanatory report to the Agreement on the Accession of the European Union to the Convention for the Protection of Human Rights and Fundamental Freedoms, Appendix V to document 47+1(2013)008 rev2 (10 June 2013) (n 3), stating that '[c]ases in which the EU may be a co-respondent arise from individual applications concerning acts or omissions of EU Member States. The applicant will first have to exhaust domestic remedies available in the national courts of the respondent member State' (para 65).

[26] Emphasis added.

[27] Draft Explanatory Report of the CDDH (n 25), para 51.

[28] The co-respondent mechanism would, however, allow an application not to be declared incompatible *ratione personae* in some of the cases where it was erroneously directed against both the EU and one or more Member States. If the relevant conditions are met, according to draft Art 3(4) either the Union or the Member State (or States) concerned may apply for their status to be changed from respondent to co-respondent: ibid (n 25), paras 43 and 56–58. At the same time, it follows from Art 36, para 4, of the Convention, as amended by the Draft Agreement, that the admissibility of an application would be assessed without regard to the participation of the co-respondent in the proceedings.

an obligation under European Union law'. While not affecting the responsibility of the Member State (or States) in question,[29] the co-respondent mechanism enables (but does not require) the Union to become a co-respondent in cases where the conduct constituting the alleged violation by the Member State (or States) concerned is ultimately based on an obligation under Union law. Cases such as *Bosphorus* (Member State acting pursuant to its obligations under a Union regulation)[30] and *Cantoni* (Member State legislation enacted pursuant to a Union directive)[31] are obvious examples. When the 'root cause' of the alleged violation lies with conduct of the Union, considerations of both accountability and enforceability (of an eventual judgment) indeed speak in favour of providing the Union with the possibility of becoming a co-respondent alongside with the Member State (or States) concerned.[32] It should be highlighted, however, that the expression 'a provision of European Union law' in Article 3(2) of the Draft Agreement is deemed to cover not only secondary but also primary law of the Union.[33] The drafting of Article 3(6) also reflects the inclusion of primary law within the scope of application of Article 3(2).[34]

(ii) No Assessment of Compatibility with the Convention of the Provision of EU Law by the CJEU has Taken Place

The prior involvement of the CJEU may only take place if 'the Court of Justice of the European Union has not assessed the compatibility with the Convention rights at issue of the provision of European Union law' (ie, the question of 'compatibility' that had initially triggered the application of the co-respondent

---

[29] Art 1(4) of the Draft Agreement reads as follows: 'For the purposes of the Convention, of the protocols thereto and of this Agreement, an act, measure or omission of organs of a member State of the European Union or of persons acting on its behalf shall be attributed to that State, even if such act, measure or omission occurs when the State implements the law of the European Union, including decisions taken under the Treaty on European Union and under the Treaty on the Functioning of the European Union. This shall not preclude the European Union from being responsible as a co-respondent for a violation resulting from such an act, measure or omission, in accordance with Article 36, paragraph 4, of the Convention and Article 3 of this Agreement'.

[30] *Bosphorus Hava Yolları Turizm ve Ticaret Anonim Şirketi v Ireland* Application no 45036/98 (ECtHR, 30 June 2005).

[31] *Cantoni v France* Application no 17862/91 (ECtHR, 11 November 1996).

[32] The logic behind the 'mirror-image' possibility of allowing EU Member States to become co-respondents is similar. Pursuant to draft Art 3(3) they have that right when the alleged violation '… calls into question the compatibility with the rights at issue defined in the Convention or in the protocols to which the European Union has acceded of a provision of the Treaty on European Union, the Treaty on the Functioning of the European Union or any other provision having the same legal value pursuant to those instruments, notably where that violation could have been avoided only by disregarding an obligation under those instruments'.

[33] Draft Explanatory Report of the CDDH, above (n 25), para 48. *Cf* Art 4 of the first Draft Agreement published by the CDDH in which the right of the Union to become a co-respondent only covered cases where an alleged violation appeared to have a substantive link with 'European Union legal acts or measures', ie, secondary law. See document CDDH-UE(2011)04 (25 February 2011).

[34] See below section II.B.ii.

mechanism). In the Draft Explanatory Report of the CDDH, the 'assessing the compatibility' is defined as meaning:

> [T]o rule on the validity of a legal provision contained in acts of the European Union institutions, bodies, offices or agencies, or on the provision of the Treaty on European Union, the Treaty on the Functioning of the European Union or of any other provision having the same legal value pursuant to those instruments.[35]

While the meaning of this second condition of the prior involvement appears self-explanatory in principle, its practical application may turn out to be more complicated.

Firstly, it may be not always be evident that an assessment of a provision of EU law in the light of fundamental rights recognised by Article 6 TEU corresponds to the assessment to be made in the light of 'the Convention rights'. Secondly, the rationale of the mechanism of prior involvement would seem to entail that the requirement concerning the absence of a prior assessment by the CJEU would have to be interpreted in the light of the *CILFIT* criteria concerning the interpretation of Article 267 TFEU.[36] In other words, the criterion should not be whether an assessment by the CJEU has *actually* taken place. The mechanism should rather only be available in those cases where a reference for a preliminary ruling *ought to have been* (but was not) made by courts or tribunals of a Member State against whose decisions there is no judicial remedy. The *CILFIT* criteria, however, are, of course, open to interpretation.

C. The Procedural Framework for the Prior Involvement of the CJEU

The text of Article 3(6) of the Draft Agreement seeks to reflect one of the central concerns raised during the negotiations in respect of the idea of prior involvement—the desire to avoid complicated procedures that would slow down the proceedings before the ECtHR.[37] While 'sufficient time' should be afforded to the CJEU to make its assessment and thereafter for the parties to make observations to the ECtHR, the Union must ensure that the assessment by the CJEU is 'made quickly so that the proceedings before the [ECtHR] are not unduly delayed'.

The more detailed implementation of the above principles is likely to take place within the rules of procedure of the respective courts. However, two additional clarifications are made in the CDDH commentary.[38] Firstly, the examination of the merits of the application by the ECtHR should not resume before the parties and any third party interveners have had an opportunity to assess properly the consequences of the ruling of the CJEU. Secondly, reference is made to the existence of the accelerated[39] procedure (provided for in Article 105 of the

---

[35] Draft Explanatory Report of the CDDH (n 25), para 66.
[36] See Case 283/81 *CILFIT* [1982] ECR 3415.
[37] See document CDDH-UE(2010)12 (12 October 2010) p 12.
[38] Draft Explanatory Report of the CDDH (n 25), para 69.
[39] As of 1 November 2012, the accelerated procedure is called the 'expedited procedure'.

Rules of Procedure) of the CJEU, possibly on the assumption that the procedure concerned could be used in the context of the prior involvement. These questions will be addressed in greater detail in section IV below.

III. ON THE RATIONALE AND JUSTIFICATION OF THE MECHANISM OF PRIOR INVOLVEMENT

A. Preliminary Remarks

The principal consequence and, indeed, the aim of the accession of the Union to the Convention would be the submission of the acts, measures and omissions of the Union to the external control exercised by the ECtHR.[40] As an obvious corollary, the decisions of the ECtHR in cases to which the EU is party will be binding on the Union's institutions, including the CJEU.[41] There is nothing peculiar about this. As the CJEU has held already some 20 years ago in an often-quoted passage from its opinion on the first Draft Agreement on the creation of the European Economic Area:

> [T]he Community's competence in the field of international relations ... necessarily entails the power to submit to the decisions of a court which is created or designated by such an agreement as regards the interpretation and application of its provisions.[42]

The most recent restatement of this principle may be found from the ECtHR's advisory opinion on the envisaged agreement creating a Unified Patent Litigation System.[43] In the actual practice, too, the EU has become a contracting party to a number of international agreements providing for the creation of courts or other third-party dispute settlement bodies. While those courts or dispute settlement bodies have jurisdiction to *interpret* the given agreement, they certainly do not have the power to rule on the *validity* of acts or measures of the Union's institutions, bodies, offices or agencies. It is clear that no such power would be vested with the ECtHR.[44] There is, therefore, nothing exceptional about Draft Agreement in this respect, either.

Nor is there anything unique or revolutionary about the fact that Article 34 of the Convention establishes a mechanism of individual applications whereby the ECtHR may receive applications from any person, non-governmental organisation or group of individuals claiming to be the victim of a violation by one of the

---

[40] See Art 59(2) of the Convention, as amended by Art 1(2) of the Draft Agreement, and Draft Explanatory Report of the CDDH (n 25), para 5.

[41] Draft Explanatory Report of the CDDH (n 25), para 21.

[42] Opinion 1/91 *Draft agreement between the Community, on the one hand, and the countries of the European Free Trade Association, on the other, relating to the creation of the European Economic Area* [1991] ECR I-6079, para 40.

[43] Opinion 1/09 *Draft agreement relating to the creation of a unified patent litigation system of the Court of 8 March 2011* [2011] ECR I-01137, para 74.

[44] See eg document CDDH-UE(2010)12 p 13.

High Contracting Parties. Article 26 of the Energy Charter Treaty,[45] for instance, provides for a system for the settlement of disputes between an investor and a Contracting Party, including the EU, by dispute settlement organs identified in the provision concerned.[46] Indeed, the mechanism of prior involvement may *never* be applied to situations where an individual application under Article 34 of the Convention is directed against acts or measures (or omissions) of the Union's institutions, bodies, offices or agencies, that is, where the EU is the (original) respondent (even if the CJEU has not yet assessed the compatibility with the Convention rights at issue of the relevant provisions of EU law (for example, as a result of the fact that the action pursuant to Article 263(4) TFEU has been declared inadmissible by the CJEU)). This shows that the prior involvement of the CJEU is not necessitated by fact that the Convention, unlike most other international agreements, establishes a mechanism of individual applications.

So, the question is what distinguishes the accession to the ECHR from all other international agreements providing for systems of courts or other dispute-settlement organs, to a degree that a special mechanism of participation by the CJEU in the dispute-settlement procedure is considered to be necessary? In order to shed light upon this question, it is appropriate first to look at the grounds put forward in favour of creating such a special mechanism (section III.B) and then make an assessment of whether they are sustainable (section III.C and section III.D). The question also arises whether the mechanism of prior involvement amounts to privileged treatment of the EU under the Convention (section III.E).

B. The Discussion Document of the CJEU and the Joint Communication of the Presidents

In the discussion document of the CJEU of May 2011,[47] the following reasons are put forward in support of the Court's proposal on a mechanism concerning prior involvement. For the sake of both accuracy and completeness the relevant passages should be quoted in full:[48]

> According to *[the] principle [of subsidiarity]*, it is for the States which have ratified the Convention to guarantee that the rights enshrined in the Convention are observed at

---

[45] [1994] OJ L380/24.

[46] See also the Optional Protocol to the UN Convention on the Rights of Persons with Disabilities which establishes a mechanism of individual applications whereby the Committee on the Rights of Persons with Disabilities is entitled to receive and consider communications from or on behalf of individuals or groups of individuals, subject to its jurisdiction, who claim to be victims of a violation by that State party of the provisions of the Convention (Art 1 of the Protocol). The Union has concluded the Convention (see [2010] OJ L23/35) but not the Optional Protocol)). For the proposal for a Council decision on the conclusion of the Protocol, see COM(2008) 530 final (Brussels, 28 August 2008), vol II.

[47] See n 19.

[48] Paras 6–10 of the document (emphasis added).

national level and for the European Court of Human Rights to verify that those States have in fact complied with their commitments.

On the basis of that principle of subsidiarity and in order to ensure that it is put into practice in the context of preparing for accession, *the Union must make sure*, as regards acts of the Union which are susceptible to being the subject of applications to the European Court of Human Rights, *that external review by the Convention institutions can be preceded by effective internal review* by the courts of the Member States and/or of the Union.

It is settled case-law that all national courts have jurisdiction to consider the validity of acts adopted by institutions of the Union, but national courts, whether or not there is a judicial remedy against their decisions in national law, do not have jurisdiction themselves to declare such acts invalid. To maintain uniformity in the application of European Union law and to guarantee the necessary coherence of the Union's system of judicial protection, *it is* therefore *for the Court of Justice alone*, in an appropriate case, to declare an act of the Union invalid.

In order to preserve this characteristic of the Union's system of judicial protection, the possibility must be avoided of the European Court of Human Rights being called on to decide on the conformity of an act of the Union with the Convention without the Court of Justice first having had an opportunity to give a definitive ruling on the point.

With respect more particularly to the preliminary ruling procedure provided for in Article 267 TFEU, it may be pointed out in this connection that [...] *it is not certain that a reference for a preliminary ruling will be made to the Court of Justice in every case* in which the conformity of European Union action with fundamental rights could be challenged. While national courts may, and some of them must, make a reference to the Court of Justice for a preliminary ruling, for it to rule on the interpretation and, if need be, the validity of acts of the Union, it is not possible for the parties to set this procedure in motion. Moreover, *it would be difficult to regard this procedure as a remedy which must be made use of as a necessary preliminary to bringing a case before the European Court of Human Rights in accordance with the rule of exhaustion of domestic remedies.*

The same arguments were later reiterated in the Joint Communication issued by Presidents Costa and Skouris of January 2011,[49] endorsing the requirement for a procedure that would ensure the possibility for the CJEU to carry out an internal review before the ECtHR carries out an external review. The relevant passages in paragraphs 2 of the Communication read as follows:

[I]f, for whatever reason, such *a reference for a preliminary ruling were not made*, the [ECtHR] would be required to adjudicate on an application calling into question provisions of EU law without the CJEU having the opportunity to review the consistency of that law with the fundamental rights guaranteed by the Charter.

---

[49] See n 22.

[T]he preliminary ruling procedure may be launched only by national courts and tribunals, to the exclusion of the parties, who are admittedly in a position to suggest a reference for a preliminary ruling, but do not have the power to require it. That means that the reference for a preliminary ruling is normally not a legal remedy to be exhausted by the applicant before referring the matter to the [ECtHR].

In order that the principle of subsidiarity may be respected also in that situation, a procedure should be put in place, in connection with the accession of the EU to the Convention, which is flexible and would ensure that the CJEU may carry out an internal review before the [ECtHR] carries out external review.

In a nutshell, therefore, the reasoning goes as follows: if (and when) the reference for a preliminary ruling is not regarded as a domestic remedy in the sense of Article 35(1) of the ECHR, the exhaustion of which is a condition for admissibility, the ECtHR may be seized by an applicant even when no reference pursuant to Article 267 TFEU has been by the national court to the CJEU. Such a scenario, the argument runs, would not only be contrary to the principle of subsidiarity under the Convention system but also pose a threat to the powers of the CJEU to maintain uniform application of EU law and to guarantee the coherence of the Union's system of judicial protection.

The above arguments will be assessed more closely in the following section.

C. On the Relevance of the Principle of Subsidiarity

For the purposes of the Convention system, the principle of subsidiarity signifies the idea that the machinery of protection established by the Convention is subsidiary to the national systems safeguarding human rights. An important aspect of this principle is the requirement concerning the exhaustion of all domestic remedies as a condition of admissibility of any application under the Convention (Article 35(1) ECHR). The purpose of that requirement is to afford the Contracting States the opportunity of preventing or putting right the violations alleged against them before those allegations are submitted to the institutions of the Convention.[50]

For present purposes attention should be drawn to the fact that the reference for a preliminary ruling under Article 267 TFEU is not to be considered a legal remedy an applicant must exhaust before making an application to the ECtHR, the explanation being that the parties to the national proceedings have no right to require a reference to be made. This is entirely a matter for the national court.[51] However, without such a preliminary ruling, the ECtHR could be required to

---

[50] See eg *Selmouni v France* Application no 25803/94 (ECtHR, 28 July 1999), para 74.

[51] The CJEU has described the procedure as one establishing 'direct cooperation between the Court and the courts and tribunals of the Member States by way of a non-contentious procedure excluding any initiative of the parties [to the main proceedings] who are merely invited to be heard in the course of that procedure'. See Case C-364/92 *SAT Fluggesellschaft mbH v Eurocontrol* [1994] ECR I-43, para 9.

adjudicate on the conformity of a provision of Union law with the Convention, without the CJEU having had the opportunity to do so.[52] 'Therefore', the CDDH commentary explains:

> [I]n order to respect the principle of subsidiarity *also in that situation*, an internal EU procedure should be put in place with a view to ensure that the CJEU may have the opportunity to review, in the form of a ruling, the conformity of the EU act at issue with fundamental rights before the ECtHR completes its review.[53]

The following comments on the role of the principle of subsidiarity are invited.

Firstly, that principle is not capable of serving an *autonomous* justification for the mechanism of prior involvement of the CJEU. This is obvious, since the justification for the mechanism of prior involvement will have to be specific to the legal or judicial order of the EU. Therefore, that principle is only deemed to come into play in conjunction with the characteristics of the procedure provided for by Article 267 TFEU (read: the uncertainty concerning the making of a reference that is up to the national court).[54] Secondly, the need for a mechanism of prior involvement could of course have been avoided entirely had it been concluded that a reference for a preliminary ruling would constitute a remedy in the sense of Article 267 TFEU. Such a hypothesis would, however, have involved a whole host of other problems at the level of both the Convention and EU law, possibly leading to an undue denial of access to the ECtHR (in cases where no preliminary reference was made).[55]

So, we must next turn to the other argument put forward in the CJEU's discussion document, that is, the prospect of a preliminary reference under Article 267 TFEU not necessarily being made 'in every case', as a justification for the creation of the procedure of prior involvement.

D. On the Prospect of Preliminary References not being Made under Article 267 TFEU

The argument that the characteristics of the preliminary reference procedure set out in Article 267 TFEU would be bound to threaten the principle of subsidiarity, unless no mechanism of prior involvement of the CJEU is instituted, is based on the concern that questions of interpretation or validity of Union law that ought to be referred by national courts to the CJEU would not for some reason be referred and, given that the reference does not constitute a domestic remedy to be exhausted, such 'by-passing' of the CJEU would be no bar for the applicant to reach the ECtHR. It should be added that a failure to submit a question for a

---

[52] Draft Explanatory Report of the CDDH (n 25), para 65.
[53] Document CDDH-UE (2011)05 (25 February 2011), para 62.
[54] See C Naômé, *Le renvoi préjudiciel en droit européen. Guide pratique* (Brussels, Larcier, 2010) 351.
[55] On the various problems, see T Lock, 'EU Accession to the ECHR: Implications for Judicial Review in Strasbourg' (2010) 35 *EL Rev* 777, 791–92.

preliminary ruling would not normally be capable of constituting a violation of Article 6 of the Convention (right to a fair trial), as the ECtHR has recently confirmed in *Ullens de Schooten and Rezabek v Belgium*.[56]

The concern about the compliance by courts or tribunals of Member States against the decisions of which there is no judicial remedy under national law with their obligation to make a reference for a preliminary ruling under Article 267(3) TFEU, is obviously not a novel one but rather one of the 'recurring' topics of EU law. In the present context, it should be of particular interest to note the observation once made by Judge Timmermans on the situation (considering the idea of a mechanism of prior involvement was first presented by him before the European Parliament in March 2010). Writing in 2004, and regarding the development and use of the preliminary procedure 'generally as a success', he observed that:

> [T]he situation is certainly not perfect. Too little is known of cases where Community law has not been applied where it should have been applied. Preliminary questions have not been raised where they should have been raised. Supremacy of Community law has only been accepted by some of the highest national Courts subject to important conditions. And of those highest Courts, some have never used the preliminary procedure or have even explicitly denied being in a position to do so.[57]

Some commentators share this view,[58] while others appear to be more optimistic.[59]

One way of assessing the 'scale' of the alleged problem could be to look at the consequences of non-compliance with Article 267(3) TFEU, provided for by EU law, that is:[60] first, the principle that a Member State is obliged to make good damage caused to individuals as a result of breaches of EU law for which it is responsible[61] and, secondly, the possibility of instituting infringement proceedings pursuant to Articles 258 and 260 TFEU where Union law is infringed by a national court.[62] However, the problem with such an approach is that the legal (or political) threshold for the application of these mechanisms has been extremely high in practice.

The Commission has been reluctant to make use of Articles 258 and 260 TFEU in respect of the failures of national courts to apply Article 267(3) TFEU, and

---

[56] *Ullens de Schooten and Rezabek v Belgium* Application no 3989/07 (ECtHR, 20 September 2011), especially paras 59–61.

[57] C Timmermans, 'The European Union's Judicial System' (2004) 41 *CML Rev* 393, 399.

[58] See eg C Baquero, 'La procédure préjudicielle suffit-elle à garantir l'efficacité et l'uniformité du droit de l'Union européenne?' in L Azoulai and L Burgorgue-Larsen (eds), *L'autorité de l'Union européenne* (Brussels, Edition Bruylant, 2006) 243.

[59] Eg T de la Mare and C Donnelly, 'Preliminary Rulings and EU Legal Integration: Evolution and Stasis' in P Craig and G de Búrca (eds), *The Evolution of EU Law* 2nd edn (Oxford, Oxford University Press, 2011) 362, 393.

[60] See Opinion 1/09 (n 43), paras 86–87.

[61] Case C-224/01 *Köbler* [2003] ECR I-10239, paras 31 and 33–36.

[62] Case C-129/00 *Commission v Italy* [2003] ECR I-14637, paras 29, 30 and 32.

there appears to be no case law from the CJEU on this issue.[63] Similarly, it follows from the judgment of the CJEU in *Köbler* that State liability, under Union law, for a failure by a national court adjudicating at last instance to comply with its obligation to make a reference for a preliminary ruling under Article 267(3) TFEU, could only be incurred in exceptional circumstances where there is a 'manifest' breach of the Treaty.[64] In other words, while national courts are subject to the principle of State liability under EU law, the threshold for establishing such liability is higher than usual[65] and, therefore, it would be a rare occurrence if a Member State were to be held liable for a failure by one of its courts to make reference for a preliminary ruling.[66] Hence, given the strictness of the fashion in which the conditions for the application of the above mechanisms are to be construed, the limited number of instances where the above mechanisms have actually been applied in practice would not seem capable of providing proof as to the degree to which Article 267 TFEU is actually complied with by national courts. This makes it difficult to assess the actual scale of the problem presented in the CJEU's discussion paper.

In any event, the argument concerning the prospect of preliminary references not being made under Article 267 TFEU as a justification for the introduction of the mechanism of prior involvement calls for the following comments.

Firstly, given that the reference for a preliminary ruling is not regarded as a domestic remedy in the sense of Article 35 ECHR, there is undoubtedly a risk that the external control exercised by the ECtHR may not always be preceded by the internal control by the CJEU. This risk exists as long as a litigant in the national court cannot enforce a reference for a preliminary ruling to be made.[67] At the same time, however, it is submitted that the test concerning the need for a specific mechanism set out in the discussion document of the CJEU would seem to be an unreasonably strict one. The mechanism is argued to be justified as 'it is not *certain* that a reference for a preliminary ruling will be made to the Court of Justice in *every* case' (emphasis added). Taken literally, such a test would seem to fail to take into account the fact that, according to the *CILFIT* case law of the CJEU, the courts or tribunals of a Member State, against the decisions of which

---

[63] See M Broberg and N Fenger, *Preliminary References to the European Court of Justice* (Oxford, Oxford University Press, 2010) 265–66. In respect of the Commission's role of supervising the application of Art 267 TFEU by national courts, attention should also be drawn to the fact that up to the year 2007 the Commission's annual Reports on monitoring the application of EU law included a specific Annex entitled 'Application of Community Law by the National Courts'. One of the questions addressed in the Annex was whether there had been cases where decisions against which there was no appeal had been taken without a reference for a preliminary ruling even though they turned on a point of Union law whose interpretation was less than perfectly obvious. The surveys for the years 1985–2007 are available at http://curia.europa.eu/jcms/jcms/Jo2_7064/.

[64] Case C-224/01 *Köbler* (n 61), para 53.

[65] See P Aalto, *Public Liability in EU Law. Brasserie, Bergderm and Beyond* (Oxford, Hart Publishing, 2011) 189–90.

[66] Broberg and Fenger (n 63) 271.

[67] Ladenburger (n 3) 49.

there is no judicial remedy, also enjoy certain discretion in deciding whether a reference should be made to the CJEU.[68] Moreover, the test put forward by the CJEU in the discussion document overlooks the function of national courts as 'Community courts of ordinary jurisdiction'.[69] The strictness of the test could even regarded as symptomatic of an attitude within the CJEU whereby national courts of Member States are not to be trusted to implement EU law but would rather need to be supervised.[70] Thirdly, one cannot help noticing that, in March 2011—that is, soon after the publication of the Court's discussion document— the CJEU, in its opinion on the envisaged Agreement creating a Unified Patent Litigation System, rejected the conferment upon the envisaged Patent Court of certain functions currently exercised by the national courts of the Member States precisely by underlining the fact that the sanctions provided for situations where Union law was infringed by a national court would not have applied to the Patent Court. (Article 48 of the Agreement provided for a preliminary ruling procedure akin to Article 267 TFEU, giving to the Patent Court the power to refer questions to the CJEU.)[71] In other words, while in the Patent Court opinion context the emphasis was on the fact that decisions of national courts of are 'subject to mechanisms capable of ensuring the full effectiveness of the rules of the European Union',[72] there is no mention of the mechanisms concerned in the context of the accession to the ECHR. In the discussion document, the emphasis is rather on the *uncertainty* as to whether Article 267 TFEU is properly applied by national courts.

E. On the Comparison of the CJEU and other Supreme or Constitutional Courts

The courts of no other contracting party to the Convention currently benefit from a mechanism similar to the one envisaged by Article 3(6) of the Draft Agreement. Therefore, even if one assumed that there existed a 'risk' of the external control by the ECtHR not being preceded by internal control of the CJEU in some cases, the introduction of the mechanism of prior involvement (or some other special mechanism) would seem to be justified only on the condition that no comparable risk exists in the case of (other) supreme or constitutional courts of the other contracting parties to the ECHR. Otherwise, the creation of the mechanism could be criticised of being an unjustified privilege granted to the EU. The comparison between the CJEU and other supreme or constitutional courts shows that such criticism would not seem to be entirely without foundation.

---

[68] See above section II.B.ii.
[69] Conclusions of Léger AG in Case C-224/01 *Köbler* (n 61), para 66.
[70] *Cf* de la Mare and Donnelly (n 59) 393.
[71] Opinion 1/09 (n 43), para 88.
[72] ibid (n 43), para 82.

Firstly, it should be noted that procedures comparable to Article 267 TFEU also exist within judicial systems of State parties to the Convention. Historically, the inclusion in Article 177 of the EC Treaty (as it then was) on the preliminary reference procedure has been explained by the existence of comparable provisions in the constitutions of some of the original European Community Member States.[73] While some of those procedures may only bear a superficial resemblance to the procedure set out in Article 267 TFEU—so that one should be forewarned to draw to any direct parallels—two mechanisms, both providing for a review of constitutionality of legislation, have been mentioned as providing for relevant points of comparison: Article 100 of the German *Grundgesetz* as well as the Article 23 Italian Law No 87 of 11 March 1953 concerning the composition and procedures of the Constitutional Court.[74] Under both procedures, unlike in the case of certain other preliminary reference procedures existing in other EU Member States, the decision to refer a question to the constitutional court is taken by the referring court and not by the parties to the main proceedings. Moreover, the procedure established by Article 23 of the Italian Law No 87 is not deemed to constitute domestic remedies in the sense of Article 35 of the Convention,[75] and the same would probably be true with Article 100 of the *Grundgesetz*.[76] Therefore, a situation where the ECtHR would be required to assess the compatibility of a measure with the Convention without the constitutional court having had an opportunity to do so first, would seem to be perfectly possible at least in Germany and Italy.[77]

Secondly, the situation where a domestic court—which is, under certain conditions, under an obligation to make a reference for preliminary ruling to a domestic (or international) court—has for some reason decided not to make a reference, has also been examined by the ECtHR in respect of Article 6 of the Convention (right to a fair trial). It emerges from the case law that, while the possibility of a breach of Article 6 is not completely excluded (in particular where such a refusal appears arbitrary), a failure to submit a question for a preliminary ruling is not normally capable of constituting a violation of the provision in question. For present purposes, however, this case law shows that a failure to refer a question for a preliminary ruling could take place not only in conjunction with Article 267 TFEU but also in the context of similar mechanisms laid down in judicial systems

---

[73] See eg M Lagrange, 'L'action préjudicielle dans le droit interne des Etats membres et en droit communautaire' (1974) 10 *Revue Trimestrielle de Droit Europeen* 268.

[74] ibid, 275–77 and DWK Anderson and M Demetriou, *References to the European Court* 2nd edn (London, Sweet & Maxwell, 2002) 5–6.

[75] *Immobiliare Saffi v Italy* Application no 22774/93 (ECtHR, 28 July 1999), para 42.

[76] The situation is therefore different from the cases of 'individual' constitutional complaints existing in German law. These have normally been regarded as remedies which the applicant must exhaust under Art 35 of the Convention. See, however, *Sürmeli v Germany* Application no 75529/01 (ECtHR, 8 June 2006), para 108.

[77] See the interventions by O de Schutter before the AFCO of the European Parliament (18 March 2010 and 10 April 2010), available at: http://www.europarl.europa.eu/committees/en/AFCO/events. html, and Besselink (n 3) 39.

of other contracting parties to the ECHR. As the ECtHR has held in a recent judgment concerning failure to make a reference under Article 267 TFEU:

> la Convention ne garantit pas, comme tel, un droit à ce qu'une affaire soit renvoyée à titre préjudiciel par le juge interne devant une autre juridiction, *qu'elle soit nationale ou supranational*[78]

Accordingly, the introduction of the mechanism of prior involvement is regarded by Professor O de Schutter as a special and privileged procedure 'giving the CJEU a chance which the national court had refused it'.[79] In the submission of the eminent author:

> [l]a situation dans laquelle se trouvera la Cour de justice de l'Union européenne à la suite de l'adhésion de l'Union ne sera donc pas véritablement spécifique, surtout si l'on considère que les juridictions nationales des Etats membres sont les premiers juges de l'application du droit de l'Union européenne. L'argument que la Cour de justice devrait nécessairement pouvoir se prononcer avant que soit soumise à la Cour européenne des droits de l'homme la question de savoir si tel acte de l'Union européenne est compatible avec les droits fondamentaux, et que ceci viserait à aligner la situation de la Cour de justice sur les juridictions nationales suprêmes des autres Parties à la Convention, doit être traité avec précaution: en réalité, l'instauration d'une procédure spéciale visant à donner à la Cour de justice de l'Union européenne une chance que la juridiction nationale lui a refusée, créerait au bénéfice de la Cour de justice une situation d'exceptionnalité qui n'a pas de précédent.

IV. ON THE IMPLICATIONS OF THE MECHANISM OF PRIOR INVOLVEMENT, ESPECIALLY FOR THE APPLICANT

An assessment of the mechanism of prior involvement should also take account of the more practical implications of the mechanism for the procedure before the ECtHR, especially from the point of view of an applicant. It may be noted that while neither the discussion document of the CJEU nor the Joint Communication of Presidents Costa and Skouris refers to such questions, they have received attention among commentators. For instance, in his General Report for the 2012 FIDE Conference, Professor LFM Besselink is highly critical of the mechanism of prior involvement from the perspective of judicial protection of the applicant, arguing that, as a result of the mechanism, the applicant is placed before a court other than to which he had addressed his application and one to which he would normally have no access. In the view of the author, this amounts to an infringement of the important procedural principle of '*gesetzliche Richter*'.[80]

---

[78] *Ullens de Schooten and Rezabek v Belgium* (n 56), para 57 of the judgment (emphasis added).

[79] See Schutter (n 77). LFM Besselink (n 3) at 39, also regards the mechanism as introducing 'procedurally a double standard, which is not convincingly argued in all respects'.

[80] Besselink (n 3) 39.

At a more practical level, the introduction of the mechanism of prior involvement could have implications of at least the following kind: firstly, the impact of the mechanism on the length of proceedings before the ECtHR; secondly, the possibility of additional costs incurred by the applicant as a result of the involvement of the CJEU; and, finally, the question as to the effects of the decision of CJEU on the status of the applicant in the proceedings before the ECtHR. While a more definitive assessment of these (and many other) questions would have to wait for the more detailed rules on the implementation of Article 3(6) of the Draft Agreement to be adopted—presumably in the context of the procedural rules of the respective courts as well as by the Union's institutions—the following remarks can none the less be made at this stage.

Insofar as concerns, first, the implications of the mechanism for the length of proceedings before the ECtHR, the immediate impression is that the length of those proceedings increases as a result of the involvement of the CJEU. Some delay to the proceedings is already implied by Article 3(6) of the Draft Agreement, providing that, once the mechanism is triggered, 'sufficient time shall be afforded for the Court of Justice of the European Union to make such an assessment and thereafter for the parties to make observations to the Court'. On the other hand, the Union 'shall ensure that such assessment is made quickly so that the proceedings before the Court are not unduly delayed'. The possible delay, it could be argued, would result from the inclusion of the following extra stages to the procedure: firstly, the proceedings before the CJEU, presumably in accordance with the expedited procedure provided for in Article 105 of the Rules of Procedure of the Court,[81] and, secondly, the requirement, laid down by Article 3(6) of the Draft Agreement, of time being afforded for the parties to make observations to the ECtHR after the CJEU has made its assessment. At a closer look, however, the impact on the overall length of the procedure before the ECtHR might not be as dramatic as one could imagine at first sight. The sequence of the proceedings could be designed in such a way that would enable the involvement of the CJEU to take place within the standard procedural phases of the procedure before the ECtHR. In cases concerning EU law relating to the Area of Freedom, Security and Justice, the procedure before the CJEU could also be further speeded up by having recourse to the urgent preliminary ruling procedure (the so-called 'PPU') provided for in Article 107 of the Rules of Procedure of the Court.[82] Most importantly, the mechanism of prior involvement could serve a function similar to the one that traditionally attributed to the requirement concerning the exhaustion of domestic remedies in international law: the preparation of the case for an international jurisdiction by the procedure in domestic courts. In this way,

---

[81] In the two cases to which the expedited (formerly, 'accelerated') procedure was applied in 2011, the duration of the proceedings was from five to six months.

[82] In 2011, the average duration of PPU proceedings was 2.5 months.

the assessment of the case made by the CJEU could even enable the matter to be handled more speedily by the ECtHR.[83]

Insofar as concerns, secondly, the possible additional financial burden faced by applicants as a result of the involvement of the CJEU, reference may only be made to the possibility of granting legal aid under both the Rules of the ECtHR[84] and the Rules of Procedure of the Court of Justice.[85]

As a third and perhaps the most complex set of issues from the perspective of the applicant, the question of the effects of the decision of the CJEU on the proceedings before the ECtHR should be considered. If no incompatibility was established by the CJEU, the situation would seem to be clear: the proceedings before the ECtHR would resume and continue in the normal way. In those cases, however, where the assessment by the CJEU leads to a finding of incompatibility, the implications of the CJEU's decision may not be equally evident. The central question is whether, and, if so, under what conditions, the decision of the CJEU could be capable of remedying the alleged violation and, as a consequence, depriving the applicant of his 'victim status' under Article 34 of the Convention.[86]

The question of the effects of the decision of the CJEU for the proceedings before the ECtHR is not explicitly addressed in the current Draft Agreement. However, it follows from the final sentence of Article 3(6)—providing that '[t]he provisions of this paragraph shall not affect the powers of the Court'—that the matter is to be determined solely by the ECtHR. In this respect, the ECtHR will obviously be guided by the principles established in its own case law concerning the loss of a victim status under Article 34. It is clear that the decision of the CJEU would not in itself be capable of depriving the applicant of his status as a victim.[87] As a rule, an appropriate and sufficient redress would have to be provided, in the first place by the national authorities of the respondent Member State. However, under EU law, a Member State could hardly be required to re-open proceedings that are *res judicata* under national law. Insofar as concerns regarding preliminary rulings under Article 267 TFEU, it is settled case law that Union law allows a national judgment to stand even if it is based on an understanding of the law which subsequently overturned by a preliminary ruling, including cases where the result reached in the national case is incompatible with Union law;[88] the legal effects of a decision of the CJEU under Article 3(6) of the Draft Agreement could hardly be any more far-reaching than those of a preliminary ruling in this respect.

---

[83] This point was highlighted by Advocate General Kokott at the Seminar in Florence.
[84] Chapter XI of the Rules of the ECtHR.
[85] Arts 115–18 of the Rules of Procedure of the Court of Justice.
[86] This question was identified in document CDDH-UE(2010)12 (12 October 2010) p 13. Under Art 34 only applicants who consider themselves 'victims' of a breach of the Convention can complain to the ECtHR, and this 'status' remains relevant for at all stages of proceedings. See eg *Scordino v Italy* Application no 36813/97 (ECtHR, 26 March 2006), paras 177 *et seq*.
[87] Ladenburger (n 3) 52.
[88] See Broberg and Fenger (n 63) 446, and the case law there cited.

Another matter is that the national law of a Member State in question could provide for the possibility of remedying the violation in such a way that the ECtHR considers the applicant to have lost his victim status. There is nothing peculiar about such a finding, as the same may happen in any proceedings brought under Article 34 of the Convention. The mechanism of prior involvement would simply provide for an additional possibility to remedy the violation. If, however, no redress was provided and the applicant retained his procedural status, the Union and/or the Member State could offer a friendly settlement or, if the applicant does not agree thereto, make a unilateral declaration (involving, for example, a commitment to amend legislation), enabling the ECtHR to strike out the case. In the mechanism of prior involvement, however, there is nothing to constrain the review conducted by the ECtHR of the compliance by the EU of its obligations under the Convention.

V. GENERAL CONCLUSIONS AND ASSESSMENT

The mechanism of prior involvement would apply to situations where the ECtHR is required to review the compatibility of provisions of EU law with the ECHR without the CJEU first having been offered the opportunity to review the consistency of those provisions with EU fundamental rights. The Joint Communication from Presidents Costa and Skouris predicts that, '[i]n all probability, that situation should not arise often'.[89] Irrespective of whether that prediction proves correct or not, the practical implications of the mechanism of prior involvement are most likely to remain relatively mundane. From the perspective of the procedural and substantive rights of the applicant, it needs to be underlined that the powers of the ECtHR would remain unaffected by the mechanism of prior involvement as envisaged by the Draft Agreement. It would only be up to that court to decide what consequences, if any, were to follow from the decision of the CJEU and whether the violation has been remedied by the respondent Member State and/or the Union.

At the same time, however, there is no escape from the fact that the mechanism set out in the Draft Agreement appears to create at least as many legal problems as it solves. The following (and other) questions would seem to arise. Who is to determine whether or not the CJEU has 'assessed' the compatibility with 'the

---

[89] See n 21. For the view that even the *co-respondent mechanism* (the application of which to the EU is a prerequisite for the application of the mechanism of prior involvement) may be expected to be applied only in a limited number of cases only, see Draft revised Explanatory report to the draft Agreement on the Accession of the European Union to the European Convention on Human Rights, document CDDH-UE(2011)11 (15 June 2011), para 38. As examples of cases which only 'might have certainly required' the application of the co-respondent mechanism, reference is made to *Matthews v United Kingdom*, Application no 24833/94 (ECtHR, 18 February 1994); *Bosphorus Hava Yollari Turizm Ve Ticaret Anonim Sirketi v Ireland*, Application no 45036/98 (ECtHR, 30 June 2005) and *Cooperatieve Producentenorganisatie van de Nederlandse Kokkelvisserij UA v the Netherlands*, Application no 13645/05 (ECtHR, 20 January 2009).

Convention rights at issue' of the provision of EU law in question? If this decision is to be taken by the ECtHR, would this be in conformity with EU law? What are the effects, under the Convention, in EU law as well as the national law of the Member State concerned, of the assessment to be made by the CJEU? If the assessment by the CJEU were to lead to an act of an institution being declared invalid or to a binding interpretation of the relevant provision of Union law, can such a power be conferred upon the CJEU without a Treaty amendment? What is the relevance of the limitations to the jurisdiction of CJEU based on Article 275 TFEU (exclusion, as a rule, of the Common Foreign and Security Policy (CFSP))? Would it be possible to confer upon the ECtHR jurisdiction to assess the compatibility of CFSP measures with the Convention even in cases where the CJEU does not have a corresponding power of review? While some of these issues will perhaps be solved in the detailed rules implementing the Accession Agreement, others may have to wait for subsequent practice.

A much more fundamental aspect of the mechanism is however the *signal* it is likely to give, or the *impression* it is likely to create, of the self-conception of the EU and its institutions towards national courts of the Member States, the other contracting parties to the ECHR and their domestic courts as well as the realm of international judicial or dispute settlement.

Insofar as concerns, first, the relationship between the CJEU and *national courts of the Member States*, the signal could be regarded as one of the CJEU's attachment to a goal of maximum uniformity. The mechanism could be seen to be based on a degree of 'suspicion' that, for whatever reason, no reference for a preliminary ruling under Article 267 TFEU would necessarily be made even when it should, and on the view that, whenever such a scenario were to materialise, the review of Union law by the ECtHR is not to be tolerated without the prior involvement of the CJEU.[90] Similar tendencies have also been identified in respect of the application of Article 267 TFEU.[91] It is clear, however, that the mechanism of prior involvement would not have been the only possible way of alleviating such concerns: EU law also contains the means of its own for enforcing the application of Article 267 TFEU, as recently recalled by the CJEU itself in Opinion 1/09. For a more subtle approach, the means utilised upon the adoption of the urgent preliminary ruling procedure (the 'PPU')—that is, the drawing of attention of national courts to the importance of considering the need for a reference whenever the question of compatibility of a Union measure with the ECHR is raised in a national court—would also have been available.[92] It therefore seems that the mechanism of prior involvement seeks to address a problem that could have been alleviated to a certain extent through internal measures of the Union.

---

[90] As the CJEU argued in the discussion document, 'it is not *certain* that a reference for a preliminary ruling will be made to the Court of Justice in *every* case in which the conformity of European Union action with fundamental rights could be challenged' (emphasis added).

[91] See de la Mare and Donnelly (n 59) 391.

[92] See the statement adopted by the Council in respect of the PPU, [2008] OJ L24/44.

Regarding, secondly, *the other contracting parties to the ECHR and their domestic courts*, it has been argued that the mechanism of prior involvement is tantamount to creating privileged treatment in comparison to courts of the other contracting parties to the ECHR. The latter cannot, as Lock has put it, 'avoid the risk of violating the Convention by obtaining a preliminary clearance from the ECtHR'.[93] However, to the defence of the mechanism, it should be pointed out that the situation of the CJEU is different from supreme courts in 'appellate' systems where the requirement of the exhaustion of domestic remedies ensures their involvement. Moreover, even to the extent other national judicial systems include mechanisms of court-to-court constitutional referral similar to Article 267 TFEU, there seem to be certain differences. In particular, the *scope* of the jurisdiction of the CJEU is far broader than, for example, that of the German Constitutional Court under Article 100 of the Basic Law or that of the Italian Constitutional Court under Article 23 of Italian Law No 87 of 11 March 1953; the latter are as a rule limited to the question of unconstitutionality of laws. In other words, the role, and the sheer volume, of the decentralised enforcement of law seem much greater in the EU than in those national systems involving mechanisms of court-to-court referral. From this perspective, the 'privilege' seems to be to some extent justified.

Thirdly, the mechanism of prior involvement also invites comparison with *other instances where an international agreement concluded by the Union provides for a court or other system of binding third-party dispute settlement*. As the CJEU itself has emphasised, the decisions of such dispute settlement bodies are binding upon the Union's institutions, including the CJEU.[94] Under no other EU agreement, however, is there a mechanism comparable to the one provided for by Article 3(6) of the Draft Agreement, nor has any such mechanism ever been proposed in any other context. What, then, is the difference between the ECHR and all other external agreements entered into by the Union that is deemed to justify the mechanism of prior involvement in the context of the accession to the ECHR (apart from the obvious difference in the volume of litigation)?

At first sight, there appear to exist none. At closer scrutiny, however, at least the following issues would seem to arise. Firstly, it will be remembered that one of central arguments behind the introduction of a mechanism of prior involvement was the conclusion that a reference for preliminary ruling under Article 267 TFEU would not be regarded as a domestic remedy under Article 35 of the Convention. Within the framework of decentralised enforcement of Union law this opens up the possibility of 'by-passing' of the CJEU along the way to 'Strasbourg' in a way that is normally not the case with supreme courts in 'appellate' systems. Under many other international agreements of importance in terms of international judicial dispute settlement there is either no requirement (eg the Energy Charter Treaty),[95] or at least no strict requirement (eg the World Trade

---

[93] Lock (n 55) 793.
[94] Opinion 1/91 (n 42), para 39.
[95] See Art 26 of the Treaty (n 45).

Organization (WTO) Agreement),[96] for the exhaustion of domestic remedies. In those systems, the CJEU does not appear to be placed in any less advantageous position as a result of the mechanism, such as the one based on Article 267 TFEU. Secondly, under some of the most relevant agreements, notably the WTO Agreement and the UN Convention Law of the Sea, the CJEU has consistently refused to acknowledge direct effect of the agreements concerned, including, under the WTO Agreement, decisions of the dispute settlement bodies set under them.[97] Among other objectives, the non-recognition of direct effect is one way of upholding the jurisdictional autonomy of the CJEU. Concluding his criticism on the CJEU's refusal to accept direct effect of a WTO dispute settlement, Eeckhout submits that the Court 'has never in its history accepted that it was bound by the decisions of another adjudicator', and hopes that this approach is not transposed to the ECHR.[98]

From this perspective, the need for the mechanism of prior involvement may also be illustrative of the acknowledgement that, in the case of the ECHR, a similar approach, including the possibility of denying direct effect, would simply not be an option: in other words, where the ECtHR has found a violation of the Convention by the EU, the CJEU *will have to be* bound by that decision when interpreting the ECHR in subsequent cases.[99] This state of affairs, combined with the uncertainty of whether there will be a reference for a preliminary ruling in every case where there should be one, explains, to a large part, the need to protect the powers of the CJEU, and, as a corollary, the emergence of the mechanism of prior involvement.

---

[96] See eg D Lovric, *Deference to the Legislature in WTO Challenges to Legislation* (The Hague, Kluwer 2009) 37.

[97] For a recent overview, see P Eeckhout, *EU External Relations Law* 2nd edn (Oxford, Oxford University Press, 2011) 331–83.

[98] ibid, 381.

[99] T Lock, 'The ECJ and the ECtHR: The Future Relationship between the Two European Courts' (2009) 8 *The Law and Practice of International Courts and Tribunals* 375, 397.

13

Worlds Apart? Comparing the Approaches of the European Court of Justice and the EU Legislature to International Law

JAN WOUTERS, JED ODERMATT AND THOMAS RAMOPOULOS[1]

I. INTRODUCTION

THE EUROPEAN UNION'S (hereafter referred to as 'the EU' or 'the Union') relationship with international law, especially questions relating to how international law is applied and interpreted within the EU legal order, is complex and ever-developing.[2] Until the changes brought about by the Lisbon Treaty, there had been only few provisions in the Treaties that gave guidance on these matters. It has therefore mostly been up to the Court of Justice of the European Union ('Court') to determine the relationship between international law and the EU legal order. On the one hand, the Court has demonstrated a degree of openness towards international law; it has reviewed whether certain measures of secondary EU law comply with international law and has interpreted EU law in the light of international law. At the same time the Court has also asserted and underlined the autonomy of the EU legal order, inviting criticism for pursuing

---

[1] Thomas Ramopoulos currently works as an official in the European Commission (DG AGRI). He contributed to this chapter before joining the Commission. His views expressed herein are strictly personal.

[2] See, inter alia: KS Ziegler, 'International Law and EU Law: Between Asymmetric Constitutionalisation and Fragmentation' in A Orakhelashvili (ed), *Research Handbook on the Theory of International Law* (Cheltenham, Edward Elgar, 2011), 268–327; E Cannizzaro, P Palchetti and RA Wessel (eds), *International Law as Law of the European Union* (Leiden, Martinus Nijhoff, 2012); C Kaddous, 'Effects of International Agreements in the EU Legal Order' in M Cremona and B de Witte, *EU Foreign Relations Law: Constitutional Fundamentals* (Oxford, Hart Publishing, 2008), 291–311; J Wouters, A Nollkaemper and E de Wet (eds), *The Europeanisation of International Law. The Status of International Law in the EU and its Member States* (The Hague, TMC Asser Press, 2008); J Wouters, 'The Tormented Relationship between International Law and EU Law' in PHF Dekker, R Dolzer and M Waibel (eds), *Making Transnational Law Work in the Global Economy. Essays in Honour of Detlev Vagts* (Cambridge, Cambridge University Press, 2010), 198–221.

an approach that gives too little weight to international law. Yet the approach of the Court represents only one part of the Union's wider relationship with international law. EU legislation often seeks to implement, or is influenced by, rules developed at the international level, and refers to international instruments within its preamble or substantive provisions, even when these instruments are not strictly binding upon the Union. The EU pursues an international agenda that includes shaping and developing international law through negotiating and entering into international agreements and by participating in international organisations and other bodies.[3] A full understanding of the EU's relationship with international law must take into account the practice, not only of the Court, but also other EU institutions. It is this chapter's central tenet that the Court's approach to international law in recent years, often seen as becoming more rigid, stands in contrast with a more open and receptive approach by the EU legislature.

We proceed in three parts. The first part turns to the Treaties to see what guidance they provide on how international law should be dealt with in the EU legal order. We argue that the references to international law and multilateral-ism, especially those included following the Lisbon Treaty, ought to be seen as constitutional principles that guide all EU institutions and bodies, including the Court and the EU legislature. The second section reviews the Court's approach to a number of international law issues. We examine some of the tools the Court has developed to apply and interpret international law, and the ways it has sought to safeguard the autonomy of the EU legal order. There is an emphasis on recent cases, such as *Air Transport Association of America and Others v Secretary of State for Energy and Climate Change*[4] (*ATAA*), which in clarifying the Court's approach with regard to certain concepts, illustrates the divergence between it and the EU legislature.[5] The third section examines the approach of the legislature regarding international law, focusing on the fields of aviation, the environment, fisheries and human health, all fields in which EU and international law have come into contact in recent years.

A comparison of the EU legislature with the Court may seem to deviate from the traditional analysis of this topic.[6] They are each tasked with different duties, and their approaches may be explained, in part, by these differing roles within the EU institutional set-up. The other institutions, the European Parliament,

---

[3] See the Treaty on the Functioning of the European Union (TFEU), Art 221(1) where it is stated that '[t]he Union shall establish all appropriate forms of cooperation with the organs of the United Nations and its specialised agencies, the Council of Europe, the Organisation for Security and Cooperation in Europe and the Organisation for Economic Cooperation and Development. The Union shall also maintain such relations as are appropriate with other international organisations'.

[4] Case C-366/10 *Air Transport Association of America and Others v. Secretary of State for Energy and Climate Change* (*ATAA*), judgment of 21 December 2011, nyr.

[5] See J Odermatt 'Case C-366/10, Air Transport Association of America and Others v. Secretary of State for Energy and Climate Change' (2013) 20(1) *Columbia Journal of European Law*, 143–65.

[6] However, see G De Baere and P Koutrakos, 'The Interactions Between the Legislature and the Judiciary in EU External Relations' in P Syrpis (ed), *The Judiciary, the Legislature and the EU Internal Market* (Cambridge, Cambridge University Press, 2012) 243–73.

the European Council, the Council of the European Union and the European Commission, have mainly political and—with the exception of the European Council[7]—legislative roles.[8] While both political and legal considerations determine the actions of these institutions, the Court has to 'ensure that in the interpretation and application of the Treaties the law is observed'[9] and must, therefore, prioritise legal and constitutional considerations. The particular attitude of these institutions towards international law should be understood in light of this.

Much of the literature aimed at examining the EU's relationship with international law has focused on the Court of Justice. Yet in order to fully understand the complexities of the EU's relationship with international law, one institution cannot be studied in isolation. A 2011 *Common Market Law Review* editorial linked the complex legal issues faced by the Court in a string of cases dealing with international law with the approach taken by the EU legislative organs. It argued that these issues 'are all basically rooted in the underlying problem of a discontinuity between the internal legislation and the external obligations of the Union'.[10] Moreover, due to the widening and deepening of the EU legal order, and the ever-expanding range of legal instruments at the international level, the fields covered by the two legal orders tend to converge. This has led to conflicts, such as when international anti-terrorism regulation conflicts with European fundamental rights norms, or when European measures to protect the environment seem to conflict with international laws regulating transport. The Union will likely be confronted with an increasing number of such conflicts. It is important to understand how the EU institutions and organs can work in a way that minimises the 'discontinuity' and prevent conflicts from arising. Although the Court is faced with the task of balancing respect for international law with the preservation of the integrity of the EU legal order, this does not require the restrictive approach to international law which it has adopted, one that puts an emphasis on safeguarding the autonomy of the EU legal order. Rather, we submit that the Court should enter into an open dialogue with international law, recognising the EU itself as part of the international legal order with its own origins in international law.

II. INTERNATIONAL LAW AND MULTILATERALISM IN THE TREATIES POST-LISBON

It is often stated that the Treaty on European Union (TEU) and Treaty on the Functioning of the European Union (TFEU) give little or no guidance on how international law is to be applied and interpreted within the EU legal order, leaving it to the Court to develop rules regulating how international law is given effect

---

[7] Art 15(1) TEU.

[8] Arts 14–17 TEU.

[9] Art 19(1) TEU.

[10] See 'Editorial Comments' (2011) 48(1) *CML Rev* 3.

within the EU.[11] While the Court undoubtedly has a central role in developing the contours of the EU's relationship with international law, the EU Treaties are not entirely silent on the matter. In contrast to the pre-Lisbon era, there are now significant references to international law. These references to international law and multilateralism may at first glance seem to consist of broad 'motherhood statements',[12] yet it is submitted that they should be taken up by the Court to further guide its approach to international law and more generally that they should serve to develop a more consistent approach to international law across EU institutions and bodies.

The EU's commitment to international law is set out in Article 3(5) TEU, which states that the Union 'shall contribute [...] to the strict observance and the development of international law'.[13] In *ATAA*, the Court interpreted this to mean that when the EU adopts an act, the Union 'is bound to observe international law in its entirety, including customary international law'.[14] The principle that the Union 'must respect international law in the exercise of its powers'[15] had already long been enshrined in the Court's case law since *Poulsen*. In *ATAA* the Court for the first time explicitly linked this duty to respect international law with the obligation set out in Article 3(5) TEU. In doing so, the Court aligned itself with the Opinion of Advocate General Kokott who, in addition to citing relevant case law, referred to the second sentence of Article 3(5) TEU to reaffirm the principle that international agreements and rules of customary international law form part of the European legal order.[16]

Article 21(1) TEU provides that the Union's 'action on the international scene' is to be guided by numerous principles, including the 'respect for the principles of the United Nations and international law'.[17] The EU must also 'promote

---

[11] See J Klabbers, *The European Union in International Law*, Institut des hautes études internationales de Paris, Université Panthéon-Assas (Paris II), Cours et travaux no 13 (2012), 72: 'As a starting point it should be noted that the TEU (nor any of the other relevant foundational treaties) says nothing whatsoever about the effect of international law within the 'internal' legal order of the EU'.

[12] Indeed, it has been observed that similar objectives can be found in national constitutions, and in some cases these foreign policy objectives have been given legally binding effect. See J Larik, 'Shaping the International Order as Union Objective' in D Kochenov and F Amtenbrink (eds), *The European Union's Shaping of the International Legal Order* (Cambridge, Cambridge University Press, 2014) 62–86.

[13] Art 3(5) TEU.

[14] *ATAA* (n 4), para 101.

[15] See Case C-286/90 *Poulsen and Diva Navigation* [1992] ECR I-6019, paras 9–10. This duty includes respect for principles of customary international law: Case C-162/96 *Racke* [1998] ECR I-3655, paras 45–46. This was confirmed in Case C-386/08 *Brita GmbH v Hauptzollamt Hamburg-Hafen* [2010] ECR I-1289: 'the Court has held that, even though the Vienna Convention does not bind either the Community or all its Member States, a series of provisions in that convention reflect the rules of customary international law which, as such, are binding upon the Community institutions and form part of the Community legal order' and Case C-308/06 *Intertanko and Others* [2008] ECR I-4057, para 51: 'as is clear from settled case-law, the powers of the Community must be exercised in observance of international law, including provisions of international agreements in so far as they codify customary rules of general international law'; *ATAA* (n 4), para 101.

[16] *ATAA* (n 4), Opinion of Advocate General Kokott, para 108.

[17] Art 21(1)TEU; see also *ATAA* (n 4), Opinion of Advocate General Kokott, para 43. There the Advocate General restricted herself to referring to the goal of the Union 'to advance respect for the

multilateral solutions to common problems, in particular in the framework of the United Nations' and 'promote an international system based on stronger multilateral cooperation and good global governance'.[18] One of the goals of the EU in its external action is to 'consolidate and support democracy, the rule of law, human rights and the *principles of international law*'.[19] These goals apply both to 'the Union's external action' and 'the external aspects of its other policies'.[20] The Treaties therefore present the EU as an international actor that takes international law seriously. The respect for international law within the EU is even presented as one of the principles which have 'inspired [the Union's] own creation' on par with principles such as democracy, the rule of law, and human rights and fundamental freedoms.[21] The respect for international law should thus be viewed as one of the Union's fundamental constitutional principles. While the Advocate General did refer to Article 21(1) TEU in *ATAA* (on a somewhat subsidiary basis), the Court did not make use of this provision, citing only relevant case law confirming that the EU has to respect international law in all external aspects of its policies.[22]

Apart from provisions outlining the EU's commitment to international law, the Treaties give little specific guidance on how international law should be applied *within* the EU legal order. Article 216(2) TFEU states that '[a]greements concluded by the Union are binding upon the institutions of the Union and on its Member States'.[23] The provisions of these agreements 'form an integral part of Community [now Union] law'[24] from the moment they enter into force[25] and do not require implementing acts at the European or national level.[26] This has been described as following a 'monist' approach to international law.[27] Yet as we argue

principles of international law in the wider world' without adding the former goal stated in Art 21 TEU, which is that the Union will be guided among others by international law in its actions on the international plane.

[18] Art 21(1) TEU, second para, and 21(2)(f).

[19] Art 21(2)(b)TEU (emphasis added).

[20] Art 21(3)TEU.

[21] Art 21(1)TEU.

[22] *ATAA* (n 4), paras 103, 123.

[23] Art 216(2) TFEU. See ex Art 300(7) TEC. The Lisbon Treaty extended the reach of this clause to Common Foreign and Security Policy (CFSP) agreements. Under the former Treaty of European Union (TEU) (Nice version), Art 24(6), these agreements were only binding on the institutions of the Union.

[24] Case 181/73 *Haegeman* [1974] ECR 449, para 5.

[25] Case C-386/08 *Brita GmbH* (n 15), para 39.

[26] See Case C-533/08 *TNT Express Nederland BV v AXA Versicherung* AG [2010] I-4107, para 60: 'In the case of international agreements, it is settled that such agreements concluded by the European Union form an integral part of its legal order'; Case C-301/08 *Bogiatzi v Deutscher Luftpool and Others* [2009] ECR I-10185, para 23; Case C-344/04 *IATA and ELFAA* [2006] ECR I-403, para 36; Case C-459/03 *Commission v Ireland* [2006] ECR I-4635, para 82.

[27] K Lenaerts and P Van Nuffel, *European Union Law* 3rd edn (London, Sweet & Maxwell, 2011) 862. It has been argued however that the monism/dualism dichotomy used to describe national legal systems may be less useful when describing the effect of international law within the EU. See RA Wessel, 'Reconsidering the Relationship between International Law and EU Law: Towards a Content-Based Approach?' in E Cannizzaro, P Palchetti and RA Wessel (eds) *International Law as Law of the European Union* (Leiden, Martinus Nijhoff, 2012) 12–13.

in the next section, the Court has developed very restrictive rules concerning how international law is given effect within the EU, pushing the EU closer towards a dualist approach.[28] International agreements entered into by the EU must also be compatible with the EU Treaties. In order to prevent the EU from entering into internationally binding commitments with third states and organisations that might be incompatible with European primary law, Article 218(11) TFEU (ex Article 300(6) TEC) allows Member States or EU institutions to obtain an opinion from the Court on the proposed agreement's compatibility with the Treaties.[29] Article 351 TFEU (ex Article 307 TEC) relates to how incompatibilities or conflicts between EU law and international agreements entered into by Member States with third States prior to their Union membership are to be dealt with. While, on the one hand, this provision confirms the *pacta sunt servanda* rule in holding that 'rights and obligations arising from [such] agreements […] shall not be affected by the provisions of the Treaties', it also obliges the Member States concerned, 'to the extent that such agreements are not compatible with the Treaties', to 'take all appropriate steps to eliminate the incompatibilities established'. The Court has interpreted this requirement to eliminate incompatibilities quite expansively, even applying it to incompatibilities that are yet to materialise.[30] Article 351 TFEU may be seen as a way in which the EU seeks to maintain a balance between respect for pre-existing Member States' international obligations and equipping the EU legal order with the conflict law rule to preserve its integrity. The Court's recent case law suggests an emphasis on the latter goal. In cases where applicants have sought to rely on Article 351 TFEU to limit Union acts, their arguments were given short shrift.[31] The EU Treaties are therefore not entirely silent on the topic of international law. Rather, the Court has either failed to make use of existing provisions putting emphasis on the EU's respect for international law, or has applied provisions dealing with international law in a restrictive or narrow fashion. The

[28] Klabbers argues that the EU follows a more dualist approach to international law: '[M]ost international law, to the extent that it is treaty-based, will not be directly applied but will somehow need to be transformed …' (Klabbers, *The European Union in International Law* (n 11) 72).

[29] Art 218(11)TFEU: 'A Member State, the European Parliament, the Council or the Commission may obtain the opinion of the Court of Justice as to whether an agreement envisaged is compatible with the Treaties. Where the opinion of the Court is adverse, the agreement envisaged may not enter into force unless it is amended or the Treaties are revised'.

[30] See Case C-205/06 *Commission v Austria* [2009] ECR I-1301, Case C-249/06 *Commission v Sweden* [2006] ECR I-1335 and Case C-118/07 *Commission v Finland* [2009] ECR I-10889; also N Lavranos, 'Protecting European Law from International Law' (2010) 15 *European Foreign Affairs Review* 265–82.

[31] See Joined Cases C-402/05 P and C-415/05 P *Yassin Abdullah Kadi & Al Barakaat International Foundation v Council and Commission (Kadi I)* [2008] ECR I-6351, para 304: 'Article 307 EC [now Art 351 TFEU] may in no circumstances permit any challenge to the principles that form part of the very foundations of the Community legal order'. See Case C-301/08 *Bogiatzi* (n 26), paras 17–19; *ATAA* (n 4), para 61: 'Although the first paragraph of Article 351 TFEU implies a duty on the part of the institutions of the European Union not to impede the performance of the obligations of Member States which stem from an agreement prior to 1 January 1958 […] that duty of the institutions is designed to permit the Member States concerned to perform their obligations under a prior agreement and does not bind the European Union as regards the third States party to that agreement'.

Court, as well as any other EU institutions and bodies, should be guided by the provisions that place a great importance on the respect for international law. Such an approach may help prevent the 'discontinuity' between the approaches of the Court and the legislature regarding international law.

III. INTERNATIONAL LAW AND THE COURT OF JUSTICE

It is difficult to make broad statements regarding the Court's general attitude towards international law. The Court only deals with the specific issues to be decided in each case, meaning that a full account of the Court's approach to international law can only be gleaned from a comprehensive analysis of its case law. The present section reviews some of this recent case law, although not exhaustively, demonstrating how the Court now adopts a more guarded or restrictive approach towards international law, one that seeks to ensure that the autonomy and fundamental principles governing the Union legal order are not jeopardised. It briefly examines the Court's approach in a number of areas: the effect of international agreements, customary international law and the role of non-binding legal instruments on the EU legal order.

A. The Effect of International Agreements in the EU Legal Order

As discussed above, international agreements entered into by the Union become part of the EU legal order and do not require implementing acts to give them binding character. This allows, under certain conditions, Member States, EU institutions or even individuals to rely on such an agreement in proceedings before the Court. Although this may appear to indicate a certain degree of openness to international law, the Court has established rather restrictive conditions determining when an agreement may be relied upon.

(i) Agreements Binding on the Union

The first step the Court takes is to examine whether the international agreement is binding on the Union.[32] This is a relatively straightforward question where the EU is a formal party to an international agreement. More difficult questions arise when the EU is not a party to an agreement but all its Member States are.[33] In this

---

[32] Joined Cases 21 to 24/72 *International Fruit Company v Produktschap voor Groenten en Fruit* [1972] ECR 1219, para 7: 'Before the incompatibility of a Community measure with a provision of international law can affect the validity of that measure, the Community must first of all be bound by that provision'. See also *ATAA* (n 4), para 52; Case C-308/06 *Intertanko and Others* (n 15), para 44.

[33] See JW van Rossem, 'Interaction between EU Law and International Law in the Light of *Intertanko* and *Kadi*: The Dilemma of Norms Binding the Member States but not the Community' (2009) 40 *Netherlands Yearbook of International Law* 183–227.

situation, it may be argued that the EU is nevertheless bound by the agreement via functional succession. This means the EU may become legally bound by an international agreement where the Member States have transferred competences to the EU in the field covered by that agreement. The Court applied this principle to the General Agreement on Tariffs and Trade (GATT) in *International Fruit Company* where it held that in circumstances where the EU has 'assumed the powers previously exercised by Member States' in the area covered by an international agreement, 'the provisions of that agreement have the effect of binding' the EU.[34] Where the EU has taken over powers previously exercised by its Member States, the entity in the position to actually implement the agreement is no longer the Member States but the Union, and it could be argued that the Union has therefore succeeded to the obligations under the agreement. The Union would therefore become bound by those obligations, preventing the situation whereby the Member States could evade their international commitments by transferring competences to an international organisation such as the EU.[35] In other words, in this manner the EU would 'contribute [...] to the strict observance [...] of international law'.

Although functional succession may seem to provide a way of solving the problem of norms binding on the Member States but not the EU, the Court has applied the principle only very rarely in practice, and under quite restrictive conditions. The principle was discussed in *ATAA* with regard to the Convention on International Civil Aviation (Chicago Convention),[36] a Convention to which the EU is not a contracting party but all EU Member States are. The Court examined whether the EU is bound by the Chicago Convention, as it has competence in the field of air transport under Article 100(2) TFEU and has legislated extensively in the fields covered by the agreement. The Member States retain powers in relatively few areas covered by the Convention, such as the award of traffic rights, airport charges, and the prohibition of territory which may be flown over.[37] In light of this the Court stated that 'in order for the European Union to be capable of being bound, it must have assumed, and thus had transferred to it, all the powers previously exercised by the Member States that fall within the convention in question'.[38] The Court reiterated, therefore, that the requirement is not for the majority of the powers to have been transferred to the Union, but for a '*full transfer* of the powers previously exercised by the Member States'[39] to have taken place. In determining whether a full transfer has taken place, the Court will look at the extent

---

[34] Joined Cases 21 to 24/72 *International Fruit Company* (n 32), para 18. This principle of succession has been confirmed on numerous occasions by the Court, most recently in *ATAA* (n 4), para 62 and cases cited therein.

[35] This was part of the reasoning in the ECtHR in *Matthews v United Kingdom* Application no 24833/94 (ECtHR, 18 February 1999), para 32.

[36] Convention on International Civil Aviation (Chicago Convention) (adopted on 7 December 1944, entry into force 4 April 1947) 15 UNTS 295.

[37] *ATAA* (n 4), para 70.

[38] ibid (n 4), para 63.

[39] Case C-308/06 *Intertanko and Others* (n 15), para 49 (emphasis added).

of EU legislative action in the field in question.[40] Even if the EU has exercised its competence in most of the areas covered by an agreement, and the Member State competence is marginal, the EU cannot be deemed to have succeeded to the obligations under this Convention and will therefore not be bound.[41]

This sets a very high threshold for functional succession to be recognised. Under this requirement, it is virtually impossible for succession to take place short of an explicit treaty change.[42] In her Opinion in *Intertanko*, Advocate General Kokott suggested that even *exclusive competence* would not necessarily be sufficient to demonstrate a succession of legal obligations short of an explicit transfer via the Treaties:

> Irrespective of whether or not the Community's competence is now exclusive, there must also be doubts as to whether such an assumption of powers resulting from the exercise of competence is sufficient as a basis on which to conclude that the Member States' obligations under international law are binding on the Community. In any event, the assumption of trade-policy powers, to which GATT related, was laid down expressly in the Treaty.[43]

Indeed, in *International Fruit Company*, the Court recognised that the EU had assumed the obligations stemming from the GATT due to, in part, the fact that the Member States had transferred powers to the EU in the fields of trade and tariff policy.[44] Such a restrictive approach to the principle of functional succession raises numerous problems. It allows a situation whereby the Member States are bound by the international agreement, and responsible for its implementation under international law, while the entity actually capable of (co-)implementing it, the EU, is not bound. Some observers have been critical of this approach, arguing that it permits 'the very situation that functional succession was designed to avoid',[45] that is, to allow the EU Member States to escape treaty commitments through creating and transferring powers to an international organisation. One way to remedy this situation would be for the EU to become a party to the international agreement alongside its Member States,[46] and in many instances this is what occurs. For example, the solution to the dilemma of the Member States being parties to the European Convention on Human Rights (ECHR) while the EU was not, has been for the EU to eventually accede to that treaty. However, as

---

[40] Case C-301/08 *Bogiatzi* (n 26), paras 29–30; *ATAA* (n 4), paras 65–68.

[41] *ATAA* (n 4), paras 69 and 71.

[42] However, De Baere and Ryngaert have raised the question whether the Court would limit functional succession to *a priori* exclusive competences enshrined in Art 3(1) TFEU, or whether shared competences that have become exclusive via Art 2(2) TFEU would also qualify. G De Baere and C Ryngaert, 'The ECJ's Judgment in Air Transport Association of America and the International Legal Context of the EU's Climate Change Policy' (2013) 18 *European Foreign Affairs Review* 389, 396.

[43] Case C-308/06 *Intertanko* (n 15), Opinion of Advocate General Kokott of 20 November 2007, para 43.

[44] Joined Cases 21 to 24/72 *International Fruit Company* (n 32), paras 16–18.

[45] BF Havel and JQ Mulligan, 'The Triumph of Politics: Reflections on the Judgment of the Court of Justice of the European Union Validating the Inclusion of Non-EU Airlines in the Emissions Trading Scheme' (2012) 37(1) *Air and Space Law* 16.

[46] See 'Editorial Comments' (n 10).

the example of EU accession to the ECHR demonstrates, this 'solution' raises its own set of complex problems. Some international agreements only allow states to become a party (for example, Article 4(1) Charter of the United Nations) and would require a treaty modification to allow EU participation. Another significant obstacle is the political and legal difficulties facing EU Member States and the institutions in agreeing on having the Union accede to international treaties. There are also questions regarding the positions of third states that are parties to the international agreement in question, who may object to an international organisation such as the EU becoming a party to a treaty.[47]

Furthermore, the requirement for a 'full transfer of powers' to have taken place is also problematic given the nature of competences within the Union. Most international agreements will regulate at least *some* fields pertaining to competences reserved to the EU Member States. Even in relation to the GATT, where the Court did find a full transfer to have taken place, it could be argued that the Agreement retained some functions for the Member States—provisions relating to meetings of the parties and modifications to the Agreement[48] still applied to the contracting parties, and could not apply to the EU. Aside from the situation of the GATT, the Court has been extremely reluctant to accept the EU's succession of obligations in other situations,[49] and the high threshold set by the Court ('full transfer of powers') means that we are unlikely to see succession take place in other situations. Perhaps the succession of the GATT should be seen as a rather exceptional case,[50] made possible due a number of factors. First, the GATT obligations relate to the common commercial policy, a field in which the European Community (EC)/EU exercises exclusive competence. Second, as the Court points out in *International Fruit Company*, not only did the EC consider itself bound by the GATT, but third states had already accepted the EC in fact acted like a contracting party to the Agreement.[51]

---

[47] On the opposition of third states to participation by the EU within an international organisation, see J Wouters, J Odermatt and T Ramopoulos, 'The Lisbon Treaty and the Status of the European Union in the International Arena: The May 2011 Upgrade at the UN General Assembly' (2011) *IEMed Mediterranean Yearbook* 166.

[48] General Agreement on Tariffs and Trade (entry into force provisionally 30 October 1947) 55 UNTS 187. Art XXV ('Joint Action by the Contracting Parties') and Art XXX (Amendments) arguably only applied to the 'Contracting Parties' to the GATT.

[49] See, for example, *ATTA* (n 4), para 63; Case C-308/06 *Intertanko and Others* (n 15), paras 48–49; Case C-301/08 *Bogiatzi* (n 26), para 33.

[50] 'The GATT is a special case ... as the transfer of commercial powers was governed expressly by the then EC Treaty'. Case C-533/08 *TNT Express Nederland BV v AXA Versicherung AG* [2010] ECR-4107, Opinion of Advocate General Kokott of 28 January 2010, para 62. De Schutter points out that the EC's succession to the GATT, 'is not unique, but remains exceptional', arguing that substitution of international obligations 'may be allowed under certain circumstances, so narrowly defined however that this would in any event remain exceptional'. O De Schutter, 'Human Rights and the Rise of International Organisations: The Logic of Sliding Scales in the Law of International Responsibility' in J Wouters, E Brems, S Smis and P Schmitt (eds), *Accountability for Human Rights Violations by International Organisations* (Antwerp, Intersentia, 2010) 63.

[51] Joined Cases 21 to 24/72 *International Fruit Company* (n 32): 'Third countries which are members of GATT accept that the Community in fact acts like a contracting party to this agreement', 1225. The actual participation of the EU in the relevant organisation, and the acceptance of succession by

The succession theory has been developed by the Court with little reference to international law. In fact, international law has surprisingly little to say on the topic of how international organisations may succeed to obligations of its members.[52] International law relating to succession of legal obligations has developed in a very state-centric manner, and applies primarily to succession from one state to another. The Vienna Convention on Succession of States in respect of Treaties (1978), for example, applies only to succession as 'the replacement of one State by another in the responsibility for the international relations of territory'.[53] De Schutter argues that the term 'succession' in this context is misleading: '[s]ince international organisations are not sovereign entities, they do not 'succeed' to their Member States as happens in situations of succession of States'.[54] Succession has also been discussed in the context of the succession by a federation to the pre-federation treaties entered into by the members of the federation.[55] The situation whereby a group of states have transferred powers to an international organisation, while yet retaining their status as sovereign states, is far less clear. Schütze argues that '[i]n the absence of a doctrine of succession in international law, only treaties to which [the EU] is a formal party will internationally bind the Union'.[56] Yet it should be remembered that becoming a party to an international treaty is only one way in which an entity may express its will to be bound under international law.[57] Uerpermann-Wittzack argues that in the case of the GATT, what actually occurred was not a real case of succession under international law, but an instance of 'implied accession'[58] by the EU.

The succession doctrine developed by the Court does not seem to stem from international law, but has origins in German legal scholarship, and the doctrine

other parties, continues to be a factor. As Kokott argues in the *ATAA* Opinion: 'there is no indication that the European Union, or the European Community before it, would act as the successor to the Member States in the context of the ICAO and that such action would be agreed to by the other parties to the Chicago Convention as in the case of the 1947 GATT', *ATAA* (n 4), Opinion of Advocate General Kokott, para 64.

[52] JF Weis, 'Succession of States in Respect of Treaties Concluded by the European Communities' (1994) 42 *Tijdschrift voor Europees en Economisch Recht* 668: '[T]here are no general legal rules on … succession between international organizations'.
[53] Art 2(1)(c) Vienna Convention on Succession of States in respect of Treaties (adopted on 22 August 1978, entry into force 6 November 1996) 1946 UNTS 3.
[54] De Schutter (n 50) 57.
[55] R Schütze, '"The Succession Doctrine" and the European Union' in A Hull, C Barnard, M Dougan and E Spaventa (eds), *A Constitutional Order of States? Essays in EU Law in Honour of Alan Dashwood* (Oxford, Hart Publishing, 2011), 462–67.
[56] ibid, 475.
[57] Klabbers argues that 'the succession theory is perfectly acceptable, under international law, as a means of expressing consent to be bound' and is in harmony with international treaty law including the Vienna Convention on the Law of Treaties, Klabbers (n 11) 73. For example, the EU may bind itself via a unilateral act, as it has with the International Health Regulations of the World Health Organization (see below).
[58] R Uerpmann-Wittzack, 'The Constitutional Role of Multilateral Treaty Systems' in A von Bogdandy and J Bast (eds), *Principles of European Constitutional Law* (Oxford, Hart Publishing, 2006) 166.

of *Funktionsnachfolge* or *funktionelle Rechtsnachfolge*.[59] The limited scholarship dealing with this topic has mainly examined the situation of the ECHR,[60] to which the EU is not (yet) a party. Arguments in favour of succession were put forward as a way to ensure that EU Member States would not create a gap in human rights protection by transferring powers to the EU. The EU Court of First Instance also relied on a version of the succession doctrine in *Kadi I* when it stated that '[b]y conferring [the powers necessary for the performance of the Member States' obligations under the UN Charter] on the Community, the Member States demonstrated their will to bind it by the obligations entered into by them under the Charter of the United Nations', basing its argument, by analogy, on *International Fruit Company*.[61] This argument that the EU had become bound by the UN Charter via succession was never discussed by the Court of Justice[62] and the notion that the EU had succeeded to the obligations under the UN Charter has been subject to criticism.[63]

Whereas the Member States are fully capable of transferring part of their powers to the EU in a certain field (which is the actual practice), they are not capable of transferring only parts of their corresponding international legal obligations. This recognises the fact that the EU is a distinct legal entity with its own legal personality, and is not merely a 'bundle of Member States jurisdictions'.[64] In *Matthews* the European Court of Human Rights (ECtHR) held that the human rights obligations of the Member States continue despite a transfer of powers: 'The Convention does not exclude the transfer of competences to international organisations provided that Convention rights continue to be "secured"'.[65] The succession theory, as developed by the Court, does not seem appropriate to the situation of the EU, where the Member States will transfer (often substantial) powers in a certain field, yet retain their status as sovereign states in international relations. The requirement for a full transfer of powers to have taken place does not take into account the nature of the EU as an example of cooperative federalism and

[59] See C Tomuschat, 'Artikel 281 EG' in H von der Groeben and J Schwarze (eds), *Kommentar zum Vertrag über die Europäische Union und zur Gründung der Europäischen Gemeinschaft* (Baden-Baden, Nomos, 2004) 1239–69, paras 53 *et seq*; W Schroeder and M Selmayr, 'Die EG, das GATT und die Vollzugslehre' (1998) 53 *Juristenzeitung* 344.

[60] See Uerpmann-Wittzack (n 58); Schütze (n 55).

[61] CFI, Case T-315/01 *Kadi v Council and Commission* [2005] ECR II-3649, para 200.

[62] *Kadi I* (n 31).

[63] See Klabbers (n 11), 74–75; F Naert, 'Binding International Organisations to Member State Treaties or Responsibility of Member States for their own Actions in the Framework of International Organisations' in J Wouters, E Brems, S Smis and P Schmitt (eds), *Accountability for Human Rights Violations by International Organisations* (Antwerp, Intersentia, 2010) 150.

[64] See Uerpmann-Wittzack (n 58) 168.

[65] *Matthews v United Kingdom* Application no 24833/94 (ECtHR, 18 February 1999), para 32. See also, *M & Co v the Federal Republic of Germany* Application no 13258/87 (ECtHR, 9 February 1990): 'The Commission considers that a transfer of powers does not necessarily exclude a State's responsibility under the Convention with regard to the exercise of the transferred powers. Otherwise the guarantees of the Convention could wantonly be limited or excluded and thus be deprived of their peremptory character'.

the political and legal reality of competences being divided between the EU and its Member States. One approach would be to develop a doctrine of succession under EU law, rather than international law, that would bind the EU to obligations of the Member States whenever it acted in a field covered by an international agreement to which all Member States are parties.[66] The Court could hold, for instance, that, since the EU substantially exercises powers in areas covered by the Chicago Convention, it would be bound by the corresponding treaty obligations in these areas as a matter of EU law. Such an approach has a number of benefits. It does not require the further development of the succession doctrine under international law, does not require the consent of third party states,[67] and would also not require the EU to actually replace the Member States within the international organisations in question (eg UN, the International Maritime Organization (IMO), the International Civil Aviation Organization (ICAO) etc). It would also fit within one of the original rationales of the succession principle in *International Fruit Company*, which was the need to avoid a conflict of obligations.[68] Such an approach is also supported by the EU Treaties, which, as discussed above, place a great deal of importance on the respect for international law, and the respect for Member States' international obligations. Furthermore, it would reflect the approach of the EU legislature which, as discussed in the next section, already places great emphasis on obligations of the Member States not strictly binding on the EU.

(ii) Direct Effect

Once it has been determined that the EU is legally bound by the agreement in question, the Court will subsequently examine whether the 'nature and broad logic' of that agreement might exclude review. This means that the Court will examine, looking at the international agreement as a whole and 'in particular [...] its aim, preamble and terms'[69] whether there are reasons that preclude its provisions from being capable of having direct effect.[70] This test was applied to the GATT/World Trade Organization (WTO)[71] and the UN Convention on the Law of the Sea (UNCLOS),[72] which were found to be incapable of having direct effect.

---

[66] A similar approach is discussed in van Rossem (n 33): 'such self-binding would lie in ruling out the eventuality of conflict between obligations of the Member States to the EU and at the international level', 214.

[67] Uerpmann-Wittzack (n 58) 172.

[68] Ziegler (n 2) 289.

[69] Case C-308/06 *Intertanko and Others* (n 15), para 54.

[70] *ATAA* (n 4), para 53; Joined Cases C-120/06 and C-121/06 *FIAMM* [2008] ECR 6513, para 110; Joined Cases 21 to 24/72 *International Fruit Company* (n 32).

[71] Joined Cases 21 to 24/72 *International Fruit Company* (n 32), paras 19–27; Case 149/96 *Portugal v Council* [1999] ECR I-8395.

[72] Case C-308/06 *Intertanko and Others* (n 15), paras 54–65.

The Court will examine whether the provisions of the agreement in question are sufficiently precise and unconditional to be capable of being used to challenge the validity of an instrument.[73] Recent case law in this field emphasises the requirement for the provision to establish rules that may provide rights capable of being relied upon by individuals. In *Intertanko*, the Court found that UNCLOS did not establish rules intended to provide rights to individuals.[74] This requirement seems to confuse two separate concepts: the concept of direct effect, designed to protect individuals, and the conditions under which the Court will determine whether EU law conforms to international legal obligations.[75] This approach has been criticised for essentially applying 'the same tests to determine whether an agreement creates individual rights and whether it can serve as a standard of legality'.[76] Rather, a distinction between the two ought to be made in line with the view that 'as long as a behavioural norm for the [Union] can be derived from an international agreement, this agreement can serve as a norm for reference when the validity of [EU] law is at stake'.[77] Some questioned whether the *Intertanko* judgment represented a significant shift in the Court's approach to the effect of international agreements and whether future case law might moderate its effects.[78] In *ATAA*, the Court closely followed the approach it took in *Intertanko*, confirming that that case was by no means an 'isolated incident'.[79]

An approach that emphasises whether an agreement can be relied upon by individuals significantly precludes the range of international instruments that may otherwise be given effect in the EU legal order. The types of agreements that the Court has found to have been capable of being relied upon by individuals have concerned trade agreements,[80] association agreements, as well as partnership and

---

[73] *ATAA* (n 4), para 54; Case C-308/06 *Intertanko and Others* (n 15), para 45; Case C-344/04 *The Queen, on the application of International Air Transport Association and European Low Fares Airline Association v Department of Transport* [2006] ECR I-00403, para 39.

[74] Case C-308/06 *Intertanko and Others* (n 15), para 64.

[75] J Wouters and D van Eeckhoutte, 'Enforcement of Customary International Law through European Community Law' in JM Prinssen and A Schrauwen (eds), *Direct Effect: Rethinking a Classic of EC Legal Doctrine* (Groningen, Europa Law Publishing, 2002), 223–25.

[76] P Eeckhout, 'Case C-308/06 *The Queen, on the application of International Association of Independent Tanker Owners (Intertanko) and Others v Secretary of State for Transport*, judgment of the Court of Justice, (Grand Chamber) of 3 June 2008' (2009) 46 *CML Rev* 2053.

[77] K Lenaerts and T Corthaut, 'Of Birds and Hedges: The Role of Primacy in Invoking Norms of EU Law' (2006) 31 *EL Rev* 298.

[78] J Wouters and P de Man, 'International Association of Independent Tanker Owners (Intertanko), International Association of Dry Cargo Shipowners (Intercargo), Greek Shipping Cooperation Committee, Lloyd's Register and International Salvage Union V. Secretary of State for Transport. Case C-308/06' (2009) 103 *American Journal of International Law* 3, at 560–61: 'In the end, future ECJ decisions will have to clarify Intertanko's reach—which will, it is to be hoped, serve as opportunities to moderate the effects of the judgment's sweeping language'.

[79] J Etienne, 'Loyalty Towards International Law as a Constitutional Principle of EU Law?', Jean Monnet Working Paper 03/11, at www.JeanMonnetProgram.org, 19: 'Whether *Intertanko* marks a new approach on the invocability of external agreements or is rather an isolated decision has still to be confirmed'.

[80] For example, provisions of the Lomé Conventions in Case C-469/93 *Amministrazione delle Finanze dello Stato v Chiquita Italia SpA* [1995] ECR 4533, para 35; and its predecessor the Yaoundé Convention, Case 87/75 *Bresciani v Amministrazione Italiana delle Finanze* [1976] ECR 129, 135.

cooperation agreements.[81] Kaddous argues that this shows how the Court has adopted 'a very open approach to the effects of international agreements within the EU legal order'.[82] However, these agreements really only represent one type of international agreement to which the EU is a party. As Klabbers argues, '[i]f there is one category of treaties that the ECJ is happy to endow with directly effective provisions, it is the group of association agreements and related instruments, such as decisions of association councils set up under those association agreements'.[83] These types of agreements tend to extend EU law principles such as free movement outside of the EU, and will often contain precise and unconditional language capable of being relied upon by individuals.[84]

Other types of international agreements, especially multilateral treaties, usually touch upon different matters and will naturally contain provisions that are worded less closely to EU standards. Moreover, such multilateral treaties will rarely contain precise and unconditional clauses capable of being relied on by individuals; rather, their provisions are generally couched in broader terms, giving the parties greater room to implement the treaty. These issues indeed arose when multilateral instruments such as the Kyoto Protocol or UNCLOS were used to challenge EU acts. As Cannizzaro argues, '[a]greements which confer rights to individuals enforceable in the international legal order are notoriously rare'.[85] Requiring an international agreement to confer rights upon individuals in order for that agreement to be used to assess the validity of EU legislative acts, Cannizzaro argues, would in effect 'nullify the domestic effect of international law'.[86] This approach practically excludes the legal effect of a great number of agreements binding on the Union. In *ATAA* the Court examined whether provisions of the Open Skies Agreement[87] and the Kyoto Protocol[88] were capable of being relied upon to

---

[81] See eg Case 17/81 *Pabst & Richarz KG v Hauptzollamt Oldenburg* [1982] ECR 1331 regarding an association agreement between the EC and Greece.

[82] Kaddous (n 2) 311.

[83] Klabbers (n 11) 81.

[84] It has also been argued that the Court has shown less willingness to use international agreements as a standard of review of EU acts compared with its stance regarding action of the Member States. See M Mendez, 'The Legal Effect of Community Agreements: Maximalist Treaty Enforcement and Judicial Avoidance Techniques' (2010) 21 *European Journal of International Law* 104.

[85] E Cannizzaro, 'The Neo-Monism of the European Legal Order' in E Cannizzaro, P Palchetti, and RA Wessel (eds), *International Law as Law of the European Union* (Leiden, Martinus Nijhoff, 2012) 49.

[86] ibid.

[87] Air Transport Agreement concluded on 25 and 30 April 2007 between the United States of America, of the one part, and the European Community and its Member States, of the other part ('Open Skies'). See Decision 2007/339/EC of 25 April 2007 of the Council of the European Union and the representatives of the Governments of the Member States of the European Union on the signature and provisional application of the Air Transport Agreement between the European Community and its Member States, on the one hand, and the United States of America, on the other hand [2007] OJ L134/1.

[88] Kyoto Protocol to the UN Framework Convention on Climate Change (UNFCCC) (1998) (adopted on 11 December 1997, entry into force 16 February 2005) 2303 UNTS 148 ('the Kyoto Protocol').

challenge the contested Directive.[89] With regard to the Kyoto Protocol, the Court held that, since the parties to the agreement are given significant scope in how to implement the agreement, it is not sufficiently precise or unconditional to be relied upon in legal proceedings to challenge the Directive.[90] The Court did find, however, that certain provisions of the Open Skies Agreement were sufficiently precise to be relied upon, since they provide rules that are designed to apply directly and immediately to airlines.[91]

B. Customary International Law

Like international agreements to which the EU is a party, customary international law is equally binding upon the Union, as confirmed in *ATAA*.[92] Customary international law has been held by the Court to act as a limit on the powers of Member States and the EU,[93] to provide rules of interpretation and to act as a 'gap filler' in the absence of European rules.[94] Another complex question in this regard is the extent to which customary international law may be invoked before the Court to review the legality of EU acts. As a first step, the Court will examine whether the rules being relied upon are recognised as being part of customary international law.[95] Upon finding that a certain rule is part of customary international law, the Court then turns to the question whether the customary law rules being invoked are capable of challenging the act in question.[96] The way in which the Court deals with customary international law in these circumstances substantially diverges from the way it handles international agreements. First, the rules of customary law being relied upon must be 'capable of calling into question the competence of the European Union to adopt that act'.[97] Second, they must be 'liable to affect rights which the individual derives from European Union law or to create obligations under European Union law in this regard'.[98] The Court justifies its different approach to customary international law on the basis that 'a principle of customary international law does not have the same degree of precision as a provision of an international agreement',[99] echoing its reasoning in *Racke* where it based the

---

[89] Directive 2008/101/EC of the European Parliament and of the Council of 19 November 2008 amending Directive 2003/87/EC so as to include aviation activities in the scheme for greenhouse gas emission allowance trading within the Community [2009] OJ L8/3.

[90] *ATAA* (n 4), paras 77–78.

[91] ibid (n 4), paras 83–85.

[92] ibid (n 4), para 101. See n 15 and the cases cited therein.

[93] See Case C-364/10 *Hungary v Slovak Republic*, judgment of 16 October 2012, nyr.

[94] Wouters and van Eeckhoutte (n 75), 186–96.

[95] *ATAA* (n 4), para 102.

[96] ibid (n 4), para 102.

[97] ibid (n 4), para 107; see also Joined Cases 89/85, 104/85, 114/85, 116/85, 117/85 and 125/85 to 129/85 *Ahlström Osakeyhtiö and Others v Commission* [1988] ECR 5193, paras 14–18; Case C-405/92 *Mondiet* [1993] ECR I-6133, paras 11–16.

[98] *ATAA* (n 4), para 107.

[99] ibid (n 4), para 110.

'manifest error' standard of review on 'the complexity of the rules in question and the imprecision of some of the concepts to which they refer'.[100] Due to this lack of 'precision' the Court limits review to 'whether, in adopting the act in question, the institutions of the European Union made *manifest errors of assessment* concerning the conditions for applying those principles'.[101] The review, in the light of customary international law, is limited to whether the EU made a manifest error regarding it competences.[102]

The notion that customary international law is less 'precise' than treaty law, and the legal consequences the Court attaches to this finding, must be questioned.[103] As discussed above, some international agreements contain detailed provisions resembling legislation, providing unambiguous rules and even rights that may be relied upon by individuals. Yet many international agreements also tend to use broad language and principles that give greater scope for implementation and in this way are hardly precise at all. Moreover, customary international law is not necessarily 'imprecise'; it may be found codified in the text of international instruments to which the EU is not a party,[104] or in draft articles and other texts or expounded by committees and experts, in academic literature, as well as in national, regional and international case law. In this way, it may be the case that a principle of customary international law is more 'precise' than a formulation in a treaty. The Court seems to determine whether a rule is precise, not by examining the content of that rule, but by whether or not it is contained in a formal international instrument.

The Court's attitude to customary international law, which has undergone quite some fluctuations in the course of its history,[105] remains puzzling today. In one sense the Court appears open to it, finding that customary international law can be used to invalidate incompatible secondary law. However, the Court's standard of review, that of a manifest error, is even more restrictive than its approach to international agreements,[106] and its justification for such a different approach is unpersuasive. The Court's current approach towards customary international law means that, in reality, the latter is rarely to be relied upon and the question may be raised whether this satisfies the Article 3(5) TEU requirement of 'strict observance ... of international law'.

---

[100] Case C-162/96 *A Racke GmbH & Co v Hauptzollamt Mainz* [1998] ECR I-3655, para 52.

[101] *ATAA* (n 4), para 110 (emphasis added). Case C-162/96 *A Racke GmbH & Co* (n 100), para 52.

[102] See J Klabbers, '*Case C-162/96 A. Racke GmbH & Co. v Hauptzollamt Mainz*, judgment of 16 June 1998' (1999) 36 *CML Rev* 179–89.

[103] See Wouters and van Eeckhoutte (n 75), 229–31.

[104] For instance, the Court of Justice has applied the provisions of the 1969 Vienna Convention on the Law of Treaties insofar as they represent customary international law. See Case C-386/08 *Brita GmbH* (n 15), 40–45.

[105] See inter alia Wouters and van Eeckhoutte (n 75); C Timmermans, 'The EU and Public International Law' (1999) 4 *European Foreign Affairs Review* 181; PJ Kuijper 'From Dyestuffs to Kosovo Wine: From Avoidance to Acceptance by the Community Courts of Customary International Law as Limit to Community Action' in IF Dekker and HHG Post (eds), *On the Foundations and Sources of International Law: Essays in Memory of Herman Meijers* (The Hague, TMC Asser Press, 2003) 151–71.

[106] Wouters and van Eeckhoutte (n 75), 223–25.

C. Other International Influences on the EU Legal Order

The discussion above focuses mainly on how norms of international law may be invoked before the Court of Justice. These cases focus on questions regarding whether the norm is binding on the Union, and if so, whether it may be given direct effect within the EU legal order. However, even where an international law norm may not be directly applied, it may still be relevant, and applied in other ways. For example, an international agreement that is not binding on the EU but to which all EU Member States are parties, can be taken into consideration by the Court in performing consistent interpretation of relevant EU legislation even when the international instrument at hand does not contain provisions that are the expression of customary international law. This was the finding of the Court in *Intertanko*, where it stated that the Directive in question should be interpreted 'taking account of'[107] Marpol 73/78,[108] although in this case the Court did not actually go on to perform such an exercise.[109] The Advocate General in *ATAA* picked up on this 'consistent interpretation' reasoning and embarked on such an exercise with regard to the Chicago Convention given that all EU Member States are parties to it. However, in *ATAA* the Court even took a step back; it merely reiterated its case law with regard to the effect of customary international law on the interpretation of EU legislation.[110]

A similar argument may be applied to international agreements binding on the EU but lacking direct effect. These may be given 'general effect'[111] or 'indirect effect'[112] when the Court interprets EU law in the light of the agreement. However, despite referring implicitly to consistent interpretation with regard to Marpol 73/78, the Court in *Intertanko* did not make a similar reference to UNCLOS, to which the EU is a party, thus 'ignor[ing] the fact that the measure to be assessed was actually implementing the two conventions'.[113] In this latter case, it can be argued that consistent interpretation is warranted in light of the fact that it is a 'corollary of the principle of primacy',[114] in this case the primacy of international agreements over EU legislation. Its application disentangles the performance of judicial control of EU legislation in accordance with international obligations of the Union from questions of direct effect. Consistent interpretation requires the Court to, as far as possible, interpret EU legislation in a manner consistent with

---

[107] Case C-308/06 *Intertanko and Others* (n 15), para 52.
[108] International Convention for the Prevention of Pollution from Ships, signed in London on 2 November 1973, as supplemented by the Protocol of 17 February 1978, 1340 UNTS 61.
[109] Eeckhout (n 76) 2056.
[110] *ATAA* (n 4), para 123.
[111] F Casolari, 'Giving Indirect Effect to International Law within the EU Legal Order: The Doctrine of Consistent Interpretation' in E Cannizzaro, P Palchetti and RA Wessel (eds), *International Law as Law of the European Union* (Leiden, Martinus Nijhoff, 2012) 396.
[112] van Rossem (n 33) 207.
[113] M Smrkolj and A von Bogdandy, 'European Community and Union Law and International Law', *Max Planck Encyclopedia of Public International Law*, at http://www.mpepil.com.
[114] Lenaerts and Corthaut (n 77) 293.

international agreements.[115] The doctrine of consistent interpretation, if properly applied, has the advantage that it both reaffirms the claim of the EU that it aims to promote the strict observance and development of international law and preserves the power of the Court to safeguard the integrity of the EU legal order while allowing the latter to enter into an open dialogue with international law. However, like other tools developed by the Court to deal with international law, the principle of consistent interpretation can likewise be applied in a narrow or broad fashion depending on the instrument at issue. If not properly applied, the doctrine runs the risk of merely being a gesture towards international law, something that allows the Court to refer to international law while continuing to deny its binding legal nature. Instead, the need for consistent interpretation should stem from a sense of constitutional obligation, in particular Article 3(5) TEU.

The Court may also be influenced by, or draw upon other principles of international law in its decisions. This may occur, for example, when the Court looks to international norms when defining a concept under EU law. In a case concerning an action for annulment of the Working Time Directive,[116] the Court examined the notion of 'public health' under EU law in light of the preamble of the World Health Organization Constitution,[117] an organization of which the EU is not a formal member.[118] The Court held that '[t]here is nothing in the wording of Article 118a [EC Treaty—now Article 153(1) TFEU] to indicate that the concepts of "working environment", "safety" and "health" as used in that provision should, in the absence of other indications, be interpreted restrictively'.[119] Yet at times the Court has decided not to follow an international decision. In *Grant v South-West Trains Ltd*[120] the Court found that 'discrimination based on sex' does not include discrimination based on a person's sexual orientation, arguably going against the understanding of 'sexual discrimination' under international human rights law.[121] The influence of non-binding norms on the EU legal order has been discussed elsewhere.[122] We point out here that a discussion of the EU's approach to international law that only examines treaty or customary international law unduly leaves

---

[115] Case C-61/94 *Commission v Germany* [1996] ECR 3989, para 52.

[116] Council Directive 93/104/EC concerning certain aspects of the organization of working time [1993] OJ L307/18.

[117] Case C-84/94 *United Kingdom v Council* [1996] ECR I-5755, para 15.

[118] Although Art 3 of the WHO Constitution only allows membership to states, the EU has established a close partnership with the WHO. See B Eggers and F Hoffmeister, 'UN-EU Cooperation on Public Health: The Evolving Participation of the European Community in the World Health Organization' in J Wouters, F Hoffmeister and T Ruys (eds), *The United Nations and the European Union: An Ever Stronger Partnership* (The Hague, TMC Asser Press, 2006) 158–59.

[119] Case C-84/94 *United Kingdom v Council* [1996] ECR I-05755, para 15.

[120] Case C-249/96 *Grant v South West Trains* [1998] ECR I-00621.

[121] Communication No 488/1992 *Toonen v Australia*, UN Doc CCPR/C/50/D/488/1992 (1994) which interpreted 'sex' to include 'sexual orientation'.

[122] J Wouters and J Odermatt, 'Norms Emanating from International Bodies and Their Role in the Legal Order of the European Union' in RA Wessel and S Blockmans (eds), *Between Autonomy and Dependence—The EU Legal Order under the Influence of International Organizations* (Springer/TMC Asser Press, 2013).

out other international norms or principles that form part of the *corpus juris gentium* and therefore should be taken into account in a proper application of Article 3(5) TEU, including decisions of international organisations, general principles and relevant case law of international courts and (quasi-) judicial bodies.

D. 'Friendliness' and 'Openness' Towards International Law?

The Court's approach towards international law has been discussed using terms such as 'international law friendly'[123] or 'openness'[124] to international law. These expressions seem to imply that the Court retains a substantial degree of discretion when deciding how international law should be treated and applied. They contrast with terms such as 'loyalty',[125] 'cooperation', 'compliance' or even 'fidelity'.[126] According to the Court's case law, the EU's approach to international law does not stem from the EU's place within a wider legal order, but is determined entirely by its own legal system. As Advocate General Maduro put it in his Opinion in *Kadi I*: 'the Community Courts determine the effect of international obligations within the Community legal order by reference to conditions set by Community law'.[127] When the Court does show 'openness' towards international law, this does not seem to stem from the binding nature of international law or its hierarchical superiority, but from some kind of benign attitude of the Court.

Recent case law shows how the Court's supposed strong commitment to international law has increasingly come into doubt. In cases such as *Kadi* the Court seeks to emphasise the autonomy of the EU legal order in a way that downplays the role of international law, while *Intertanko* and *ATAA* demonstrate that the Court's supposed 'openness' to international law is rather restrictive in practice. One of the reasons for such an approach can be traced back to the Court's conception of an 'autonomous' Community legal order. Recent cases discussed in this

---

[123] See C Eckes 'International Law as Law of the EU: The Role of the European Court of Justice' in E Cannizzaro, P Palchetti and RA Wessel (eds), *International Law as Law of the European Union* (Leiden, Martinus Nijhoff, 2012) 363.

[124] PJ Kuijper, 'Customary International Law, Decisions of International Organisations and Other Techniques for Ensuring Respect for International Legal Rules in European Community Law' in J Wouters, A Nollkaemper and E de Wet (eds), *The Europeanisation of International Law: The Status of International Law in the EU and its Member States* (The Hague, TMC Asser Press, 2008) 105–6; Cannizzaro (n 85) 50.

[125] Etienne (n 79).

[126] See G de Búrca, 'The European Court of Justice and the International Legal Order After *Kadi*' (2010) 51(1) *Harvard International Law Journal* 41: 'the strong pluralist approach that underpins the judgment of the ECJ is at odds with the conventional self-presentation of the EU as an organization which maintains particular *fidelity to international law* and institutions, and it is an approach that carries certain costs and risks for the EU'. Also, M Mendez, 'The Enforcement of EU agreements: Bolstering the Effectiveness of Treaty Law?' (2010) 47 *CML Rev* 1751: 'The general immunization of EU norms from review ... reflects badly on the EU's carefully cultivated image of *fidelity to international law* ...' (emphasis added).

[127] *Kadi I* (n 31), Opinion of Advocate General Maduro, para 23.

chapter can be understood as the Court developing tools to limit and circumscribe the effects of international law. Its approach to issues such as functional succession, direct effect of treaties, customary international law and consistent interpretation, can all be seen as methods whereby the Court guards the way in which international has an effect within the EU legal order. We submit that such an approach to autonomy is unwarranted, and undermines the EU's commitment to international law. Bruno de Witte has argued rightly that the Court's appeals to autonomy can be considered an example of it being 'rather unfriendly towards the "rest" of international law'.[128] He argues that the concept of autonomy, as developed by the Court, in fact means two different things: 'either that EU law, as a specialised international legal order, *deviates* from the general rules of international law ... or that the European Union fails to comply with specific international obligations and gives priority to its own internal rules'.[129] In recent cases autonomy has been a key concept in locating the EU's place within the international legal order. This approach has been described as 'robustly pluralist ... to international law and governance, emphasizing the separateness, autonomy, and constitutional priority of the EC legal order over international law'.[130] At a time when some of the EU's international partners have questioned the EU's commitment to international law,[131] the Court's approach does little to allay such concerns.

IV. INTERNATIONAL LAW AND THE LEGISLATURE

Whereas the Court's approach to international law is a source of rich academic debate, less attention is given to that of other EU institutions and bodies. The practice of the EU legislature, charged with actually implementing the EU's international legal obligations, deserves careful consideration. Like the Court, the EU

---

[128] B de Witte, 'European Union Law: How Autonomous is its Legal Order?' (2010) 65 *Zeitschrift für öffentliches Recht* 150.

[129] Ibid, 151.

[130] de Búrca (n 126) 7.

[131] The EU's Emission Trading Scheme as applied to airlines, is the latest example of a measure seen by some third states as a measure breaching international law. See Joint declaration of the Moscow meeting on inclusion of international civil aviation in the EU-ETS, 22 February 2012, at http://www.ruaviation.com/docs/1/2012/2/22/50/; 'India Joins China in Boycott of EU carbon scheme', Reuters, 23 March 2012, at http://www.reuters.com/article/2012/03/23/uk-india-eu-emissions-idUSLNE82L02220120323; '10 Airlines Snub Europe's Emissions Rule', *New York Times*, 15 May 2012, at http://www.nytimes.com/2012/05/16/business/global/10-airlines-snub-europes-emissions-rule.html; see also HR 2594 'European Union Emissions Trading Scheme Prohibition Act of 2011' (US legislation in the process of enactment), at http://thomas.loc.gov/cgi-bin/bdquery/z?d112:h.r.2594. See M Petersen, 'The Legality of the EU's Stand-Alone Approach to the Climate Impact of Aviation: The Express Role Given to the ICAO by the Kyoto Protocol' (2008) 17 *Review of Community and International Environmental Law* 196; BF Havel and JQ Mulligan (n 45) 3–33; B Mayer, 'Case C-366/10, *Air Transport Association of America and Others* v. *Secretary of State for Energy and Climate Change*, Judgment of the Court of Justice (Grand Chamber) of 21 December 2011, nyr' (2012) 49 *CML Rev* 1113–40; E Denza, 'International Aviation and the EU Carbon Trading Scheme: Comment on the Air Transport Association of America case' (2012) 37 *EL Rev* 314–26.

legislative organs have a complex relationship with international law, shaped very much by their role within the EU legal order. Of course, the legislative organs are political actors that pursue their interests and objectives and are by no means completely virtuous when it comes to international law. Nevertheless, the practice of the EU's legislative institutions tends to show a much more open attitude towards international law compared to that of the Court. This attitude seems to resemble more closely the way the EU seeks to present itself; as an international actor that takes international law seriously. In the present section we focus on the way international law is being handled by the EU legislature in the enactment of Union legislation, focusing on the fields of aviation, the environment, fisheries and human health. While obviously only a fraction of the EU's legislative practice, these areas illustrate how the EU legislature takes into account developments on the international plane. Moreover, these fields are subject to regulation at both the international and European level and have also given rise to considerable case law, including the many legal issues touching on environmental and aviation law which the Court faced in *ATAA*.

A. EU Legislation in Light of Developments in International Law

(i) Chicago Convention

In light of the almost complete transfer of national competences in the fields covered by the Chicago Convention, the European Commission made a proposal as early as 2002 to the Council for authorisation to open negotiations for the EC to accede to the Chicago Convention.[132] This has not been followed through by the Council, due to disagreements among Member States.[133] Although the EU has not become a party to the Convention, and is therefore not strictly bound by its provisions, the EU legislature nevertheless takes account of the Chicago Convention's provisions and of the 'international standards and recommended practices and procedures' adopted and amended by the ICAO according to Article 37 of the said Convention.[134] This is

---

[132] Recommendation from the Commission to the Council in order to authorise the Commission to open and conduct negotiations with the International Civil Aviation Organization (ICAO) on the conditions and arrangements for accession by the European Community, 9 April 2002, SEC/2002/0381 final. On page 2 of the explanatory memorandum to this recommendation the European Commission observed that an EU accession to ICAO 'will put the Community in a position to meet its obligations as regards external competences and to guarantee consistency between Community law and international law in these two sectors of particular economic importance'.

[133] The European Commission still aims at full membership in international organisations where this will improve its capacity to pursue EU policies. See in this regard, 'White Paper: Roadmap to a Single European Transport Area—Towards a competitive and resource efficient transport system', European Commission, 28 March 2011, COM(2011) 144 final, 66.

[134] The situation is very similar in the area of maritime transport and the work of the IMO. See in this regard 'White Paper: European Transport Policy for 2010: Time to Decide', Commission of the European Communities, 12 September 2001, COM(2001) 370 final and 'Strategic Goals and Recommendations for the EU's Maritime Transport Policy until 2018', Communication from the

illustrated in the European Commission 2001 White Paper on a European transport policy for 2010, where it observed that the Union had 'little room for manoeuvre' in the exercise to strike a balance between growth in air transport and the protection of the environment since 'account must be taken of the international commitments entered into by the Member States within the International Civil Aviation Organisation (ICAO)'.[135] Further, when it discussed the question of imposing an aviation fuel tax within the EU, it insisted on avoiding 'calling into question the international rules' and prioritised efforts to work within ICAO in this direction.[136] True to this spirit of opting for multilateral solutions through international instruments, once a breakthrough was made within ICAO in the field of aviation emissions, the European Commission agreed to limit the scope of the EU emissions trading system (ETS) to flights within the European Economic Area (EEA) until 2016. It will reassess its options after that date in light of developments in ICAO.[137]

In addition, recent EU legislation in this area generally follows developments in ICAO. Regulation 216/2008 on common rules in the field of civil aviation which further established the European Aviation Safety Agency (EASA) is one example of this.[138] The Regulation aimed to respect fully and ensure the adequate implementation within the EU of the international legal framework created by the Chicago Convention and the work of ICAO.[139] It was amended by Regulation 690/2009 'in order to reflect the changes to the Chicago Convention'.[140] A further indicative example is Regulation 691/2010 on air navigation services and network functions for general air traffic, whose application is 'without prejudice to the rights and duties of Member States under the 1944 Chicago Convention',[141]

Commission to the European Parliament, the Council, the European Economic and Social Committee and the Committee of the Regions, 21 January 2009, COM(2009) 8 final. See also, EU legislation covering maritime security, maritime safety and environment, seafarers and short sea shipping among others.

[135] 'White Paper: European Transport Policy for 2010: Time to Decide', Commission of the European Communities, 12 September 2001, COM(2001) 370 final, 39.

[136] ibid, 40.

[137] See in this regard, European Commission, 'Stopping the Clock of ETS and Aviation Emissions Following Last Week's International Civil Aviation Organisation (ICAO) Council', 12 November 2012, MEMO/12/854. See also European Commission, 'Proposal for a Directive of the European Parliament and of the Council amending Directive 2003/87/EC establishing a scheme for greenhouse gas emission allowance trading within the Community, in view of the implementation by 2020 of an international agreement applying a single global market-based measure to international aviation emissions', 16 October 2013, COM(2013) 722 final.

[138] Regulation (EC) No 216/2008 of the European Parliament and of the Council of 20 February 2008 on common rules in the field of civil aviation and establishing a European Aviation Safety Agency, and repealing Council Directive 91/670/EEC, Regulation (EC) No 1592/2002 and Directive 2004/36/EC [2008] OJ L79/1.

[139] Regulation (EC) No 216/2008 (ibid), Arts 5.6(d), 8.6, 9.1, 9.4(a), 9.5(a), 9.5(d)(i), 17.2(e), 20.1, 27.3.

[140] Commission Regulation (EC) No 690/2009 of 30 July 2009 amending Regulation (EC) No 216/2008 of the European Parliament and the Council on common rules in the field of civil aviation and establishing a European Aviation Safety Agency, and repealing Council Directive 91/670/EEC, Regulation (EC) No 1592/2002 and Directive 2004/36/EC [2009] OJ 199/6, preamble, point (3).

[141] Commission Regulation (EU) No 691/2010 of 29 July 2010 laying down a performance scheme for air navigation services and network functions and amending Regulation (EC) No 2096/2005 laying down common requirements for the provision of air navigation services, Art 1.6(a), [2010] OJ L201/1.

whereas its review should 'tak[e] appropriate account of work carried out by ICAO in this field'.[142] In the same line the (then) EC concluded a Memorandum of Cooperation (MoC) with ICAO with regard to security audits/inspections and related matters, thereby harmonising its legislation with international standards and 'preserving the universality and integrity of the ICAO [Universal Security Audit Programme]'.[143] According to the MoC, ICAO assesses European inspections in order to verify their compliance with the relevant international standards.[144] In other words, the EU accepted with the MoC the authority of a third party to assess the implementation of EU legislation in light of a standard set by an international legal instrument. It is indicative of the EU legislature's multilateral approach to norms governing air transport, that even when Union legislation goes further than relevant international rules, it still makes reference to these rules and partly conditions its amendment on further international developments.[145]

This approach stands in stark contrast with the attitude of the Court in *ATAA*, where it refused to take into consideration international obligations stemming from the Chicago Convention and non-binding recommended practices and procedures agreed upon in the ICAO.[146] Having found that the EU was not bound by the Convention via functional succession, the Court avoided delving in an exercise of consistent interpretation, which would have been very much in line with the behaviour of the EU legislature.

(ii) Protection of the Environment from Harmful Chemicals

EU legislation on the protection of the environment from harmful chemicals provides another illustrative example of the openness shown by the EU legislative organs towards international efforts to introduce obligations based on common principles and guidelines. At the end of 2008, the European Parliament and the Council adopted Regulation (EC) No 1272/2008 on classification, labelling and packaging of substances and mixtures,[147] which fully incorporates the relevant legally non-binding criteria set at UN level called Globally Harmonised System of Classification and Labelling of Chemicals (GHS). The Regulation 'follow[ed] various declarations whereby the Community confirmed its intention to contribute

---

[142] ibid, Art 24.

[143] Memorandum of Cooperation between the European Community and the International Civil Aviation Organisation regarding security audits/inspections and related matters [2009] OJ L36/20, preamble.

[144] ibid, point 1.2.

[145] Council Regulation (EC) No 2027/97 of 9 October 1997 on air carrier liability in the event of accidents [1997] OJ L285/1, preamble, point (15).

[146] *ATAA* (n 4), paras 57–72.

[147] Regulation (EC) No 1272/2008 of the European Parliament and of the Council of 16 December 2008 on classification, labelling and packaging of substances and mixtures, amending and repealing Directives 67/548/EEC and 1999/45/EC, and amending Regulation (EC) No 1907/2006 [2008] OJ L353/1.

to the global harmonisation of criteria for classification and labelling, not only at UN level, but also through the incorporation of the internationally agreed GHS criteria into Community law'.[148] Therefore, '[t]he terms and definitions used in this Regulation should be consistent [...] with the definitions specified at UN level in the GHS, in order to ensure maximum consistency in the application of chemicals legislation within the Community in the context of global trade. The hazard classes specified in the GHS should be set out in this Regulation for the same reason'.[149] What is more, 'the Commission should be empowered to adapt this Regulation to technical and scientific progress, including incorporating amendments made at UN level to the GHS'.[150] In the same line, in the intersection between environment and international trade the EU implements fully the Convention on International Trade in Endangered Species of Wild Fauna and Flora (CITES). The Union has been enacting and amending legislation, the so-called Wildlife Trade Regulations, which implements CITES, whereas in some respects it even goes beyond it.[151] This is so despite the fact that the Union is not yet a party to this Convention, although all its Member States are.

(iii) Human Health

In the field of health the Union's action is influenced by developments at the WHO, a UN specialised agency with which the EU cooperates closely without being a formal member.[152] Two important WHO instruments have shaped European legislation in this field: the Framework Convention on Tobacco Control (FCTC),[153] to which the EU is a party since 2005 together with its Member States, and the International Health Regulations (IHR),[154] to which the EU cannot be

---

[148] ibid, preamble (6).

[149] Regulation (EC) No 1272/2008 (n 147), preamble (12).

[150] ibid (n 147), preamble (77).

[151] Council Regulation (EC) No 338/1997 of 9 December 1996 on the protection of species of wild fauna and flora by regulating trade therein [1997] OJ L61/1; Commission Regulation (EU) No 101/2012 of 6 February 2012 amending Council Regulation (EC) No 338/97 on the protection of species of wild fauna and flora by regulating trade therein [2012] OJ L39/133; Commission Regulation (EC) No 865/2006 of 4 May 2006 laying down detailed rules concerning the implementation of Council Regulation (EC) No 338/97 on the protection of species of wild fauna and flora by regulating trade therein [2006] OJ L166/1, consolidated version; Commission Regulation (EC) No 100/2008 of 4 February 2008 amending, as regards sample collections and certain formalities relating to the trade in species of wild fauna and flora, Regulation (EC) No 865/2006 laying down detailed rules for the implementation of Council Regulation (EC) No 338/97 [2008] OJ L31/3; Commission Regulation (EU) No 828/2011 of 17 August 2011 suspending the introduction into the Union of specimens of certain wild fauna and flora [2011] OJ L211/11.

[152] Eggers and Hoffmeister (n 118) 155–68.

[153] WHO Framework Convention on Tobacco Control, World Health Organization, adopted at the fifty-sixth World Health Assembly on 21 May 2003, available at http://www.who.int/tobacco/framework/WHO_FCTC_english.pdF See also Council Decision of 2 June 2004 concerning the conclusion of the WHO Framework Convention on Tobacco Control (2004/513/EC) [2004] OJ L213/8.

[154] International Health Regulations (2005), World Health Organization, adopted at the fifty-eighth World Health Assembly on 23 May 2005, available at http://whqlibdoc.who.int/publications/2008/9789241580410_eng.pdf.

a party according to the Constitution of the WHO but EU Member States have given their consent to be bound in the interest of the Union.[155] With regard to the former, the Union institutions follow up recommendations adopted at the Conference of the Parties to the Convention in establishing and updating relevant internal legislation.[156] They thereby strengthen this international regime, whereas they transform non-binding recommendations at the international level to binding EU legislation. In the case of the IHR, although only the Member States are bound by the Regulations, EU legislative institutions are nevertheless open to their application. This is illustrated by the fact that the European Commission has adopted a Communication before the entry into force of the IHR recommending the early voluntary implementation of some aspects of these within the EU.[157]

(iv) Fisheries

In the field of fisheries the EU has been particularly active internationally.[158] The attitude of the legislature is reflected in Regulation No 44/2012 on fishing opportunities, which states that:

> [T]he Union is a contracting party to several fisheries organisations and participates in other organisations as a cooperating non-party. [...] Those fisheries organisations have recommended the introduction for 2012 of a number of measures, including fishing opportunities for EU vessels. Those fishing opportunities should be implemented in the law of the Union.[159]

The Regulation goes on to describe the decisions of international maritime organisations (IMAO) that should be implemented within the EU. In doing so it even refers to the Inter-American Tropical Tuna Commission of which the EU is not a member, whose measures and resolutions 'should be implemented in the law of the Union'.[160] In addition, EU legislation refers to the Convention for the International Council for the Exploration of the Sea (ICES) to define terms.[161] The Commission also bases its proposals on total allowable catches (CATs) in

---

[155] See Eggers and Hoffmeister (n 118) 162–68.

[156] See Commission Directive 2012/9/EU of 7 March 2012 amending Annex I to Directive 2001/37/EC of the European Parliament and of the Council on the approximation of the laws, regulations and administrative provisions of the Member States concerning the manufacture, presentation and sale of tobacco products [2012] OJ L69/15.

[157] Communication from the Commission to the European Parliament and the Council on the International Health Regulations, 26 June 2006, COM(2006) 552 final.

[158] J Wouters et al, 'Study for the Assessment of the EU's Role in International Maritime Organisations' Final Report, April 2009, Leuven Centre for Global Governance Studies, 30.

[159] Council Regulation (EU) No 44/2012 of 17 January 2012 fixing for 2012 the fishing opportunities available in EU waters and, to EU vessels, in certain non-EU waters for certain fish stocks and groups of fish stocks which are subject to international negotiations or agreements [2012] OJ L25/57, preamble (19).

[160] ibid, preamble (21).

[161] Council Regulation (EU) No 1256/2011 of 30 November 2011 fixing for 2012 the fishing opportunities for certain fish stocks and groups of fish stocks applicable in the Baltic Sea and amending Regulation (EU) No 1124/2010 [2011] OJ L320/3; Council Regulation (EU) No 43/2012 of 17 January

order to achieve maximum sustainable yield level (MSY) for fishing on the relevant approach adopted by the ICES.[162] This is so despite the fact that only some of the EU Member States are parties to ICES whereas the Union is not.

B. Reconciling the Approaches of the Court and Legislature

The discussion above demonstrates some of the ways in which the EU legislature's approach to international law often stands in contrast with that of the Court. First, the legislature demonstrates openness by referring to international law within its legislation, either within the preamble or the substantive provisions. But it goes further than simply mentioning international law, which by itself does not necessarily indicate an 'international law friendly' approach. Its openness to international law is particularly evident when it seeks to incorporate international law developments that are not binding upon it. Here we should distinguish between two groups of international instruments. The first comprises instruments binding on all or some EU Member States, like the Chicago Convention and obligations undertaken within ICAO, CITES, and the WHO (IHR). The second group includes instruments that are non-binding in nature but have been agreed upon in multilateral fora where the EU or its Member States (or both) are represented, such as the ICAO recommended practices and procedures, the GHS and the FCTC Conference of the Parties. Our analysis above shows how in both these groups EU legislation tends to incorporate international developments. What is less clear, however, is the extent to which the legislature incorporates these norms out of a sense of *obligation* and respect for international law stemming from Articles 3(5) and 21 TEU. The EU often helps shape, either directly or indirectly, developments at the international level and therefore has an interest in accepting international norms it had a hand in developing. For instance, in the field of financial regulation, the EU legislature has been extremely open towards incorporating norms developed within the G20 framework. This phenomenon is less remarkable, however, when one considers the extent to which many of the EU's G20 commitments were actually heavily influenced by the EU and its Member States at various G20 summits.[163]

With regard to instruments binding upon the Member States but not the Union, the EU legislature has adopted a pragmatic approach, contrasting with the rigid approach adopted by the Court. A number of international instruments and

---

2012 fixing for 2012 the fishing opportunities available to EU vessels for certain fish stocks and groups of fish stocks which are not subject to international negotiations or agreements [2012] OJ L25/1.

[162] Communication from the Commission to the Council concerning a consultation on Fishing opportunities for 2013, 7 June 2012, COM(2012) 278 final.

[163] See J Wouters, S Van Kerckhoven and J Odermatt, 'The European Union at the G20 and the G20's Impact on the EU' in B Van Vooren, S Blockmans and J Wouters (eds), *The EU's Role in Global Governance: The Legal Dimension* (Oxford, Oxford University Press, 2013).

organisations lack provisions that would allow the EU to become party to them, or their parties are not willing to grant the EU such a right, even where the EU has competences in some or all the fields covered by this instrument. It may also be the case that EU Member States parties to such agreements or members of such organisations do not wish to see the Union as a full party or member to them. EU political institutions endeavour to overcome such political obstacles to the accession of the Union to such agreements. They continue to make sure the EU is present at such fora at least as an observer while they coordinate with EU Member States for the representation of the interests of the Union there. At the same time they continue to update the relevant EU legislation according to developments in these organisations.

The approach of the legislature also helps to prevent a situation where EU Member States would have conflicting legal obligations at the European and international levels. The fact that it does, largely confirms Eeckhout's point that:

> [T]he Community cannot, in its legislative activity, disregard the Member States' international obligations. The Community would not be a responsible international actor if it required the Member States to breach international law whenever the latter does not suit its legislative objectives.[164]

Thus, the EU legislature presents itself as being responsible and receptive to international legislative efforts in harmonising its activities with international instruments that bind EU Member States. It does so not only in explicitly referring to international law developments in the preamble of EU legislation,[165] but also in its operative parts. However, when the international regime is not as developed as the EU would want it to be, the EU goes further with its internal legislation as in the cases of ICAO and CITES.

The approach of the Court and the legislature towards international law are in many ways determined by the differing roles of each organ. The restrictive approach of the Court can be understood in part by a desire to protect the integrity and autonomy of the EU legal order, while much of the legislature's openness can be understood in light of the desire of the EU political organs to present the EU as a responsible international actor who shapes developments at the international level. Despite these differences, the Court and the legislature should seek to reconcile these approaches, taking as a starting point the requirement to respect international law enshrined in the EU Treaties. For instance, taking into account the legislature's openness to international law, it seems only logical that the Court interpret EU legislation in the light of international legal developments. As discussed above, the Court has shown hints that it could move in this direction through developing the principle of consistent interpretation, however the

---

[164] Eeckhout (n 76) 2052.

[165] See the discussion in J Wouters and J Odermatt, 'Norms Emanating from International Bodies and Their Role in the Legal Order of the European Union' in RA Wessel and S Blockmans (eds), *Between Autonomy and Dependence—The EU Legal Order under the Influence of International Organisations* (Springer/TMC Asser Press, 2013).

principle has yet to be properly implemented in practice. Similarly, the Court's approach to the issue of functional succession is too restrictive, and does not to take into account the openness of the legislature towards norms that are not strictly binding upon the Union. The restrictive approach developed by the Court regarding these matters appears to be out of sync with attitudes in Brussels.

The changes to the Court's approach to international law issues advocated in this chapter would also be in line with the approach of the EU to international law in its external relations. As discussed above, the Treaties themselves place the respect for international law as an important principle for the EU. Yet the respect for international law is also viewed as a tool by which the Union pursues its objectives. In many cases, the international norms being applied before the Court are those that the EU itself had a hand in shaping, and the Union has a strong interest in seeing them respected at the international level. The Union sees the respect for international law as something that is part of its own self-interest; the European Security Strategy, for instance, states that the Union is 'committed to upholding and developing International Law'.[166] By developing a more rigid approach towards international law, the Court risks undermining a broader goal of the Union to enhance and uphold the international multilateral system. Some scholars, especially in the wake of the *Kadi* judgment, noted how the Court's approach 'sits uncomfortably with the traditional self-presentation of the EU as a virtuous international actor'.[167] The EU is a party to hundreds of international agreements, ranging from bilateral agreements to multilateral treaties on a range of issues, including UNCLOS,[168] the UN Framework Convention on Climate Change (UNFCC)[169] or the Convention on the Rights of Persons with Disabilities.[170] The EU is also a member, observer or enhanced observer in international organisations, and has sought to upgrade its status at certain international bodies.[171] The EU often has a significant role to play in the negotiation and drafting of these multilateral treaties. A judicial approach that is overly restrictive when it comes to international law contrasts with and goes against the Union's broader goal to further develop and strengthen an international system based on respect for international law.

---

[166] European Security Strategy, 'A Secure Europe in a Better World', Brussels, 12 December 2003.

[167] See de Búrca (n 126) 3.

[168] United Nations Convention on the Law of the Sea (UNCLOS), Council Decision of 23 March 1998 concerning the conclusion by the European Community of the United Nations Convention of 10 December 1982 on the Law of the Sea and the Agreement of 28 July 1994 relating to the implementation of Part XI thereof [1998] OJ L179/1.

[169] Council Decision of 15 December 1993 concerning the conclusion of the United Nations Framework Convention on Climate Change [1994] OJ L33/11.

[170] Council Decision of 26 November 2009 concerning the conclusion, by the European Community, of the United Nations Convention on the Rights of Persons with Disabilities [2010] OJ L23/35.

[171] M Emerson, R Balfour, T Corthaut, J Wouters, PM Kaczynski and T Renard, *Upgrading the EU's Role as Global Actor: Institutions, Law and the Restructuring of European Diplomacy* (Brussels, Centre for European Policy Studies, 2011).

The above analysis is based on indicative examples in order to demonstrate broader trends rather than an exhaustive examination of all case law and legislation dealing with international legal developments. One can point to instances where the Court has shown openness towards international law,[172] or where legislation is arguably out of line with international legal developments. Still, our discussion provides a broad picture of the differing attitudes of the EU legislature and judicature in this field of law. Furthermore, it allows us to open the debate of how the Court can reposition itself towards the status of international law within the Union legal order.

V. CONCLUSION

Given their differing functions, a comparison of how the Court and the EU legislature deal with international law may at first glance seem to provide only limited insight. However, such a comparison is warranted, especially given the new post-Lisbon text of the Treaties containing a number of references to international law, the growing convergence between regulatory efforts on the international and European levels, as well as recent case law of the Court that demonstrates a more reticent attitude towards international law. Although the TEU sets out that the EU 'shall contribute [...] to the strict observance and the development of international law',[173] the approach of the Court and the legislature show remarkably different attitudes to international law. Thus, despite the guidance given by the Treaties, the EU does not seem to be consistent in its dealings with international law both internally and abroad.

The first part of this chapter examined how provisions in the Treaties, including numerous references to international law and multilateralism, should be used as a starting point to guide the EU institutions and bodies in their relationship with international law. These broad goals have as of yet not been taken up fully by the Court, which has progressively defined the contours of the EU-international law relationship through its case law. The principle of respect for international law could be used to guide both the Court and the other EU institutions, to minimise inconsistencies in their respective attitudes, and reduce the chance of normative conflicts.

The Court has the tools to embark on an open debate with international law. Instead of adopting judicial avoidance techniques, it has every interest in tackling the effects of international law within the EU legal order while preserving the integrity of the EU constitutional order. For instance, a more pragmatic

---

[172] *Hungary v Slovak Republic* (n 93), has been presented as an example of the Court 'stepping back from *Kadi*'s broad dualist language', see 'Case C-364/10, Hungary v. Slovak Republic, 2012 ECJ EUR-Lex LEXIS' (2013) 126 *Harvard Law Review* 2425, 2434. Case C-386/08 *Brita GmbH* (n 15) could also be considered such an example, although Klabbers argues that this is an example of a case 'where the answer is obvious and international law only plays a cosmetic role': Klabbers (n 11) 7.

[173] Art 3(5) TEU.

approach towards functional succession would ensure that the EU implements commitments entered into by Member States where the EU has in effect taken over their powers in a certain field, thereby giving greater respect to international law commitments. The Court's approach to the direct effect of international law is not an appropriate method to determine the invocability of international treaty and customary law within the EU. The Court should also further develop and apply the principle of consistent interpretation of EU law in light of international treaty and customary obligations. Moreover, the Court should not take an overly narrow view on the types of international norms it takes into account. International law includes more than treaty and customary international law—general principles of law, decisions of international organisations and other bodies, decisions of (quasi) judicial bodies at the international level and other international norms should also be taken into account. Importantly, such an approach should not stem from a benevolent attitude or 'international law-friendly' approach of the Court and only applied in cases where it is in the EU's interests to see international law applied. Rather, this approach should stem from a sense of constitutional obligation to respect international law, recognising the EU's place within the wider international legal order.

A full understanding of the EU's relationship with international law requires an analysis, not only of the Court, as the body that interprets and applies international law, but also the other EU institutions, in particular the EU legislature, which is influenced by, and seeks to implement, international law. When it comes to their relationship with international law, however, they remain worlds apart. As the Court continues to develop rules that progressively restrict the application of international law within the EU legal order they may move further apart. A more consistent approach, one that recognises respect for international law as a fundamental constitutional principle of the EU legal order, would serve to reassure all that the EU genuinely aims to 'contribute [...] to the strict observance and the development of international law'.

Index

www.ingramcontent.com/pod-product-compliance
Lightning Source LLC
Chambersburg PA
CBHW060152280326
41932CB00012B/1736